# CHEMICAL DEPENDENCY COUNSELING

# CHEMICAL DEPENDENCY COUNSELING
## A PRACTICAL GUIDE

Robert R. Perkinson

**SAGE** Publications
*International Educational and Professional Publisher*
Thousand Oaks   London   New Delhi

*For information address:*

SAGE Publications, Inc.
2455 Teller Road
Thousand Oaks, California 90321
E-mail: order@sagepub.com

Sage Publications Ltd.
6 Bonhill Street
London EC2A 4PU
United Kingdom

Sage Publications India Pvt. Ltd.
M-32 Market
Greater Kailash I
New Delhi 110 048 India

Printed in the United States of America

*Library of Congress Cataloging-in-Publication Data*

Perkinson, Robert R.
    Chemical dependency counseling: a practical guide  /  author,
Robert R. Perkinson.
        p.  cm.
    Includes bibliographical references and index.
    ISBN 0-7619-0859-5 (pbk.: alk. paper)
    1. Substance abuse—Patients—Counseling of.   2. Dual diagnosis—
Patients—Counseling of.   I. Title.
RC564.P47   1997
362.29′186—dc21                                              96-51207

98  99  00  01  02  03  10  9  8  7  6  5  4  3

| | |
|---|---|
| *Acquiring Editor:* | Jim Nageotte |
| *Editorial Assistant:* | Kathleen Derby |
| *Production Editor:* | Michèle Lingre |
| *Production Assistant:* | Karen Wiley |
| *Typesetter/Designer:* | Janelle LeMaster |
| *Indexer:* | Teri Greenberg |
| *Design Director:* | Ravi Balasuriya |
| *Print Buyer:* | Anna Chin |

# Contents

Appendix Contents     xv

Foreword     xvii

Preface     xix

Acknowledgments     xxi

**1.**    **The First Hours**     1

How to Greet Patients     1

How to Handle Family Members     2

Beginning the Therapeutic Alliance     2

    The Importance of Trust     2

    Dealing With Early Denial     3

    Example of an Initial Contact     3

How to Check for Organic Brain Dysfunction     4

The Initial Assessment     4

    American Society of Addiction Medicine (ASAM)
    Patient Placement Criteria     6

    *DSM* Criteria for Diagnosis     7

    How to Determine the Level of Care Needed     9

    How to Share the Diagnosis With the Patient     12

Assigning a Treatment Buddy     13

The Intoxicated Patient     14

    How to Determine the Level of Intoxication     14

    The Patient's Reaction to Intoxication     14

    What to Do With an Intoxicated Patient     15

Detoxification                                                          16
    How Patients React in Detox                     16
The AMA Threat                                                         17
    Example of an AMA Intervention                  17
    How to Use the AMA Team                         18
    How to Use In-House Intervention                19
    How to Respond to Patients Who Leave AMA        19

**2.**    **The Biopsychosocial Interview**                  21

How to Conduct the Interview                                           22
Summary and Impression                                                 27
Diagnosis                                                              27
Disposition and Treatment Plan                                         28
A Sample Biopsychosocial Interview                                     28

**3.**    **The Treatment Plan**                             37

How to Build a Treatment Plan                                          37
The Diagnostic Summary                                                 37
The Problem List                                                       38
    How to Develop a Problem List                   38
Goals and Objectives                                                   38
    How to Develop Goals                            39
    How to Develop Objectives                       39
    How to Evaluate the Effectiveness of the Treatment   41
    How to Select Goals and Objectives              41
    Examples of Goals and Objectives                41
Treatment Plan Review                                                  42
Documentation                                                          43
    How to Write Progress Notes                     43
    Formal Treatment Plan Review                    44

**4.**    **Individual Treatment**                           47

The Therapeutic Alliance                                               47
    How to Develop a Therapeutic Alliance           47
    How to Be Reinforcing                           48
    How to Use Empathy                              49
Transference and Countertransference                                   49
    Examples of Empathetic Statements               50
    How to Be Confrontive                           50
Behavior Therapy                                                       50
    How Patients Learn                              51

The Behavior Chain                                            52
    The Importance of Reinforcement                      53
    How to Use Punishment                               53
    Why We Concentrate on Behavior Therapy              55
Cognitive Therapy                                             55
    How Chemically Dependent People Think               55
    Applying Cognitive Therapy                          57
    How to Correct Inaccurate Thoughts                  59
Interpersonal Therapy                                         64
    How to Develop Healthy Relationships                64
    How Patients Use Feelings Inappropriately           66
    How Patients Learn Relationship Skills              66
    How to Change Relationships                         66
    How to Handle Grief                                 67
    How to Choose the Therapeutic Modality              67

**5.**    **Group Therapy**                                     69

Benefits of the Group Process                                 69
Preparation for Group                                         70
    The Preparation Statement                           71
    The Agenda                                          71
The Honesty Group                                             73
    Example of an Honesty Group                         73
    Uncovering the Lies                                 74
    How to End Each Group                               75
The Euphoric Recall Group                                     75
    How to Uncover Euphoric Recall                      75
    How to Get Real                                     76
The Reading Group                                             77
Relapse Prevention Groups                                     77
    The Trigger Group                                   78
    The Inaccurate Thinking Group                       79
    The Feelings and Action Group                       79
    The Slips Group                                     80
The Spirituality Group                                        82
    Group Preparation                                   82
    How to Develop a Healthy Relationship               82
    How to Develop a Healthy Relationship With God      83
    The Eleventh-Step Group                             83
    The Meditation Group                                83
The Childhood Group                                           85
    How to Explore Early Parental Relationships         85

How to Begin to Heal Early Childhood Pain                    86

The Men's Group/Women's Group                                87

The Community Group                                          87

The Personal Inventory Group                                 87


**6.  The Contracts**                                        89

The Chemical Use History                                     89

Honesty                                                      90

Love, Trust, and Commitment                                  90

Feelings                                                     91

Relationship Skills                                          92

Addictive Relationships                                      93

Communication Skills                                         94

Self-Discipline                                              94

Impulse Control                                              96

Relapse Prevention                                           97

Stress Management                                            98


**7.  The Steps**                                            101

The Committee                                                102

Step One                                                     102

Step Two                                                     104

How to Help Patients Accept a Higher Power                   104

Step Three                                                   105

How to Help Patients Embrace Step Three                      106

Step Four                                                    107

Step Five                                                    108


**8.  The Lectures**                                         111

The Disease                                                  112

Chemical Dependency Is Not a Moral Problem                   112

Chemical Dependency Is Not Due to a Weak Will                112

Chemical Dependency Has Genetic Links                        112

Chemical Dependency Is a Social Problem                      112

Chemical Dependency Is a Psychological Problem               113

Chemical Dependency Is a Physiological Problem               113

The Obsession                                                113

The Problems                                                 114

Defense Mechanisms                                           114

Minimization                                                 114

Rationalization                                              115

Denial 115
How to Begin to Live in the Truth 116
The Great Lie 116
How the Great Lie Works 116
Truth 117
Normal Development 118
The Primary Caregiver 118
The Struggle for Independence 118
The Fear of Abandonment 118
Learning the Rules 118
The Development of Insecurity 118
The Peer Group 119
Adolescence 119
Adulthood 119
Physical Addiction and Recovering 120
How Drugs Affect the Cell 120
How Drugs Affect Behavior 121
Tolerance 121
Cross-Tolerance 121
Withdrawal 121
How We Learn 122
Alcoholics Anonymous 122
A Spiritual Awakening 122
Two Alcoholics Talking to Each Other 123
The Big Book 123
The Twelve Steps 124
Meetings 124
Feelings 124
Feelings Are Adaptive 125
How to Be Assertive 126

**9. Special Problems** 127
The Psychiatric/Psychological Assessment 127
How to Develop the Treatment Plan 128
The Depressed Patient 128
How to Assess Depression 129
How to Treat Depression 129
Suicide 137
The Angry Patient 138
How to Handle a Violent Patient 138
How to Handle an Angry Patient 138
Assertiveness Skills 139

|  |  |
|---|---|
|     The Importance of Forgiveness | 139 |
|     How to Teach Patients to Recognize Their Anger | 140 |
|     How to Keep Your Cool as a Counselor | 141 |
|   The Homicidal Patient | 141 |
|     The Duty to Warn | 141 |
| Personality | 142 |
|   What Is Personality? | 142 |
|   The Antisocial Personality | 143 |
|     The Impulsive Temperament | 143 |
|     A Disorder of Empathy | 143 |
|     How to Treat Antisocial Personality | 143 |
|     How to Deal With a Rule Violation | 144 |
|     Moral Development | 145 |
|     How to Deal With the Family | 145 |
|   The Borderline Patient | 146 |
|     Interpersonal Relationships | 146 |
|     Affective Dysregulation | 146 |
|     How to Treat Borderline Patients | 146 |
|   The Narcissistic Patient | 148 |
|   The Anxious Patient | 149 |
|     How to Measure Anxiety | 150 |
|     The Psychological Component of Anxiety | 150 |
|     How to Use Relaxation Techniques | 151 |
|     The Daily Log | 152 |
|     Cognitive Therapy | 152 |
|     Panic Attacks | 153 |
|   The Psychotic Patient | 153 |
|     Hallucinations and Delusions | 153 |
|     How to Treat the Psychotic Patient | 154 |
|     The Family | 155 |
| Acquired Immune Deficiency Syndrome (AIDS) | 156 |
|   High-Risk Patients | 156 |
| Patients With Low Intellectual Functioning | 157 |
|   How to Treat Patients With Low Intelligence | 157 |
|   Patients Who Can't Read | 157 |
|   The Family | 158 |
| The Elderly Patient | 158 |
| Patients With Early Childhood Trauma | 159 |
|   How to Deal With Sexual Abuse | 159 |
|   Cognitive Therapy | 160 |
|   How to Learn Forgiveness | 160 |
| Love in the Treatment Center | 161 |

The Importance of Unit Rules    161
How to Deal With Patients in Love    161

**10.   Adolescent Treatment**    163

The Normal Adolescent    163
    Ages 13 to 16    164
    Ages 16 to 19    164
The Chemically Dependent Adolescent    165
The Adolescent Chemical Dependency Counselor    166
The Point System    166
The Primary Elements in Adolescent Treatment    167
    The Rules    167
    Communication Skills    167
    Honesty    168
    Exercise    168
    Fun in Sobriety    168
    The Reinforcers    169
    Spirituality    169
    Group Therapy    169
    Peer Pressure    170
    Continuing Education    170
    Continuing Care    170
    The Parents' Support Group    171
    The Behavioral Contract    171
    Phases of Adolescent Treatment    171

**11.   The Family Program**    173

The First Contact    173
How to Handle Early AMA Risk    174
The Family Process    174
    Codependency    174
    Guilt    175
    Loss of Control    175
    Shame    175
    Caretaking    175
    Enabling    175
    Inability to Know Feelings    176
    Inability to Know Wants    176
    Lack of Trust    176
    People Pleasing    176
    Feelings of Worthlessness    176

|  | Dependency | 177 |
|  | Poor Communication Skills | 177 |
| How to Treat Family Members | | 177 |
| The Family Program Schedule | | 178 |
| How to Work With the Family in Group | | 179 |
| The Conjoint Session | | 180 |

**12. The Clinical Staff** 181

The Physician 181
The Psychologist/Psychiatrist 182
The Nurse 182
The Clinical Director 183
The Clinical Supervisor 183
The Chemical Dependency Counselor 183
The Rehabilitation Technician or Aid 184
The Activities Coordinator 184
Clinical Staffing 184
    How to Present a Patient 185
Team Building 186
    Commitment to Coworkers 187
    Boundaries 187
Staff-Patient Problems 188
    When a Patient Doesn't Like a Counselor 188
    When a Patient Complains About a Rule 189
The Work Environment 189

**13. Discharge Summary and Aftercare** 191

Outpatient Discharge Criteria 192
Inpatient Discharge Criteria 193
    How to Develop a Discharge Summary 194
    The Discharge Summary 195
    Saying Good-bye 195

**14. The Drugs** 197

CNS Depressants 197
CNS Stimulants 197
The Hallucinogens 198
The Reinforcing Properties of Drugs 198
Tolerance and Dependence 198
Cross-Tolerance 199
Alcohol 199

Alcohol-Induced Organic Mental Disorders   199

Sedatives, Hypnotics, and Anxiolytics   201

Opioids   201

Cocaine and the Amphetamines   202

Pattern of Use   203

The Cocaine Abstinent Syndrome   203

Phencyclidine (PCP)   204

Hallucinogens   204

The Psychedelic State   205

Cannabis   205

Inhalants   206

Nicotine   207

Polysubstances   208

Treatment Outcome   208

**15.**   **The Good Counselor**   211

Being Loving   211

Loving Counselors Enjoy Their Work   211

Loving Counselors Don't Become Overly Involved   212

Loving Counselors Don't Lie   212

Loving Counselors Are Gentle   212

Good Counselors Love Themselves   212

Sensitivity   212

The Sixth Sense   213

Good Counselors Don't Become Overly Emotional   213

Active Listener   213

Good Counselors Don't Talk Too Much   214

Boundaries   214

Patience   215

Interpersonal Relationship Skills   215

Sound Code of Ethics   216

List of Appendixes   219

References   401

Index   413

About the Author   431

# Appendix Contents

  1. Cognitive Capacity Screening Examination      221

  2. Short Michigan Alcoholism Screening Test (SMAST)      223

  3. CAGE Questionnaire      225

  4. *DSM-IV* Psychoactive Substance Use Disorder      227

  5. Clinical Institute Withdrawal Assessment of Alcohol Scale      229

  6. Narcotic Withdrawal Scale      233

  7. Sample Biopsychosocial      235

  8. Chemical Use History      239

  9. Honesty      243

10. Love, Trust, and Commitment      247

11. Feelings      253

12. Relationship Skills      257

13. Addictive Relationships      261

14. Communication Skills      263

15. Self-Discipline      267

16. Impulse Control      271

17. Relapse Prevention      277

18. Step One      287

19. Step Two      299

20. Step Three      307

21. Step Four      315

22. Step Five      323

23. Adolescent Unit Level System      325

24. Peer Pressure      329

25. The Behavioral Contract      333

26. Family Questionnaire      337

27. Codependency      345

28. Personal Recovery Plan      353

29. Sample Discharge Summary      357

30. Stress Management      361

31. The Beck Depression Inventory      369

32. Biopsychosocial Assessment      373

33. Anger Management      383

34. Narcissism      395

# Foreword

At no time in history has such a wealth of clinical information been available to those working in the field of addiction. Yet such a body of information is meaningless unless it is organized and presented in a manner that affords the addiction clinician the ability to integrate this knowledge into his or her daily clinical practice.

Regardless of one's educational background in the medical and behavioral sciences, it is essential that those individuals working with psychoactive substance abusers have both an in-depth understanding of the dynamics of addiction as well as the essential clinical processes involved in assessing and treating the illness. The purchasers of health services are correctly calling for objective data supporting both the appropriateness of the treatment and the effectiveness of the care provided.

The addiction clinicians of today must be disciplined professionals who have mastered a body of addiction-based knowledge and demonstrated effective therapeutic interventions and skills. Such professionals must be able to interface clinically and effectively with abusers of psychoactive substances to help them arrest their addiction and achieve meaningful abstinence from the defeating use of mood-altering chemicals.

Addiction clinicians are now recognized by licensing, registering, certifying, and accrediting authorities as being specialists in assessing and effectively treating individuals with a biopsychosocial addictive disease. With such recognition comes accountability. The scope of the present book clearly addresses those critical areas that external reviewers and purchasers of addiction services expect from a professional addiction clinician.

This counseling book by Dr. Perkinson assists the counselor in learning essential assessment, treatment-planning, and treatment-intervention processes. The book also gives helpful guidelines in developing a therapeutic alliance with the addict and methods of working with behavioral stances of both the adolescent and adult addict that tend to undermine or sabotage abstinence.

The very nature of the assessment and treatment-intervention processes necessitates the coordinated effort of a skilled interdisciplinary team working with all aspects of the addictive disease. This requires that the addiction clinician master the skills needed to produce substantive and timely documentation that affords team members, supervisors, and external reviewers the ability to use the medical record to evaluate the appropriateness and effectiveness of the interventions used.

The text of *Chemical Dependency Counseling* aids all clinicians in translating their insights into written measurable benchmarks to evaluate the process and outcome of treatment. In addition, the use of the guidelines noted in this book will enhance the ability of all clinicians' to reflect the use of critical clinical, intelligence in the provision of essential services.

—Richard D. Weedman, MSW, FACATA
President, *Healthcare Network, Inc.*

# Preface

On May 11, 1935, Bill Wilson met with Dr. Bob Smith, and the basic premise of Alcoholics Anonymous was born. The two men were supposed to get together for 15 minutes, but they talked for more than 6 hours. Bill Wilson had recently had his spiritual awakening, but it was not enough to keep him sober. He needed another alcoholic to share with. The common bond of one drug addict talking to another became the core of recovery.

Twelve years later, in 1947, the idea of Hazelden was born as a way to keep alcoholic priests sober. The Hazelden Foundation was formed in 1949 with the expanded purpose of keeping professional alcoholics sober. Lynn Carroll was the first counselor and program director of Hazelden. He initiated and ran the program, based on Alcoholics Anonymous principles. Mr. A. A. Heckman, one of the original members of the Hazelden Foundation, stated, "I think we all agree that the effectiveness of the treatment at Hazelden is due, to a large extent, to the unusual skill of Lynn Carroll. This is fine, except that we do not know to what extent the skills possessed by Carroll can be taught to others" (McElrath, 1987, p. 36).

Lynn Carroll spent 17 years as program director at Hazelden. He married Mitzi Carroll in 1970 and started the Keystone Treatment Center in 1973. Along with Mitzi, as clinical director, Lynn continued to develop the program of recovery. Both Lynn and Mitzi believed in a strong spiritual base. Alcoholics Anonymous has always been a spiritual program.

There was little in the field that this couple didn't try at one time or another; they discarded some things, changed some, and kept some. The program is multidisciplinary, as all good chemical dependency treatment must be. All of the people at Keystone Treatment Center, past and present, have played a part in the development of this program. Their individual contributions are too numerous to mention. The purpose of this text is to teach counselors the skills necessary to treat chemical dependency effectively.

After Lynn's death in 1982, Mitzi continued to fine-tune the program. She worked closely with national and state chemical dependency counselors, was a charter fellow of the American College of Addiction Treatment Administrators, and spent 6 years on the Board of Directors of the National Association of Addiction Treatment Providers. She was a certified Clinical Director, a certified chemical dependency counselor, Level III, and served as Vice President of the South Dakota Chemical Dependency Association. In 1991, she was awarded the Distinguished Service Award of the South Dakota Chemical Dependency Association.

In 1988, Mitzi added psychological services to the program and that was me—I am the clinical director. I spent long hours with Mitzi, her head nurse Carol Regier, and the counseling staff of Keystone Carroll, to learn the program. In time, I added to the program from my own experiences as a psychologist.

Mitzi often commented, with that excited but weary look of hers, that she wanted to write a book for the chemical dependency counselor. She had started a book several times, but these attempts had ended up in boxes in her basement. In March 1991, Mitzi developed terminal cancer, and I promised her that I would write this book. She was delighted. Mitzi died in October 1991. My hope is that the spirit of Lynn and Mitzi Carroll will live on through this program.

This text is not meant to be everything a counselor needs to know to pass his or her state or national certification examination. It is not a theory book and it does not cover all of the programs that can help the substance abuser. Other treatments like Rational Recovery can be effective, but they are rarely used in treatment centers. This book is the traditional treatment outlined by the American Society of Addiction Medicine in *Principles of Addiction Medicine* (1994). The text details the essentials necessary to provide high-quality treatment demanded by state and national accrediting bodies. The program works through the first five steps of AA/NA, and it is designed for all levels of care, even individual counseling. Outpatient professionals will work through fewer steps, though the more the better. Some programs will work through only the first step and some will work through all five. The policies and procedures outlined in this manual have been used by Keystone Treatment Center to become Accredited With Commendation by the Joint Commission on Accreditation of Healthcare Organizations (JCAHO).

It must be emphasized that this program can never be static; it must be fluid, ever changing to fit the particular situation and patient. No two patients can ever be treated alike. By working through the exercises, it is hoped that counselors will learn how to develop exercises on their own. This is the way to individualize treatment. The counselor must learn to use his or her own unique skills.

—Robert R. Perkinson

# Acknowledgments

This manual was shaped by many professionals trying to develop a text we could be proud of and use daily. The work of training new staff is exhausting for everyone in the field and it became necessary to have a standard text that everyone coming on board could read and understand. It had to be a practical book, simple and easy to use, not bogged down by theory or extraneous material. The following professionals played a role in text development, sharing their training and expertise, and often going over the manual in fine detail. I want to thank each of them from the bottom of my heart:

Nancy Waite-O'Brien, PhD, Clinical Director, Betty Ford Center at Eisenhower

Daniel Anderson, PhD, President Emeritus, Hazelden

Linda Kaplan, Executive Director, National Association of Alcoholism and Drug Abuse Counselors

Michael Ford, President, National Association of Addiction Treatment Programs

Richard Weedman, President, Healthcare Network, Inc

Eleanor Sargent, Project for Addiction Counselor Training

Robert Carr, PhD, Director, Substance Abuse Program, VA Regional Hospital, Sioux Falls, SD

Terry O'Brien, Board of Directors, Hazelden

Carol Davis, Counselor, Betty Ford Center at Eisenhower

Carol Regier, Executive Director, Keystone Treatment Center

Mona Sumner, Chief Operations Officer, Rimrock Foundation

Chris O'Sullivan, PhD, Assistant Professor, University of South Dakota

Robert Bogue, Clinical Supervisor, Keystone Treatment Center

Jim Nageotte, Sage Publications

Julie Braaten, Accreditation Coordinator, Keystone Treatment Center

All of the staff, past and present, of Keystone Treatment Center

CHAPTER
ONE | # The First Hours

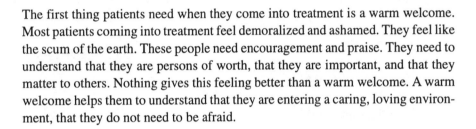

The first thing patients need when they come into treatment is a warm welcome. Most patients coming into treatment feel demoralized and ashamed. They feel like the scum of the earth. These people need encouragement and praise. They need to understand that they are persons of worth, that they are important, and that they matter to others. Nothing gives this feeling better than a warm welcome. A warm welcome helps them to understand that they are entering a caring, loving environment, that they do not need to be afraid.

## How to Greet Patients

You need to convey to patients that you understand how they feel, that you will do everything in your power to help them. It is as if you welcome a long-lost brother or sister back into your family. This person is not different from you; this person *is* you. Treat the person the way you would want to be treated yourself. The more your patients sense your goodwill and unconditional positive regard, the less alienated and frightened they will feel.

When you speak to your new patients, reach out and touch them. This physical touch says a lot about you, and a lot about the patient. Patients often think no one wants to touch them again. You prove this thinking is inaccurate.

Use your own judgment to tell when and where to touch. Be sensitive, some people can be hugged, but some cannot. Some patients you can touch on the arm. If you feel that you can only shake their hand, do this. Make it a warm handshake. As you do these things, you are developing your therapeutic alliance, and you are giving the patient the most important thing he or she needs—love.

The initial words you choose are important. Patients remember your words. Patients come back after years and describe their first few hours in treatment. They remember the exact words people said. They seal them inside their heart. You want them to remember the good things.

Introduce yourself and say something like the following:

"Welcome to (name of treatment center). You've made a good choice. I'm proud of you."

"This is a new start. Good going." Give the thumbs-up sign.

"Good job. We are going to take good care of you."

"I know this was a difficult decision for you, but you won't be sorry. This is the beginning of your new life."

Notice how each of these statements welcomes the patient, and enhances his or her self-esteem: Welcome. You are a good person. You made a good choice. We are going to take good care of you.

Ask if the patients want anything. How can you help? Nothing shows you care better than to offer to get them something small, juice, food, milk, coffee. This shows you care, and that they are worth caring for. You are giving these patients new ideas. Treatment is not going to hurt. You are willing to respond to their needs. "This treatment thing might be okay," they begin to think. "I just might be able to do this."

## How to Handle Family Members

When you have all the information that you need from the family, they should be encouraged to leave the treatment setting. To have them linger unnecessarily can be detrimental to the patient's transition. The patient needs to focus on herself or himself and to orient to treatment. Family members who cling are rare, but they do exist. These people need to be separated from the patient and given reassurance that the patient is in a safe place.

## Beginning the Therapeutic Alliance

Your patients are learning some important things about you. You are friendly, and you are on their side. You have introduced yourself as their counselor. They see you as a concerned professional. They have hope that you can help them. The therapeutic alliance is built from this initial foundation of love and trust.

Let the patients know that you will be with them throughout treatment. They do not have to feel alone. You are there. Neither of you can do this by yourself. Both are needed, in cooperation with each other. Patients know things that you do not know. They have knowledge that you do not have. They know themselves better than anybody, and they need to learn how to share themselves with you. Likewise, you know things that they do not know. You know the tools of recovery. You have to share these tools and help the patient to use them. This is a cooperative effort. It is as if you are on a great, wonderful journey together.

### The Importance of Trust

The patients must develop trust in you. To establish this trust, you must be consistent. You must prove to the patients, time and time again, that you are going to be actively involved in their individual growth. When you say you are going to do something, you do it. When you make a promise, you keep it. You never try to get something from the patients without using the truth. You never manipulate, even to get something good. The first time your patients catch you in a lie, even a small one, your alliance is weakened.

The patients must learn that the staff works as a team. What patients tell you, even in confidence, they tell the whole team. Patients will occasionally test this. They will tell you that they have something to share, but they can only share it with you. They want you to keep it secret. This is a trap that many beginning counselors fall into. The truth is that all facts are friendly, and all accurate information is vital to treatment. You must explain to the patients that if they feel too uncomfortable sharing certain information with the clinical team, they should keep it secret. Maybe they can share this sensitive information in their Fifth Step. No matter what the patients decide to do, you are going to share everything they tell you with the clinical staff. You trust the team, and you encourage the patients to do the same. Most patients will share the information when they see how much you trust each other.

Patients must understand that you are committed to their recovery, but you cannot recover for them. You cannot do the work yourself. You must work together, cooperatively. You can only teach the tools of recovery. The patients have to use the tools to establish abstinence.

## Dealing With Early Denial

The first few hours of treatment are not a time for harsh confrontation. It is a time for support and encouragement. The great healer in any treatment is love, and love necessitates action in truth. All patients are in some form of denial. They have been dishonest with themselves and others. They are lying, and they will lie to you. Your job is to reveal the lie, as gently as possible, reflecting truth. Particularly at first, this must be done very gently. You do not want to hurt the patients, or incur their wrath, but you must be dedicated to the truth. This program demands rigorous honesty.

Patients lie to themselves in many ways. They do not want to see the whole truth because the truth makes them feel anxious. They keep this anxiety under control by deceiving themselves. They distort reality just enough to feel reasonably comfortable. They defend themselves against the truth with unconscious lies called *defense mechanisms.* "As long as we could stop using for a while, we thought we were all right. We looked at the stopping, not the using" (*Narcotics Anonymous,* 1988, p. 3).

Patients minimize reality by thinking the illness is not so bad. Then they rationalize by thinking they have a good reason to use drugs. Then they deny by stubbornly refusing to see the problems at all. Treatment is an endless search for truth. "Those who do not recover are people who cannot or will not completely give themselves to this simple program, usually men and women who are constitutionally incapable of being honest with themselves. There are such unfortunates. They are not at fault; they seem to have been born that way. They are naturally incapable of grasping and developing a manner of living which demands rigorous honesty" (*Alcoholics Anonymous,* 1976, p. 58).

The job of a chemical dependency counselor is to love the patients in truth, knowing that the truth will set them free.

## Example of an Initial Contact

Approach the patient. Reach out and take the patient's hand. "Hi, Ralph." Use the patient's first name. "I'm _____ (your name), "I'm going to be your counselor. How are you doing so far?"

The patient may look at the floor and then at the wall. Know the importance of silence and wait.

The patient finally looks up. "I'm okay . . . I guess."

"When I came into treatment, I was feeling scared too. The first 3 days are going to be the hardest. After that, it's going to be all downhill. This is the beginning of recovery. Is there anything I can do for you right now to make you feel more comfortable?"

"I don't think so," Ralph says, looking relieved.

Lean forward and touch the patient's arm. "If you feel uncomfortable, I want you to tell me or the nurse, okay? We want you to feel as good as possible even in withdrawal. How you feel is important to us." The therapeutic alliance is being established.

The patient may never have experienced unconditional positive regard before. It may seem strange to him. To many it is unbelievable. Patients come into treatment with preconceived ideas about how treatment is going to go. Many think they are going to be shamed or punished. When they are greeted with love and affection, it comes as a great surprise. Your words of support and concern are as soothing as a warm bath.

All chemically dependent patients, at some level, want to punish themselves. They feel guilty about what they have done, and they are waiting for the executioner. They expect to be treated poorly, blamed and shamed. When you treat them with respect, they ask themselves why people are treating them so nicely. "Could it be that I am worth it?"

Tell the patients that they are important. The staff cares about how they feel and what they want. You are here to help. You want to help. You are going to respond to the patient's needs. It might be tough for a while, but things are going to get better.

## How to Check for Organic Brain Dysfunction

■

Patients need to be checked for medical problems, particularly organic brain syndrome. Some patients coming in to treatment are organically compromised, and they need immediate medical treatment to prevent further damage. Patients may be intoxicated, in withdrawal, or they may have a serious vitamin deficiency called Wernicke's encephalopathy.

You should be familiar with how to check a patient for these cognitive problems. The Cognitive Capacity Screening Exam (Appendix 1) is an excellent way to screen for organic brain problems (Jacobs et al., 1977). The Mini-Mental State Exam is a similar assessment test (Folstein, Folstein, & McHugh, 1975). Either of these tests is a brief 10-minute assessment of how the brain is functioning. The tests are simple and they come up with a score. If the patient falls below the cut-off score, inform medical professionals of the organic problems. If you notice anything unusual about how the patient moves, acts, or speaks, tell a physician or nurse. Always count on your medical staff or the patient's family physician. They are more skilled at these examinations than you are.

## The Initial Assessment

■

In the first few hours, you must determine if patients fit into your program. Do they have a problem with chemicals? Do they have the resources necessary for treatment? Are they well enough to move through your program? This criterion for admission is different for different facilities. For the most part, you will start by asking yourself certain basic questions: Does this person have a problem with chemicals? Does she or he need treatment? What kind of treatment does she or he need?

Two quick screening tests for alcoholism have been developed: the Short Michigan Alcoholism Screening Test (SMAST), in Appendix 2 here, and the CAGE Questionnaire, in Appendix 3 (Ewing, 1984; Selzer, Winokun, & van Rooijen, 1975). SMAST is a 13-question version of the original Michigan Alcoholism Screening Test (MAST). The SMAST has been shown to be as effective as the MAST. It has greater than 90% sensitivity to detect alcoholism. It can be administered to the patient or the spouse.

The Substance Abuse Subtle Screening Inventory (SASSI) was developed to screen patients who are defensive and in denial. The SASSI measures defensiveness and the subtle attributes that are common in chemically dependent persons. It is a difficult test to fake, unlike the MAST or the CAGE. The SASSI gives the patients the opportunity to respond honestly about their problems with chemicals, but it also measures the patients' possible abuse, using questions that do not pertain to chemicals (Creager, 1989; Miller, 1985). Patients can complete the SASSI in 10 to 15 minutes and it takes only a minute or two to score. It identifies accurately 98% of patients who need residential treatment, 90% of nonusers, and 87% of early-stage abusers (Miller, 1985).

The Addiction Severity Index (ASI) is a widely used structured interview that is designed to provide important information about what might contribute to a patient's alcohol or drug problem. The instrument assesses seven dimensions that typically are of concern in chemical dependency: medical status, employment/support status, drug/alcohol use, legal status, family history, family/social relationships, and psychiatric status. The ASI is designed to be administered by a trained technician and takes about an hour (McLellan, Luborsky, & Woody, 1980).

The Recovery Attitude and Treatment Evaluator (RAATE) is a measure of patient readiness. It assesses patient resistance and impediments to treatment. The instrument is a structured interview that measures five scales: degree of resistance to treatment, degree of resistance to continuing care, acuity of biomedical problems, acuity of psychiatric problems, and extent of social/family/environmental systems that do not support recovery (Mee-Lee, 1985, 1988).

Laboratory tests can be used to corroborate suspicions about excessive alcohol use that have been generated by the history and physical. None of the tests alone or in combination can diagnose alcoholism, but they add to the certainty of the diagnosis and warn the patient of physical complications. High serum levels of liver enzymes can represent alcohol-induced hepatic injury. Gamma-glutamyl transferase (GGT), is elevated in two thirds of alcoholics. Aspartate aminotransferase (AST) and alanine aminotransferase (ALT) are elevated in about one half of alcoholics. Alteration of fat metabolism causes elevated serum triglycerides in about one fourth of alcoholics. Alkaline phosphatase is elevated in about one sixth of alcoholics. Total bilirubin is elevated in about one seventh of alcoholics. Mean corpuscular volume (MCV) is elevated in about one fourth of alcoholics. Uric acid is elevated in about one tenth of alcoholics (Brostoff, 1994; DuPont, 1994; Wallach, 1992).

*American Society of Addiction Medicine (ASAM) Patient Placement Criteria*

All patients need to be assessed in the following six dimensions:

1. Acute intoxication and or withdrawal complications
2. Biomedical conditions and complications
3. Emotional/behavioral conditions and complications
4. Treatment acceptance/resistance
5. Relapse/continued use potential
6. Recovery/living environment

These are the areas of assessment that have been developed by the American Society of Addiction Medicine (ASAM) (1996) in their new handbook, *Patient Placement Criteria for the Treatment of Psychoactive Substance Use Disorders* (PPC-2). All counselors need to have a copy of this manual, and use these criteria in deciding which level of care a patient needs. A copy of the criteria can be obtained by contacting the American Society of Addiction Medicine, 4601 North Park Avenue, Upper Arcade, Suite 101, Chevy Chase, Maryland 20815. The manual details specific criteria for admission, continued stay, and discharge for all levels of treatment, adult and adolescent.

For brevity, the present manual will concentrate on the criteria for admission and discharge of outpatient and inpatient treatment. These are the criteria that a counselor will use the most often. The criteria are as objective and as measurable as possible, but some clinical interpretation is involved. Psychoactive disorders are no different from any other medical evaluation. Assessment and treatment are based on a mix of objectively measured criteria and professional judgment. Six dimensions need to be assessed:

1. Acute intoxication and/or withdrawal complications
   a. What risk is associated with the patient's current level of intoxication?
   b. Is there significant risk of severe withdrawal symptoms, based on the patient's previous withdrawal history, amount, frequency, and recency of discontinuation of chemical use?
   c. Is the patient currently in withdrawal? To measure withdrawal, use the Clinical Institute Withdrawal Assessment of Alcohol or Benzodiazepine Scale (CIWA) or the Narcotic Withdrawal Scale (ASAM, 1996; Fultz & Senay, 1975).
   d. Does the patient have the supports necessary to assist in ambulatory detoxification, if medically safe?
2. Biomedical conditions or complications
   a. Are there current physical illnesses, other than withdrawal, that may need to be addressed, or that may complicate treatment?
   b. Are there chronic conditions that may affect treatment?
3. Emotional behavioral complications
   a. Are there current psychiatric illnesses or psychological, emotional, or behavioral problems that need treatment or may complicate treatment?
   b. Are there chronic psychiatric problems that affect treatment?
4. Treatment acceptance or resistance
   a. Does the patient object to treatment?
   b. Does the patient feel coerced into coming to treatment?
   c. Does the patient appear to be complying with treatment only to avoid a negative consequence, or does he or she appear to be self-motivated?

5. Relapse potential
    a. Is the patient in immediate danger of continued use?
    b. Does the patient have any recognition of, understanding of, or skills with which he or she can cope with his or her addiction problems to prevent continued use?
    c. What problems will potentially continue to distress the patient if the patient is not successfully engaged in treatment at this time?
    d. How aware is the patient of relapse triggers, ways to cope with cravings, and skills to control impulses to continue use?
6. Recovery/living environment
    a. Are there any dangerous family members, significant others, living situations, or school/working situations that pose a threat to treatment success?
    b. Does the patient have supportive friendships, financial resources, or educational vocational resources that can increase the likelihood of treatment success?
    c. Are there legal, vocational, social service agency, or criminal justice mandates that may enhance the patient's motivation for treatment?

Patients must be able to understand treatment. They must be intellectually capable of absorbing the material. They must be physically and emotionally stable enough to go through the treatment process. They must not be actively harmful to themselves or others. They cannot be overtly psychotic. They cannot have such a serious medical or psychiatric problem that they cannot learn.

*DSM Criteria for Diagnosis*

To make a diagnosis, use the criteria listed in the latest addition of the *Diagnostic and Statistical Manual of Mental Disorders (DSM)* published by the American Psychiatric Association. Order a copy of this from the American Psychiatric Association, 1400 K Street, NW, Washington, DC 20005. A new edition comes out every few years, so there will be changes in the criteria from time to time. The 1994 criteria are listed in Appendix 4.

*Diagnosis: Drug Abuse*

A maladaptive pattern of psychoactive substance use leading to clinically significant impairment or distress indicated by one (or more) of the following, occurring within a 12-month period:

1. Recurrent substance use resulting in a failure to fulfill major role obligations at work, school or home (e.g., repeated absences or poor work performance related to substance use; substance-related absences, suspensions, or expulsions from school; neglect of children or household)
2. Recurrent use in situations in which use is physically hazardous (e.g., driving an automobile or operating a machine when performance is impaired by substance use)
3. Recurrent substance-related legal problems
4. Continued substance use despite having persistent or recurrent social or interpersonal problems caused or exacerbated by the effects of the substance (e.g., arguments with spouse about consequences of intoxication, physical fights)

The symptoms never met the criteria for Psychoactive Substance Dependence for this class of substance.

*Questions to Ask the Patient*

1. What are your drinking and drug habits?
2. Was there ever a period in your life when you drank or used drugs too much?
3. Have drugs or alcohol ever caused problems for you?
4. Has anyone ever objected to your drinking or drug use?

If you are unable to diagnose abuse, check with the family. This patient may be in denial, and you may get more of the truth from someone else. Family members, particularly a spouse or a parent, may give you a more accurate clinical picture of the problems.

If you diagnose abuse, move on to the dependency questions.

*Diagnosis: Chemical Dependency*

Chemical dependency is a maladaptive pattern of substance use, leading to clinically significant impairment or distress, as manifested by three (or more) of the following, occurring at any time in the same 12-month period:

1. Tolerance, as defined by either of the following:
   a. A need for markedly increased amounts of the substance to achieve intoxication or desired effect.
   b. Markedly diminished effect with continued use of the same amount of the substance.
2. Withdrawal, as manifested by either of the following:
   a. The characteristic withdrawal syndrome for the substance.
   b. The same (or a closely related) substance is taken to relieve or avoid withdrawal symptoms.
3. The substance is often taken in larger amounts or over a longer period of time than was intended.
4. There is a persistent desire or one or more unsuccessful efforts to cut down or control substance use.
5. A great deal of time spent in activities necessary to get the substance (e.g., visiting multiple doctors or driving long distances), use the substance (e.g., chain smoking), or recover from its effects.
6. Important social, occupational, or recreational activity given up or reduced because of substance use.
7. The substance use is continued despite knowledge of having a persistent or recurrent psychological or physical problem that is likely to have been caused or exacerbated by the use of the substance (e.g., current cocaine use despite recognition of cocaine-induced depression, or continued drinking despite recognition that an ulcer was made worse by alcohol consumption)

Specify if

*with physiological dependence*: evidence of tolerance or withdrawal,
*without physiological dependence*: no evidence of tolerance or withdrawal.

Explain to the patients that the diagnosis is your best professional judgment. It is important that the patients make up their own minds. Patients need to collect the evidence for themselves and get accurate in their thinking. Do they have a problem or not? This is a good time to explain about denial and how it keeps patients from seeing the truth.

*How to Determine the Level of Care Needed*

Once you know the patient has a significant problem, you must decide the level of care the patient needs. There are five levels of care generally offered across the United States:

Level 0.5. *Early Intervention.* Early intervention is an organized service delivered in a wide variety of settings designed to explore and address problems or risk factors that are related to substance use and to assist the individual in recognizing the harmful consequences of inappropriate substance use. Patients who need early intervention do not meet the diagnostic criteria of either chemical abuse or chemical dependency, but they have significant problems with substances. The rest of the treatment levels include patients who meet the criteria for psychoactive substance abuse or dependency.

Level I: *Outpatient Treatment.* Outpatient treatment takes place in a nonresidential facility or an office run by addiction professionals. The patient comes in for individual or group therapy sessions, usually fewer than 9 hours per week.

Level II: *Intensive Outpatient/Partial Hospitalization.*
    Level II.1: Intensive Outpatient Treatment. This is a structured day or evening program from 9 or more hours of programming per week. These programs have the capacity to refer patients for their medical, psychological, or pharmacological needs.
    Level II.5: Partial Hospitalization. Partial hospitalization generally includes 20 or more hours of intense programming per week. These programs have ready access to psychiatric, medical, and laboratory services.

Level III: *Residential/Inpatient Services.*
    Level III.1: Clinically Managed Low-Intensity Residential Services. This is a halfway house.
    Level III.3: Clinically Managed Medium-Intensity Residential Services. This is an extended care program oriented around long-term management.
    Level III.5: Clinically Managed High-Intensity Residential Services. This is a therapeutic community designed to maintain recovery.
    Level III.7: Medically Monitored Intensive Inpatient Treatment. This is a residential facility that provides a 24-hour-a-day structured treatment. This program is monitored by a physician who manages the psychiatric, physical, and pharmacological needs of her patients.

Level IV: *Medically Managed Intensive Inpatient Treatment.* This facility is a 24-hour program that has the resources of a hospital. Physicians provide daily medical management.

*Criteria for Outpatient Treatment (Adults)*

Adult patients qualify for outpatient treatment if they meet the diagnostic criteria for Psychoactive Substance Use Disorder as defined by the current *DSM* and if they meet all six of the following criteria:

1. Patient is not acutely intoxicated and is at minimal risk of suffering severe withdrawal symptoms.
2. All medical conditions are stable and do not require inpatient management.
3. All of the following:
   a. The individual's anxiety, guilt, and/or depression, if present, appear to be related to substance related problems rather than to a coexisting psychiatric/emotional/behavioral condition. If the patient had psychiatric/emotional/behavioral problems other than those caused by substance use, the problems are being treated by an appropriate mental health professional.
   b. Mental status does not preclude the patient from comprehending and understanding the program or participating in the treatment process.
   c. Patient is not at risk of harming self or others.
4. Both of the following:
   a. Patient expresses a willingness to cooperate with the program and attend all scheduled activities.
   b. The patient may admit that he or she has a problem with alcohol or drugs, but the patient requires monitoring and motivating strategies. The patient does not need a more structured program.
5. Patient can remain abstinent only with support and can do so between appointments.
6. One of the following:
   a. Environment is sufficiently supportive to make outpatient treatment feasible. Family or significant others are supportive of recovery.
   b. The patient does not have the ideal support system in his or her current environment, but the patient is willing to obtain such support.
   c. Family or significant others are supportive, but they need professional interventions to improve chances of success.

*Criteria for Inpatient Treatment (Adults)*

Adult patients need inpatient treatment if they meet the *DSM* diagnostic criteria for Substance Use Disorder and meet at least two of the following criteria:

1. Patient presents a risk of severe withdrawal or the patient has had past failures on entering treatment after detox.
2. Patient has medical conditions that present imminent danger of damaging health if use resumes or concurrent medical illness needs medical monitoring.
3. One of the following:
   a. Emotional/behavioral problems interfere with abstinence and stability to the degree that there is a need for a structured 24-hour environment.
   b. There is a moderate risk of behaviors endangering self or others. Current suicidal/homicidal thoughts with no action plan and a history of suicidal gestures or homicidal threats.
   c. The patient is manifesting stress behaviors related to losses or anticipated losses that significantly impair daily living. A 24-hour facility is necessary to address the addiction.

    d. There is a history or presence of violent or disruptive behavior during intoxication with imminent danger to self or others.

    e. Concomitant personality disorders are of such severity that the accompanying dysfunctional behaviors require continuous boundary-setting interventions.

4. Despite consequences, the patient does not accept the severity of the problem and needs intensive motivating strategies available in a 24-hour structured setting.

5. One of the following:

    a. Despite active participation at a less intensive level of care or in a self-help fellowship, the patient is experiencing an acute crisis with an intensification of addiction symptoms. Without 24-hour supervision the patient will continue to use.

    b. The patient cannot control her or his use as long as alcohol or drugs are present in the environment.

    c. The treatments necessary for this patient require this level of care.

6. One of the following:

    a. Patient lives in an environment in which treatment is unlikely to succeed (e.g., chaotic environment, rife with interpersonal conflict, which undermines the patient's efforts to change, nonexistent family, or other environmental conditions, or significant others living with the patient manifest current substance use and are likely to undermine the patient's recovery).

    b. Treatment accessibility prevents participation in a less intensive level of care.

    c. There is a danger of physical, sexual, or emotional abuse in the current environment.

    d. The patient is engaged in an occupation where continued use constitutes a substantial imminent risk to personal or public safety.

*Criteria for Outpatient Treatment (Adolescents)*

Adolescent patients qualify for outpatient treatment if they meet *DSM* criteria for Substance Use Disorder and the following dimensions:

1. Patient is not intoxicated and presents no risk of withdrawal.

2. The patient has no biomedical conditions that would interfere with outpatient treatment.

3. Patient's problem behaviors, moods, feelings, and attitudes are related to addiction rather than to a mental disorder, or the patient is being treated by an appropriate mental health professional. Patient's mental status is stable. Patient is not at risk for harming self or others.

4. Patient is willing to cooperate and attend all scheduled outpatient activities. Patient is responsive to parents, school authorities, and the staff.

5. Patient is willing to consider maintaining abstinence and recovery goals.

6. A sufficiently supportive recovery environment exists that makes outpatient treatment feasible.

    a. Parents or significant others are supportive of treatment and the program is accessible.

b. Patient currently does not have a supportive recovery environment, but he or she is willing to obtain such support.

c. Family or significant others are supportive but require professional intervention to improve chances of success.

*Criteria for Inpatient Treatment (Adolescents)*

To qualify for inpatient treatment the adolescent must meet the *DSM* criteria for Substance Use Disorder, all of the dimensions for outpatient treatment, plus at least two of the following dimensions:

1. The risk of withdrawal is present.
2. Continued use places the patient at imminent risk of serious damage to health, or biomedical condition requires medical management.
3. History reflects cognitive development of at least 11 years of age and significant impairment in social, interpersonal, occupational, or educational functioning as evidenced by one of the following:
   a. Current inability to maintain behavioral stability for more than a 48-hour period.
   b. Mild to moderate risk to self or others. Current suicidal/homicidal thoughts with no active plan and a history of suicidal/homicidal gestures.
   c. Behaviors sufficiently chronic and/or disruptive to require separation from current environment.
4. Patient is having difficulty acknowledging an alcohol or a drug problem and is not able to follow through with treatment in a less intense environment.
5. Patient is experiencing an intensification of addiction symptoms despite interventions in a less intense level of care; or patient has been unable to control use as long as alcohol or drugs are present in the patient's environment; or if abstinent, the patient is in crisis and appears to be in imminent danger of using alcohol or drugs.
6. One of the following:
   a. Environment is not conducive to successful treatment at a less intense level of care.
   b. The parents or legal guardians are unable to provide consistent participation necessary to support treatment in a less intense level of care.
   c. Accessibility to treatment precludes participation in a less intense level of care.
   d. There is a danger of physical, sexual, or emotional abuse in the patient's current environment.

*How to Share the Diagnosis With the Patient*

You need to discuss your findings with the patient and, if possible, with the patient's family. If you are in recovery yourself, this is not a good time to share much of your story. This may frighten the patient, and make her or him wonder about your own state of health. Patients need a stable, well-adjusted counselor. You can tell a patient that you are recovering, but don't get into war stories about your drinking and using days.

As you share the diagnosis with the patient, make sure to take the time to encourage and reinforce him or her for having the courage to come into treatment.

Check out how the patient feels. It is not good to be suffering, and the patient has been in misery for a long time. It was scary to come into treatment, but he or she made it. You are proud of him. Most persons who complete their first inpatient treatment ultimately achieve a stable recovery. They might have to come into treatment again, even again and again, but the first treatment is a major turning point. Patients learn things in the first treatment that they never forget. They learn that there is a disease called chemical dependency, that there is treatment for it, that the treatment doesn't hurt, and that people can live happy, sober lifestyles.

*Example of How to Share the Diagnosis*

After the initial assessment, talk with the patient. "Ralph, I have diagnosed you as having alcohol dependence and cannabis dependence. Do you have any questions?"

"I don't think the pot has ever been a problem for me," the patient says with a concerned look on his face. The patient apparently wants to hold onto his use of marijuana. He wants to give up the alcohol, that's caused him a lot of problems, but he wants to keep the option open on using cannabis.

You understand and immediately intervene. "That's a common belief. You think that because alcohol has given you most of the problems that it is the only problem. We have found that all mood-altering chemicals are a problem. You can't just quit the booze and smoke a little dope. Studies shows that if you were to quit drinking and just use pot, then the pot would ultimately lead you back to drinking. This is called cross-tolerance. Both drugs, alcohol and cannabis, do essentially the same thing, they are downers. They are a way of treating feelings inappropriately. What we learn in treatment is how to use our feelings appropriately."

## Assigning a Treatment Buddy

Once you have made your initial assessment and feel you have the beginnings of a therapeutic alliance, introduce the patient to a treatment buddy. If your facility allows access to other patients, check the patient list and come up with a patient of the same sex who is doing well in the program. This person will usually be a few weeks ahead of your new patient in the program. Try to match personalities a bit so the two people will have a good chance of hitting it off. Get the cooperation from the buddy first, and then introduce them. Tell the patient that the buddy will give him or her a tour of the treatment setting and introduce her or him to the staff and the other patients. Tell the buddy to share her or his experience, strength, and hope with the patient. Do not leave the patient alone. The worst thing for someone just coming into treatment is to be left alone where the illness can work unencumbered. Patients who isolate themselves have a much higher chance of leaving treatment against medical advice.

Tell the treatment buddy to stick with the patient until the patient adjusts to treatment. This will take a varying amount of time depending on the patient. If the patient is resisting, you will have to be more aggressive and keep him or her with the buddy longer. You may have to trade off buddies, particularly if this is a difficult patient. This Twelfth Step work is good for all parties concerned, the patient and the buddies. There is nothing like working with someone in early recovery to solidify your own program.

**The Intoxicated Patient**

The intoxicated patient can be difficult for everyone to deal with. Intoxication is the organic brain syndrome that is produced by the ingestion of high doses of all classes of psychoactive substances except nicotine. Central nervous system depressants, such as opiates, inhalants, alcohol, barbiturates, and benzodiazepines create intoxicated states characterized by slurred speech, incoordination, and an unsteady gait. Central nervous system stimulants, like cocaine and amphetamines, create signs such as agitation, talkativeness, vigilance, and grandiosity. Cannabis produces euphoria and an altered time sense. Hallucinogens produce hallucinations, usually of a visual nature. Inhalants produce a light-headed feeling and confusion (Schuckit, 1984).

*How to Determine the Level of Intoxication*

Patients who have taken enough of a drug to compromise their vital signs are experiencing a toxic reaction. This is a drug overdose where they have taken so much of a drug that their bodies cannot function properly.

Patients who demonstrate a drug-related syndrome, with relatively stable vital signs, and who show signs of withdrawal, are said to be in withdrawal. Withdrawal is evidenced by physical and psychological symptoms that develop when a physically addicting drug is stopped too quickly.

Patients with stable vital signs, and no symptoms of withdrawal, who have a drug-induced confusion, are experiencing an organic brain syndrome. Organic brain syndrome is characterized by confusion, disorientation, and decreased intellectual functioning (Schuckit, 1984).

*The Patient's Reaction to Intoxication*

Patients in these acute organic states can seem relatively normal or extremely bizarre. They can be actively psychotic or in a panic. They can experience intense flashbacks. High doses of amphetamines, cocaine, and phencyclidine (PCP) may produce organic delirium. Delirium is characterized by reduced ability to maintain attention and by disorganized thinking. The patient will not be able to follow a conversation. The disorganized thinking will be manifested by rambling, irrelevant, or incoherent speech. This delirium is usually brief (less than 6 hours) after amphetamine or cocaine use, but it can last up to a week after PCP use (American Psychiatric Association, 1987; Schuckit, 1984).

Acute use of amphetamines, cocaine, or PCP may result in a delusional state. Delusions are false beliefs that are intractable to logic. The patient may feel that someone or some group is out to get him or her. They may think they have strange or unusual powers. These delusions are usually brief, lasting from several hours to several days, but in some patients they can last up to a year, even in the absence of further drug use. Hallucinogen use can result in the development of delusions (Vardy & Kay, 1983). Brief psychotic states have also been reported following cannabis use (Hollister, 1986).

During acute intoxication and withdrawal it is not unusual for a patient to complain of hallucinations. These hallucinations are usually visual or tactile, rarely auditory. This is a transient psychotic state. Patients may see trailing of objects (e.g., when they move their hand they can see a brief image extend behind the solid object like a jet contrail). The walls or floor may seem move, or the patients may see bugs or other things that are not there. They may feel something unusual on or under their skin. These hallucinations are usually brief, but the patient will need to be reassured and supported. The patient's brain is chemically correcting.

These negative experiences can be used to give patients evidence that they need to stop abusing chemicals.

*What to Do With an Intoxicated Patient*

Never argue with intoxicated patients; this will get you nowhere. They're probably not going to remember the conversation anyway. Briefly introduce yourself, let the medical staff examine them, and let them sleep it off. Intoxicated patients, and patients in withdrawal, will mainly be the responsibility of the medical staff. They will be watching the patients carefully and monitoring their vital signs.

There is an old idea that has been floating around the field for years that the patient should hurt. The theory goes that this will help a patient to learn that he or she has a problem. Doing this would be a medically unsound practice. It is inappropriate to subject patients to severe withdrawal symptoms just to teach them a lesson; some of them would die. Patients should be medicated to a point where they stay in mild withdrawal—this hurts enough.

Intoxicated patients who want to talk will have to be reassured and educated. They are not bad people; they are sick. If they want to talk a lot, let some of the other patients do the talking. Join in if you have to. The patients will definitely need to trade off. This is very tiring work, but it is beneficial for them to see the intoxicated patient so messed up. It reinforces for the other patients that they never want to go through this again.

Patients need to be educated about withdrawal. What can they expect? The main thing they need to hear is that things are going to get better. With every hour that passes, things are going to improve. The staff is not going to let them feel too uncomfortable. It is going to feel uncomfortable sometimes, but the staff is not going to allow the pain to reach intolerable levels.

Many of the patients' thoughts and feelings now are chemically induced. Patients need to understand that they are going to have some wide swings in mood in acute withdrawal. Most patients will be feeling at various times depressed, agitated, irritable, and crabby. They need their fears and concerns put to rest. Let them talk. Answer their questions. Listen. These patients need a lot of attention.

*Example of a Conversation With an Intoxicated Patient*

As a counselor walks into the patient's room, there might be a heavy sweet smell of booze in the air.

"Hi, Barbara, how are you doing?"

"Not good," the patient says. There is a pained look on her face.

"It will get better," you might respond, reaching out and squeezing the patient's arm. "I promise you that. You're going to get free of this thing."

"I hope so."

"It's going to happen," you say. "Either you will hook into this program or you'll die. It's as simple as that."

"I don't want to do that."

"I know you don't. No one wants to feel miserable. Looks like you've been feeling pretty bad."

"Yeah."

"Well, that's all over now. The nurse will keep you as comfortable as possible, and when you're ready, we'll start to work."

"Okay."

Stay and chat for the next 20 minutes or so. It's all casual and comforting, no heavy stuff. All questions need to be answered. Then you should close the session. "There will be a lot of people looking in on you for the next few days, Barbara. Don't hole up in here by yourself. There's an old AA saying: What we cannot do alone we can do together." Then stand up and put your hand on the patient's shoulder. "Hang in there. I'll be in to see you pretty often. If you need to talk, my office is right down the hall."

## Detoxification

Except for the hallucinogens, PCP, and the inhalants, prolonged drug or alcohol use is accompanied by the development of drug tolerance and physical dependence. In the case of withdrawal from the central nervous depressants (alcohol, barbiturates, and benzodiazepines), tremulousness, sweating, anxiety, and irritability may give way to life-threatening seizures and delirium. Opioid withdrawal, although the patient feels uncomfortable, is not life-threatening (Group for the Advancement of Psychiatry Committee on Alcoholism and the Addictions, 1991). Withdrawal from central nervous system stimulants may be accompanied by a "crash," characterized by depression, fatigue, increased need for sleep, and increased appetite (Gawin & Ellinwood, 1988).

You must be able to determine where your patient is in withdrawal. This is best accomplished by using the Clinical Institute Withdrawal Assessment of Alcohol Scale (Appendix 5). This scale can be modified to rate withdrawal from the benzodiazepines. To score withdrawal from narcotics, use the Narcotic Withdrawal Scale (Appendix 6; Fultz & Senay, 1975). Patients who are in moderate to severe withdrawal need to be assessed every hour until the symptoms are under control (Adinoff, Bone, & Linnolila, 1988).

Detoxification is the gradual, safe elimination of the drug from the body. Some drugs, like alcohol, are detoxified quickly, usually within a few days, but the benzodiazepines may take weeks or months (Burant, 1990; Schuckit, 1984). Many patients are suffering from polysubstance withdrawal and this can complicate the clinical picture. The drugs most likely to cause serious physical problems are the depressants. These patients can deteriorate rapidly.

## How Patients React in Detox

Most any physical or mental symptom can present itself in withdrawal. No heavy confrontation is necessary. These patients are sick and irritable. They are sleeping poorly. They have powerful cravings. This is where many patients walk out of treatment. They feel they can't stand the symptoms anymore. These patients need medication, reassurance, and support. You must be gentle. Keep telling them over and over that it will get better. If they stay clean and sober, they will never have to go though this misery again.

During withdrawal, patients feel restless and they have strong cravings. This physiological and psychological need for the substance is the primary motivating force behind drug addiction. The patients' bodies are driving them to return to their drug of choice. The cells are screaming for relief. They have been in withdrawal hundreds of times before, but they have always treated it by getting intoxicated again. Now they are going to stick it out, striving for recovery. All of these patients think about leaving treatment, but when they get to feeling a little better, they reach the highest chance of actually going out the door. You must be on top of this by constantly assessing where the patient is physically and psychologically.

Detoxification should be managed in a room without excessive stimulation. The area needs to be quiet without bright lights. Familiar people, pictures, a clock, and clothes are helpful. Soft conversation that reassures the patient and keeps him or her oriented is best. The staff should display a positive attitude of mutual respect. Reassuring touches (e.g., taking pulse, hand on shoulder) are helpful (Baum & Iber, 1980).

Once the acute withdrawal syndrome has passed, patients remain in a protracted abstinence syndrome for weeks or even years. Relapse is higher during this period of physiological adjustment. The protracted abstinence syndrome varies depending on the drug of dependency. Typically it is a symptom constellation opposite of that which the patient was using the drug to produce (e.g., the patient using stimulants to increase energy will experience lethargy; Geller, 1990).

## The AMA Threat

Patients in an inpatient or an outpatient setting can present an AMA threat. They can leave treatment *Against Medical Advice.* They usually isolate themselves first from their treatment peers and the staff. The addictive thinker must lie to himself or herself, and believe the lie is the truth, for the illness to work. The addiction cannot exist in the light of the truth. The disease has a much better chance of working in isolation. That is why patients must not be left alone in early treatment until they have stabilized.

The illness cooks a stew of inaccurate information: minimization (My use is not that bad); rationalization (I have a good reason to use); projection (It's not my problem; it's their problem); and denial (a stubborn refusal to see truth). All of these defenses are used to distort reality.

You may first get wind of an AMA threat as you assess the patient, or you may learn of it from another patient or from a member of the staff. The patient shares that he or she is thinking about leaving treatment. You must intervene when you see this problem developing. As patients tell more and more lies to themselves, they become convinced that the lies are the truth. They keep collecting information that proves the illness is right.

Most of the patients' reasons will be inaccurate. They are distortions of reality. Patients may not be aware that the real reason they are leaving treatment is to use their drug of choice. Patients delude themselves. They are craving, but many of them don't know it. They believe the inaccurate thinking.

## Example of an AMA Intervention

The intervention desperately needed here is the truth. Every time the patient brings up a reason for leaving treatment, you challenge her with the truth. Be gentle, the truth is on your side, and a big part of the patient wants to know the facts. Don't talk to the illness side of the patient; talk to the side that wants to get well.

*Patient:* I can quit on my own.

*Counselor:* You've tried that before, and you have always failed.

*Patient:* This time I can do it.

*Counselor:* Your alcoholism is worse now than it's ever been. It's not better, it's worse.

*Patient:* I'll go to meetings.

*Counselor:* You may do that for awhile, but it's my opinion that you won't be able to make it out there.

*Patient:* I think I can.

*Counselor:* You have had that thought a hundred times before. Give the disease some credit. It's stronger than you are. Alcoholics Anonymous says no human power can remove our alcoholism. You will never lick this thing on your own.

*Patient:* I'll go to church.

*Counselor:* You need treatment.

*Patient:* I've got some marital problems that I need to work out. I can't do that in here.

*Counselor:* The best thing you can do for your marriage is to stay in here and get into a stable recovery. Why don't we call your wife and see if she wants you to leave?

*Patient:* I don't fit in here.

*Counselor:* What can you do to improve that situation? Maybe you can help someone else.

*Patient:* I'm not like these people. Their problems are much worse than mine.

*Counselor:* Didn't you get two DWIs?

*Patient:* Yes.

*Counselor:* But you're not like these people?

*Patient:* No.

*Counselor:* You have a lot of skills. You can do this.

This conversation can go on for quite some time. The longer you expose the lies the patient is telling him- or herself, the better the chance of keeping the patient in treatment. If you have to, see if the patient will agree to stay in treatment one more day or even one more hour. The longer the patient stays, the more opportunity you have to turn him or her around.

*How to Use the AMA Team*

The AMA team is a group of three or more of the treatment peers who have been selected by the staff to help other patients who are in trouble of leaving treatment early. Have them share their experience, strength, and hope with the patient. Often this group is more effective than you are. It is easier for the patient to trust people who have just gone through treatment. In an outpatient setting, if you don't have an AMA group, maybe one of the patients further along in the program will agree to encourage the patient to stay.

If there are any consequences the patient will face if he or she leaves treatment, this is the time to bring these things out. The patient may have been court-ordered into treatment. The patient's employment may be in jeopardy. The spouse or parent may have given the patient an ultimatum, "Get treatment or else." Use every angle you can as long as it is based in the truth.

The patient must be confronted with the truth until he or she hears it. There is a healthy side of the patient, the side that is sick of this problem and wants to recover. The truth is a very powerful tool. It is even more powerful when delivered in an atmosphere of loving support.

Some counselors feel that they have to hammer away at a patient's denial aggressively until they literally "break through it," but it can't be like a war where each person tries to attack the other. The aggressive technique is not recommended. The therapeutic alliance is too important to weaken. The therapeutic alliance must be built on mutual acceptance, trust, and unconditional positive regard. It is impossible to trust someone who is verbally beating on you. Raising your voice in anger is rarely beneficial to patients. This behavior harms your relationship and makes your job even harder than it is already. You will get angry with patients—that's normal, everyone does—but don't act abusive. Treat the patient the way you would want to be treated.

| *How to Use In-House Intervention* | If all else fails, you may have to arrange an in-house intervention. Here you gather the patient's family and concerned others together and have them tell the patient why they want the patient to stay in treatment. |
|---|---|

Have each of the participants write a letter stating how the patient's chemical dependency has adversely affected them. They need to give specific examples of how they were hurt when the patient was intoxicated or hung over. They share how they are feeling now and ask for what they want. They write down exactly what they are going to do if the patient doesn't agree to stay in treatment. A spouse may state she has been humiliated in front of friends. If the patient doesn't stay in treatment, she will divorce him. An employer may say he's weary of the patient calling in sick. If the patient doesn't stay in treatment, he will be fired. The kids could say that they have been embarrassed by the patient and want out of the home. A parent could talk about the lies and mistrust in the home and say they are going to withdraw their financial support.

In an intervention, the family is going to need a lot of encouragement. You need to help them with their letters and practice the intervention without the patient present. Once the group is gathered, bring the patient in and have each member share his or her letter. If the patient is still unwilling to stay in treatment, you can open the group up for discussion. Again, every time the patient gives the family a good reason for leaving, you and the family will tell the patient the truth.

| *How to Respond to Patients Who Leave AMA* | Do everything in your power to keep the patients in treatment, but if they decide to leave early, wish them well and invite them to come back if they have further problems. Many patients will leave for a time and then return. Whatever happens, remember that when the patient was in treatment you told that person the truth. A patient leaving treatment is no reflection on you or your skills. You did not lose; you planted a seed of the truth that will grow later. |
|---|---|

Programs that are more genuinely loving will keep more patients than programs that are confrontive. The key balance to be struck is to confront the patient in an atmosphere of support. A loving environment is attractive and everyone wants more of it. You will know that you have struck the right balance when many of your patients are reluctant to leave treatment at the end of their stay. They have felt so accepted, loved, and supported that they don't want to leave an environment where they have achieved major growth.

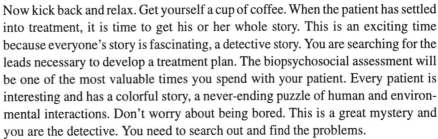

CHAPTER
TWO

# The Biopsychosocial Interview

Now kick back and relax. Get yourself a cup of coffee. When the patient has settled into treatment, it is time to get his or her whole story. This is an exciting time because everyone's story is fascinating, a detective story. You are searching for the leads necessary to develop a treatment plan. The biopsychosocial assessment will be one of the most valuable times you spend with your patient. Every patient is interesting and has a colorful story, a never-ending puzzle of human and environmental interactions. Don't worry about being bored. This is a great mystery and you are the detective. You need to search out and find the problems.

The purpose of the biopsychosocial interview is to find out exactly what the problems are, where they came from. Then you need to decide what you are going to do about them. All diseases have biological, psychological, and social factors that contribute to dysfunction. These ingredients mingle together, leaving the patient in a state of dis-ease. The patients don't feel easy, they feel dis-easy. All major psychiatric diseases have biopsychosocial components. All chemical dependency affects the cells (biology), the emotions, attitudes, and behavior (psychology), and relationships (sociology).

To conduct your biopsychosocial interview, you will need the biopsychosocial form (Appendix 32) and a quiet place where you will not be disturbed. The interview will take at least an hour, maybe two, maybe more. Many beginning counselors get bogged down in this interview, because they become overwhelmed with information, or they try to begin to treat the problems too early. This interview is not for treatment, it is for assessment. The best way to avoid these traps is to let the patients do most of the talking. You ask the questions and let them tell their story while you write it down. Ask for more information only if you are confused or uncertain about what they are describing. You must understand the story and how the patient feels.

It will take you a while to become a skilled interviewer. It takes keen insight to see the problems clearly as they develop. You will get better at this as you become more experienced.

21

**How to Conduct the Interview**

■

Begin the biopsychosocial interview by telling the patient what you are going to do.

"The purpose of this interview is to see exactly what the problems are, where they come from, and what we are going to do in treatment. From this information, we will develop your treatment plan. You need to keep me real accurate here. Don't make things bigger than they were, or smaller than they were, just tell me exactly what happened. Any questions? Let's begin."

Now relax and begin your interview. Don't be in a hurry. This is fascinating and fun. Ask the following questions and write the answers down in the blank provided on the biopsychosocial form.

*Date:*
*Patient name:*
*Age:*
*Sex:*
*Marital status:*
*Children:*
*Residence:*
*Others in residence:*
*Length of residence:*
*Education:* Mark highest grade completed.
*Occupation:*
*Characteristics of the informant:* Mark down whether or not you trust the information the patient is giving you. Is the patient reliable? If so, write, "Reliable informant." If you do not trust the information for some reason, write down why you mistrust it. You may want to write, "Questionable informant."
*Chief complaint:* The chief problem that brought the patient to treatment. Use the patient's own words. If someone else gives you the chief complaint, list that person as the informant. "What was the chief problem that brought you to treatment?"
*History of the present problem:* Everything that pertains to the chief complaint. One good approach with histories is to say something like this: "As they are growing up, kids have a real accurate idea when things are right with them, and at home with their mom and dad, and when things are wrong. Go back into your childhood, and tell me where you think things began to go wrong for you. From that point, tell me the whole story, including what is bringing you into treatment now."

Let the patient tell his or her story, and for the most part you just copy it down. Use as many direct quotes as you can. Guide the patient only when you need to. You want the story to flow in a roughly chronological order. Most patients will do this naturally, but everyone jumps around a little. Stop them if they are going too fast or if you don't understand something. Don't let them ramble and get caught up in irrelevant details. Look for the problem areas.

The history of the present problem must contain the following information:

- *Age of onset:*
- *Duration of use:*

- *Patterns of use:* How do they drink? Are they binge drinkers or daily drinkers? Do they drink all day or only after work? How often do they drink?
- *Consequences of use:* Physical, psychological, or social problems caused by or exacerbated by drinking.
- *Previous treatment:* Whom did they see? What was the treatment? What were the results?
- *Blackouts:*
- *Tolerance:*
- *Withdrawal symptoms:*

*Past history:* History of the patient's life from infancy to the present is the next phase of the interview. The categories include:

- *Place of birth:*
- *Date of birth:*
- *Developmental milestones:* "Did you have any problems when you were born? Problems walking, talking, toilet training, reading, or writing? Did anyone ever say that you were a slow learner?" Cover developmental problems and intellectual problems here. Determine as best you can whether the patient can understand the material presented in your program. Most AA material is written at a sixth-grade level. Patients who read two grade levels below this are going to need help.
- *Raised with:* Primary caregivers, brothers, sisters, and what it was like to live with them?
- *Ethnic/cultural influences:* "What's your ethnic heritage? Are you French, Dutch, German?" (A black inner-city teenager is going to be verydifferent from a midwestern farmer.) You need to know something about the culture. How does the culture relate to such things as time orientation, family, sharing, cooperation, and taught customs that guide relationships? (For further information on cultural differences, read the book *Counseling the Culturally Different* by Sue & Sue, 1990.)
- *Home of origin:* "When you were growing up, how did it feel in the house where you were raised?"
- *Grade school:* "What kind of a kid were you in grade school? How did you get along with the other kids and the teachers?"
- *High school:* "What kind of a student were you in high school?"
- *College:* "What were you like in college?"
- *Military history:* "Were you ever in the armed services? How long? What was your highest rank? Did you get an honorable discharge?"
- *Occupational history:* "Briefly tell me about your work history. What kind of work have you done?" Include longest job held and any consequences of drug or alcohol use.
- *Employment satisfaction:* "How long have you been at your current job? Are you happily employed?"
- *Financial history:* "How is your current financial situation?"

- *Gambling:* "Have you ever had a problem with gambling?"
- *Sexual orientation:* "How old were you when you first had sex? Have you ever had a homosexual contact?"
- *Sexual abuse:* "Have you ever been sexually abused?"
- *Physical abuse:* "Have you ever been physically abused?"
- *Current sexual history:* "Are you having any current sexual problems?"
- *Relationship history:* Briefly describe this patient's relationship and friendship patterns. Does he or she have any close friends? Is he or she in a romantic relationship now? How is that going? Include consequences of chemical use. Some helpful questions include, "Do you have close friends? Have you ever been in love? How many times? Tell me a little bit about each relationship."
- *Social support for treatment:* "Does your family support you coming into treatment? What about your friends?" Thoroughly assess the patient's recovery environment. How supportive are family and friends going to be about recovery?
- *Spiritual orientation:* "Do you believe in God or a higher power or anything like that? Do you engage in any kind of religious activity, go to church or anything like that?"
- *Legal:* "Are you having any current problems with the law? Have you ever been arrested?"
- *Strengths:* "What are some of your strengths, some of your good qualities?"
- *Weaknesses:* "What are some of your weaknesses, some of your qualities that aren't so good?"
- *Leisure:* "What do you do for play, entertainment, or fun? What has been the affect of your chemical use?"
- *Depression:* "Have you ever felt depressed or down most of the day almost every day for more than 2 weeks?" If the patient has signs of depression, this needs to be flagged for the medical staff.
- *Mania:* "Have you ever felt so high or full of energy that you got into trouble or people thought you were acting strangely?" Mania is a distinct period of abnormally elevated, expansive, or irritable mood. This mood must be sustained for at least 2 full days.
- *Anxiety disorders:* "Have you ever been anxious for a long time? Have you ever had a panic attack?"
- *Eating disorder:* "Have you ever had any problems with appetite or eating, gorging, purging, starving yourself, or anything like that?"

*Medical history*

- *Illnesses:* "Have you ever had any physical illnesses, even the small ones, measles, mumps, chicken pox?"
- *Hospitalizations:* "Have you ever been in a hospital overnight?" Write down the reason for each hospitalization.

- *Allergies:* "Do you have any allergies?"
- *Medications at present:* "Are you taking any medication?"

*Family history*

- *Father:* "How old is your father? Is he in good, fair, or poor health? Any health problems? What's he like? How did he act when you were growing up?"
- *Mother:* "How old is your mother? Is she in good, fair, or poor health? What was she like when you were growing up?"
- *Other relatives with significant psychopathology:* "Did anyone else in your family have any problems with drugs or alcohol or any kind of mental disorder?"

*Mental status:* This is when you formally test the patient's mental condition.

- *Description of the patient:* Describe the patient's general appearance. How would you be able to pick the patient out of a crowd? Age, skin color, sex, weight, hair color, eye color, scars, glasses, mustache, etc.
- *Dress:* How are they dressed? Describe what they are wearing and how they are dressed. Are they overly neat, sloppy, casual, seductive, formal?
- *Sensorium:* Is the patient fully conscious and able to use her or his senses normally or does something seem to be clouding the patient's sensorium? Is he or she alert, lethargic, drowsy? Intoxicated patients will not have a clear sensorium.
- *Orientation:* A person is oriented to person, place, and time if they know their name, location, and today's date.
- *Attitude toward the examiner:* What is the patient's attitude toward you: cooperative, friendly, pleasant, hostile, suspicious, defensive?
- *Motor behavior:* Describe how the patient is moving. Anything unusual? Does the patient move normally, restlessly, continuously, slowly? Do they have a tremor or tic?
- *Speech:* How does the patient talk? Any speech or language problems? Does the patient talk normally, is he or she overly talkative, or minimally responsive? Do you detect a speech disorder?
- *Affect:* How is the patient's affect during the interview: appropriate, blunted, restricted, labile, dramatic overproduction?
- *Range of affect:* What is the patient's capacity to feel the whole range of feelings? Affect ranges from elation to depression. During the interview, you should see the patient cover a wide range of affect. Does the patient's range of feelings seem normal, constricted, blunted, flat?
- *Mood:* What is the feeling that clouds the patient's whole life? They might be calm, cheerful, anxious, depressed, elated, irritable, pessimistic, angry, neutral, or absorbed in any other sustained feeling.
- *Thought processes:* Does the patient have a normal stream of thought? Is she or he able to come up with clear ideas, form these ideas into speech,

and move the speech into the normal conversation? If the patient is hard to follow, write down why. Describe what the person is doing that makes the conversation difficult. Are the patient's thought processes logical and coherent, blocked, circumstantial, tangential, incoherent, distracted, evasive, persevered?

- *Abstract thinking:*

    Ask "What does this saying mean to you: People who live in glass houses shouldn't throw stones." An abstract answer is, "don't talk about people because you might have problems yourself." A concrete answer is, "they might break the glass."

    Ask "How are an egg and a seed alike?" An abstract answer is, "things grow from both." A concrete answer is, "they are both round." Using such questions, determine the patient's ability to abstract. Is it normal or is it impaired?

- *Suicidal ideation:* "Have you ever thought about hurting yourself or anything like that?" Describe all suicidal thoughts, acts, plans, or attempts.

- *Homicidal ideation:* "Have you ever thought about hurting someone else?" All thoughts, acts, plans, or attempts should be described.

- *Disorders of perception:* Disorders in how the patient perceives can be assessed by asking such questions as: "Have you ever seemed to hear things that other people couldn't seem to hear, like whispering voices, or anything like that? Have you ever seemed to see things that other people couldn't seem to see, like a vision? Have you ever smelled a strange smell that seemed out of place? A strange taste? Have you ever felt anything unusual on or under your skin?"

- *Delusions:* "Have you ever felt that anyone was paying special attention to you or anything like that? Have you ever felt that someone was out to hurt you or give you a hard time? Have you ever felt like you had any strange or unusual powers? Have you ever felt like one of the organs in your body wasn't operating properly?" A delusion is a false belief that is fixed.

- *Obsessions:* "Have you ever been bothered by thoughts that didn't make any sense and that kept coming back even when you tried not to think about them? Have you ever had awful thoughts like hurting someone or being contaminated by germs or anything like that?" Obsessions are persistent ideas, thoughts, impulses, or images that are experienced, at least at first, as intrusive and senseless.

- *Compulsions:* "Was there anything that you had to do over and over again and you couldn't stop doing it, like washing your hands over and over again, or checking something several times to make sure you had done it right?" Compulsions are repetitive, purposeful, and intentional behaviors that are performed in response to an obsession, or according to certain rules, or in a stereotyped fashion.

- *Intelligence:* Estimate the patient's level of intellectual functioning: above average, average, below average, borderline, retarded.

- *Concentration:* Describe the patient's ability to concentrate during the interview: Normal, mild, moderate, severe impairment.

- *Memory:*

  Immediate memory: Ask the patient to do this: "Listen carefully, I'm going to say some numbers. You say them right after me: 58931." After the patient has completed this task, ask her to do this: "Now I'm going to say some more numbers, this time I want you to say them backward, 439." Patients should be able to do five digits forward and three backward.

  Recent memory: Ask the patient to do this: "I'm going to give you three objects that I want you to remember: A red ball, an open window, and a police car. Now you remember those and I'll ask you what they are in a few minutes." Patients should be able to remember all three objects after 5 minutes.

  Remote memory: Patients should be able to tell you what they had for dinner last night or for breakfast this morning. They should know the names of the last five presidents of the United States. They should know their own past history.

- *Impulse control:* Estimate the ability of the patient to control his or her impulses.

- *Judgment:* Estimate the patient's ability to make good judgments. If you can't estimate from the interview, ask the patient a question. "If you were at the movies and were the first person to see smoke and fire, what would you do?" Patients should give a good answer that protects both themselves and the other people present.

- *Insight:* Do they know that they have a problem with chemicals? Do they understand something about the nature of the illness?

- *Motivation for treatment:* Is the patient committed to treatment? Estimate the level of treatment acceptance or resistance.

## Summary and Impression ■

Begin with the patient's childhood and summarize all you have heard and observed. Include all the problems you have seen and give your impression of where the patient stands on each of the following dimensions:

1. Acute intoxication and/or withdrawal complications
2. Biomedical conditions or complications
3. Emotional/behavioral complications
4. Treatment acceptance or resistance
5. Relapse potential
6. Recovery environment

## Diagnosis ■

Diagnose the problem using the *Diagnostic and Statistical Manual of Mental Disorders.*

**Disposition and Treatment Plan**

■

List and describe all of the problems that need treatment and how you plan to treat each problem.

**A Sample Biopsychosocial Interview**

■

Now let's go through an actual interview so you can see how it works. We'll describe how you should be thinking as we go through the interview.

The patient comes into the office. She is tall and thin, dressed in white jeans, and a white sweat shirt. She smiles as she sits down. She makes good eye contact and relaxes. Her face is pretty. She does not appear to be in any acute distress.

*Counselor:* Give me your full name, all three names please, and spell them all.

*Patient:* Patty P-A-T-T-Y Jean J-E-A-N Robbins R-O-B-B-I-N-S.

*Counselor:* How old are you?

*Patient:* Twenty-eight. (*The patient seems to relax even more. She sits further back in the chair and crosses her legs.*)

*Counselor:* Are you married?

*Patient:* No.

*Counselor:* Have you ever been?

*Patient:* No.

*Counselor:* Do you have any kids?

*Patient:* No.

*Counselor:* What's your current hometown?

*Patient:* Watertown, South Dakota.

*Counselor:* Who lives with you?

*Patient:* No one.

*Counselor:* How long have you lived there?

*Patient:* About 5 years.

*Counselor:* How much education do you have?

*Patient:* High school.

*Counselor:* Are you currently employed?

*Patient:* Yes.

*Counselor:* What do you do?

*Patient:* I am a beautician for The Cut Above.

*Counselor:* What was the chief problem that brought you to treatment?

*Patient:* I knew I couldn't go on drinking the way I was.

*Counselor:* When kids are growing up, they have a real accurate idea when things are right with them and wrong with them. Go back into your childhood as early as you feel is important and tell me, where do you think things began to go wrong with you in your life? From that point? Tell me the whole story, including what brings you to treatment now.

*Patient:* I think that as a child, I don't remember an awful lot about my childhood. I don't remember a lot of good things. I didn't have a bad childhood. I have never been abused physically or sexually or anything like that. I always felt left out, abandoned, lost, alone a lot. (*This is when the problems started. The patient grew up feeling left out, abandoned, lost, and alone.*)

*Patient:* I think I knew that I was loved, but I wasn't shown it very much. Going to a Lutheran school was hard on me. I never felt like I was like the other kids. (*The patient continues to feel isolated in school.*)

*Patient:* One year I was a class officer and that made me feel real good. I wasn't sports minded. I didn't feel that anyone was working with me, with what I could do. My father died when I was a baby. My mother didn't listen to me. I would ask her a question and she would just look at me. I could never get any answers. I remember asking her about how boys and girls were different. She just said, "Don't you know?" I remember I never got any information about my periods. I didn't get it until I was pretty old anyway, about seventeen, and by then I had to find out some things from my friends. I read a book about how to take care of myself. (*The patient is angry at her mother and harbors some resentments; this may or may not have influenced her drinking. It certainly increased her feelings of isolation and loneliness, and influenced her ability to establish and maintain close interpersonal relationships.*)

*Patient:* I hear from other members of my family that my father was strict. I didn't hear good things about him, but I didn't hear bad things either. He didn't like drinking and Mom would hide her alcohol from him. (*The patient seems to long for her father. It's in the sadness of her voice. Her mother might have had a drinking problem; it sounds like it caused some family conflict.*)

*Patient:* I think my mom talked to me about this. She may have had a problem. She hid her wine bottle down in the basement. Going through school was hard because I didn't fit in with the group. I remember making up stories and trying to buy clothes like the ones they wore to fit in, but I never did. They all caught on about what I was trying to do. It didn't work. I couldn't afford a lot of things. When I was older I was real glad to get out of the house. I didn't date much, but when I did, I immediately fell in love. I felt like, great, somebody likes me. When they would go out with others I was devastated. I kept grasping at them to come back. (*These relationships sound addictive. This is a problem. Listen to the powerful feeling statements she makes: "When they would go out with others I was devastated. I kept grasping at them to come back." The patient begins to use relationships to fill the empty void within herself. She is trying to replace her dead father and her distant mother with a relationship with a man.*)

*Patient:* One day my girlfriend and I were eating lunch and these guys came up to us. They asked if we wanted to go out for a ride and have a few drinks with us. They were pretty cute, you know, so we decided to go. There was this one; he said his name was Mark. He was older, and we got along really well. I was impressed by him. I could tell he liked me really a lot, more so than anyone else I had ever dated. I ended up going with him for quite a while. About a year later, I found out he was married. His name wasn't Mark, it was Andy. He had a wife and a kid. I finally called him up and told him that I knew the truth but that I loved him anyway. This was a very passionate man. He loved me. He showed me he loved me. I don't care what you say, he was able to love two people at the same time. (*The patient falls victim into another addictive relationship. This time it is with a man who is addictive himself. The intense sexual excitement this man offers fools her into thinking that he really loves her.*)

*Patient:*   We continued that relationship for a long time. There was a lot of pain in that relationship. I just broke up with him about 2 years ago.

*Counselor:*   When did you start dating him?

*Patient:*   About 21. I went with him for 4 years. Two of those years he was married, two he wasn't. (*This is addictive, but is it also passive and dependent? She doesn't look passive, she makes good eye contact, and seems to feel comfortable. We'll have to let the story unfold to get the answer.*)

*Counselor:*   How old were you when you first had a drink?

*Patient:*   It was in my early teens, at a party.

*Counselor:*   Did you drink much in high school?

*Patient:*   No, only very occasionally.

*Counselor:*   Okay, go on with your story. You're going out with Andy and Andy's married.

*Patient:*   We kept seeing each other. He kept promising that he was going to get a divorce. He didn't want to lose me. It kept going on for years and years. I would get angry at him when I found out that he was seeing somebody else, other than me and his wife. I would blow up and then I'd finally settle down, and we would continue to see each other. Every time I would get frustrated with him, I would seek someone else out. (*Again the quick addictive fix.*)

*Patient:*   I would find someone else who was interested in me. I had several affairs. Andy would get very angry if he found out that I was dating someone, but I felt he didn't have the right to get angry, he was married. (*There is an honesty problem here. The patient was lying to both men.*)

*Patient:*   I went out with this guy once. He was everything I had ever dreamed of. He was tall and dark with a hairy chest. He was beautiful. I went out with him for quite a while. He really liked me, but I kept seeing Andy. The relationship with this guy, the new guy, Rob, began to get abusive. The relationship with Andy was abusive too. They'd both hit me, slap me, sometimes. They both tried to choke me. A couple of times they raped me out of anger. Andrew wasn't ever a violent person, but then all of a sudden he got violent. He put me down a lot. He put me down all the time.

*Counselor:*   Did he make important choices for you? (*The counselor probes the dependency problem.*)

*Patient:*   No, I never did that.

*Counselor:*   Is it hard for you to make decisions without some sort of reassurance from someone else?

*Patient:*   No, I don't have any problem there, but I am attracted to men with power. They can tell me anything and I'll believe it. I don't know what it is about powerful men, but I'm real attracted to that. Andy finally got a divorce, and I lived with him. He's a banker and very wealthy. I thought, "Things are going to be a lot better now." He was still controlling and manipulative, but I thought everything was going to improve. I always knew that sooner or later I was going to be abandoned. (*Here we see the fuel for the addictive relationship. The patient chronically fears abandonment like she felt as a child. This leaves her feeling anxious and vulnerable. She will do anything to keep her man, but at the same time, she fears she will lose him.*)

*Patient:*   He was very demanding, but I could get what I wanted by being very diplomatic. It took me a long time to learn how to do that. He always wanted me to do all kinds of things. I kept the house and the grounds immaculate. I worked and kept house and did the yard and worked at my job. (*The patient is not assertive. She has learned how to lie and manipulate to get what she wants.*)

*Patient:*   All this time I was drinking a lot. I was hiding my drinking. I would hide my beer cans. Sometimes he would come home, and I'd be drunk.

*Counselor:*   How much were you drinking then?

*Patient:*   At least a six pack.

*Counselor:*   Did you ever have a blackout?

*Patient:*   Oh, yeah, I had plenty.

*Counselor:*   Did you ever have a real bad hangover?

*Patient:*   Yes.

*Counselor:*   Hands ever get shaky?

*Patient:*   No, but I would be sick. I would feel terrible. Headache, upset stomach.

*Counselor:*   What happened then?

*Patient:*   I came home one night and caught him with another woman. He denied what was going on, but I knew. I could tell from her reaction that she didn't know about me. I talked to her, and in time we both got together with him again. I swear to God he has the ability to love two women at the same time. I can tell he loves me.

*Counselor:*   Healthy relationships are based on trust.

*Patient:*   I know that. This woman and I were never mad at each other. We both knew that he was so intense that he could love us both.

*Counselor:*   It's never loving to lie.

*Patient:*   I like that. That makes sense. I finally broke up with him. I didn't know anyone. It was real hard, but I did it. He was furious. That was the last time he raped me. He was out of his mind.

*Counselor:*   You don't rape somebody that you love either.

*Patient:*   It was finally over. I fell in love with a new guy, Dave. I fell in love so fast. He was a dream come true. We had long talks about things. This guy didn't work out because I realized that I was doing all of the giving again. I'm starting to realize my pattern. I do all the giving, and I love men with power. It took me a long time to realize that. He would go to my house and watch TV and eat all my food. He never took me anywhere. I said, "Are you getting tired of me or what?" I realized that there was something I wasn't getting here. I had such feelings for David. I can't remember ever feeling like that. He was such a heartthrob.

*Counselor:* It's easy to get love and lust confused. (*The counselor continues to teach the patient and to show her how she has been confused about relationships. Notice that these interventions are very brief. This is not the time for therapy, it is the time for the assessment.*)

*Patient:* That relationship ended and I started going out with another guy. He was an alcoholic in recovery so I cut down on my drinking some. I only saw him once a week. It was nice. One night Andy just walked in on us. It was really crazy. He just came right in as if he owned the place. I had my own place then. I was finally making the break with him, and he couldn't believe it. Dave handled it real well. Andy finally left. You know, I like a man with power. I have this thing about a man with power. I don't know what it is.

*Counselor:* Well, you've felt pretty powerless in your life. Someone with power would make you feel safe.

*Patient:* Yeah, a strong man makes me feel safe. Anyway, my drinking kept on increasing and my relationships [are] going to hell and here I am.

*Counselor:* Anything in particular bring you into treatment now?

*Patient:* I went out and got drunk again, and I woke up with such a hangover. I said to myself, I've got to do something about this, now. I made the call right then.

This concluded the history of the present problem. Then the counselor moved right into the past history:

*Counselor:* Where were you born?

*Patient:* Livingston, South Dakota.

*Counselor:* When is your birthday?

*Patient:* June 28, 1963.

*Counselor:* Did you have any trouble when you were born?

*Patient:* No.

*Counselor:* Any trouble walking, talking, toilet training, reading, writing?

*Patient:* No.

*Counselor:* You were raised with whom?

*Patient:* My mother and two younger sisters.

*Counselor:* What is your ethnic heritage, Irish, German? Do you know?

*Patient:* I'm Irish.

*Counselor:* Your home of origin, growing up with your mother and sisters—how did it feel in that house?

*Patient:* I felt alone. I didn't like it.

*Counselor:* What kind of a kid were you in grade school?

*Patient:*   I was timid, not very outgoing.

*Counselor:*   What kind of a kid were you in high school?

*Patient:*   I was scared. Scared to relate.

*Counselor:*   You seem to have made real progress with that timid thing. You don't seem timid anymore.

*Patient:*   Yeah, I really have. I don't think I'm timid anymore.

*Counselor:*   Great. Were you ever in the armed services?

*Patient:*   No.

*Counselor:*   Ever go to college.

*Patient:*   No.

*Counselor:*   Give me a brief occupational history. What kind of work have you done?

*Patient:*   I worked as a secretary for 5 years. I've been at my current job for 10 years.

*Counselor:*   Are you happily employed?

*Patient:*   Yeah, I like my job.

*Counselor:*   How is your current financial situation?

*Patient:*   Good. I'm not rich but I get along okay.

*Counselor:*   Do you have any sexual problems?

*Patient:*   No.

*Counselor:*   Have you ever had a homosexual contact?

*Patient:*   No.

*Counselor:*   Are you currently involved with a guy?

*Patient:*   Yes.

*Counselor:*   How long has that been going on?

*Patient:*   About 3 months.

*Counselor:*   And how is that going?

*Patient:*   Great.

*Counselor:*   Do your friends and family support your coming into treatment?

*Patient:*   Yes.

*Counselor:*   Do you feel like there is any kind of a higher power or God or anything?

*Patient:*   I believe in God.

*Counselor:*   Do you attend church?

*Patient:*   I go to the Lutheran church.

*Counselor:*   Are you having any problems with the law?

*Patient:*   No.

*Counselor:*   Have you ever had any problems with the law in the past?

*Patient:*   No.

*Counselor:*   What are some of your strengths, some of your good qualities?

*Patient:*   I'm caring. I get along with people real well. I think I'm intelligent.

*Counselor:*   What are some of your weaknesses?

*Patient:*   A drinking problem.

*Counselor:* What do you enjoy doing for fun?

*Patient:* I enjoy biking. I hike and jog.

*Counselor:* Have you ever had a period of time where you felt down or depressed most of the day most every day?

*Patient:* No.

*Counselor:* Have you ever felt real anxious?

*Patient:* No.

*Counselor:* Ever felt so high or filled with energy that you got into trouble or people thought you were acting strangely?

*Patient:* No.

*Counselor:* Ever had any eating problems, gorging, purging, starving yourself, anything like that?

*Patient:* No.

*Counselor:* Are you intensely afraid of anything?

*Patient:* No.

*Counselor:* Ever had any illnesses, even the small ones, measles, mumps, chicken pox?

*Patient:* Measles, mumps, chicken pox.

*Counselor:* Ever been in a hospital overnight?

*Patient:* No.

*Counselor:* Do you have any allergies?

*Patient:* No.

*Counselor:* Are you taking any kind of medication here?

*Patient:* They have me on a Valium come-down schedule.

*Counselor:* For what?

*Patient:* I have been taking Valium for about 5 years. I'm withdrawing from that. (*Current problems are supposed to be covered in the history of the present problem. The counselor didn't know about the Valium until now. This happens often. The counselor now has to flip back to the history of the present problem and add this part.*)

*Counselor:* How much of the Valium were you using?

*Patient:* I was using it every day for sleep.

*Counselor:* Did you find yourself using more?

*Patient:* Yes, I had to increase what I took so it would work.

*Counselor:* Twice as much?

*Patient:* More.

*Counselor:* Did you ever stop using?

*Patient:* No.

*Counselor:* How much would you take every night?

*Patient:* I got up to about 30 mg. (*Once this information was gathered the counselor resumed the patient's past history.*)

*Counselor:* Okay, how old was your father when he died?

*Patient:* In his twenties.

*Counselor:*   How old is your mother?

*Patient:*   Fifty-three.

*Counselor:*   Is she in good, fair, or poor health?

*Patient:*   She's in good health.

*Counselor:*   What kind of a person is your mom?

*Patient:*   She's quiet, demanding.

*Counselor:*   Has anyone else in your family had any problems with alcohol, drugs, or any other kind of mental disorder?

*Patient:*   I think my mother had a drinking problem.

That concludes the past history. Now you would complete the mental status, which we won't bore you with, and you are ready to dictate the biopsychosocial. The patient has said a lot, and it was important for her to share these things, but you need to tell the story in an abbreviated form. Keep the main parts of her story but exclude all the details. At the end of the biopsychosocial come up with a problem list and a preliminary treatment plan.

For Patty's biopsychosocial as it was completed, see Appendix 7.

# The Treatment Plan

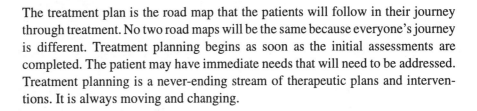

The treatment plan is the road map that the patients will follow in their journey through treatment. No two road maps will be the same because everyone's journey is different. Treatment planning begins as soon as the initial assessments are completed. The patient may have immediate needs that will need to be addressed. Treatment planning is a never-ending stream of therapeutic plans and interventions. It is always moving and changing.

## How to Build a Treatment Plan

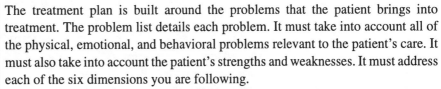

The treatment plan is built around the problems that the patient brings into treatment. The problem list details each problem. It must take into account all of the physical, emotional, and behavioral problems relevant to the patient's care. It must also take into account the patient's strengths and weaknesses. It must address each of the six dimensions you are following.

The treatment plan details the therapeutic interventions, what is going to be done, when it is going to be done, and by whom. It must consider each of the patient's needs and come up with clear ways to deal with each problem. The treatment plan flows into discharge planning, which begins from the initial assessments.

## The Diagnostic Summary

After the interdisciplinary team assesses the patient, they meet and develop a summary of their findings. This is the diagnostic summary. This is where the clinical team—the physicians, nurses, counselors, psychologists, psychiatrists, recreational therapists, occupational therapists, physical therapists, dietitians, family therapists, teachers, pastors, pharmacists, and anyone else who is going to be actively involved with the patient's care—meet and develop a summary of the patient's current state and needs. They discuss each of the patient's problems and how best to treat them. From this meeting, the diagnostic summary is developed. This details what the problems are, where they came from, and what is going to be done about them. It is much better to do this as a team. As you see your team function, you will see how valuable it is to have many disciplines involved.

**The Problem List**

The treatment team will continue to develop the problem list as the patient moves through treatment. New problems will come up and be added. Nothing will stay the same. A problem list and treatment plan must be fluid, it must be modified as conditions change.

*How to Develop a Problem List*

A treatment plan must be measurable. It must have a set of problems and solutions that the staff can measure. The problems can't be vague. They must be specific. A problem is a brief clinical statement of a condition of the patient that needs treatment. The problem statement should be no longer than one sentence and describe only one problem.

All problem statements are abstract concepts. You cannot actually see, hear, touch, taste, or smell the problem. Low self-esteem, for example, is a clinical statement that describes a variety of behaviors exhibited by the patient. You can see the behaviors and conclude from them that the patient has low self-esteem, but you can't actually see low self-esteem.

Problems are evidenced by signs (what you see) and symptoms (what the patient reports). The problems on the treatment plan should be followed by specific physical, emotional, or behavioral evidence that the problem actually exists. List the problem and then add "as evidenced by," or "as indicated by," then describe the concrete evidence you see that tells you that the problem exists.

*Examples of a Problem List*

*Problem 1:*  Inability to maintain sobriety outside of a structured facility
As evidenced by:  Blood alcohol level of .23
As evidenced by:  The patient's family report of daily drinking
As evidenced by:  Alcohol withdrawal symptoms
As evidenced by:  Third DWI
As evidenced by:  History of third treatment for chemical dependency

*Problem 2:*  Depression
As evidenced by:  Beck Depression Inventory score of 29
As evidenced by:  Psychological evaluation
As evidenced by:  Patient has made two suicide attempts in the past 3 months
As evidenced by:  Depressed affect

*Problem 3:*  Acute alcohol withdrawal
As evidenced by:  Course hand tremors
As evidenced by:  BP 160/100, pulse 104
As evidenced by:  Restless pacing. Self-report of strong craving
As evidenced by:  Profuse sweating. Mild visual disturbances

**Goals and Objectives**

Once you have a problem list, you need to ask yourself what the patient needs to do to restore him- or herself to normal functioning. A person who has a drinking problem needs to stop drinking and learn the skills necessary to maintain a sober lifestyle. A person who is depressed needs to reestablish normal mood. People who are dishonest need to get honest with themselves and others.

*How to Develop Goals* | A goal is a brief clinical statement of the condition you expect to change in the patient or in the patient's family. You state what you intend to accomplish in general terms. Specify the condition of the patient that will result from treatment. All goals label a set of behaviors you want to create.

Goals should be more than the elimination of pathology; they should be directed toward the patient's learning new and more functional methods of coping. Focus on more than just stopping the old dysfunctional behavior; concentrate on replacing it with something more effective.

*Examples of Developing Goals*

*Instead of:* The patient will stop drinking.
*Use:* The patient will develop a program of recovery congruent with a sober lifestyle. (The patient is learning something different.)
*Use:* The patient will learn to cope with stress in an adaptive manner.

*Instead of:* The patient will stop negative self-talk. (Patients don't learn or use something differently; they just avoid something they already know.)
*Use:* The patient will develop and use positive self-talk. (Now the patient learns something different that is incompatible with the old behavior.)
*Use:* The patient will develop a positive self-image.
(The patient learns something new and more adaptive.)

The patient or the patient's family must be the subject of each goal. No member of the staff, or intervention by the staff, should be mentioned. Identify one goal and condition at a time. Make all goals one sentence.

*Examples of Goals*

1. The patient will learn the skills necessary to maintain a sober lifestyle.
2. The patient will learn to express negative feelings to his or her spouse.
3. The patient will develop a positive commitment to sobriety.
4. The patient will develop a healthy diet and begin gaining weight.
5. The patient will learn how to tolerate uncomfortable feelings without using chemicals.
6. The patient will learn to share positive feelings with others.
7. The patient will develop the ability to ask for what he wants.
8. The patient will develop the ability to use anger appropriately.
9. The patient should sleep comfortably on a regular basis.
10. The patient will learn healthy communication skills.

*How to Develop Objectives* | An objective is a specific skill the patient must acquire to achieve a goal. The objective is what you really set out to accomplish in treatment. Objectives are concrete behaviors you can see, hear, smell, taste, or feel. An objective must be stated so clearly that almost anyone would know when he or she saw it. Goals are usually abstract statements that you can't actually see happen. You can't see someone learn or see his or her self-esteem. You can see individuals express ten positive things about themselves. One way to see if you have a goal or an objective is to use the "See Johnny" test developed by Arnold Goldman. "If you can see Johnny do it, it's an objective; if you can't it's a goal."[1]

Remember, if you can see it, it will usually be an objective. If you can't, it's a goal.

Can you see the patient read about Step One in the Big Book? Yes. (Objective)
Can you see him understand the illness of chemical dependency? No. (Goal)
Can you see him gain insight? No. (Goal)
Can you see him improve his self-esteem? No. (Goal)
Can you see him complete the Step One Exercise? Yes. (Objective)
Can you see him keep a daily record of his dysfunctional thinking? Yes. (Objective)
Can you see him share his feelings in group? Yes. (Objective)

All goals and objectives are aimed at change. Individuals must change how they feel, what they think, or what they do. Each goal should have one or more objectives. The best way to develop goals is to ask yourself this question: How can I know for sure the patient has achieved the goal? What must the patient say or do to convince you that the treatment goal has been completed?

State the goal aloud and then add on the words, as evidenced by, or as indicated by, then complete the sentence describing the specific objectives that will tell you that the goal has been reached. Each goal will need at least one objective. Each goal and objective will need a number or a letter that identifies it. Each objective will need a completion date. This is the date by which you expect the objective will be completed. If the patient passes this date without completing the objective, the treatment plan may have to be modified.

*Examples*  *Goal A:* The patient will develop a program of recovery congruent with a sober lifestyle, as evidenced by:
1. The patient will share in contracts group three times when he or she tried to stop drinking but was unable to stay sober.
2. The patient will make a list of the essential skills necessary for recovery.

*Goal B:* The patient will learn to use assertiveness skills, as indicated by:
1. The patient will discuss the assertiveness formula and will role-play three situations where he or she acts assertively.
2. The patient will keep an assertiveness log and will share the log with the counselor daily.
3. The patient will practice assertiveness skills in interpersonal group.

Objectives must be measurable. You must be able to count them. Thoughts, feelings, and actions can all be counted by you or the patient. Patients can count their thoughts by keeping a daily record of their thinking. They can count feelings by keeping a feelings log. You can keep a record of every time a patient acts angry around the unit.

To achieve the goal of maintaining a sober lifestyle, an alcoholic may need to develop one or more of the following skills:

1. Verbalize that they have a problem. Verbalize an understanding of the problem.
2. Develop and practice new behaviors that are incompatible with the problem. Read the Big Book.
3. Practice the Twelve-Steps of Alcoholics Anonymous.

4. Go to meetings.
5. Learn how to cope with uncomfortable feelings.
6. Develop a relapse prevention plan.

Patients who are depressed may need to do develop one or more of the following skills:

1. Learn how to say positive things to themselves.
2. Develop recreational programs to add fun to their lives.
3. Grieve—learn how to accept the deaths of loved ones.
4. Get accurate in their thinking.
5. Improve the dysfunctional interpersonal relationship with their spouses.
6. Take antidepressant medication.

*How to Evaluate the Effectiveness of the Treatment*

In treatment it is vital to keep score of how you are doing. It is the only way you will know whether the treatment is working. Feelings, thoughts, and behaviors need to be counted. The staff can count them or the patient can count them. Thoughts and feelings, being internal states, must be recorded by the patient. Behaviors can be recorded by the patient or by the staff. Patients and staff will record feelings, thoughts, and behaviors and keep a log of these data. The staff log is called the *patient record* or the *chart*.

*How to Select Goals and Objectives*

Goals and objectives are infinite. It takes clinical skill to decide exactly what the patient needs to do to establish a stable recovery. Every treatment plan is individualized. Everyone is different and every treatment plan is different. For the same goal you may have widely different objectives. You need to ask yourself two questions:

1. What is this patient doing that is maladaptive?
2. What does the patient need to do differently?

These questions, asked carefully, will uncover your goals. Once you have your goals, ask yourself this question: What does the patient need to do to achieve this goal? These are your objectives. Each patient will need to do the following three things:

1. Identify that they have a problem.
2. Understand exactly what that problem is and how it affects them.
3. Apply healthy skills that will reduce or eliminate the problem.

*Examples of Goals and Objectives*

*Problem 1.* Pathological relationship with alcohol as indicated by a blood alcohol level (BAL) on admission of .32, three DWIs, family report of daily drinking.

*Goal:* Develop a program of recovery congruent with a sober lifestyle, as evidenced by:
*Objective 1:* Norman will identify with his counselor ten times that alcohol use negatively affected his life, by 6-1-92.

*Objective 2:* Norman will complete his chemical use history and share in group his understanding of his alcohol problem, by 6-1-92.

*Objective 3:* Norman will share his powerlessness and unmanageability with his group, by 6-10-92.

*Objective 4:* Norman will share in group his understanding of how he can use his Higher Power in sobriety, by 6-15-92.

*Objective 5:* Norman will discuss with the clergy how he plans to use this Step Three in sobriety, by 6-20-92.

*Objective 6:* Norman will develop a written relapse prevention plan, by 6-25-92.

*Objective 7:* Norman will develop a written aftercare plan using the problems he identified in treatment, by 6-30-92.

In developing goals and objectives, the patient must move through the following events:

1. Identify that they have a problem.
2. Understand how the problem negatively affects them.
3. Learn what they are going to change.
4. Practice the change.

Let's take another problem.

*Problem 2.* Poor impulse control as indicated by numerous fights, abusive to spouse, self-report that he loses control when angry.

*Goal:* Learn to use angry feelings appropriately as evidenced by:

*Objective 1:* Thomas will discuss with his counselor five times when he used anger inappropriately, by 7-2-92.

*Objective 2:* Thomas will share his understanding of what he needs to do differently to cope with his anger, by 7-10-92.

*Objective 3:* Thomas will visit the staff psychologist and discuss his anger problem, by 7-2-92.

*Objective 4:* Thomas will keep a daily log of his angry feelings and discuss the log with his counselor once a week.

*Objective 5:.* Thomas will share his hurt and his angry feelings in group, by 6-21-92.

*Objective 6:* Thomas will practice sharing his hurt and his anger with his spouse in a conjoint session. This will be completed by 7-30-92.

*Objective 7:* Thomas will attend a violence group once a week.

Samples of a complete biopsychosocial, diagnostic summary, and treatment plan are given in Appendix 7.

## Treatment Plan Review

■

The interdisciplinary team reviews the treatment plan at regular intervals throughout treatment. At a minimum, the treatment plan is reviewed at all decision points. These points include the following:

1. Admission
2. Transfer
3. Discharge
4. Major change in the patient's condition
5. The point of estimated length of treatment

Most facilities have a daily staffing where the patient's progress is briefly discussed and a weekly review where the treatment plan is discussed. It is at these meetings that the treatment plan will be modified. Problems, goals, and objectives will change as the patient's condition changes. Treatment team review is where the staff finds out how the patient is doing in treatment and what changes need to be made.

## Documentation

The staff keeps a journal of the patient's progress through treatment. This document is called the *patient record*, commonly called the *chart*. The staff keeps progress notes that document what happens to the patient during treatment.

Each progress note needs to be identified with one or more treatment objectives. For example, a progress note on Goal A, Objective 7, would begin with the notation "A(7)." This helps the staff keep track of how the patient is doing with each objective.

Progress notes include the following data:

1. The treatment plan
2. All treatment
3. The patient's clinical course
4. Each change in the patient's condition
5. Descriptions of the patient's response to treatment
6. The outcome of all treatment
7. The response of significant others to important events during treatment.

## How to Write Progress Notes

Keep your progress notes short. They must include just enough detail to describe accurately what's going on with the patient. For the most part, describe things in behavioral terms. All entries that include your opinion or interpretation of events must be supplemented by a description of the actual behavior observed. What did you see, hear, smell, taste, or touch that lead you to that conclusion? Describe exactly what the patient did or said. Direct quotations from the patient make excellent progress notes.

The patient's progress in meeting the goals and objectives must be regularly recorded. The efforts of the staff in helping the patient to meet treatment goals and objectives are recorded. The progress notes will be used by the staff to see how the patient is doing. A person who has never met the patient should be able to know the patient's story by reading the patient record. Before you chart, ask yourself this question: If I were a counselor just coming in to take over this case, what would I need to know? It is a good idea to write a short progress note on each patient each day. This is not absolutely essential, but it will keep you thinking about the treatment plan and the patient's progress through the treatment plan on a daily basis.

*Examples of Progress Notes*

6-12-91 (10:30 a.m.)

B(3): Patty discussed her denial exercise in group. She verbalized an understanding how denial had adversely affected her, stating, "I can't believe how dishonest I was to myself. I really didn't think I had a problem even after all that trouble. I lied to Andy, too, about everything." The patient was able to see how denial was a lie, a lie to herself and to others. After the session, the patient was able to verbalize her need to get honest with herself and others. "I've been lying about everything. It's about time I got honest with myself."

6-14-91 (3:15 p.m.)

A(1): Patty was tearful in an individual session. She mourned the loss of her love relationship with her past partner. The group helped her to see how destructive the relationship had been for her. The treatment peers reinforced that Patty was worth being treated better than her partner was treating her. Patty expressed that she is extremely angry at her mother. "I hate her. She never spent any time with me. She only wanted me as a slave. She wanted a housekeeper, not me." It seemed to give Patty some relief to hear other patients express that they had similar feelings about their mothers. "I thought I was the only one who felt like that," Patty stated.

6-15-91: (11:00 a.m.)

C(2): Patty's facial expression is sad. She has been isolating herself. She didn't eat breakfast. She was seen crying alone in her room. I went in and she was able to express her feelings. "I'm so ashamed of myself. I'll never be able to live this down." Patty expressed she was feeling guilty about sharing with group her anger at her mother. I reassured Patty and told her to bring up her feelings in group this afternoon.

*Formal Treatment Plan Review*

Once a week the staff will do a formal treatment team review. This requires a more detailed look at how the patient is doing on in each problem area. The staff members present must be identified, with their credentials.

6-16-91 (11:45 a.m.)

*Treatment Plan Review:* Present, Dr. Roberts, MD; M. Smith, CCDC Level II; T. Anderson, RN; F. Mark, CCDC Level I, Dr. Thomas; M. Tobas, PhD; E. Talbot, RN; A. Stein, LPN. The staff feels that Patty is adjusting well to treatment. She is more talkative and seems to feel more comfortable. She has made some friends with several treatment peers, including her roommate. Her mother came to see her on Sunday, and Patty reported that this visit went well.

*Problem 1:* Patty continues on her Valium come-down schedule. She has reported only mild withdrawal symptoms. She is sleeping well. She continues to be mildly restless. She was encouraged to increase her level of exercise to 20 minutes daily.

*Problem 2:* Patty has completed her Chemical Use History and Step One Exercise. She shared in interpersonal group her powerlessness and unmanageability. She was open in group, and she verbalizes that she has accepted her disease of chemical dependency. She was somewhat more reluctant to accept her problem with Valium, but the group did a good job explaining cross-tolerance. The patient should complete the cross-tolerance exercise and report her findings to her group.

*Problem 3:* Patient continues to take her iron supplement. Her hemoglobin is within normal limits.

*Problem 4:* The patient is over her cold. Problem 4 is completed.

*Problem 5:* Patient has written a letter to her mother and father describing how she felt about her childhood. The patient shared her letter in group, and she was surprised to find out that many of the other patients had similar experiences. The patient states she is feeling more comfortable sharing in group, and she appears to be gaining confidence in herself. Patty met with her counselor, and the counselor encouraged Patty to accept her new AA/NA group as the healthy family she never had. Patty expressed hope in becoming involved with this healthy family.

*Problem 6:* Patty is working on the Relationship Skills Exercise. She has been practicing asking for what she wants. It is still very difficult for her to share some of her feelings, particularly her anger, in group. When she shares her anger, she tends to feel guilty.

*Problem 7:* Patty completed the Honesty Exercise and the Chemical Use History that opened her eyes about how dishonest she has been. Patty made a contract with her group to be honest and asked the patients to confront her if they felt she was being dishonest. Patty is keeping a daily log of her lies and when she is tempted to lie. She has been able to identify many lies she was telling in her life and is able to verbalize her understanding of how the lies keep her isolated from others.

*Problem 8:* Patty is working on the assertiveness skills exercise. She is practicing the assertiveness formula. She tends to feel guilty, when she says no but she is getting better at it. She will say no to someone five times per day for 3 days and keep a log of how she feels about each situation.

Note     1. Goldman gives lessons on treatment planning in *Accreditation and Certification: For Providers of Psychiatric, Alcoholism and Drug Abuse Services*, available from P.O. Box 742, Bala Cynwyd, PA 19004. Richard Weedman has also done a lot of work in this area. He wrote *Patient Records in Addiction Treatment: Documenting the Quality of Care*, which can be obtained from the Joint Commission on Accreditation of Healthcare Organizations at the following address: 1 Renaissance Boulevard, Oakbrook Terrace, IL 60181. These materials should be read if you have problems with treatment planning.

# CHAPTER FOUR

# Individual Treatment

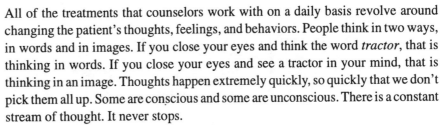

All of the treatments that counselors work with on a daily basis revolve around changing the patient's thoughts, feelings, and behaviors. People think in two ways, in words and in images. If you close your eyes and think the word *tractor*, that is thinking in words. If you close your eyes and see a tractor in your mind, that is thinking in an image. Thoughts happen extremely quickly, so quickly that we don't pick them all up. Some are conscious and some are unconscious. There is a constant stream of thought. It never stops.

Feelings give us the energy and direction for problem solving. All feelings have a specific movement attached to them. The feeling of fear gives us the energy and direction to run away from an offending stimulus. The feeling of sadness gives us the energy and direction to recover a lost object. Good problem solving necessitates using feelings appropriately.

Behavior is movement. Anytime people move, they are exhibiting behavior. Speech is movement. Drinking is movement. Going to AA meetings is movement. These are all behaviors. Behaviors are the easiest things to see, count, and record. Whenever possible, conduct your treatment using the patent's behavior as your guide. Behavior will tell you if your treatment is working.

## The Therapeutic Alliance

All individual treatment will revolve around the relationship you have with your patient. This is called the *therapeutic alliance*. If the patient likes and trusts you, he or she will listen to you and want to change to please you.

### *How to Develop a Therapeutic Alliance*

The therapeutic alliance should be growing and improving from the first moment you meet a patient. You need to be constantly encouraging and supportive. In this way, you will give patients the feeling that you are going to walk with them through treatment. This relationship must be based on love and trust. Patients are afraid to tell anyone the truth. They have probably never told anyone the whole truth. You are going to be different. You are going to be confidential and consistently act in the patients' interest. You are going to show them unconditional positive regard. No matter what they do, you are going to be there for them when they need you. You are not always going to tell patients what they want to hear; that wouldn't be loving. You are going to tell them the truth, and you are going to encourage them to see the truth in themselves. You are going to expect them to improve, and you are going to act like it. You are going to encourage them to see the fact that they can recover if they work at a program of recovery. You feel that they have the resources necessary or you wouldn't have accepted them as your patients. You believe they can do it.

The patients will have great doubts about themselves. They have tried to lick their addiction before, many times, and they have always failed. They hope they can recover but they don't have much confidence in themselves. Self-efficacy is where a patient learns, "I can do it." This confidence is carefully built over the weeks of treatment by constantly reinforcing patients when they complete some small part of the program. This may be as little as someone coming to breakfast on time or as big as someone confronting their parents with their real feelings.

The solid basis of a good therapeutic alliance is constantly being reinforcing. Counselors look for good behavior from a patient. When they see the patient doing something right, they point it out and praise the patient for it.

*How to Be Reinforcing*

"Good job. I knew you could do it."

"You're doing great. I'm proud of you."

"That took great courage."

"This is going to pay off for you."

"Keep coming. You can do it."

These statements reinforce patients. You are going to support them warmly, and as often as you can. Touch them if you feel this is a reinforcer, but don't force yourself on anyone. Be sensitive to their needs. Constantly ask yourself this question: If I were in this patient's situation, how would I want to be treated? Then treat the patient that way.

Make good eye contact when you give praise or make a point. Patients have learned that they can't trust anyone. They don't even trust themselves. You are going to prove to them, with your actions, that they can trust you.

Be gentle. Don't hammer your points home aggressively; that weakens the therapeutic alliance. Let the power of the truth work for you. A whisper of truth is much more powerful than an angry confrontation. Your patients are injured. They don't need to be attacked. They need to heal in an atmosphere of love and trust.

Aid patients to move toward greater self-understanding. Help them to identify exactly how they have kept themselves isolated and teach them new ways of reaching out to others. These patients have been hiding from themselves for a long time. They have been feeling lost and alone. They need to come out from the darkness created by the disease into the light of the truth.

*How to Use Empathy*

Empathy is understanding how someone feels from their frame of reference. Whenever you put yourself in someone else's position, you are practicing empathy. It is often helpful to recognize a feeling or thought of the patient that stimulates something from your own experience. You do not have to experience the same intensity of feelings that grip the patient, but you need to relate to the feelings and understand them. Feel yourself walking in the patient's shoes. What if this were happening to you? How would you feel? What would you be thinking? What would you need? What would you want? Your empathic responses will not always be correct, you can misperceive a patient, but they will improve over time. A good test of empathy is that your comments should deepen the patient's narrative flow (Havens, 1978). Empathic accuracy can be further determined by reflecting the patient's feelings. Repeat to patients your understanding of they have just said. Patients will usually clarify any misunderstanding. The patient's words and behavior should continually deepen your understanding of them (Bettet & Maloney, 1991).

Be sensitive to your own feelings. How is the patient affecting you? Are some of your own issues being triggered? How can this give you insight into yourself and your patient?

**Transference and Countertransference**

■

Transference is when patients respond to you with the same feelings, thoughts, and behaviors, that they developed for someone else in their life. Countertransference is when you respond to the patient the way you responded to someone else. We all have internal maps about how the world and people function. We trust these maps to help us navigate. We learned these maps from our primary caregivers and from significant others in our life. If you had a father that was demanding, you learned that people, particularly men, are demanding. If you had a mother that you couldn't trust, you learned that people, particularly women, are not trustworthy. These maps profoundly affect therapy. Sometimes they are accurate and sometimes they are inaccurate. You have to check your own maps and the patient's maps constantly for accuracy.

Some counselors are insensitive to themselves and others. These counselors can do great damage to their patients. They are impatient and demand immediate self-disclosure before the patient is ready. They are not sensitive enough to know that the patient is not ready to share. Patients should only be given the opportunity to share. They should never be forced or manipulated. The best intervention for someone who is keeping a secret is to tell them they can keep the secret; that is their right. You don't have to share everything with everyone, but there is a consequence for keeping secrets: If you cut someone off from the truth, you cut yourself off from feeling close to that person. The formula is this: The more you can share, the closer you can get, and the closer you can get, the more you can share. Intimacy can only occur in an atmosphere of truth. It's impossible to love without truth.

Some of the keys to developing a positive therapeutic alliance are a forward-leaning posture, good eye contact, a reinforcing facial expression, good listening skills, unconditional positive regard, and the skill of engaging the patient on a feeling level. It helps if you can engage the patient using your own feelings. This increases the feeling of intimacy.

*Examples of Empathetic Statements*

"Bob, you scare me. I have to wonder how your wife and kids must feel when you raise your voice like that."

"I feel very close to you right now."

"I'm confused, what do you want from me right now?"

"That makes me feel really sad. I'm sorry that happened to you."

"I can feel that you're angry, what happened?"

"Ralph, I'm scared for you."

*How to Be Confrontive*

A good confrontation is when one individual states how another person is making them feel. The formula is as follows:

1. I think _____. (Describe the patient's behavior.) "That's the third time that you have said that nothing is wrong."
2. I feel _____. (Tell the patient how the behavior makes you feel.) "I feel a bit frustrated."
3. I want _____. (Describe exactly what you want the patient to do.) "I want you to describe how you are feeling."

These actions must be described in behavioral terms. Exactly what did the person do to make you have a certain feeling.

"I hear you deny you've been drinking. I feel frustrated. I want you to look at what what's really been happening in your life. Didn't you just get your third DWI?"

"I feel scared when I hear you say that you want to hurt yourself. What are your alternatives?"

"When I see you sit there with that blank look on your face, I feel sad. You seem to want to cry. Can you tell me what you are thinking?"

A positive therapeutic alliance fosters mutual independence. It is an intense investment of energy. There is a lack of defensiveness and a sense of mutual positive regard. You develop similar modes of communication. You are on the same wavelength. You constantly affirm the patient's worth as an individual.

## Behavior Therapy

In treatment, counselors concentrate on change. The patients have maladaptive feelings, thoughts, and behaviors that keep them from functioning normally. The patients are unable to reach their full potential in life because of something they are doing wrong. When there is something wrong with their actions, behavior therapy is used. All behavior is movement. Changing how patients move will help them to function better. Patients who always lash out in physical violence when they are mad are in for a world of hurt. They must understand how to do something differently when they are mad. They must practice this new behavior until it becomes automatic.

*How Patients Learn* | To understand all types of therapy, you need to know how the brain works. The brain is like a jungle. Imagine, for a moment, that you have crash-landed an airplane in the jungle. There are thick branches and vines everywhere. All you see is thick vegetation. As you recover from the crash you get thirsty. You hear a creek running to the right of the nose of the plane. You look for the easiest way to the creek but you only see jungle. The jungle is the same thickness in all directions. Finally, your thirst overcomes your fear, and you strike out for the creek. When you do, you make a pathway. It's not much, and it won't last long, but it's there. By passing through the jungle once, you have made a pathway of least resistance. Naturally, on the way back, you take that pathway again, it's the easiest way. As you go through again and again, you make more of a pathway, until in time, you have a nice smooth trail. Every time you go to the creek, you take the easiest way. That is exactly how the brain works and that's how learning takes place.

*Habits* Humans are creatures of habit. Habits are learned behaviors. They are easy pathways in the brain. Habits must be practiced to remain active parts of the person's behavior. Let's say someone has a drinking problem. This is a habit. It has this wide pathway in the brain. We could call this the drinking pathway. When this person feels uncomfortable, she or he takes a drink. The person has been doing this for years. We need to teach this person another way to relax. The first time the person takes the new way in the brain, it is going to be difficult. Just like the jungle, there are thick vines and branches in the way, it hurts, and all the time, the person has this other way, tempting him or her back to drinking. The old pathway is better established. As the counselor, you encourage patients to try something new. You support them, and you reward them, and finally, they try the new way. It's not easy, but they do it. Now you encourage them to try it again, and again. They begin to build a new pathway in the brain, and as they do, the old pathway gradually begins to grow over. It will never grow over completely. Patients may think about drinking. This will be tempting sometimes, but the more they take the new pathway, the more it becomes the pathway of least resistance. Soon it will be the easiest way and the patient will take the new way automatically.

You can see from this analogy that every time you go one way in the brain, it is important. Each time you go through the brain the same way, you are making a better, more long-lasting pathway.

*Changing a Habit* People drink for a reason. Let's say they drink when they feel tense. Every time they feel tense, they reach for a drink. Once they come into treatment, they decide that they can't drink anymore, but they still have times when they feel tense. They need to learn a new way of dealing with that tension. They need to learn a new skill. They may learn that every time they feel tense they can talk about it, or exercise, or go to an AA meeting. The more a patient practices the new behavior, the more comfortable and habitual it becomes. Soon, the new behavior will become second nature. Every time patients feels tense, they use the new skill.

*What Is a Reinforcement?*   New behavior is learned by encouraging the patient to try something new and then reinforcing the new behavior. Reinforcement increases the frequency of a behavior. It increases the chances that the new behavior will happen again. A reinforcer does one of two things for the patient:

1. It gives the patient something positive.
2. It allows the patient to escape from something negative.

Behavior does not exist, nor does it continue to exist, without reinforcement. If you take the reward away, the behavior will vanish, it will extinguish.

*What Is a Punishment?*   Punishment decreases the frequency of a behavior. It works in two ways:

1. It introduces something negative.
2. It removes something positive.

The best punishment for someone is to allow him to suffer the natural consequences of his behavior. For example, someone who does a poor job completing a step exercise has to do it over again. This is usually punishment enough. There are some bad things about punishment, and you need to use it sparingly. Punishment cannot teach someone a new behavior; it can only teach her to avoid an old behavior. Punishment takes the patient's mind off of what she or he did, and puts it on to what you are doing. The patient can miss the point. Treatment centers need to be set up with a clear consequences for maladaptive behavior. The rules have to be carefully spelled out and the consequences for breaking the rules specified.

## The Behavior Chain

To understand people and behavior therapy you need to understand the behavior chain. At every point along the chain, patients can change, they can do something differently. Treatment is learning what to do and when to do it; these are the tools of recovery.

The first event in the chain is the *trigger*. This is the stimulus or event that triggers a patient's response. After the trigger, comes *thinking*. Here the person evaluates what the stimulus means. Much of this thinking is so fast that it is not consciously experienced. The thoughts generate *feelings*. The feelings give energy and direction for action or *behavior*. All behavior has positive or negative *consequences*. The behavior chain looks like this:

Trigger → Thinking → Feeling → Behavior → Consequence

Let's take an example. Larry is addicted to cocaine. He is riding down the street and he hears a particular song on the radio (trigger). He begins thinking about the good old days when he enjoyed using cocaine (thinking). This thinking leads him to crave cocaine (feeling). Larry decides to ride over to a drug dealer's house just to see how his "old friend" is doing (behavior). Larry uses cocaine (consequence).

Now let's plug in some tools of recovery. Larry is riding down the street and he hears a particular song on the radio. Larry recognizes this song as one of his triggers. He tells himself that he no longer has the option of using cocaine (new thinking). He thinks about the misery that cocaine caused him (new thinking). He experiences some craving, so he decides to give his sponsor a call (new behavior). He goes to a meeting with his sponsor (new behavior). He does not use cocaine (new consequence).

*The Importance of Reinforcement*

Every time you encourage people, or pay attention to them, you reinforce them. You must try to reward patients only when they act in the way that you want them to act. If possible, you must ignore, or give negative consequences to, all maladaptive behavior. Behavior therapy is going on constantly in treatment. You need to look for positive things to reinforce. Reward your patients as often as you can. See yourself as someone who is constantly looking for behavior to reinforce.

*Examples of Reinforcing Statements*

"I liked what you did in group today."

"Thank you for joining in this afternoon."

"You look better after you exercise."

"You told the truth. That's great!"

"I saw you working on your assignments this afternoon. Good going."

*How to Use Punishment*

When maladaptive behavior is displayed, the first thing you need to do is share your feelings. Remember the formula. I feel _____. When you _____. I would prefer it if _____. This tells patients how you are feeling, what they are doing that is causing you to have that feeling, and what you want them to do differently.

"Tom, I feel frightened when you raise your voice. I would prefer it if you speak more quietly." (If the maladaptive behavior continues, warn the patient of an impending consequence.)

"Tom, if you don't lower your voice I'm going to leave the room." (If the behavior continues, administer the consequence: Leave the room.)

Let's go through another example.
Tim, an adolescent patient, begins to throw food.

"Tim, it makes me angry when you throw food. I would prefer it if you would eat normally." [*Tim keeps throwing the food. He laughs with the other adolescents.*]

"Tim, if you don't stop throwing food, you will be restricted to your room for one hour." [*Tim defiantly throws food again.*]

"Go to your room. You are restricted to your room for one hour."

*When a Patient Breaks a Rule*    If a rule is broken, a consequence must be given. To let the behavior slide tells the patients that rules don't count. It is a common early mistake for counselors to want to avoid giving consequences. They don't want to hurt the patient's feelings, and they want to be seen as the patient's friend. If you will examine this desire carefully, you will see how wrong it is. A good counselor does not want to teach someone to do bad things. You do not want to let patients continue their maladaptive behavior that is helping them stay sick.

Let's go through a few behavioral objectives. Remember, in behavior therapy you want to teach the patient to do something differently.

*Objective 1.* Patient will go to five treatment peers and share the Feelings Exercise with them. (This exercise comes with a built-in reward because sharing feelings brings people closer together. As patients share their feelings, they draw closer to others. This is a powerful reinforcement.)

*Objective 2.* Patient will list 10 times he lost his temper with his children. He will discuss each situation with his counselor. He will verbalize other means of dealing with his anger by 9-20-91. (In this objective, patients also feel closer as they share the truth. You would also want to reinforce patients for being honest and ask them how they feel after the disclosure.)

*Objective 3.* Patient will keep a feelings log for the next 5 days. Completed by 9-15-91. (In a feelings log, patients chart their feelings. This allows them to keep up on their improvement. This is a powerful reinforcement.)

*Objective 4.* Patient will give a 20-minute speech to his group on his powerlessness and unmanageability by 9-25-91. (Giving the group a talk is a good way to have patients learn new material. If they are going to teach something to others, they first need to learn it themselves.)

*Objective 5.* Patient will meet with his counselor and his spouse in five conjoint sessions before the end of treatment. (During each session you would want to reinforce each person for building better communication skills. When someone compromises, reinforce them.)

*Objective 6.* Patient will ask two treatment peers a day for help with his program. He will record each situation and share weekly with his counselor. (Patients who are reluctant to ask for help need practice in doing so. The illness tells them that they are not worth helping, that other people don't want to help them. Nothing works better to dispel these inaccurate beliefs than to have people actually help them.)

*Objective 7.* Patient will give three treatment peers a compliment a day. He will keep a log of each situation and discuss with his counselor by 9-25-91. (By having a patient say reinforcing things to others, you set up a natural reinforcing situation. You need to talk with the patient about how the other people responded.)

*Objective 8.* Patient will keep an anger log and share weekly with his counselor by 9-30-91. (Keeping an anger log will make patients more aware of their anger.

If they are more aware, they can to catch the anger at an earlier time and use a specific skill to deal with the feeling. Every time they get angry, for example, they could back away from the situation until they can get accurate in their thinking. Then they can do something different, for instance, talk about their anger.)

*Why We Concentrate on Behavior Therapy*

The reason why behavior therapy is so good is you can see it happen. The new behavior either occurs or it doesn't. The more you reinforce a new behavior, the quicker it develops into a habit. It is important to reinforce the behavior as quickly as you can after it occurs. Practice is important. The more a patient practices a behavior, the more of a habit it will become. You can role-play certain situations to solidify and practice the new skills. We ask for progress, not perfection. Most old behaviors fall away slowly. It will be months before the triggers stop creating old responses.

Don't drink or use drugs, read the Big Book, go to meetings, seek a Higher Power, call your sponsor, share how you feel, ask for what you want, be loving, tell the truth, all of these are essential parts of the program. They can all be placed in behavioral terms. They can be monitored. They can be changed and counted as they change. If you monitor behaviors you will know exactly how your patient is doing in treatment.

## Cognitive Therapy

Another essential element in chemical dependency treatment is how people think. Thoughts precede feelings, and feelings initiate action. Patients have to think about drinking before they drink. People think in words or in images. If I were to ask you to close your eyes and think the word *wagon*, you could do that. If I were to ask you to close your eyes and see a wagon, you could close your eyes and see some sort of an image of a wagon; that is thinking in imagery.

*How Chemically Dependent People Think*

Patients who are chemically dependent do not think accurately. They have separated themselves from reality. They are distorting the truth to protect themselves. Most patients come into treatment in some form of denial.

"I don't think I have a drinking problem."

"I never had any problems with marijuana."

"Everybody I know drinks as much as I do."

"My husband is overly sensitive. His dad was a heavy drinker."

"Anybody can get a DWI."

"I may have an alcohol problem, but I'm not an alcoholic."

The patient who said these things had a severe drug problem. All of these thoughts were inaccurate. She was addicted to alcohol and cannabis. She was drinking and using cannabis all day, every day.

The psychology of chemical dependency demands repressing the truth from consciousness. Repression is a mental process where we keep the facts hidden from ourselves. This information is kept secret to protect us from the painful reality of our situation. If drug addicts see the whole truth, they will see their addiction. They will see that they are dying from chemical dependency. This truth creates tremendous fear. The addicted individuals protect themselves from experiencing this fear by not seeing reality. They may have gotten their eighth DWI, but they still don't think they have a problem. They may see only half-truths, they may see that the police are out to get them, or the spouse is overreacting, but they don't see the whole truth, the seriousness of their addiction.

*Defense Mechanisms*    The illness of chemical dependency cannot operate without lies. People must lie to themselves until they believe the lie or the illness cannot continue. All of the lies are inaccurate ways of thinking. Cognitive therapy corrects the thoughts and gets the patient accurate. Cognitive therapy is a fearless search for truth.

*Minimization* distorts reality and makes it smaller than it actually is. Minimizing says, "It's not so bad." When alcoholics pour whiskey, they do not use a shot glass, they pour. If we take that poured drink and measure how many shots are in it, we would find four or five shots in the glass. To the alcoholic, this is *one* drink. But, it's not one drink, it's five drinks. "I'm only having three," he says innocently to himself. "What's the problem?"

*Rationalization* is a good excuse for drinking or using drugs. Probably the most common excuse is, "I had a hard day." Therefore, for the addict, "anyone who has had a hard day, needs to relax." Therefore, "I need a few."

Patients can rationalize almost anything. Rationalization can also be called blaming.

"The police were out to get me."

"My wife doesn't understand me. That's why I drink."

"I've been having financial problems."

"I can't sleep if I don't drink."

"My boss really gets on my nerves, I need a drink."

The essential element here is that the patients are fooling themselves. They really believe that their behavior is not their fault. Something else is to blame. In treatment, they need to accept the responsibility for their own behavior. Being an adult means making all of your own decisions and living with the consequences.

*Denial* is the most common defense in chemical dependency. It is primitive and distorts reality more than any other defense mechanism. In denial, the patient refuses to experience the full impact of reality. Suppose you are walking downtown on a hot summer's day. Along the sidewalk, people are standing holding buckets of ice water. As you walk past, they throw the ice water in your face. You see the water, you see the people, but you don't experience the full shock of the water. Denial is a disassociated unreal world. A drug addict may be losing his spouse, children, job, friends, money, and freedom, but he doesn't experience the full impact of this reality. He doesn't see what everyone is worried about.

All patients who come into treatment are in some form of denial. They are not seeing what is right in front of their face. It is incredible how strong denial can be. Patients can be at death's door and still believe that they are fine.

*Applying Cognitive Therapy* | Cognitive therapy corrects the lies patients have been telling themselves. It is the process of getting the thinking accurate. The counselor helps the patient to see the truth. First, the patient needs to see the lies in operation. Have the patient do the following exercise in your office or in group.

Place a chair in the center of the room and explain to the patients that they have an internal dialogue going on all the time. The dialogue is between the illness and the healthy side of themselves. The illness wants to use alcohol or drugs. The healthy side wants to be healthy and happy. Have the patient sit in one chair and just be the illness. Have the illness side talk the healthy side into drinking or using drugs. It will be helpful if you model the exercise first. The dialogue will go something like this:

"John, you've had a pretty hard day. Nobody is going to know if you have just a couple of beers. Your wife is not going to find out. Why don't you stop by the bar for just a couple? It would taste pretty good. You can handle a couple of beers. You can stop whenever you want to. Remember all the good times we had drinking? Remember the women? You can talk to them better if you've had a couple of beers. You don't have to call your wife. She won't know. You can hide it. It won't matter."

As the patient talks you can see all of the lies he is telling himself:

"I've had a hard day."

"Nobody is going to know."

"Just a couple."

"You can handle it."

"You can stop."

"Remember all the good times?"

"Remember the women, they liked you better when you were drunk."

"You can talk to women better when you've had a couple."

"You don't have to call your wife."

"She won't know."

"You can hide it."

"It won't matter."

Now you challenge each of the patient's inaccurate statements:

"Do you think that having a hard day is worth risking your life?"

"When is the last time you went in a bar and just had a couple?"

"Haven't you proven to yourself that you can't stop? If you could stop, what are you doing in here?"

"How are you going to feel if you start hiding from your wife again?"

Again and again, the patient's inaccurate thoughts have to be challenged. In treatment and in recovery patients must be committed to reality. They have to live in reality and solve problems using the whole truth.

Patients are not only inaccurate about their drugs, they are also inaccurate about their self-images. They may call themselves stupid, inadequate, or ugly. They may have an exaggerated sense of their own importance. The best way to correct these inaccurate thoughts is in group, but individual therapy is also valuable. People who think they are worthless, helpless, and hopeless, need to see what is real. Many patients will argue with you about these things; the inaccurate thoughts seem to have a life of their own.

*Patient:*   I can't live without Bob, I can't.

*Counselor:*   You can't? What would happen to you if you were shipwrecked on an island in the South Pacific? There is no one on this island but you. You have plenty of food and water, but you're all alone.

*Patient:*   Oh, I'd be okay.

*Counselor:*   But Bob wouldn't be there. Wouldn't you die?

*Patient:*   That's different. That's a different situation.

*Counselor:*   No, it's not. You just said you *can't* live without Bob. Now you tell me you could live without anyone.

*Patient:*   Well, I don't *want* to live without him.

*Counselor:* That's better, but that's not quite accurate either. Would you kill yourself if you didn't have Bob in your life? Is it really impossible to live without Bob?

*Patient:*   No, it's possible to live without Bob, but I love Bob. I want Bob in my life.

*Counselor:*   Good, that's accurate. You want Bob in your life. You don't need him in your life for survival. Seeing the relationship more accurately will give you more accurate feelings. If you need Bob for your survival, and Bob leaves you, you will die. That's pretty scary. It's too scary and it's not accurate.

*Automatic Thoughts*   Thinking occurs extremely quickly. There is a never-ending stream of conscious and unconscious thought flowing though our mind. Most of this thought is not registered on the screen of consciousness. The more a behavior or thought process is practiced the more unconscious and automatic it becomes. You do not have to think consciously of each of the hundreds of little decisions you make while driving a car. You make most of these decisions unconsciously, out of habit. How to turn the wheel. When to put on the brake. When to speed up a little bit. These decisions are all made without conscious thought.

Beck, Rush, Shaw, and Emery (1979) found that many people who were depressed were having certain thoughts that were leading them to feel depressed. It was the private way that these individuals were interpreting events that was critical to their uncomfortable feelings. They were thinking inaccurate things that were involuntary, persistent, plausible, and often contained a theme of loss. It was this thinking that was keeping them down. Most of these thoughts occurred automatically, totally out of the patient's awareness. The important thing to note here is that these thoughts profoundly affect feelings and behavior.

Beck (1967, 1972, 1976) reported that three elements were essential to the psychopathology of depression. These are the cognitive triad, silent assumptions, and logical errors.

*The cognitive triad* consists of patients' negative views about themselves, their world, and their future. Generally, depressives view themselves, their world, and their future as lacking something that is a prerequisite for happiness. For example, they may view themselves as inadequate, incompetent, or unworthy. They may view their environment as demanding and unsupportive. They may view the future as hopeless, frightening, and full of inevitable pain.

*Silent assumptions* are unarticulated rules that influence the depressive's feelings, thinking, and behavior. For example, the patient may believe one or more of the following:

"I will only be happy if I'm good-looking, intelligent, or wealthy."

"When I make a mistake, people think less of me."

"It is weak to ask for help."

"I have to please everyone all the time."

These stable beliefs develop from early experience and influence the individual's responses to events. They give rise to automatic thoughts.

*Logical errors* are the inaccurate conclusions patients draw from negative thinking. They can overgeneralize, drawing conclusions about their ability, performance, or worth from one incident. "He doesn't love me, so I am unlovable." They can magnify or minimize, by exaggerating or diminishing the importance of an event. "The class laughed. Everyone thinks I'm a fool. I got all A's this quarter, but 2 years ago I got a C. I can't do college work like other people."

*How to Correct Inaccurate Thoughts*

Let's go through an example of how to correct automatic thoughts. The first time patients hear about interpersonal group, they usually feel frightened. They may not stop and think, "Why am I afraid?" They just feel scared. Feeling like this, they may try todo something to prevent themselves from going to group. They may fake being sick or tired.

*Uncover the Thoughts and Feelings*

Using cognitive therapy, you would first ask them, how they were feeling. Write each feeling down. Then ask, "What were you thinking between the time that you heard about interpersonal group and the feeling you felt? What thoughts came to mind?" The patient may be able to respond here, or you may have to suggest some thoughts. In cognitive therapy, you will have to constantly suggest to patients thoughts that they could have been having. Don't stop until you have brought out a short list of thoughts such as the following:

1. "The people in group won't understand me."
2. "I'll make a fool of myself."
3. "This is going to be humiliating."
4. "They are going to put me on the hot seat."
5. "They are going to make me talk."

Pull on the patient's automatic thoughts. Ask and then make suggestions. Remember, these are thoughts that the patient doesn't try to have; they are unconscious and happen automatically. Once you see the powerful negative message that these thoughts give the patient, you will understand why he or she feels afraid.

*Score the Inaccurate Feelings*

It will help to have the patient to score each feeling on a scale of 1 (*as little as possible*) to 100 (*as much as possible*). Let's say the patient felt fear at 90. Ask if the patient was feeling any other feelings and ask him or her to score each of these. Our patient was also feeling angry at a score of 50. She was angry because the group was going to try to "make me talk." She was also feeling sad at a score of 70 because, "This is going to be humiliating. I'm going to make a fool out of myself. These people won't understand me." If we add up all the negative feelings, the patient was feeling 210 units of distress.

*Getting the Thoughts Accurate*

Now we help the patient challenge her automatic thinking. We know that many of these thoughts are inaccurate.

*Counselor:* Your thought was, "These people won't understand me." What do you think is accurate?

*Patient:* Well, they have the same problem as I do, they should be able to understand me. At least they'll try to.

*Counselor:* How about, "I'm going to make a fool out of myself."

*Patient:* I don't really think I'm going to make a fool out of myself. It could be a little embarrassing.

*Counselor:* Yeah, you could do something a little embarrassing. What do you think would happen if you did?

*Patient:* I don't know.

*Counselor:* Do you think the other patients might understand and be sympathetic.

*Patient:* I think they would try to understand.

*Counselor:* So, even if you did do something a little embarrassing, it wouldn't be the end of the world.

*Patient:* No.

*Counselor:* Now what about, "This is going to be humiliating." Do you think the group is going to humiliate you?

*Patient:* No, I don't. I've met a few of the patients already and they seem very nice. I do feel humiliated though, just being here . . . you know, in treatment.

*Counselor:* Do you think the other group members could relate to that?

*Patient:* Sure.

*Counselor:* How about, "They're going to put me on the hot seat."

*Patient:* Well, they might. I've heard about these groups where they hound you and attack you, until you spill your guts.

*Counselor:* Let me assure you that the staff here doesn't work like that. We don't have a hot seat. We give people the opportunity to talk. If they don't want to talk, that's fine. What if it was one of those heavy confrontational groups, could they make you talk if you didn't want to?

*Patient:* Probably not.

*Counselor:* So what's accurate here?

*Patient:* I can talk if I want to. I really want to talk. I want to get better.

*Counselor:* Good, let's go back and score your feelings again using accurate thoughts. You hear that there is an interpersonal group at 10 o'clock. You think, these people are nice; they have the same illness as I do; they should be able to understand me; I want to talk and get better.

*Scoring the Accurate Feelings*

*Counselor:* Now, thinking accurately, how much fear do you feel?

*Patient:* About 35, I guess.

*Counselor:* How much anger?

*Patient:* None.

*Counselor:* How much sadness?

*Patient:* 40.

*Compare Inaccurate and Accurate Thoughts and Feelings*

*Counselor:* When you were thinking automatically, you were feeling 210 units of distress, but when you get accurate, your pain drops to 75. That's a drop of 135 points.

*Patient:* Amazing.

*Counselor:* Yes, and these thoughts go on all the time. You automatically think the worst, so you feel bad. There is some real reason to feel uncomfortable, bad things could really happen, but if you get accurate, you can live in reality. You can feel the real world. You have been living and feeling in a world created by your distorted thoughts.

*Uncovering the Themes*

As patients keep track of their negative thoughts, you will see that their thinking ends up with certain themes. These are stable attitudes or beliefs that develop over time. They can usually be traced to early childhood experiences. These beliefs are very tenacious. People who believe, "I don't get along with people," may base that belief on something that happened to them as a small child. The inaccurate thinking keeps them from seeing reality. Themes are based on evidence that patients have collected over a number of years. Patients act on these beliefs as if they are absolute facts. They no longer challenge them. The automatic thoughts are used as evidence from which these inaccurate conclusions are drawn. You must help the patient uncover these distorted attitudes and beliefs; they are not accurate, and they need to be corrected.

Patients may believe that they are unlovable. They are convinced in of their own thinking that this is a fact, "I am unlovable." Patients will begin to build evidence from their experience that will support this belief. They will begin to tell themselves things like, "I'm unlovable because I'm ugly, I'm stupid, I'm bad." None of these things are true, but the patient believes they are true. Naturally this leads to uncomfortable feelings. Patients who think they are unlovable feel depressed and lonely.

In cognitive therapy, your job is to get patients thinking accurately. Most of their thinking is automatic and you will have to train them to keep track of their thoughts. *Feeling Good: The New Mood Therapy* by David Burns (1980) is an excellent overview of the various forms of cognitive therapy. Reading this is a good way to begin thinking in cognitive terms. In time, you will pick up patients' inaccurate thinking quickly. You will rarely want inaccurate thinking to pass by unnoticed. Stop patients at every opportunity and correct them.

*Patient:* I've messed up my whole life.

*Counselor:* Your whole life?

*Patient:* Yeah.

*Counselor:* Is any part of your life still intact?

*Patient:* No, I've screwed up everything.

*Counselor:* You still have your job.

*Patient:* Well, yeah.

*Counselor:* You still have your wife and kids.

*Patient:* Yeah, they're still with me.

*Counselor:* And your boss is supporting your treatment.

*Patient:* Yeah.

*Counselor:* So, let's get accurate. You haven't messed up everything, you just feel like you have.

*Patient:* (Laughs) Now that I think about it, I have a few things left: I still have my job, my wife, my kids, my house.

*Counselor:* You have a lot of things. You haven't messed everything up. Why don't we make a list of the things you still have? Carry this list around with you and when you think you messed everything up, take out the list and read it to yourself.

This is cognitive therapy at its best. The patient corrects inaccurate thinking, develops accurate thought, and then practices accurate thinking.

*Solidifying Accurate Thinking*

It is helpful to have patients carry around note cards with accurate thoughts written on them. When they feel bad, they take out the cards and read them to themselves. Sometimes they need to look at themselves in the mirror and read it to themselves. Patients won't catch the inaccurate thinking at the thinking stage; thinking happens too quickly. They will have to catch the inaccurate thoughts at the uncomfortable feeling, then backtrack to find out what the thoughts were. Have patients keep a feelings log, they jot down every time they have a significant feeling and the situation that caused the feeling. Then have them score each feeling on the 1-to-100 scale. Once they have a few days of a log, call them in, and begin to filter out what thoughts were occurring during a given situation.

John came in with his feelings log. On Thursday at lunch, he felt hurt and angry when a treatment peer made the following comment about his sweater: "Where did you steal that!" John felt angry at 70 and hurt at 80. He felt 150 units of emotional distress.

*Example of a Cognitive Therapy Session*

*Counselor:* What were you thinking when he said that?

*Patient:* He doesn't like me.

*Counselor:* What else?

*Patient:* That's about it.

*Counselor:* Were you thinking that people don't like you very much?

*Patient:* Yeah, I was.

*Counselor:* Were you thinking, Nobody likes me.

*Patient:* Exactly.

*Counselor:* Nobody has ever liked me?

*Patient:* (Nods his head.)

*Counselor:* How about, Nobody will ever like me?

*Patient:* Well, I know that.

*Counselor:* Bob says to you, "Where did you steal that sweater?" and you think, He doesn't like me. Nobody likes me. Nobody will ever like me.

*Patient:* Yes.

*Counselor:* Now, what's accurate? Bob says, "Where did you steal that thing?" What do you think is an accurate way of thinking about that situation.

*Patient:* Bob was making a joke.

*Counselor:* So, to get you to like him, Bob tells a joke.

*Patient:* I think so.

*Counselor:* Why does Bob tell you a joke?

*Patient:* Because he want's me to like him.

*Counselor:* Right, Bob likes you and wants you to like him, so he tells you a joke. He ribs you about your sweater. Your automatic thinking takes over and says, He hates me, everyone hates me, everyone will always hate me. Thinking these thoughts, you feel hurt and angry. Now, thinking accurately, how do you feel?

*Patient:* I feel pretty good. Bob likes me.

*Counselor:* Right.

**Interpersonal Therapy**

■

Chemical dependency wounds relationships. Interpersonal therapy heals relationships and restores an atmosphere of love and trust. In recovery, patients are encouraged to love God, love others, and love themselves. If one of these relationships is not healed, patients will continue to feel uncomfortable, and they will be vulnerable to relapse.

*How to Develop
Healthy Relationships*

In the AA/NA program, when we are talking about relationships, we are talking about spirituality. Spirituality is defined as the innermost relationship we have with ourselves and all else. The first thing a patient must do in developing a healthy relationship is to surrender. Step One demands an admission of powerlessness and unmanageability. Without surrender, patients will continue to try to control themselves and other people. This leads to disaster, "self will run riot" (*Alcoholics Anonymous*, 1976, p. 62).

The next step is to believe that a Power greater than ourselves can restore us to sanity. This relationship with a Higher Power is an essential part of the AA/NA program. Patients must seek God, as they understand him, and establish a relationship with their Higher Power.

Relationships with God, self, and others are based on love, trust, and commitment. Love is not a feeling, it is an action. Trust necessitates truth, and commitment takes consistency of action. Action without truth is not enough, truth without action is not enough.

*Building a Relationship
With God*

In building a relationship with God, a patient must be willing to accept that some sort of a Higher Power is possible. The best way to show this is to ask the patient a question: "Do you think that there is a Power greater than yourself?" For most patients this is enough, but for some you have to demonstrate. "If you wanted to leave this room, and the group was determined to keep you in, could you leave?" The answer here is obvious to even the most stubborn. The group has greater power.

Now, can the patient *begin* to turn her or his will and his life over to this new Power? This will start with the group. Can the group be trusted? Does the group make good decisions? If patients can begin to deal with doubt and faith in a group, they have come a long way in developing trust in a Higher Power. They must see the group members love each other. They must see the group be committed to the truth even when it hurts.

Much later in the program, the patients are encouraged to begin thinking about God. Willingness, again, is the key. If patients will seek God through prayer and meditation, they will begin to make progress in this area. Some patients will want to do some reading about spirituality, and all of them need to talk with a member of the clergy familiar with the Twelve Steps.

*Developing a Relationship
With Self*

The relationship with self begins to heal when patients begin to treat themselves well. They stop hurting themselves with drugs and alcohol. They stop saying bad things to themselves. They begin eating three meals a day. They sleep properly. They begin to get regular exercise. All of these simple skills have a profound effect on the patients' feeling of self-worth. A person of great worth is worth treating well.

*Building Relationships* Interpersonal relationships heal when patients use good interpersonal relationship
*With Others* skills.

1. They must share how they feel.
2. They must ask for what they want.
3. They must be honest.
4. They must be actively involved in the other person's individual growth.

If one of these skills is missing, the relationship will be unstable. It will feel unstable and the individuals involved will feel frightened. Each of these skills needs to be developed and practiced.

Patients must practice identifying and sharing their feelings. This takes education, individual therapy, and group work. There are only a few primary emotions. Robert Plutchic (1980) theorizes that there are eight:

1. Joy
2. Acceptance
3. Anticipation
4. Anger
5. Fear
6. Surprise
7. Disgust
8. Sadness

Other emotions are various combinations of the basic eight. Jealousy, for example, is feeling sad, angry, and fearful all at the same time. All feelings give energy and direction for movement. Feelings motivate behavior that is directly related to survival. Fear, for example, activates escape behavior. Escape protects the organism from a dangerous situation. Surprise activates orienting behavior. Sadness gives the organism the energy and direction to recover the lost object.

In therapy, you must educate patients about their feelings. In many homes, for example, anger is an unacceptable emotion. A child learns that anger is dangerous, so the child learns to repress anger; they do not feel it. They may feel fear every time that they feel angry. Patients need to use all of their feelings to function normally. People who cannot feel anger, cannot express anger. People who cannot express anger are handicapped. They cannot adequately protect themselves. Anger is necessary to establish and maintain boundaries around ourselves. If we cannot do this, people will violate our boundaries and we will be victimized.

Have the patients list situations where they felt each feeling and then discuss how the patients could have responded properly. You will find that cultural differences abound. In America, for example, women are not supposed to act angry, so when they feel angry, they cry. Men are not supposed to cry, so when they feel sad, they act angry.

As the counselor, you are teaching the patients to use feelings in problem solving. When patients have a feeling, they should listen to this feeling. What is the feeling telling them to do? They should then consider options of action.

*Patient:* I got so mad.
*Counselor:* What did you do?

*Patient:* I just stood there. I didn't know what to do.

*Counselor:* What were your options.

*Patient:* I could have hit him.

*Counselor:* What else could you have done?

*Patient:* I could have walked away.

*Counselor:* What else?

*Patient:* I was so mad, I didn't know what to do.

*Counselor:* Could you have told him you were mad?

*Patient:* Oh, yeah, but he wouldn't have cared.

*Counselor:* You could have told him you were mad and what he did that made you mad.

*Patient:* What good would that have done?

*Counselor:* We have to hold people accountable for what they do. That's what anger is for, anger gives us the energy and direction to fight for our rights. One of the best ways to use your anger is to tell people you're angry. That holds them accountable.

*How Patients Use Feelings Inappropriately*

Many patients use their feelings inappropriately. They make the wrong movements when they have a feeling. People who are fearful can constantly be withdrawing. They shy away from everything. People who are angry can always be fighting. They fight everybody about everything. These patients need to learn how to use their feelings appropriately. Their feelings can get to be the problem. Some of these patients need behavior therapy. They need to learn how to act appropriately when they feel certain feelings. A patient who was abused and terrified by his father, may respond to all people with fear. This patient needs to identify and understand how the relationship with his father influences how he responds to everyone. He needs to understand that most people are going to treat him well.

*How Patients Learn Relationship Skills*

People learn what to expect from the world by the experiences they have had. It is from these experiences that we draw maps about what the world is like. We learn what to do in certain situations. Childhood experiences are very powerful. They condition us and give us attitudes about what the world is like. The most important relationship for us was with our primary caregiver. This person was usually the mother, but it could have been someone else. If this person was healthy and loved us, we felt safe and important. We grew up feeling that the world was a safe, loving place. If our primary caregiver was not healthy, we learned other things. We may have learned that the world was an abusive place or a sad place. The first relationship is very important. The counselor must help the patient develop accurate maps of the world.

*How to Change Relationships*

In therapy you will see the patients' relationship maps in how they relate to you. Patients will react to you just as they reacted to significant others in their past. This is called transference. When you react to the patient using your old maps, that's countertransference. As the patients respond to you, watch for the inaccurate way they interpret what you do. If they act frightened of you when there is nothing to be frightened about, you can be pretty sure that you are dealing with a transference issue. As you treat patients with encouragement and love, they will have an opportunity to redraw their maps. Maybe the world is a safe place after all. In the relationship with you, patients will see how healthy persons relate to each other. They will observe and be able to model themselves after you. You will teach them how to communicate and how to relate to another person with love and trust.

Patients may have a relationship problem that they will need to address with some other person. In the family program you will have the opportunity to work with the family. Here you can teach them all healthy communication skills. You can teach them how to listen to each other and to develop empathy for each other. Have them repeat each other's thoughts and feelings. This makes sure each person understands what the other is saying. Teach them to use "I feel" statements. Teach them how to reinforce each other. Teach them how to inquire for more information until they understand. The *Feeling Good Handbook* by Burns (1990) has some communication exercises that can be helpful if you are interested in pursuing this therapy further.

*How to Handle Grief* | Grief issues can need attention in interpersonal therapy. When patients have lost a significant other, they will have to work through the grief. They will have to experience their pain and say good-bye to the lost loved one. Having patients talk about the good and bad times they had is important. Have them write a letter of good-bye. Have them read the letter to you or to their interpersonal group. They need to gain the support of other people. The Higher Power concept can be greatly beneficial here. God knows everything, and everything fits into God's plan. "Nothing, absolutely nothing happens in God's world by mistake" (*Alcoholics Anonymous,* 1976, p. 449). The patient can be encouraged to trust in God's judgment. Step Three work and grief work go together. We turn our will and our lives over to the care of God as we understand God. Grief work is a good time to build a closer relationship with the Higher Power.

*How to Choose the Therapeutic Modality* | Individual therapy helps prepare patients for group work. They will transfer what they learn from you in individual therapy to the group as a whole. Patients will transfer what they have learned from the group to people in society. Individual therapy gives you an opportunity to discuss some things with the patient that are not appropriate for the group. There is no need for a patient to share every intimate detail in group; some things are best left for individual therapy. Sexual abuse and other sensitive issues can generate a great deal of shame, and the group may not understand. If patients decide to share something with you, but they do not want to share this issue with their group, they should be given this opportunity, but remember, everything of importance must be discussed with the clinical staff. The patient doesn't have to talk to the staff, but you do. You need the help of your colleagues, particularly in sensitive situations.

Individual therapy gives patients the opportunity to have a healthy interpersonal relationship with another person. This is very healing. They will finally tell someone the whole truth and see that person's reaction. As you continue to care for them, even when they tell you the worst, it teaches them something that they have never known: They are people who are worthy of love. Nothing battles the disease better than this fact.

CHAPTER FIVE | # Group Therapy

The most powerful motivation for change in most chemical dependency programs is the group. The group is a microcosm of the world. In the group, there are people we identify with mother, father, brothers, sisters, friends, and enemies. You can grow in group in ways that you cannot grow in individual therapy. The group serves as a healthy family from which patients can develop normal social interaction. From the treatment center group, the patient transfers the relationships to the AA or the NA group. Chemical dependency requires long-term treatment, and this is how it occurs. Long-term treatment is necessary for the underlying character defects. In AA/NA the treatment is good, it's supportive, and it's free. The group has special characteristics that make it uniquely effective in helping patients to overcome their problems.

**Benefits of the Group Process**

1. *Healthier members instill hope.* Certain patients in the group are further along in treatment. These patients look better and act better. They use effective communication skills. They do not deny their disease. They confront other patients gently and with the truth. They encourage each other. They are not afraid to share. This has great impact on patients coming into treatment. They see that people get better as they stay in treatment longer.

2. *Patients can model healthy communication skills.* They see members sharing their feelings and asking for what they want. Group members are not shamed for having feelings or thoughts. The world doesn't end if someone gets angry or cries. The patients watch as the problems and feelings are worked through until they are resolved.

3. *Patients become aware that they are not alone in their pain.* They hear the stories of the other patients and the stories are very similar. The group can laugh

together about the mutual pain. No one else but fellow alcoholics would understand riding around the block waiting for the liquor store to open, or hiding the bottle so well even you couldn't find it. It is a great relief for the patients to hear someone else discuss a shameful situation that they have experienced themselves.

4. *Information is exchanged.* Patients share their experience, strength, and hope. In these stories are examples of how to handle difficult situations. Group members learn from each other's experiences. If a member has never relapsed, it is informative to hear about someone who has had that experience.

5. *A feeling of family develops.* The group feels close. The members accept each other, and try to love each other. Interpersonal trust and intimacy develops. Patients carefully keep each other's confidentiality and learn how to watch out for each other.

6. *Patients learn that they can be accepted for who and what they are.* Even when they are at their worst, the group still accepts them. They are supportive and loving. This comes into direct conflict with what the patients have always believed, that if they told the truth, they would be rejected.

7. *Patients learn the power of the truth.* Using real feelings, in real situations, with real people, patients learn to solve real problems. People don't go away from the group sulking or worse off than when they came in. They go away feeling loved and supported. It is the counselor's responsibility to make sure that every group ends in a positive light.

8. *Patients can freely express their feelings.* They can express their pain in a loving atmosphere. They can ventilate feelings and still feel accepted. They can practice sharing feelings to see if they are appropriate to the situation. Someone who has never acted angry, can act angry, and see the positive effect of their anger.

9. *By listening to each other and sharing together, the patients feel a new sense of self-worth.* They begin to feel worthy of the group's time and energy. The group members show each other that they are all worthwhile individuals.

10. *Patients learn what works, and what does not work, in interpersonal relationships.* They see what brings people together. They come to understand that the more you share the closer you can get, and the closer you can get the more you can share.

## Preparation for Group ■

Before each group meeting, the counselor has someone read a statement about the group process. This sets the stage for the group and prepares the members for the work ahead. It sets a few simple rules about how the group will operate.

*The Preparation
Statement*

Interpersonal group is an experience designed to help us learn more about how we feel, think, and act. Chemical dependency blinds us to the truth about ourselves. It keeps us from experiencing reality. We develop defenses that keep us from seeing ourselves as we really are. We present to the world a false front that we ourselves believe to be true. If we are ever going to accept ourselves, and begin the process of recovery, we must know who we are. We can do this only by learning how other people see us. The group members will act as mirrors, showing to us those parts of ourselves that we do not see. They will reflect our feelings, thoughts, and behaviors.

The spirit of this group is love. We share, care, and help each other to grow as individuals. With all of our heart, we encourage you to share your experience, strength, and hope. Be open to listen and to talk. Our experience has shown that only those who participate fully recover.

A main focus of the group is feelings. Many of us have never dealt honestly with our feelings before. We know that doing this is frightening, and painful, but it is necessary. You must be willing to be yourself. It is a tremendously rewarding experience to be accepted for who you really are.

The group has only two rules:

1. There will be no physical violence. We need to feel free to express ourselves without the fear of physical harm.
2. Confidentiality. What you see here, what you hear here, let it stay here. We will now begin the session by introducing ourselves and stating why we are in treatment.

The reader of the preparation statement gives his or her first name and the reason why he or she is in treatment. Example: "I'm Shirley, and I'm an alcoholic." If someone in the group does not want to call themselves an alcoholic or chemically dependent, that's fine, but they do have give a reason why they are in treatment. Example: "I'm Frank, and I got a DWI."

*The Agenda*

The counselor then has each group member choose an agenda and someone in the group to share it with. The agenda is a current matter of concern for the patient. It has to be real problem that generates real emotion. Some patients will try to choose something easy, but don't let them. If they won't or can't choose something important, you choose something for them. The counselor writes down all the agenda items on the blackboard or a large pad for everyone to see.

| Patient | Agenda | Share With |
|---|---|---|
| 1. Bob | Feeling confused | Frank |
| 2. Frank | Scared about family program | Shirley |
| 3. Shirley | Mad at treatment peers | Tom |
| 4. Tom | Disgusted with self | Jose |
| 5. Jose | Fear about going to jail | Nancy |
| 6. Nancy | Sad about loss of marriage | Francis |
| 7. Francis | Angry at staff | Mory |

*How to Choose the Order of the Agenda*

Once the agendas are up on the board, the counselor chooses an agenda that seems to be the most therapeutic. Choose something that will generate emotion and will teach the patients about chemical dependency. The best agendas are usually those that deal with problems the group members are having with each other. It is always best to deal with the here and now rather than with the there and then.

The group will start with the agenda item that the counselor chooses and move as far through the list as they can. Each time the counselor chooses the next agenda. You will have a pretty good idea which agendas need to be dealt with during a particular day. The patient starts off by telling the person he or she has chosen to share the problem with. For example, Shirley talks to Tom about being mad at her treatment peers. Tom answers first, and then anyone in the group can add what they feel is important. The counselor watches for and reinforces appropriate feedback.

*How to Give Good Feedback*

A person giving good feedback will do the following:

1. Talk about the specific behavior.
2. Give feedback in a caring manner.
3. Give the other person a chance to explain.
4. Avoid being judgmental.
5. Use "I feel" statements.
6. Share the positive too.
7. Does not give advice.

*How to Receive Feedback*

To receive feedback appropriately, patients must do the following:

1. Ask for it.
2. Receive it openly.
3. Acknowledge its value.
4. Be willing to discuss it.
5. Does not make excuses.
6. Indicate what they intend to do with it.
7. Listen to everyone.

*How to Run the Group*

As the counselor, you shouldn't talk much in group. You should intervene only when necessary to keep the group moving along therapeutically. As long as the truth is coming out, and people are being loved for it, the group is doing well. It is a common early mistake for counselors to talk too much. This discourages the other members from sharing. Let the silent periods raise the group's anxiety. Someone will talk if you wait. If you always talk, no one else will.

For the most part, the patients who are doing the most sharing are getting the most out of group. You must encourage quieter members to share. A simple question such as, "Tom, how do you feel about that?" is often enough to get them started.

If someone is becoming a problem in the group, let the group handle it. Don't try to handle everything yourself. That's what the group is for. Asking a question such as, "How do the rest of you feel about Bob right now?" is enough to let the group work for you.

The counselor needs to make sure that no one gets harmed in the group process. If things are getting too hot and angry, focus on the patient's pain. Hurt comes before anger, and it defuses anger to talk about the pain. If someone is getting hurt, you must step in and give the group direction. Statements like, "How would you want to be treated right now?" go a long way in giving the group solid direction.

*How to Know Which Therapy to Use*

Behavior, cognitive, and interpersonal therapy can all be used in a group setting. The skill of the counselor is to know exactly which therapy is necessary and then to be able to plug the treatment into place. If the patients are moving in a way that is maladaptive, behavior therapy comes into play. If they are thinking inaccurately, cognitive therapy is necessary. If the problem is in a relationship, interpersonal therapy is most appropriate.

## The Honesty Group

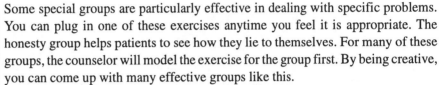

Some special groups are particularly effective in dealing with specific problems. You can plug in one of these exercises anytime you feel it is appropriate. The honesty group helps patients to see how they lie to themselves. For many of these groups, the counselor will model the exercise for the group first. By being creative, you can come up with many effective groups like this.

In the honesty group, the counselor says, "Today we're going to see how the illness operates inside of your thinking. We all have a constant dialog going on inside of our heads. This conversation is between the illness, that just wants to drink or use drugs, and the healthy side that wants to get clean and sober." Place an empty chair in the center of the group. "We are going to put a chair in the center of the group. In this chair, we are going to put our illness. This is the side of us that wants to get high. In the chair that we are currently sitting in, we are going to put the healthy side of us, the side that wants to stay clean and sober. Now each of us are going to spend some time in each chair. We are going to start in the illness chair and try to convince the healthy side of us to drink or use drugs. I'm going to go first."

*Example of an Honesty Group*

The counselor, Judy, sits in the center chair and leans toward the empty chair she was just sitting in. From the illness side of herself, she tries to talk herself into drinking or getting high. She might say something like this:

> Judy, you're doing great. I'm real proud of you. You've been sober for a long time. You've been going to meetings. That's great. You've got your life back together. You know, when you feel like it, I'd like to do something. I want to go for a ride in the car. Maybe a nice spring day. I'm not in any hurry, I can wait. I want to go for a ride, relax, and drink three beers. No one is going to know. Nothing bad is going to happen. You need to relax, Judy. You've been working too hard. You deserve a break. Come on, it's just three beers. Remember all the good times we had drinking? Remember how good it felt?

Judy looks at the group. "That's how my illness still tries to get me drunk. Now, I'm going to trade chairs and answer the illness from the healthy side of me." She moves to her original chair and leans back.

Well, illness, you seem to forget a few things. You always forget. You remember selectively. See, I remember the misery. I remember trying to drink three beers and throw up three beers at the same time. I remember losing my husband and my kids. I remember the shame of losing my job.

She sits forward in her chair.

I also remember that we have tried this before, about a hundred times. We have tried drinking only three beers, or two, or one, and it goes okay for awhile, but sooner or later, I get drunk and bad things happen. Illness, I know how good I feel in recovery. I have regained my self-respect. I have my children back. I have a good job that I'm proud of. I have found God for the first time in my life. And you want me to give all of this up for three beers? You keep your three beers. I don't want to have anything to do with you.

Now the patients should have the idea. The counselor picks someone that he thinks can do a good job and the exercise is repeated. Most of the patients won't have as long a dialog as the counselor, but it is important to see each person's illness at work. This exercise is excellent at uncovering who has a good recovery program and who is still struggling.

The patients will usually feel more comfortable playing the illness role. This may show how little it is going to take the patient to go back to using. You will see all manner of seductions perpetrated by the illness. It good for the patients to see how they have been deceiving themselves.

*Uncovering the Lies*   About halfway through the group, hand each of the patients a blank piece of paper. Then tell them this. "It is important that you see how the illness works. The illness must lie to operate. It cannot exist in the truth. You must lie to yourself, and believe the lie, before you can ever go back to drinking or drugging. What we are going to do now is uncover the lies. Every time you hear the illness lie, I want you to wave your paper. This is your white flag of surrender. Wave it loud so it rattles." The counselor asks the next patient to start another dialog.

Bob smiles at the group and sits in the illness chair. "Well," says Bob, "you've had a hard day" (group members rattle their papers). "Why don't you stop by the bar and have a couple of beers? That's not going to hurt you" (group members rattle their papers again). "Your wife won't know" (group members rattle their papers and laugh. Bob laughs with them). "You can drink just a few" (rattle), "just a couple" (rattle). "Remember all the good times we had" (rattle). "You need to relax and enjoy yourself" (rattle).

This is educational and fun. The patients will never forget those white flags going up after they speak to themselves. When the patients speak from their healthy side, the flags stay quiet. It is a sobering event to experience the lies trying to work, in front of your treatment peers.

Have the group discuss the exercise. In which role did they feel the most comfortable? Why? What are they going to do to keep from lying to themselves? How can they begin to keep the illness in check? How do they feel about the illness part of themselves and the healthy part of themselves? What is the goal of the illness? What is the goal of the healthy side? What's it like to have what seems to be two people in the same body?

*How to End Each Group* | End each group with a chance for the members to share the positive things they learned about themselves. Keep this sharing time positive. At Keystone we begin each group with the serenity prayer and end with the Lord's Prayer. The group members put their arms around each other or hold hands as they pray.

## The Euphoric Recall Group

This group examines euphoric recall and how it differs from reality. The counselor stands at the blackboard and asks patients to give an example of what drinking or using drugs did for them when they first started using. The counselor pulls out all the positive things the patients were getting from early use.

*How to Uncover Euphoric Recall*

"Tony, what did drinking do good for you? What was it giving you that was good?"

"It made me relax."

"Good," the counselor says. He writes *made me relax* on the blackboard. Then he moves to the next person in the group. "How about you, Sally. What did drugs do good for you?"

"It was easier for me to talk to people," Sally says.

"Okay, good." The counselor writes *easier to talk* on the board.

The counselor goes around the group at least twice. You need a long list of the positive things chemicals did for the group members. Don't put down the same thing twice. You should come up with a list that looks something like this:

1. It made me relax.
2. It was easier to talk to people.
3. I felt more intelligent.
4. I felt stronger.
5. It made me brave.
6. It made me feel wanted.
7. I felt more attractive.
8. I could sleep.
9. I felt happy.
10. I could be creative.
11. My problems didn't bother me anymore.
12. I could get along.
13. I was funny.
14. I felt comfortable.
15. People liked me.
16. I could talk to women/men.

The counselor makes as long a list as the blackboard will allow and then states, "Now, here are some of the good things drinking and drugs did for you. I assure you that we could make a longer list of the good things that chemicals gave us early in use. This is why we were drinking and using drugs."

*How to Get Real* | The counselor then draws a line down the middle of the board.

"Now, let's see what happened to each of these things when chemical dependency set in. Tony, after you became an alcoholic did alcohol still make you relax?"

"I was more tense. I couldn't relax," Tony says.

"How about it, Sally, after drug addiction took over was it still easier for you to talk to people, or did you feel more isolated?"

"Lonely, I felt lonely."

The counselor writes down what each person says. Be sure to read off what good the patients got out of early use before you ask them what happened when drug addiction took over. What the group is going to find out is once chemical dependency set in, they ended up with the opposite of what they were using for. People who were drinking to sleep, can't sleep. People who were using to be social, ended up alone. Your second list will look like this:

1. I felt more tense.
2. I couldn't talk to anyone. I was lonely.
3. I felt stupid.
4. I felt weak.
5. I felt inadequate.
6. I felt like no one wanted me.
7. I felt ugly.
8. I couldn't sleep.
9. I was very sad.
10. I couldn't think.
11. I had more problems.
12. I couldn't get along with anybody.
13. I wasn't funny anymore. I was sad.
14. I couldn't get comfortable.
15. I felt like no one liked me.
16. I couldn't talk to anybody.

The group needs to take a long look at both sides of the blackboard. The counselor emphasizes that the illness side of themselves will use euphoric recall to seduce them into using drugs and alcohol again. The patients have to get in the habit of seeing through the first drink. They need to remember the painful consequences that comes with continued use. The group discusses what they learned for a brief period then the counselor needs to speak again.

"You see how the illness uses the good stuff to get you to use again. Now, what are you going to do when the illness side of you begins to gain strength? What are the tools of recovery that will put hurdles in the way of the first drink."

"Call your sponsor," says Tony.

"Go to a meeting," says Bob.

"Turn it over [to your Higher Power]," says Sally Ann.

The counselor writes each of the new coping skills on the blackboard.

1. Call your sponsor.
2. Go to a meeting.
3. Turn it over to your Higher Power.
4. Get some exercise.
5. Talk to someone.
6. Read some AA/NA material.
7. Remember the bad stuff.
8. Remember how good you have felt clean and sober.
9. Ask for God's help.
10. Do something else you enjoy.

Help the patients make a long list and then discuss with the group fully.

**The Reading Group**

In a reading group the patients read a portion of *Alcoholics Anonymous* (The Big Book) or the *Twelve Steps and Twelve Traditions* (The Twelve and Twelve) and discuss it with each other. It is necessary to have a counselor present to facilitate this discussion. Gently encourage all members of the group to share. People don't have to share, but if they do they get more out of treatment. The first 164 pages of the Big Book, and all of the steps in the Twelve and Twelve, should be read during treatment. There will be patients who don't feel comfortable reading for one reason or another. Encourage all who can comfortably read to do so. If patients feel too uncomfortable reading, they can pass. This material can be taken chapter by chapter, paragraph by paragraph, or line by line. The patients discuss the subject matter to help them to understand and internalize the material.

**Relapse Prevention Groups**

A relapse prevention group should be run once a week. This group concentrates on high-risk situations and develops coping skills for dealing with each situation. The first group introduces relapse and concentrates on the triggers that might trigger using. These are the environmental situations that make a patient vulnerable to using drugs and alcohol. Patients are told that there is such a thing as lapse, the use of a mood-altering chemical, and relapse, continuing to use the chemical until the full-blown illness becomes evident again. For most patients, the time period between lapse and relapse is less than 30 days. If lapse occurs, immediate action must be taken to prevent relapse. All patients must develop coping skills for dealing with a lapse.

Hunt, Barnett, and Branch (1971) studied relapse rates following a variety of addiction programs. They found that 33% of patients lapsed within 2 weeks following treatment. Sixty percent lapsed within 3 months, and 67% lapsed within 12 months. This study should be reported to the patients and the percentile figures placed on the board. The patients are typically not happy when they hear these figures. They may tend to think, What's the use? You must point out that most patients lapse early, within the first 3 months after treatment. This does not *have* to happen, but it can happen. If the patients use their new skills, it will not happen. The patients cannot use their new skills and their drug of choice at the same time; these behaviors are incompatible.

*The Trigger Group*

The five situations that trigger relapse are placed on the board. These are the high-risk situations developed by Marlatt and Gordon (1985). To the side of each of these situations the counselor writes the percentage of time this event tends to trigger relapse.

1. Negative emotions—35%
2. Social pressure—20%
3. Interpersonal conflict—16%
4. Positive emotion—12%
5. Test personal control—5%

*How to Uncover the Triggers*

Each of these triggers needs to be carefully discussed with the group. The patients are asked to list the feelings that make them vulnerable to using. In what situations do they continue to use? How do they feel before they use? Are they more vulnerable when they are angry, frustrated, bored, lonely, anxious, happy, joyful?

Social pressure can occur in two ways, direct social pressure, and indirect social pressure. Direct social pressure is when someone directly encourages the patient to use. Indirect pressure is being in a social situation where people are drinking or using drugs.

*The Drug Refusal Exercises*

After discussing the triggers, the group goes through drug refusal exercises. One member of the group is encouraged to use by the other members while she tries to say no. The first time patients go through this, anxiety and craving are usually generated. Their first attempt at refusal tends to be rather pathetic, but with practice they get better. Patients need to practice until they can say no and feel reasonably comfortable.

The group has a lot of fun with these exercises, but this role-playing delivers a powerful message: It is hard to say no and feel good about yourself. It is a new skill and it has to be practiced until it feels reasonably comfortable. The exercise provides excellent protection against relapse if patients can continue the exercises until they feel comfortable saying no. For each patient, try to reenact the exact situation that makes him the most vulnerable to relapse. If the patient is vulnerable to a sexual situation, for example, set up this situation as exactly as you can. A situation where a significant other encourages him to use is not difficult to set up. What is he going to say? What is he going to do? What if the other person gets mad? Have him go through each situation until the group feels he has developed the skills necessary to say no, then have the group make a long list of the hurdles that the patient can put in the way of the first drink or use. What can the patient do that will prevent use even when in a high-risk situation?

*The Inaccurate Thinking Group*

The second group focuses on thinking. What thinking occurs between the trigger and the feeling of craving? This is where the patient's inaccurate thinking takes over. "It won't hurt to have a couple of beers. No one will know. I can handle it. I never had any problem with pot. I can use a little pot. I never really had a problem anyway. I deserve a drink. I had a hard day. I'll show them." All of these, and more, can be given as examples of inaccurate thinking at work.

Have the group discuss what they think about before they use chemicals. How is the sick part of themselves trying to trick them into thinking that they can still drink or use drugs normally. Use the chair technique again. Have the patients talk to the empty chair and talk the healthy side of themselves into using drugs or alcohol. Each of these thoughts must be placed on the board and exposed for the lie that it is. Discuss the inaccurate thoughts carefully until the patients understand that they are all lies. Then replace the inaccurate thoughts with accurate thoughts and have the patients practice the accurate thinking. Go over exactly what new thoughts the patients are going to use. They are all taught a sentence to plug into their thinking whenever they feel the desire to use alcohol or drugs: "Drinking (or using drugs) is no longer an option for me!"

Have the patients practice thinking this sentence to themselves several times. Have them write it down and carry it with them. Every time they feel craving in treatment, they are to first think this new thought and log the situation that triggered the craving. These triggers can be discussed in further groups. Every time patients are in a high-risk situation, they will think the new thoughts then consider the other options for dealing with the situation. Drinking and using drugs are no longer an option so what are they going to do? If they are in a high-risk situation, they need to use their new coping skills. Have the group put on the board a variety of options available other than drinking or using. The board will end up looking something like this.

1. Call someone.
2. Turn it over to your Higher Power.
3. Think, "That's no longer an option for me."
4. Call your sponsor.
5. Go to a meeting.
6. Think through the first use.
7. Think about how good you feel in recovery.
8. Remember how miserable you were before treatment.
9. Exercise.
10. Call the treatment center.

*The Feelings and Action Group*

The third group focuses on feelings and the behaviors. The group needs to know that most chemically dependent persons are particularly vulnerable to anger and frustration. How are they going to handle these feelings in sobriety?

Feelings are used to give the patients energy and direction for problem solving. Have the group discuss the feelings that make them vulnerable to relapse and come up with coping skills to deal with each feeling. Any number of positive or negative feeling states can lead to relapse. The patients need to learn how to cope with good and bad feelings without chemicals.

When patients are having intense feelings, they need to share their feelings with someone. This allows them to feel accepted and supported. They need to develop better problem-solving skills and to practice problem solving in treatment. The following steps need to be followed when solving a problem:

1. Stop and think. Exactly what is the problem?
2. Consider the options. What is the best thing you can do for yourself and/or the other person right now?
3. Develop an action plan.
4. Carry out the plan.
5. Evaluate the effect of your action.

*The Slips Group*

The fourth group is a slips group. What are the patients going to do to prevent a slip, and what are they going to do if they have a slip? How are they going to feel, and specifically what are they going to do? What hurdles are they going to put in the way after the first use to prevent continued use? Remember for most patients the elapsed time between lapse and relapse is less than 30 days.

The group puts on the board the action they are going to take to prevent a slip. Make a long list and have all the patients copy the list down to take home with them.

1. Work a daily program of recovery.
2. Attend regular meetings.
3. Read AA/NA material.
4. Daily meditation.
5. Daily contact with sponsor or other AA/NA member.
6. Get daily exercise.
7. Develop enjoyable hobbies.
8. Attend church or work on spiritual program.
9. Pray daily.
10. When wrong, promptly admit it.
11. Be honest. Don't lie.
12. Eat right.
13. Get enough sleep.
14. Take a daily personal inventory.

Have the patients make an emergency card of phone numbers to call if they are feeling vulnerable. Have them carry this card in their wallet or purse at all times. The phone numbers should include the following: sponsor, several members of their AA/NA group, the treatment center, the local AA/NA hotline, a religious contact, any other person that may be able to respond to them positively.

In group the patients should role-play calling these numbers and practice asking for help. This is a very difficult skill for some people and they need to be desensitized to the situation. Have someone else in the group play the other party. Patients need to get in the habit of calling someone when they feel uncomfortable. Just out of treatment, they should call someone every day until they feel comfortable. They should make every attempt to go to an AA/NA meeting every day for 90 days. The first 3 months out of treatment are when the patients are the most vulnerable to relapse. Every effort should be made to stay sober these first 90 days. After the first 3 months, patients can discuss with their sponsor and aftercare group how and when to cut back on meetings.

Signs and symptoms of impending relapse developed by Gorski (Gorski, 1989; Gorski & Miller, 1986) should be given to patients and their significant others. Each symptom should be discussed so the patients understand and can identify the symptom. These warning signs include the following:

1. Apprehension about well-being
2. Denial
3. Adamant commitment to sobriety
4. Compulsive attempts to impose sobriety on others
5. Defensiveness
6. Compulsive behavior
7. Impulsive behavior
8. Tendencies toward loneliness
9. Tunnel vision
10. Minor depression
11. Loss of constructive planning
12. Plans begin to fail
13. Idle daydreaming and wishful thinking
14. Feeling that nothing can be solved
15. Immature wish to be happy
16. Periods of confusion
17. Irritation with friends
18. Easily angered
19. Irregular eating habits
20. Listlessness
21. Irregular sleeping habits
22. Progressive loss of daily structure
23. Periods of deep depression
24. Irregular attendance at meetings
25. Development of an "I don't care" attitude
26. Open rejection of help
27. Dissatisfaction with life
28. Feelings of powerlessness and helplessness
29. Self-pity
30. Thoughts of social use
31. Conscious lying
32. Complete loss of self-confidence
33. Unresolved resentments
34. Discontinuing all treatment
35. Overwhelming loneliness, frustration, anger, and tension
36. Start of controlled using
37. Loss of control

The patients and their significant others should be given a copy of the warning signs. It is possible to prevent relapse. In taking a daily inventory, patients should list any relapse symptoms they see in themselves and come up with a plan for dealing with the symptoms as soon as possible. Any symptoms resistive to change should be discussed with the sponsor or AA/NA group.

Patients may not recognize the early warning signs and someone else may need to check them. That's why a sponsor, the aftercare group, and regular attendance at meetings are so essential. The patient needs to listen to everyone. A closed mind is a sure way to end up in trouble.

The patients must understand that relapse is a process. It does not begin with using alcohol or drugs. Some of the symptoms will occur long before actual drug use begins. The one symptom that everyone should pick up on is a reduced attendance at meetings. Any reduction in meetings attended should be carefully discussed with the patient's family, sponsor, and group.

## The Spirituality Group

Spirituality group should be conducted every week. This group should be run by a clergy person trained in the group process or by a member of the counseling staff who has a solid spiritual program.

### Group Preparation

At the beginning of each group, the group leader, or someone he or she has chosen, reads the following to prepare the group for the spiritual process:

> Spirituality is the innermost relationship we have with ourselves and all else. Religion and spirituality are different. Religion is an organized system of faith and worship. Spirituality deals with three intimate relationships. We will explore how to improve our relationship with ourselves, others, and a Higher Power. We are going to call this Higher Power, God. You may call your Higher Power something else if you like. We only ask that you be willing to consider the possibility that there is a Power greater than yourself. We will begin the group by giving our names and the reason why we are here.

### How to Develop a Healthy Relationship

The first group discusses the concept of healthy relationships. What are the essential components of a good relationship? What are the patients' past experiences with relationship with self, others, God, Higher Power, religion? What hurdles seem to stand in the way of these relationships? What makes them worse? What makes them better? Many patients, for example, see God as punitive. They see God as they saw their father or their mother. These transferences, attitudes, and beliefs need to be discussed with the group. The pastor or counselor should be free to discuss his or her own relationships with self, others, and God.

As the counselor, you must be willing to accept how other people experience God. You will see a wide variety of individual beliefs. This is good, each person has his or her own understanding of what the Higher Power is like, and what the Higher Power can do. In the atmosphere of unconditional acceptance, the group members can freely explore their own concept of God. They must see that God and religion are not going to be shoved down their throats in this program.

It is a mistake to allow formal religious doctrine to enter this group. Do not allow one member try to convince another about some religious principle or belief.

Alcoholics Anonymous and Narcotics Anonymous have no religious affiliation. People can talk about their religious preferences, but for the most part, they should discuss spirituality rather than religion. They need to talk about their own spiritual journey.

*How to Develop a Healthy Relationship With God*

The second group specifically delves into the relationship with God. The group members write a letter to God and ask God for what they want and share how they feel. They may come up with questions that they would ask God if God were sitting next to them. The group members share this material with each other. The group is encouraged to view the relationship with the Higher Power as essential to the program. Patients are encouraged to share their knowledge of God with each other. What do they want God to be like? What does God want from them? How can people have a relationship with God?

The group needs to process through how God communicates with them. The relationship with God needs to be presented as a simple dialogue between two people. Patients can be taught to contact God in a variety of ways. Nature, scripture, prayer, meditation, church, and other people, are all ways that God can speak to them. Each of these ways needs to be discussed and have patients in the group give examples of when they felt close or far away from their Higher Power.

*The Eleventh-Step Group*

The third group seeks ways to improve conscious contact with God. Prayer and meditation are defined and discussed. *Prayer* is described as talking to God, whereas *meditation* is described as listening for knowledge of God's will. Patients are encouraged to begin to talk to God. They need to discuss various methods of prayer and meditation. They are encouraged to look for God in themselves and in each other. What do they see in themselves that is loving and good? Patients explore the moral law. We all know what is right and wrong. How come we all have the same laws? Is it possible that some life force gives us this law? If that is possible, what might that force be? Patients are asked to explore several philosophical questions: If there is a God, how come God didn't make God more knowable? If there is a God, and God is all good, how come bad things happen?

*The Meditation Group*

The fourth group does an exercise in an attempt to contact God directly. The patients are told that God may communicate with them in many different ways, thoughts, feelings, images, other people, scripture, music, nature, and so on. God often communicates with them inside of their own mind. That God may contact them in words or in images in their own thinking. They are told that the group will try to establish a conscious contact with God, as they understand Him, and they will try to receive a direct communication from God. It is explained that God may communicate with them in one of three ways.

1. In words inside of their thinking
2. In images inside of their thinking
3. No words or images but they will know the communication

Each member of the group is given a piece of paper and told to write down any communication they receive. The counselor then plays some soft music and takes the group through this imagery exercise. Speak these words slowly and rhythmically:

> Close your eyes and concentrate on your breathing. Just feel the cool air coming in and the warm air going out. As you concentrate on your breathing, you will begin to relax. Your arms and legs will begin to feel heavy and warm. See as completely as you can in your own way, an image of ocean waves. Don't worry about how you are seeing these waves, just try to see them as completely as you can. See the wave build, as you inhale, and wash ashore as you exhale. There is no right way or wrong way to do this exercise, there is just your way. God knows exactly what you need to experience. Feel yourself relax more as you see the waves build, and wash ashore. You begin to feel more at peace.
>
> Picture an island inside of your mind, with palm trees and lush green vegetation. See yourself standing on a white sandy beach watching the ocean, watching the waves. There is a trail on this island, and you see yourself turn, and take this trail. You walk under the palm trees. You are not in a hurry. You have plenty of time. You walk to a hill that is covered with wild flowers. You climb the hill, and as you do, you become more tired, your arms and legs feel heavy.
>
> At the top of the hill, is a huge field of flowers. You can see all the way down to the sea. You sit in the center of the field, and feel yourself relax in the sun. You call out for the Higher Power of your choice three times. You may call out for God, or Jesus, or Higher Power, you choose, but call out three times.
>
> A person dressed in white walks out of the trees and begins to walk to you. The person is looking right into your eyes. You know who this person is: This is your Higher Power. The person comes to you and you stand up and you embrace God. You have waited for God all your life. God sits across from you, and takes your hands, and looks you right in the eyes. God has a communication for you. Open yourself up in every way you know how, and receive the communication from God. I will give you 5 minutes to receive the communication. I will count off the minutes for you.

The counselor then is silent and speaks only to count off the minutes. At 2 minutes, the counselor states. "If you are only receiving silence, stretch yourself into the silence and seek your communication." At 4 minutes the counselor states, "You may have questions for God. Ask them and God may answer them for you."

At the end of the 5 minutes, the counselor states. "Now stand up in the field and place God into your heart where your Higher Power will stay. Walk down the hill and back to the beach. Watch the ocean waves. Feel yourself in your chair. Wiggle your toes and your fingers. Feel your eyelids flutter, and when you feel comfortable, go ahead and open your eyes, and write down the communication you received."

After the patients have written down their communications, go around the group and have them each share what they received. If they received no communication, have such patients discuss what happened when things were silent. How did they feel? What did they think? What did they see in their mind?

When they have shared their communications, have the group decide whether or not they feel this communication came from God. Have them describe the characteristics of the person who delivered the message. What was that person like? Do they feel that this is a person who can be trusted?

All of the spirituality groups should begin with the serenity prayer and end with the Lord's Prayer. Those patients who do not feel comfortable praying can remain silent. At all points in a spirituality group, the counselor needs to concentrate on spirituality not on religion. You must encourage patients to find their own unique relationship with God. They are all seeking the God of their own understanding.

## The Childhood Group

In the childhood group, the patients come to understand how they developed the tendency to lie about themselves. They come to understand the great lie. The great lie is, "If you tell people the whole truth about you, they won't like you." The truth is the opposite of this, if you don't tell people the truth about you, they cannot like you. Most of the patients have been living their life as if the great lie were the truth. They need to hear that they were created in perfection, in the image of God. There is no reason for them to lie. The group needs to see that they couldn't be themselves, they pretended to be someone else. They wore a variety of social masks and roles. It was the only way they thought they could ever be loved.

### How to Explore Early Parental Relationships

The group explores early parental relationships. The patients had to pretend to be someone else to their parents. They knew that their parents would not love them for who they were. This belief system resulted in the patients feeling empty and unloved. They did not get what they wanted from their home of origin. Chemical dependency is an attempt to avoid this empty feeling. Most chemically dependent persons come out of their childhood's feeling inadequate and unloved by parents and others.

The group members write a letter to their parents. This work is based on some of the work of John Bradshaw (1990). The counselor introduces the exercise like this. "Write a letter to your parents, using your nondominant hand. This makes the letter look like a small child wrote it. Write them about how you felt as a child growing up. Tell them how you were feeling, and what you wanted that you didn't get."

After the members write theie letters, have them read their letters to the group. Then have the other members of the group, each in turn, respond as if they were the *healthy* parent hearing the letter. If the patients feels comfortable, have the group members reach out and touch them as they respond. The group should sound something like this.

John reads his letter. "Dear Mom and Dad, Mom, I wanted you and Dad to stop fighting. I wanted you to pay more attention to me. Dad, I wanted you to take me fishing and tell me you loved me. I wanted you to stop drinking. I wanted you to tell me everything was going to be all right. I was afraid."

Joyce, a group member, reaches out and touches John's arm. She speaks as if she is John's healthy mother. "John, I'm sorry your dad and I were fighting. We were having problems. It wasn't your fault. I love you."

Meg, another group member, leans over to John. She too plays the role of a healthy mother. "I'm sorry your dad and I were fighting. We didn't mean to frighten you. We both love you very much."

Frank speaks as the healthy father, "John, I'm sorry I was drinking. I'm sick. I'm going to try to get some help. I'd love to go fishing with you."

*How to Begin to Heal Early Childhood Pain*

After all have read their letters, the counselor takes the group through this imagery exercise. This exercise must be positive! It must emphasize that the patients are now going to be their own champion in recovery. They are going to take over the parental role. They are going to try to forgive their parents and reach for their Higher Power. The counselor should speak very slowly pausing briefly after each sentence.

Close your eyes and relax. Feel yourself becoming more comfortable. See yourself drift back through time. See your high school. What was that building like, was it brick or wood? See yourself walking the halls of that school. How did you feel at that time in your life? Did you feel happy? Did you feel frightened? Feel the feelings you were feeling then. See your grade school. See the playground. See a special friend. What are they wearing? See yourself playing a favorite game with them. How did you feel in that school? Reexperience the feelings you were having at that time.

See yourself walk up the street where you lived as a small child. See your house up ahead. You walk up the front walkway and peek in your window. Which room was yours? Go inside of your house and see yourself as a small child. How did you feel in that house? Did you feel safe? Did you feel loved? Feel the feelings you were feeling then. See your mother. How did you feel when she was there? See your father. How did you feel about him?

Walk over to yourself as a child and smile. Imagine that the child looks up at you. Tell the child, "I am from your future. I am going to be your champion from now on. You can trust me. I am going to keep you safe. I am going to see to it that good things happen to you. You are important. You matter to me. I want to listen to how you feel. I care about what you want." Tell the child that it is time for you to leave. You are growing up. You're not going to blame your parents anymore, that wouldn't do any good. They were trying as hard as they could to love you. You pick the child up, and the child wraps his or her arms around you. You carry the child out of the house. Your parents come out on the porch and wave good-bye. Your Higher Power appears beside you. Your new AA/NA group is ahead. "Come on," they say. "You can do it. We'll help you." You walk up the street, feeling confident, trusting in yourself, trusting your Higher Power, trusting your new support group. You feel happy and at peace. Everyone is smiling. You and the child are laughing together. You take the child and place her or him into your heart where the child will stay. You feel yourself coming back to this time. Back to the treatment center. Back to your chair. Take a deep breath. Feel your toes wiggle, and your eyelids flicker. When you feel comfortable, open your eyes.

The group then discusses the exercise. It is important that the group not delve deeply into old childhood pain. They need to concentrate on early recovery, but you do want to connect them to their feelings. You want them to feel supported by themselves, their new group, and their Higher Power. This will give them new hope that even the old pain can be resolved.

## The Men's Group/ Women's Group

A men's group and a women's group are run once a week. In these groups, men and women can gather and discuss things that would be more difficult in mixed company. Sexual issues and sexual abuse issues can be more easily shared in this atmosphere. The special relationship of a mother to a daughter, or a father to a son, can be explored in greater depth in these groups. How can you be a good mother or father? What did you want from your parents? What did you want to say to your mother or father that you never said? What did you want the relationship with your father or mother to be like? What is it like to be a man? What is it like to be a woman? What are the special problems that men and women face?

The group needs to discuss how to have healthy relationships with the opposite sex. They need to consider addictive, dependent, and normal relationships, and how they differ. Women can discuss premenstrual syndrome which may make some of them more vulnerable to relapse. The men need to discuss anger, and how to use their anger appropriately. Men and women can role-play various situations. Both groups need to discuss boundaries and how to establish and maintain appropriate boundaries around themselves.

## The Community Group

Community group is where the patient population meets to discuss problems they are having with each other or the staff. This group is usually run first thing in the morning and lasts only a few minutes. Some programs run this group daily and some weekly. A daily group is best, if the patients feel supported.

A daily meditation should be read during this group. Any rules of the treatment center that have been broken need to be outlined and discussed. Have the group join hands or put their arms around each other and commit themselves to helping each other through treatment.

## The Personal Inventory Group

At the end of every treatment day, the patients have a personal inventory group. In this group, the patients evaluate their day. They need to consider how they grew in the program and how they slipped backward. At the minimum, they need to consider each of the following points:

1. What did I do to love myself today?
2. What did I do to love others today?
3. What did I do to love my Higher Power today?
4. Was I honest?
5. What uncomfortable feelings did I have?
6. What did I do with my feelings?
7. What character defects caused me problems?
8. How have I been doing in my program?
9. What am I grateful for?
10. What do I need to do differently tomorrow?

Once the patients have considered their personal inventory, they need to share positive experiences from the day. Then they need to go through a relaxation exercise to wind down. This exercise can be taped or given by a counselor. Have the patients sit in a comfortable place and pay attention to their breathing. Then have them imagine a relaxing scene. They can imagine that they are at the beach, or in the mountains, down by a river, or in the desert. Take them through the scene for about 20 minutes and call it a night.

CHAPTER
SIX | # The Contracts

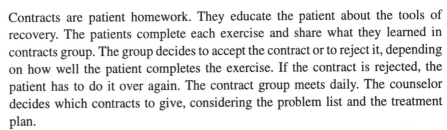

Contracts are patient homework. They educate the patient about the tools of recovery. The patients complete each exercise and share what they learned in contracts group. The group decides to accept the contract or to reject it, depending on how well the patient completes the exercise. If the contract is rejected, the patient has to do it over again. The contract group meets daily. The counselor decides which contracts to give, considering the problem list and the treatment plan.

Contracts can be listed as specific objectives. They help the patient to identify a problem, understand the problem, and learn new skills to overcome the problem. These are tools of recovery and they are individualized for each patient. The types of contracts are infinite. You will want to develop some of them on your own. A few contracts you will use more often, and some, such as the Chemical Use History, you will use with every patient. This chapter includes the contracts that you will use most often. You can order a wide variety of other contracts from treatment facilities such as Hazelden, Educational Materials, P.O. Box 176, Center City, MN 55012.

**The Chemical Use
History**

The Chemical Use History (Appendix 8) is designed to give the patient and the counselor a detailed account of the patient's use of drugs and alcohol. This is an excellent way to break through the patient's denial. It is very beneficial for patients to see the whole thing written down at one time. There is nothing like writing down the history of their chemical abuse and presenting it in front of their treatment peers, for breaking through the denial system.

The patients need to address each drug that they took and process through any problems that the drug caused them in their life. They need to identify specifically when they started using and detail their pattern of use. Where do they use, with whom? What happens when they use? What are the consequences? Each problem caused or exacerbated by use needs to be identified and discussed with the group.

Most patients will hedge, at least to some degree, in presenting their Chemical Use History. Remember, these patients come into treatment in denial; they do not know what the truth is. The counselor and the group need to be ready to press the patient when they feel he or she is not being completely honest. The group members can give examples of how they answered certain questions when they came into treatment. This confirms that the patients are not trying to lie; they are just fooled by the denial process.

As you work through the Chemical Use History, you will be able to firm up the patient's diagnosis. Period of intense intoxication, blackouts, withdrawal symptoms, using to avoid symptoms of withdrawal, and all consequences in the home, work, or school are covered. The feeling of shame and humiliation needs to be identified, and the group needs to support patients when they have these feelings. Patients need to feel like they are not alone, that they are now with their brothers and sisters in this program.

**Honesty**

The Honesty Exercise (Appendix 9) helps patients see how they have been distorting reality. All patients use denial, in its many forms, to keep themselves from experiencing the pain that the truth would bring. If they were to see the whole picture about themselves, they would realize that they are deathly ill and need treatment. This fact would create tremendous fear in them, and they would have to do something about their problem.

Patients keep from feeling this fear by minimizing, rationalizing, denying, blaming, distorting, projecting, intellectualizing, diverting, and a hundred other ways of not seeing the truth. The other patients in a contracts group will need help with this exercise. Patients cannot uncover unconscious denial without help from the group. The Honesty Exercise just gets them started in this process. Treatment should be an endless search for the truth.

It is an eye-opening experience for patients to realize just how much they have been lying to themselves and to others. Patients usually feel guilty about lying to others, but they do not realize that the person that they have lied to the most was themselves.

Patients need to process how they feel about themselves when they lie and learn the consequences of dishonesty. If they lie, they will be lonely, and they will not be able to solve problems in the real world. They need to understand why dishonesty leads to empty relationships. If you tell people lies about yourself, they cannot know you, and you will feel unloved, empty, and alone. If patients lie to themselves about the real world, they can't use the facts to solve problems. If problems are not solved, they escalate, until the patient goes crazy, gets sick, or uses drugs.

**Love, Trust, and Commitment**

The Love, Trust, and Commitment Exercise (Appendix 10) builds self-esteem. Patients come into treatment not understanding what love is. They may have love confused with sex. They need to develop a new positive relationship with themselves. They have been saying bad things to themselves for a long time. "I'm no good. I'm bad. I'm stupid. I'm ugly. I'm unlovable." These thoughts dominate the patients' thinking and keep them feeling discouraged, depressed, and anxious.

Using the Love, Trust, and Commitment Exercise, patients build a positive relationship with themselves and others. For this, they will need to understand the essential ingredients in a healthy relationship. They need to understand where their original feelings of inadequacy and rejection come from. They need to explore their first relationship with their parents or primary caregivers and how this relates to their current relationship with themselves and others.

Patients need to learn what it means to trust themselves and to commit themselves to their own individual growth. What do they need to see from themselves that will show them that they are trustworthy? What do they need to see from themselves that will show them that they are committed to their own recovery.

Patients need to learn how to be loving to themselves and to others. They need to say positive, loving things to themselves. They need to give themselves a lot of praise whenever they try to do something well. These skills will need to be practiced on a daily basis.

Many patients will have considerable difficulty working through this exercise. Some may even fight, and say that there is nothing positive to say about them. They have a hard time thinking up anything good to say about themselves. Such patients need the help of the group. Each group member may have to come up with something positive to say about the patient. It may be a long time before patients believe these things, but if they keep trying, the new ideas will begin to take hold.

They need to develop a personal plan that will help them treat themselves well. They need to act as if they are a person worthy of good things. They need to learn how to praise themselves, and others, and they need to practice this skill. A group's compliments are often helpful to get this process started. In this group, each member comes up with positive things to say about each other.

**Feelings**
■

The Feelings Exercise (Appendix 11) is designed to help the patients identify their feelings, and to use their feelings appropriately to solve problems. The patients are told that all feelings are motivators; they give energy and direction for movement. Each feeling is connected to a specific motor activity. Fear, for example, gives the energy and direction to run away from danger. If patients can't use their fear, they can't run, and they are handicapped. Similarly, if they can't act appropriately on their anger, they are more vulnerable to the world. If they can't feel, they can't adapt to their environment.

Chemically dependent people treat their feelings with drugs or alcohol. They do not use their feelings to solve problems. The Feelings Exercise takes the patients through each feeling, connects them with the physical cues that accompany each feeling, and teaches them how to problem solve.

The main point the patients need to get is this: Each feeling needs to be carefully processed. They need to stop, think, and plan before they act. Each feeling is directing them to take some sort of action. They must have the skill of identifying each feeling, and understand what each feeling is directing them to do. Then they need to work through their options of action, decide which is the best, and then act.

Patients in treatment need a lot of practice properly identifying their feelings. They have old skills that will constantly get in the way. Men, for example, when they feel hurt or frightened, often act mad. That is confusing. Once they are able to identify the real feeling, the pain, they can address the problem more accurately.

Women often cry when they are angry. This is confusing to them, and to others, and it muddies the waters of problem solving. The husband may react to the tears, when the real problem is that the woman is angry. The group and the counselor help the patients get at the core feeling, and then work through the feeling to resolve the problem.

Bob may come to group and he is acting angry and sullen. When it comes time for him to talk, he may not talk about the anger at all, he may talk about his fear. Bob may not even be aware that he is angry. Perhaps in his home of origin, he could not get angry, or he would incur the wrath of his father. As a child, it was dangerous for Bob to feel angry, so he didn't feel it, he repressed it, and he felt scared instead. The group may need to teach Bob how he is really feeling by processing the situation with him. What happened to Bob that caused the feeling? How would the rest of the group have felt in a similar situation? Bob's anger is reflected to him by the member of the group: "Bob, you say you feel scared, but you look angry."

Patients who have felt feelings for the first time in their lives can in group express their feelings in a nonthreatening environment. They are not rejected for their feelings; they are accepted and loved, no matter how they feel.

Patients need to know that all of their feelings are friendly and are great wise counselors that need to be listened to and acted on. Acting too quickly on feelings is a mistake; this causes impulse control problems, which makes the patients vulnerable to relapse. Feelings need to be processed carefully and acted on rationally. That takes a lot of practice.

## Relationship Skills

Patients who are chemically dependent have poor interpersonal relationship skills. They manipulate, distort, accuse, blame, shame, project, sulk, rage, and harbor deep-seated resentments. They are trying to control the planet Earth and everyone on it, and they are furious when everything is not going their way. The Relationship Skills Exercise (Appendix 12) has been designed to teach, and practice, healthy interpersonal relationship skills.

The patients learn that love is not a feeling—it is an action in truth. You cannot love and lie. Love is the interest in, and the active involvement in, a person's individual growth. Self-love is the interest in and the active involvement in your own individual growth. To love, you have to be there for yourself, or for the other person. Chemically dependent people can't do this. Sometimes they are too intoxicated or hung over. No drug addict is completely trustworthy.

The patients are taught that commitment means stability over time. Commitment is developed by working a daily program of recovery. Patients must take the time necessary to nourish themselves and others.

They need to be encouraging and reinforcing to themselves and others. They practice the skill of giving praise. Some patients will need specific social skills training. They need to learn how to do simple things, like make good eye contact, or to stand at an acceptable interpersonal distance. As patients practice good interpersonal skills, it is important that they recognize how they feel when they are using healthy skills compared to the old skills they have been using.

It is inevitable that they will use their old methods of coping with conflict while in treatment. When this happens, the counselor and the group can help patients stop and use their new skills. Nothing solidifies learning better than watching the consequence of the old behavior compared to the new. The patients will see that the new skills work better and result in better problem solving. The old skills tend to make the problem worse.

The patients will need a lot of practice in sharing how they feel and asking for what they want. Most of them are trying to tell people what they want to hear rather than the truth. This results in the patients' feeling unknown. They need to share their feelings and watch the other members of the group respond appropriately.

Many patients are reluctant to share their feelings. They have never asked for what they wanted. They have been taught this is selfish, or that other people simply don't care. It is a new experience for these patients to see the power of the truth.

Compromise is necessary for healthy relationships. The patients have to practice working through an issue until every party is satisfied with the result. This is called a "win-win scenario." The members of the conflict share how they feel, and what they want, until the problem is resolved. New options have to be constantly given by the group for consideration. The primary principle is this: Treat other people the way you want to be treated.

The patients are taught that all people need to be respected equally, regardless of race, color, creed, education, or belief system. Healthy relationships demands caring for how other people feel and caring about what they want.

## Addictive Relationships

Many patients coming through treatment for chemical addiction are just as addicted to some other person as they are to their drug. Addictive relationships can be as destructive as alcohol or drugs. They leave the patient feeling empty, abandoned, and unlovable. People can be so hooked on someone else that they can't see the truth.

The Addictive Relationship Exercise (Appendix 13) is designed to teach patients the difference between healthy and addictive relationships. It teaches them what they need to do if they are in a relationship that is addictive. These unhealthy relationships are fueled by powerful sexual feelings that patients mistake for love. They become caught up in the excitement of an emotionally chaotic relationship.

Addictive relationships are characterized by the same loss of reality involved in chemical dependency. Patients are unaware that the relationship is bad for them, and convinced that it is the best thing that has ever happened in their life. Lies permeate these relationships, which are filled with feelings of intense fear, anger, and pain.

To operate, the addictive relationship must use lies to keep going. The partners must feel that they have to stay in the relationship to feel normal. Without the relationship, they fear that they will be lonely forever. "I will never have anything as good as this. I can't live without her."

Addictive relationships are filled with verbal and physical abuse. They are demoralizing and end in feelings of anger and abandonment. Patients who have addictive relationships will typically have a pattern of these relationships rather than just one.

They use the relationship as drugs are used. The relationship distracts them from their real pain and fills their life with something to obsess about. The patient will need to make the decision to get out of an addictive relationship or to take the relationship into long-term treatment.

## Communication Skills ■

The Communication Skills Exercise (Appendix 14) teaches healthy communication skills. It is essential that these skills be practiced in group, and in individual sessions. The patients need to be constantly reminded to use these skills.

Basically, good communication necessitates being able to listen well and to speak clearly. Active listening pulls out more of a person's communication, until all of the message is perceived.

Words are symbols for thoughts and feelings. They are accompanied by nonverbal cues that are often more accurate than the words themselves. Patients who tell you they are doing well, with a flat unemotional voice and downcast eyes, are telling you with their words that they are fine, but with their actions they are telling you another thing entirely.

To develop good listening skills, patients need to practice repeating what each other has said until the communication correct. Many times people have different communication patterns, or family rules, that other people don't understand. In certain cultures, for example, friends argue vehemently about things, that's just how they communicate. In other cultures, this behavior may be considered insulting. Patients who are used to using an angry tone of voice to get their point across, need to hear how it adversely affects other people. They may not know how scary it is.

Many patients need to develop empathy skills. They have to practice understanding and personally relating to how other people are feeling. This will take a lot of trial and error. They need to try to relate personally to what the other person is saying by directly relating it to their own personal experience.

As the patients watch you validate the other members of the group, they will begin to be more reinforcing to each other. Patients need to be encouraged to use "I feel" statements when they speak. Many chemically dependent persons constantly blame others for their problems. "*You*" is perceived as the problem rather than "*I*." Statements that begin with "*you*" are usually headed for trouble. In the great scheme of things, we know much more about "*I*" than we do about "you."

Patients need to be reminded to be positive in their interactions with each other. A positive attitude needs to be soundly reinforced by all members of the staff. Patients who are not positive need to see how their attitude clouds their whole day. They need to practice saying positive things to themselves, and to others, even if they don't feel that way.

Patients with poor communication skills need to go through the Communication Skills Exercise with at least five of their treatment peers. These skills have to be practiced over and over again until they are used automatically. The more the patients practice, the better communicators they will become.

## Self-Discipline ■

The Self-Discipline Exercise (Appendix 15) is for those individuals who have a difficult time delaying gratification and accepting the responsibility for their own actions. They constantly blame other people for their problems. They think they would be fine if other people would leave them alone. Patients with these problems often have antisocial traits. They have had no experience with success. They have never worked at anything long enough to reach a goal.

To best treat these individuals, they need to see themselves achieve objectives in gradually escalating steps. They can accomplish things if they settle down and try. Most of these individuals have a low frustration tolerance and they have serious problems with impulse control. They act out too quickly on their feelings, particularly anger and frustration.

Begin with a simple task, such as one of the contracts, and walk the patients through it. Don't get frustrated with them when they procrastinate; that's all they know how to do. Have them sit down for a few minutes at a time and work through a page of the exercise. When they have accomplished something, reinforce them. Tell them that they can do it if they try. You have confidence in them. These patients need to see themselves be successful. They need to feel like they can do things that are difficult. Self-discipline is not an easy skill and many times it will be frustrating, but remember, if the patient gets reinforced for doing something, the behaviors will increase.

The patients need to see how poor self-discipline leads to failure. To accomplish this objective, the patients need to process through several of their problems with you. Take a problem that caused them quite a bit of pain, like getting arrested, or failing at something they really wanted, and walk them through the problem. Where did they go wrong? What else could they have done? Who was responsible?

Let's take someone who got arrested for drunk driving. They may be blaming the police. "They have always been out to get me." But, who was drunk? Did the police make them drive drunk? Where are the patients responsible?

The patients must understand that if someone else is responsible for everything bad that happens to them, then someone else is in control of their lives. They need to reachieve control by taking back the responsibility for their own behavior.

Patients with poor self-discipline do not understand the rules. They break the rules of society to get their own way. They do not understand that the rules are there to keep them safe. The spiritual part of the program can be a benefit here. The patients need to understand that God didn't make the rules to keep us from having a good time; God made the rules so we can be safe and happy. The same thing goes for the laws of the state. The legislature makes the rules to protect its citizens.

These patients will usually break some rule in treatment and will blame someone else for it. You must walk them through this violation and help them see that it was their choice to break the rule. Breaking the rule resulted in their getting caught and experiencing pain. If they could learn how to obey the rules, they would feel better all the time.

Patients with self-discipline problems have poor problem-solving skills. They go for the pleasure first, being unable to delay gratification long enough to achieve long-term goals. They need to process several problems with you while in treatment. If they want job training, how are they going to get that? Specifically, what are they going to have to do? If they want to stay sober, how are they going to do that? They must learn and practice working on a problem, on a daily basis, until the problem is solved. These individuals usually have such low frustration tolerance that they are unable to feel much pain without acting impulsively. People who can tolerate little pain cannot work at anything very long. They must see themselves take off a small piece of a problem, and work on it, until the whole problem is resolved.

**Impulse Control**

■

Patients who have impulse control problems act too quickly on their feelings. They need only a little of a feeling to move into action. If they feel angry, they act angry, immediately. This leaves them vulnerable to relapse. Craving is a feeling. If they move too quickly when they crave, they will relapse into using substances. The Impulse Control Exercise (Appendix 16) helps the patients to develop control over their feelings.

These patients need to stop, think, and plan before they act. This takes a great deal of practice, particularly when the patient is feeling strong emotions.

Patients must be able to identify each feeling, understand why they are having the feeling, consider the options of action, plan their response, and then act. When they are having strong feelings, they need to stop and analyze their feelings carefully. They can't continue to act too quickly on their feelings, for that leads to disaster.

Patients need to understand the behavior chain and practice analyzing their behavior carefully. They need to understand how their poor impulse control led to excessive drinking and drug use. They have developed a habit of moving immediately from craving to drug use. They will need to develop another plan and practice that plan many times in treatment.

These individuals are particularly vulnerable when feeling angry and frustrated. They have a low frustration tolerance, and they desire immediate gratification. They need to understand how this has lead to them into trouble. Most of them will have to work through the Self-Discipline Exercise.

They will need to learn assertiveness skills and they need to role-play interpersonal conflict. When they act impulsively in treatment, they need to process through the situation until they understand how they could have handled the situation better.

As the patients become more skilled at identifying their feelings, they can begin addressing their real feelings. What underlies most anger is pain. As they begin to solve real problems in real time, with real people, they feel less frustrated and more in control.

When angry, these patients must take a time-out and walk away from the situation. They cannot stay in a situation where they have lost control before. Teach them and their significant others to use the "time-out" sign of a referee when they are feeling too angry. They can also say the word "Time-out" as they make the sign. The partner then agrees to say nothing except, "Okay, time-out." The patients then leave the situation to get their thinking accurate. They may have to call someone to process the problem with a third party before they come back into the original situation. They must promise to come back within a previously specified length of time to continue to work on the problem. Both members of a couple need to write this plan down and follow it every time they have a significant conflict. People who get angry know before they explode that they are beginning to lose it. At the earliest possible opportunity, one of the people needs to make the "time-out" sign and then follow the prearranged contract.

All anger fueled by pain is there to make the pain stop. To be angry, patients must find someone to blame. They must think that the other person purposely did something wrong that hurt them. This is rarely accurate: Other people are just trying to meet their own needs, they are rarely trying to hurt someone.

Patients with impulse control problems will need to come up with a written plan that they carry with them at all times. When they are feeling strong emotions, they need to carry the plan out. They can call their sponsor, go to a meeting, read some AA/NA material, turn the situation over to their Higher Power, talk with a friend, and so on.

## Relapse Prevention

Relapse prevention is one of the most important aspects of chemical dependency treatment. Approximately two thirds of patients will use their drug of choice within a year of leaving treatment: 33% within the first 2 weeks, 60% within the first 3 months, and 67% within the next 12 months (Hunt et al., 1971).

Most patients (60%) lapse within 3 months of leaving treatment. This is the period of highest risk and needs the greatest attention. The patients must be willing to do almost anything to prevent relapse during this period of time. They need to see themselves as clinging to an ice-covered cliff with their recovery group holding the only rope. The most important thing they can do is go to meetings. Patients who are working a daily program of recovery will not relapse. You can't work the program and use at the same time; they are incompatible.

Relapse is a process that begins before the first use. Patients begin to feel themselves under stress. Their new tools of recovery are not used, so the problems continue to escalate. They reach a point where they think their only option is to drink or use drugs.

The Relapse Prevention Exercise (Appendix 17) draws on the work of Gorski and Miller (1986) and Marlatt and Gordon (1985) to develop a relapse prevention plan. Relapse prevention takes working a daily program of recovery. Patients must take personal inventories at the end of each day. If any of the relapse symptoms becomes evident, immediate action must be taken.

Gorski and Miller (1982) developed a list of 37 relapse warning signs. Patients should check this every day for symptoms that they are having problems. They must have a written plan detailing the exact thing they are going to do if they get into trouble. They carry an emergency card, with telephone numbers of people they can call in case they have problems.

Other people need to be encouraged to check the patient daily for relapse warning signs. This is a good reason to go to daily meetings and hang around other recovering persons. Often, other people can see what patients are unable to see for themselves.

The patients need to identify high-risk situations that may trigger relapse and to develop coping skills to deal with each situation. The more patients can practice these skills, the better off they are. In groups, the patients need to role-play high-risk situations and help each other make relapse prevention plans.

Each patient will be different, but Marlatt and Gordon (1985) found that most relapse occurs when patients are experiencing the following high-risk situations:

1. *Negative emotions.* Particularly anger and frustration. This could be negative emotions such as boredom, jealousy, depression, anxiety, etc.
2. *Social pressure.* Being in a social situation where people are using, or being directly encouraged to use by someone.
3. *Interpersonal conflict.* This can be a conflict with a parent, spouse, child, boss, friend, and so on.

4. *Positive emotions.* Something positive happens and the patient wants to celebrate. This can be a promotion, wedding, birth of a child, graduation, etc.

5. *To test personal control.* The patients use to find out if they can control the alcohol or drug again.

Using the relapse exercise, patients develop the skills necessary to deal with each of the high-risk situations, and they practice the skills until they become skilled at them. All patients must role-play drug refusal situations until they can say no and feel relatively comfortable. They must examine and experience all of their triggers, see through the first use, and learn about euphoric recall.

All patients must develop a plan for a slip. What are they going to do if they use again? Who are they going to contact? What are they going to say? This must be role-played in group, so they can see that the person on the other end of the phone is not going to be angry at them.

The patients must understand the behavior chain and develop skills for changing their thoughts, feelings, and actions when they have craving. Using imagery and drug paraphernalia, they need to experience craving and learn experientially that craving will pass if they move away from their drug of choice.

When you are discussing relapse with your patient, you might want to discuss the benefits of Naltrexone. Naltrexone is a opioid antagonist that can be helpful in many patients, particularly those with a chronic history of relapse. Naltrexone blocks the reinforcing properties of alcohol by blocking the action of endorphins (opiumlike chemicals that exist naturally in the brain to kill pain). Endorphins give addicts the euphoric effects that trigger craving. Several studies have shown that alcoholics who take Naltrexone daily can decrease relapse rates by 50%. The alcoholics still may drink, but the intense craving is not triggered, so they can bring the drinking under control more quickly (O'Malley et al., 1992; Volpicelli, Alterman, Hayshida, & O'brian, 1992).

## Stress Management

The Stress Management Exercise (Appendix 30) helps patients cope with stress. The inability to deal with stress effectively fuels chemical dependency. Patients have been using chemicals to deal with the uncomfortable feelings caused by stress.

Stress is the physiological response of the organism to a stressor. A stressor is any demand made on the body. This can include psychological or physiological loss, absence of stimulation, excessive stimulation, frustration of an anticipated reward, conflict, or the presence or anticipation of painful events (Zegans, 1982).

Hans Selye (1956) found that if rats were presented with a problem, to which there was no solution, they got sick. There was a generalized stress response that affected most organ systems. Initially the body's response to stress is adaptive, but chronic stress is damaging. Severe stress has been linked with many diseases, including kidney impairment, malignant high blood pressure, atherosclerosis, ulcers, anxiety, depression, increased infections, and cancer (Selye, 1956; Zegans, 1982).

To learn how to deal with stress more effectively, chemically dependent patients need to do three things: (1) relax twice a day, (2) maintain regular exercise, and (3) learn coping skills for dealing with stressors.

Many patients resist developing these programs and some will be unable to do so, but as many as possible need to be encouraged to practice these techniques. The patients who have the most trouble will have problems with self-discipline. They have not learned how to work toward a long-term goal. They will moan and complain whenever you mention the exercise or relaxation program. What they are really complaining about is they don't want to be told what to do. What is behind this is the inability to stick to things that they want to do. They have just failed too much, and they are unwilling to go to any length to stay clean and sober. Many of these patients will have antisocial traits. You have to show them, over and over again, why it is important to develop these programs.

If people relax twice a day for 10 to 20 minutes, they reap many benefits. They learn how to control their feelings, decrease tension, and decrease psychosomatic problems. Generally, they are happier and healthier. They learn that there is something that they can do to make them feel normal (Benson, 1975).

The patients can go through one of the formal relaxation techniques listed in the Stress Management Exercise or they can pray and meditate quietly twice a day. The important thing is they practice relaxing. The more they do this, the better they will feel.

Once patients know what it feels like to relax, they can develop techniques to stay more relaxed during the day. If something stresses them, they can use one of the techniques to recapture their serenity. The Higher Power can be used as an adjunct to this process. The patients can turn things over to their Higher Power and relax.

It is very difficult to get some chemically dependent individuals to maintain an exercise program. This is like pulling teeth for some people, but you should encourage them. Research has shown that exercise is important, not only for cardiovascular fitness but for a sense of psychosocial well-being (Folkin & Sime, 1981; Greist et al., 1979; Ledwidge, 1980; Stern & Cleary, 1981).

It has been demonstrated that hospitalized alcoholics can increase fitness levels in as little as 20 days. This increase enhances not only their physical fitness but their self-concept (Gary & Guthrie, 1972). A strong exercise program is important for developing a new sense of self-efficacy. Many chemically dependent people come into treatment thinking they can't do anything. When they see their strength develop, they feel a new sense of power and control. They feel like they can do it. This is a key, particularly for adolescent patients who are concerned about their body image.

Rigorous exercise produces natural opioids in the body that will give patients a natural high (Appenzeller, Standefer, Appenzeller, & Atkinson, 1980). They feel better all day after working out. Patients must be encouraged to develop a stretching, strength, and cardiovascular fitness program. The exercise or recreational therapist will help them individualize the program.

In learning new coping skills, the patients need to learn assertiveness skills, social skills, and how to increase their involvement in pleasurable activities. They need to be shown what they are doing that makes their life difficult. If they are frowning at everybody all the time, they are not getting a positive response from the world. They need to learn how to be pleasant, and had to ask for what they want. They need to practice sharing how they feel.

The Stress Management Exercise helps patients to develop more pleasurable activities in their lives. They need to learn how to have fun clean and sober. They must be encouraged to reach out and try something different. If they sit at home and wait for the wonders of sobriety to overtake them, they are going to be disappointed. They must reach out to others and become actively involved in their AA/NA group and community.

Many of these patients don't know how to have fun without chemicals. This has been their whole life, and it's all they know. They need to be shown that sobriety can be fun. This will be very difficult for many patients, as they are grieving the loss of their drug of choice. The pleasure of the drug must be replaced by pleasure from the environment. This requires doing something new.

The best way to get patients motivated is to show them that drugs and alcohol are no fun for them anymore. Once chemical dependency clicks in, the drugs loose their ability to make the patient feel better. The patient feels miserable, intoxicated or clean. A new lifestyle must be developed to help patients enjoy their sobriety. New hobbies and interests have to be tried until patients develop a leisure program that fits their needs.

| # The Steps

The Twelve Steps are the core of treatment for chemical dependency. More individuals have recovered using the principles of Alcoholics Anonymous than with any other treatment program. Alcoholics Anonymous currently has 1.5 million active members worldwide, including over 700,000 members in the United States. Alcoholics Anonymous works and it's free. The only requirement for membership in AA is the desire to stop drinking. Narcotics Anonymous and all of the other twelve-step groups developed their program directly from the Twelve Steps of Alcoholics Anonymous. The programs are almost identical. The program, as it is called by twelve-step groups, has been broadened to cover many types of problems, including Narcotics Anonymous, Gamblers Anonymous, Overeaters Anonymous, Drugs Anonymous, Cocaine Anonymous, and Pills Anonymous (Emrick, 1987).

Treatment programs differ in which steps they address in treatment. Some programs address only Step One, some the first three steps, and others the first five. This must be individualized. Some patients will only be able to embrace Step One, and that's fine, if they do a good Step One. For most patients, it is a benefit to complete at least the first three steps while in treatment. The more steps patients can do well, the better off they are in recovery, and the further along they are in the program. Working through the Fifth Step takes a great burden off of patients. If they complete the Fifth Step, they will not have to carry this burden into early sobriety.

If your center only works on the First Step, that will give you more time to work on powerlessness and unmanageability. In this text, we will teach you to take the patient through the first five steps, assuming that some inpatient programs will go this far; rare is the program that goes further.

As you take patients through the steps, you must make sure that they are internalizing the material. They must be able to identify each problem, understand the problem, and learn coping skills for dealing with the problem. They must be able to verbalize to you a solid understanding of each step, and how they are going to apply the step in their life.

You will be able to tell when patients are complying, and when they are understanding and internalizing the material. Their level of commitment to sobriety will be evident in their behavior, in what they do, and in what they say. If you watch how they act with you and with their treatment peers, you will have a good idea whether they are internalizing the information. If you are hearing one thing in individual sessions, and the patient's peers are hearing another thing, one of you is not getting the truth. Patients have to be confronted in group with the inconsistency of their behavior.

## The Committee

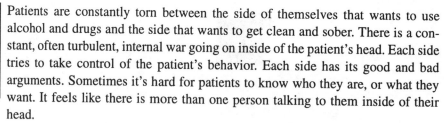

Patients are constantly torn between the side of themselves that wants to use alcohol and drugs and the side that wants to get clean and sober. There is a constant, often turbulent, internal war going on inside of the patient's head. Each side tries to take control of the patient's behavior. Each side has its good and bad arguments. Sometimes it's hard for patients to know who they are, or what they want. It feels like there is more than one person talking to them inside of their head.

It is useful to label the three voices. Freud called them the id, ego, and superego. In treatment we call the voices the disease, God, and me. One train of thinking is the disease process. This side only wants the patient to use drugs or alcohol and it doesn't care how it gets the patient to do that. If the patient feels miserable, this is all the better. Another voice is the voice of God. God only wants people to love themselves and others, and to reach for their full potential in life. This voice is incredibly supportive and loving. The third voice is the patient's own thinking. Here patients are trying to figure out things for themselves.

As you move patients through the steps, you must be sure not to continue to the next step until they have a solid foundation of the step below. If they have not completed a good Step One, it is no use in moving on to Step Two. If you have to work on Step One the whole time the patient is in treatment, that's fine, but don't try to move up in the steps until you have a firm foundation on the steps below. The steps must be build one on top of the other. The first building block is Step One.

## Step One

"We admitted we were powerless over alcohol—that our lives had become unmanageable" (*Alcoholics Anonymous,* 1976, p. 59). Please read the Step One Exercise in Appendix 18 before continuing with this chapter.

It is vital that all patients complete a solid Step One in treatment. Step One is the most important step, because without it recovery is impossible. Step One necessitates a total surrender. Patients must accept as true that they are chemically dependent, that their lives are unmanageable as long as they use mood-altering chemicals. Until this conscious and unconscious surrender occurs, they cannot grow. As long as they feel that they can somehow bring their lives under control and learn to use alcohol or drugs normally, they have not accepted their disease, they are stuck in the illness, and they cannot break free.

Step work is mainly group work. The patient completes the step exercise and presents the exercise in a group makeup. The group helps the patient with the step, asks questions, and helps the counselor decide whether or not the step is completed successfully. The counselor should not usually make this decision without the support of the group. Particularly in an inpatient setting, things go on in treatment that the counselor is not aware of. Patients may be complying with treatment, may be pretending that they are working, when they really aren't internalizing anything. The treatment peers are more likely to see these lies. They see the patient in casual interaction and pick up the inconsistencies.

In Step One, patients must learn to accept, as fact, that they are chemically dependent, that they are powerless, that their lives are unmanageable. They must understand that they cannot live normally as long as they use mood-altering substances.

The best way to convince patients to surrender is to show them, over and over again, that they get into trouble when they drink or use drugs. They don't get into trouble every time, just sometimes, but they can never predict when the trouble is going to occur. They may drink a couple of beers and go home, or they may drink more and get arrested for drunk driving. They must work through many of their problems in detail, until they realize that they have never been able to predict when they were going to have drug or alcohol problems. This is one of the primary reasons for processing through Step One.

How does the patient feel about having a blackout? It is very scary to know that you were awake doing things and you cannot remember what you did. Did the patients do something embarrassing while intoxicated? What was it, and how do they feel about what they did? How do they feel about not doing things with the family, at school, or at work because they were too intoxicated or hung over? You must get at the real story, exactly what happened, and examine how the patients feel. Talk about the shame, humiliation, depression, and anxiety caused by the drug use. How depressing is it, to know that the family is falling apart? How did it feel to be unable to keep promises?

Sometimes the patients used chemicals more, or for a longer period of time, than they had originally intended. Once they began using, the addiction took control. Even when they promised themselves that they were going to stop or cut down, they kept on using. They must understand that once they start using, they never know what they are going to do.

Most chemically dependent patients want to hold onto the delusion that they are still in control. No one wants to admit that they are powerless, that their lives are unmanageable. They were having problems sometimes, they think, but only occasionally. The fact is that when they had problems, it was almost always directly related to chemical use. They got into trouble obtaining the substance, using the substance, or recovering from the substance use. Chemically dependent persons do things when they are intoxicated that they would never do when sober. They need to take a look at each of these things and see the painful consequences of their addiction. They need to take a careful look at their chemical use history, at the lies, the crimes, the inconsistencies, and the people they have hurt. They need to understand that as long as they use drugs or alcohol they will hurt.

**Step Two**

■

"Came to believe that a Power greater than ourselves could restore us to sanity" (*Alcoholics Anonymous*, 1976, p. 59). Please read the Step Two Exercise in Appendix 19 before continuing with this chapter.

The beginning of the patient's spiritual program is Step One. This is the surrender step; it is essential for the patient to accept powerlessness and unmanageability before reaching toward a Higher Power. The essential ingredient of Step Two is willingness. Without willingness to seek a Power greater than themselves, patients will fail. "There is one thing more than anything else that will defeat us in our recovery; this is an attitude of indifference or intolerance toward spiritual principles" (*Narcotics Anonymous*, 1988, p. 18). The patients have admitted that they are powerless and their life is unmanageable; they must now see the insanity of their disease, and search for an answer to their problem.

The word *sanity* in Alcoholics Anonymous means soundness of mind. To have a sound mind, a person must be able to see and adapt to reality. They must be able to see what is real. No one who is chemically dependent sees reality accurately. They are living in a deluded world of their own creation. The mind of a chemically dependent person is irrational. They cannot see what is real so they cannot adapt to reality.

In Step Two, patients take a look at their insane behavior, they see how crazily they were acting, and reach out for an answer. They must conclude that they cannot hold onto their old ways of thinking. If they do, they will relapse into old behavior.

*How to Help Patients Accept a Higher Power*

Many patients rebel at the very idea of a Higher Power. They must be gently encouraged to open the door, just a little, and seek God. They must be encouraged to be honest, open-minded, and willing. They need power. They are powerless. They need someone else to manage. Their lives are unmanageable.

At first, the counselor encourages the patient to see that some sort of a Higher Power can exist. Patients must look at their interpersonal group and see that the group has more power than they do. The counselor can say something like this: "If you wanted to leave this room, and the group wanted to keep you in, do you think you could leave?" The matter becomes obvious, the group could force the patient to stay inside the room. It might take some wrestling, but the group has more physical power than the patient does. The patient is then asked to be willing to place trust in the higher power of the group.

Trust is a difficult issue for most chemically dependent persons, and they will need to process their lack of trust with the group. This is a good issue for group work. If patients cannot trust the group as a whole, can they trust someone in the group? If they cannot trust anyone, can they trust themselves? Are they willing to try to trust, to be open to the possibility? If they are unable to trust themselves and they are unable to trust anyone else, they are lost. They will have to start somewhere. This reality will have to be driven home.

Patients cannot trust themselves, not really; that should be obvious. There were times when they are out of control, powerless, their lives were unmanageable.

The best way to have a patient learn to trust the group is to develop a loving group. This is a group where the members are actively interested and involved in each other's growth. They gently help each other to search for the truth. The group is kind, encouraging, and supportive. The group is never hostile and aggressive.

They don't put each other down; this is counterproductive. If you have an aggressive, highly confrontive group, you will destroy trust. People must learn to confront each other in an atmosphere of love and unconditional positive regard. It is your job to teach the group this process.

Once patients trust the group, they can begin to transfer this trust to the AA/NA group. They should attend meetings while in treatment, as many meetings as possible. Gradually, they will feel safe and will begin to share; this builds trust. As the group is interested in the patient, as they show love to the patient, confidence in the group grows. This is probably the first time in the patients' lives when they have told someone the absolute truth. When the group doesn't abandon them, it is a tremendous relief. This will show on the patient's face and it will be etched into the heart.

The patient sees people further along in the program doing better—they look better and sound better. Patients cannot miss the power of the group process—it changes people right in front of their eyes. They will see new members come in frightened or hostile, and watch them turn around. They will observe the power of group support. Soon they will be offering new patients encouragement. They will learn how helpful it is to share their experience, strength, and hope.

Once they see how insane they were acting and accept that the group has the power to restore them to sanity, they have come a long way toward embracing Step Two. By trusting the group, the patient opens the door to God. This basic building block of trust is vital to good treatment. Patients who move too quickly to the concept of God miss out on the power of the group. They miss seeing God in others. These patients, on discharge, may feel that God is the only answer they need. They may think that they don't have to go to meetings as long as they have a good spiritual program. These patients will not work a program of recovery and they will ultimately relapse. All patients must be encouraged to trust the group process. We need other people to flag for us what we do not see in ourselves.

**Step Three**

■

"Made a decision to turn our will and our lives over to the care of God as we understood Him" (*Alcoholics Anonymous*, 1976, p. 59). Please read the Step Three Exercise in Appendix 20 before continuing with this chapter.

Most patients will have some difficulty with Step Three. They need to be reminded to turn problems over to their Higher Power. Chemically dependent people are self-centered and they need to learn how to be God-centered. Patients can be so self-centered that they constantly set themselves up for unnecessary pain. They think the whole world and everyone in it should revolve around them. When people don't cooperate with their self-aggrandizing plans, they are furious. They think their spouse, children, and friends should always obey their every whim. Previous relationships their partner has been involved in are seen as humiliating and self-degrading. They believe that everything should go exactly the way they want it to go. They feel they are deserving of special honor and privileges. They care very deeply about what they want and how they feel, but their ability to empathize with others is seriously impaired (Robert Carr, personal communication, 1992).

Patients might get furious when someone does something simple, like turning up the heat or failing to fix the car. When the world doesn't cooperate by doing exactly what they want, they fly into a rage. A more serious form of this character defect is called narcissistic personality disorder.

Patients can correct this defect by learning empathy for others and turning their will and their lives over to the care of a Higher Power. "Our program is a set of spiritual principles through which we are recovering from a seemingly hopeless state of mind and body" (*Narcotics Anonymous,* 1988).

The worst thing the counselor can do is push the patients faster than they are ready to go. The decision to turn things over (to a Higher Power) is the patients' decision. All you can do is encourage them.

You have one big thing going for you in Step Three. When patients finally do turn something over to a Higher Power, they feel immediate relief. They feel this relief emotionally and this is the most powerful way to learn. They will feel the stress of trying to figure the problem out reduced. The pressure will be off, and they will feel better. Nothing works better than to show them how this tool of recovery works. If you give chemically dependent people a good feeling, they will want to re-create the feeling. That's what they were doing with chemicals, seeking immediate relief from pain. The Third Step is the new answer they have been waiting for. They must experience it to believe it.

Many patients will resist Step Three stubbornly. Even people who have been in the program for years have difficulty with Step Three. Meetings are full of people talking about turning the controls over, and then taking them back. Step Three is a decision that must be made every day.

There is great hope for patients in Step Three, and they will feel it. If there is a God, and God loves them, and God will help them, that's great.

This newfound hope must not be shattered by religion. Religion can make people feel guilty. Religious doctrine must be kept out of the program as much as possible. If patients want to use a religious structure, that is encouraged, as long as it sets them free and does not immerse them in guilt and remorse. The Higher Power is presented to patients in an atmosphere of forgiveness.

*How to Help Patients Embrace Step Three*

The key to Step Three is willingness. Once patients are willing to seek a Higher Power of their understanding, they have come a long way toward completing Step Three. They will find relief in talking about a God who loves them and forgives them.

When you hear patients say they are willing to "turn it over to God," you can tell them that they are well on their way to recovery. The problems might not be immediately solved, but they are moving in the right direction.

Patients need to trust and to turn things over to the group. The group has more collective wisdom than the patient, and the group members can be helpful in solving problems. As patients use the power and support of their group, they are learning about how to turn things over to their Higher Power.

Some patients have serious problems with the word *God*, and that's fine; they don't have to use the word if they don't want to. Many of them have had the word *God* crammed down their throats for so long as children that they are sick of it. If you try to do the same thing, they will revolt. Remember, even God gives total freedom of thought and action.

**Step Four**

"Made a searching and fearless moral inventory of ourselves" (*Alcoholics Anonymous,* 1976, p. 59). Please read the Step Four Exercise in Appendix 21 before continuing. Much of this exercise was developed by Lynn Carroll during his years at Hazelden and at Keystone.

Step Four is where the patients make a thorough housecleaning. They rid themselves of the guilt of the past and look forward to a new future. Detail is important here; you must encourage them to be specific. They must put down exactly what they did. They will share their Fourth Step with someone of their choice in the Fifth Step. They will go over the assets part of the Fourth Step in group. The assets part of the Fourth Step allows them to share the good things about themselves with their treatment peers. This keeps them from decompensating into a negative attitude. The Fourth Step can be very painful for many patients, and they must be encouraged to look at the good parts of themselves.

The Fourth Step was developed directly from spiritual principles. To get rid of guilt, someone admits their wrongs, and asks God for forgiveness, and God wipes the slate clean. You should discuss the grace of the Higher Power with your patients. They need to know that there is no way to earn God's forgiveness, God offers it for free. God wants to set us free and give us an opportunity to start over again.

To do this, we must be honest. We must share our wrongs with God, ourselves, and one other person. The other person is necessary because the patients need to see a nonshaming face respond to their wrongs. Remember, the illness has been telling them that if they tell anyone the whole truth about themselves they will be rejected. The only way to prove this wrong is to do it. Patients will no longer be excessively burdened with guilt if they do their Fourth and Fifth Steps properly. They may have a difficult time forgiving themselves, but God will forgive them. Faith can do for them what they cannot do for themselves.

There will be a tendency for patients to leave something they consider bad out of the Fifth Step. The Big Book says that this is not a good idea. "Time after time newcomers have tried to keep to themselves certain facts about their lives. Trying to avoid the humbling experience, they have turned to easier methods. Almost invariably they got drunk" (*Alcoholics Anonymous,* 1976, pp. 72-73).

Patients are encouraged to share everything that they think is important, no matter how trivial it may seem. If it causes them any degree of guilt or shame, it needs to be examined. They need to come face to face with themselves. All of the garbage of the past must be cleaned out. Nothing can be left to fester and rot. The patient who leaves things out will feel unforgiven.

The Fourth Step is where patients identify their character defects. Once they are identified, the patients can work toward resolving these defects. Often patients will come on material suppressed for years. As memory tracks are stimulated, deeper unconscious material will surface.

The patients need to concentrate on the exact nature of their wrongs rather than accuse or blame someone else. This is a time to take full responsibility. They do not make excuses; they ask for forgiveness. Yes, there were mitigating circumstances, but this is not a time to find out who was right and who was wrong—it is the time to dump the guilt and the shame.

The illness of chemical dependency projects patients' errors on the screen of the consciousness. This makes patients feel bad. By drowning in their guilt and shame, they cannot pull free; they wallow in self-pity.

Patients who get too depressed doing their Fifth Step need to stop and concentrate on their good qualities. It's not all bad: They need to be shown that they are valuable persons who deserve to be accepted and loved. Some patients may have to wait quite a while before doing their Fifth Step. Absolute honesty is a requirement of their readiness.

Some patients are so used to being negative about themselves that they cannot come up with their assets. These patients need to have the group help them see the positive things about themselves.

Step Four must be detailed and specific. Patients must cover the exact nature of their behavior. This is the only way for them to see the full impact of their disease. They should not color their story to make themselves seem less guilty or responsible.

Most of all, Step Four, like all of the steps, is a time of great joy. Patients finally face the whole truth about themselves. The truth is that they are a wonderful creation of God. As they rid themselves of the pain of the past they are ready to move forward to a new life filled with hope and recovery.

## Step Five ■

"Admitted to God, ourselves, and to another human being the exact nature of our wrongs" (*Alcoholic Anonymous,* 1976, p. 57). Read the Step Five Exercise in Appendix 22 before continuing.

The counselor's job in the Fifth Step is to help patients match up with the right person with whom to share the Fourth Step Inventory. Who this person is, and what he or she is like, is vitally important. This person stands as a symbol of God and all of the people on Earth. This step directly attacks the core of the disease of chemical dependency. If it is done properly, the patient will be free of the past. The person chosen should be in the clergy, if at all possible, because a minister better symbolizes a Higher Power. Others in the program will do, if they are chosen carefully and they have a good spiritual program. The persons chosen need some experience in hearing Fifth Steps, and they must have an attitude of acceptance and unconditional positive regard. They must be nonjudgmental and strictly confidential. It is helpful if they themselves are working on a twelve-step program. They should not look uncomfortable when the patient is sharing sensitive material. If they look uncomfortable, the patient may take this negatively. The patient needs to see a nonshaming face.

The purpose of the Fifth Step is to make things right with self, others, and God. Patients should see themselves accurately, all of their positive and negative points, all at the same time. At the core of the illness of chemical dependency is a firmly held belief: "If I tell anyone the truth about myself, they won't like me." This is not accurate, but the patients have been living as if it were true. They have not been honest with themselves and others for a long time, perhaps since childhood. They have pretended to be somebody else to get the good stuff in life. The only way to prove to someone that this held belief is wrong, is to show them. This is the purpose of having another human being hear the Fifth Step. If this person does not reject the patient, the belief is proved wrong. A new, accurate thought replaces the old one: "I have told someone the truth and that person still likes me." This is a tremendous relief to patients. They have been living their lives convinced that they were totally unacceptable to others. This is a deeply held conviction, and it causes great pain. Patients must come to realize that unless they tell the truth, they will never feel loved.

During the Fifth Step, the person must come to realize that they are a good person. They have made mistakes, they have done bad things, but they are not bad, they are good. God will forgive them, and they can forgive themselves. They can start over, clean and new. Patients have varying degrees of spirituality and religious beliefs. The clergy and counselor must help the patient see that forgiveness has taken place. All religious systems provide for the forgiveness of sin.

Many patients will be tempted to hold something back in their Fifth Step. They don't want to share some part of their past; they don't think anyone can understand. Patients must be warned against this tendency. If they hold anything back, the illness is still winning. All the illness needs to stay in operation is something important kept secret. All major wrongs must be disclosed. The whole truth must come out. They must stop living a double life.

After the Fifth Step, most patients experience a feeling of relief. The truth sets them free. In time, the patient will need to process the feelings with the counselor. Some patients feel no immediate relief, but if they were honest, they will feel the relief later—sometimes this takes a little while to sink in. The Fourth and Fifth Steps make for a profoundly humbling experience, but once it is over, there is a profound feeling of relief. The person giving the Fifth Step should be encouraged to end the step with a prayer asking for forgiveness. The person listening to the step should also end the session in prayer. Persons who have heard the step should tell the patient that they understand what they have heard, that God forgives him or her, and that they believe in the patient's basic goodness.

CHAPTER
EIGHT | # The Lectures

Once a day, the patients go to lecture. The lectures last 30 minutes to an hour. All professional staff members will take their turn in educating the patients about the program. The physician will lecture on medical aspects, the psychologist on psychological aspects, the dietitian on diet, and so on. As the counselor, you will be responsible for lecture topics relevant to chemical dependency. You can use any of the exercises in this text to come up with your speech. If the patients hear the material more than once, that's all the better. Each of the Twelve Steps should be presented in lecture. Other topics include the disease concept, spirituality, relapse, feelings, relationship skills, communication skills, defense mechanisms, and so forth.

Many of these topics have been discussed already, and it would be redundant to present them again. You can use any of this information in developing your lecture program.

The lecture schedule should be flexible enough to allow for what the current patient population needs. You should read the Big Book and *The Twelve Steps and Twelve Traditions* to round out your lectures. It is not difficult to talk to the patient population, and you will soon learn to breeze through it. For those of you who are frightened of public speaking, you will need to make an outline of each talk, and follow it carefully. The structure will give you the confidence you need.

I will give examples of several lectures, but it is important to develop your own personal style. You must use your creativity. Only the important points of each lecture will be given. Your job is to fill in the lecture with examples and stories of your own. It is best to speak from personal experience. You can use your own stories, or stories you have heard from patients. The patients do not need to hear a lot of confusing research in these lectures. They will be less confused if you put forth the facts in a simple straightforward manner. Begin each lecture with the Serenity Prayer, and end with the Lord's Prayer, just as you do for a meeting.

**The Disease**

This morning we are going to talk about the disease concept of chemical dependency. It is important for you to know that you have an illness. This illness has a certain set of signs and symptoms. Not one of you asked to be chemically dependent. It's not your fault. You should not feel guilty. That would be unduly hard on yourself. You wouldn't blame someone for having cancer, or heart disease, even though some of their behaviors may have contributed to their disease. If you eat a certain way, or smoke cigarettes, you increase your chances of coronary artery disease. If you drink or use drugs, you increase your chances of becoming chemically dependent.

*Chemical Dependency Is Not a Moral Problem*

*Dorland's Illustrated Medical Dictionary* (1965) defines *disease* as, "A definite morbid process having a characteristic train of symptoms; it may affect the whole body or any of its parts, and its etiology, pathology, and prognosis may be known or unknown." In the late 1940s, E. M. Jellinek began to study alcoholism in over 2,000 members of Alcoholics Anonymous. He found that alcoholism had a characteristic set of signs and symptoms, and it had a definite progressive course. In 1956 the American Medical Association formally recognized alcoholism as a disease. Up until that time, medical science, and society in general, thought that someone who was chemically dependent was a person with a moral problem or someone with a weak will.

*Chemical Dependency Is Not Due to a Weak Will*

Please do not think that a weak will had anything to do with your chemical dependency. We find that alcoholics and drug addicts are strong and resourceful people. Over 90% of chemically dependent persons are able to keep functioning even when they are deathly ill. You know how it goes, you come to work and you've got this incredible hangover, your head is throbbing, you feel like you are going to throw up. Your coworker comes in and asks how you're doing. "Fine," you say cheerfully. You are there, you feel terrible, but you made it to work. That takes a person with a strong will.

*Chemical Dependency Has Genetic Links*

There is no major psychiatric disease that does not have genetic links. We are all genetically predisposed to certain physical and mental illnesses. We are more likely to acquire the same diseases as the members of our family have had. Cancer and coronary artery disease run in families, depression and anxiety run in families, and chemical dependency runs in families. For example, cells are programmed at birth to do certain things when alcohol is in the body. Many sons of alcoholics need to drink more before they feel intoxicated. They have a programmed need to drink to get the same effect. You may have noticed in your drinking or drug use that you could use more than other people could. This is because some people who are predisposed to chemical dependency metabolize drugs differently. It seems that many people who are chemically dependent were predisposed to the illness before they were born (Anthenelli & Schuckit, 1994; Woodward, 1994).

*Chemical Dependency Is a Social Problem*

To become chemically dependent, you need to use chemicals. This is a psychosocial issue. In some societies, drinking and drug use is not tolerated. Muslims and Mormons, for example, have a strong religious belief against the use of drugs. They consider use to be a sin. There is less chemical dependency in these groups.

In France, drinking is a regular part of life. It is not uncommon for a Frenchman to have wine with lunch and dinner. Understandably, then, France has a higher incidence of alcoholism.

*Chemical Dependency Is a Psychological Problem* | Certain psychological factors also have to come into play. There is no specific alcoholic personality, but people do have to drink to become alcoholic. Alcohol is reinforcing to some people and to some people it is not. You have to like drinking to drink. Drinking behavior naturally increases if it is reinforced.

Chemical dependency is a biopsychosocial disease. It has biological components, psychological components, and social components. Two or more of these elements appear to be necessary for chemical dependency to exist.

Someone has a drug problem if they continue to use a drug despite persistent physical, psychological, or social problems associated with that drug. Anyone who continues to use despite persistent problems is an abuser. Obviously, if you get into trouble when you use chemicals, you shouldn't use chemicals.

*Chemical Dependency Is a Physiological Problem* | Chemical dependency is characterized by tolerance and withdrawal symptoms. As you use cocaine, the cocaine tells your brain to wake up. The cells of your body gradually catch on to this abnormal wake-up signal, and they produce chemicals that tell the brain to go to sleep! The cells counteract the drug. Ultimately, it will take more of the drug to produce the same effect. As you take in more of the drug, the cells counteract even further. This is a vicious cycle called tolerance. You will find that you are using more of the drug now than when you started.

People who are having a chemical problem know it, at least on some level, and they try to cut down. They may change from beer to wine or from hard liquor to beer. They may decide to use only after five o'clock or only on weekends. They may even move or change jobs.

*The Obsession* | People who are having problems with chemicals will find that more and more of their time is taken up using the substance. People on cocaine use only recreationally at first. They occasionally use at parties. As their illness progresses, however, they find themselves using more often, during the week, even when they are alone. More and more of their time is spent in getting cocaine, using cocaine, and withdrawing from cocaine. The more they use, the more they need. The more they need, the more they use.

People who are chemically dependent find themselves intoxicated or hung over when they need to do something else. The homemaker may be high when she is supposed to be taking care of the children. She may be drunk at work. She may have to call in sick because she is too hung over to work. More and more, usually over a long period of time, the disease takes over. The drug becomes the center of the universe. Dinner time revolves around those first drinks. There begins a morning hangover ritual and an evening get-high ritual. Eventually, people give up normal activities. They don't go fishing. They don't go camping. They quit school or get fired. Sexual activity decreases. Recreational activity decreases. Time with the children decreases. Any activity can go, but the drug stays and grows more and more important.

*The Problems*

Sooner or later, problems begin to develop. There are social consequences caused by the drug use. Problems with the spouse. Problems with the law. Problems at school. Problems with friends. Problems with parents. The problems begin to mount but the chemically dependent persons keep dealing with the problems in the same way. They get relief, the only way they know how, with their drug of choice. The drug becomes their best friend. It's the only thing they can count on. It always helps to ease the pain. It works, and it works every time.

By this time, people around the chemically dependent person are complaining. They are warning that something is wrong. Someone may even have the unmitigated gall to talk to us about our problem. When someone does this, the chemically dependent person hammers them to the floor. "It's not my problem," they shout. "It's your problem." The lies escalate and the addict begins to get caught in the lies. People challenge us with the truth. All of this leads to more drug use, and the cycle goes on.

Finally, some crisis breaks through the lies we have been telling ourselves. Some glimmer of the truth slips in, and we come into treatment. We are still in denial. We are still lying to ourselves. We still can't see the full impact of our disease, but here we are, in treatment.

Chemical dependency is the third leading cause of death in this country. Most people who are chemically dependent die of it; very few make it into treatment. Of those who do make it into their first treatment, most will achieve a stable program of recovery. You either will abstain from drugs and alcohol or you will die.

You will find this treatment center dedicated to the truth. We must tell the truth to get clean and sober. We must give up all that control we have been working on and turn our will and our lives over to the care of someone else. If you work this program, you will find relief. If you hang on to your old ways, you will be miserable. The choice is yours.

## Defense Mechanisms

Today we are going to talk about where all the lies come from. How did we end up being such liars? In chemical dependency we tell incredible lies. We lie when we think we have to, and we lie when we don't have to. We lie to get out of trouble, and our lies get us into more trouble. We lie to increase our pleasure and we lie to wallow in our self-pity.

This illness must lie, and it must continue to lie or it cannot exist. The illness cannot live in the light of the truth. You can't tell the truth to yourself and continue be chemically dependent. With the truth, you would realize your problem and get some help for it.

All of the lies exist to protect us from a painful truth. The truth is, we are out of control, and if we keep up the addictive behavior, we are doomed. The truth causes us great anxiety so we defend ourselves from the truth. We distort the truth just enough to feel like nothing is wrong.

*Minimization*

The first lie we tell ourselves is called *minimization*. This is when we take reality and make it smaller. We think the problem is not that bad. If an alcoholic takes an 8-ounce glass and fills it up with ice, and takes a shot glass full of whiskey, and pours it over the ice, and holds the glass up to the light, she will be disappointed.

A shot glass full to the brim with whiskey makes a disgustingly small splash in an 8-ounce glass.

If you are an alcoholic, you are not going to use a shot glass. If you have a shot glass at home, it is gathering dust. You are going to pour your whiskey until you see some color in that glass. Now, if we were to take this drink, and measure how many shots are in it, we are going to find four, maybe five, shots in the glass. Here's how we minimize: We think, and believe, that this is a drink, one drink, but it's not one drink—it's four drinks.

We can do the same thing with beer cans. If you are a beer drinker, you have a considerable collection of empty beer cans at the end of the week. When you take the garbage out, you have maybe two big plastic trash can bags full of cans. As you are going out to take out the garbage, you may think, "Boy, I hope the garbage person doesn't think I'm drinking all this beer." At that time, you may put one of the bags on your garbage pile, and the other one on your neighbor's pile.

Those of you who are into cocaine, remember when you have just picked up your stash. You have this nice big pile of cocaine on your kitchen table. You feel self-satisfied. You have more than enough. Your treasure chest is full. You are content. You feel a great peace. This is going to last a long time. But the next morning you're wondering who got into your stash. Where did it all go? You used it all, that's where it went.

We can minimize our mounting problems. Everyone gets a couple of DWIs. Almost everybody gets a divorce. It's not so bad to spend a couple of nights in jail. We're a good person, we're not bad, we were just unlucky, the cops were after us. We take what is real and make it look smaller. We lie to ourselves, and we believe the lie.

*Rationalization* | The next lie we tell is called *rationalization*. This is where we have a good excuse. Probably the most commonly used excuse for drinking is, "I had a hard day." It follows, therefore, that if I had such a hard day, I deserve to get blasted. Anyone who had the hard day that I had, would need to relax. Let's have a few beers, a couple of joints. In rationalizing, we may blame our problems on someone else. "If you would just lighten up," we might say, "I could straighten things out." We may think remorsefully of all we could have been, if we had been born wealthy, or been given the right breaks. We look at all those successful people, and we hate them. We never had such a chance, we tell ourselves. There's no God. If there was a God, where was God when I needed God.

*Denial* | The last type of lie that we tell ourselves, and this one is the most characteristic of chemical dependency, is *denial*. Denial is a stubborn, angry refusal to see the truth. Here we refuse to see what is right before our eyes. We block out what is real until we really don't see it at all. The best way to show you how this works is to give you an example. You are walking down the street and it is a very hot day. It's 95 degrees in the shade. Sweat is pouring down your face. As you walk up the road, watching the heat waves rise from the asphalt, people are standing along the side of the road with pails full of ice water. As you pass each of them, they throw their bucket full of reality in your face. "Your wife's divorcing you! That's your third DWI! The boss won't put up with you anymore! You're in trouble with your parents again!" You see the pails of water, you see them throw them in your face, you hear the words that are shouted at you, but you do not experience the full reality of what's happening, you don't get the full emotional impact of the problems. With your whole life falling apart, you are walking up the street as if nothing was happening at all. The people around you are amazed. Why doesn't he see? Why doesn't she understand? Why can't he see what's happening to him?

*How to Begin to Live in the Truth*

You can't see what's happening to you because you are lying to yourself. You can't see the truth because you are believing the lies. You are completely fooled. In treatment the full reality of what has been happening to you will be put before you. It will be painful, but the truth will set you free. Treatment is an endless search for the truth, and you must be willing to listen to what others say. You must try to be open to what people tell you about yourself. We will reflect to each other what we see. We will try to find the truth together. What we cannot do alone, we can do together.

## The Great Lie

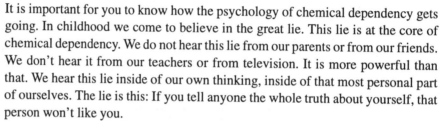

It is important for you to know how the psychology of chemical dependency gets going. In childhood we come to believe in the great lie. This lie is at the core of chemical dependency. We do not hear this lie from our parents or from our friends. We don't hear it from our teachers or from television. It is more powerful than that. We hear this lie inside of our own thinking, inside of that most personal part of ourselves. The lie is this: If you tell anyone the whole truth about yourself, that person won't like you.

Once we hear this lie and believe this lie, we know that we will never be loved for who we are. Therefore to get any of the good stuff out of life at all, we have to pretend to be someone that we are not. We try to be someone else. We watch those people who are popular and we copy them. We are very careful about what kind of clothes we wear. We copy people's mannerisms and their fine little gestures. We find ourselves cocking our heads in a certain way when we laugh or smile. We are hoping to fool people. We hope that they cannot see the real me. We want them to see the pretend me.

*How the Great Lie Works*

As this coping behavior occurs, it works. Some people do like us for the new me we are trying to be. We become pleased to know that we are not going to be alone. The people we are fooling will love us. We begin to wear specific costumes and to play certain roles. We may wear the nice girl costume or the cowhand costume. We may wear the hippie costume or the yuppie costume. We know it is a costume, we know it's not us, but the people are fooled, and the lie goes on.

*We Never Feel Accepted*

You must look carefully at what is happening. We have fooled people into liking us, but they don't really like us, they don't know us; we are keeping who we are secret. As we keep doing this, making this effort to be loved, our emptiness grows, our pain increases. We try hard. We copy everyone who looks cool. We put on the best false front we can, but in time, we realize it isn't going to work. We feel more and more lonely and isolated. We have known all along that we weren't going to be loved, not for the real us. No one was going to love us.

THE LECTURES ■ 117

*The Promise of the Disease*    When we are lonely enough in this process, when we are isolated enough, when we are hurting enough, the illness comes along and offers us a smorgasbord of answers to our pain. Sex, money, power, influence, drugs, gambling, and alcohol, are all there, and more, and we begin to feed from this cafeteria of sin. For a while, things get better. All these things relieve the pain for a little while. We find ourselves irresistibly drawn to this table of wrongs. We spend more time doing it. We eat drink, stuff, cram, push, and shove. We find that more and more of our life centers around the use of these things. We get up on the table and stuff ourselves. We begin to lose our morals and values. We eat, and consume, and vomit, and stuff ourselves even more. In time, there is never enough. There is not enough sex. There is not enough money. There is not enough power. There is not enough booze. AA says, one drink is too much and a thousand are never enough.

*Truth*    Finally, we begin to get sick from this cafeteria of wrongs. We realize an awful fact: The answer is not in these things. It is a terrible point of grief when we finally realize that the answer is not in our drug of choice. This is not a happy time, but by now we are addicted, we can't stop. You may be addicted to sex, and you want to stop what you are doing, but you can't stop. You may be addicted to money, and you want to stop chasing money, but you can't stop. You want to stop drinking. You promise yourself that you'll stop, but you can't stop, you're addicted.

Somehow, by the grace of God, you finally come to treatment. Maybe you are ready to surrender—I hope so, because if you aren't, you are in for a lot more misery. If you are ready to surrender, if you are ready to try something new, this program is for you.

*A Program of Rigorous Honesty*    One of the things you must be willing to do is tell the truth all the time. Nothing else will stop the great lie. God says, "The truth will set you free." You are enslaved to your addiction, but the truth will set you free of your chains.

In treatment, probably for the first time in your life, you will have the opportunity to get honest. If you don't, if you hold anything back, you will return to chemicals. You don't have to tell everyone the truth, but there is a psychological law at work. The law is this: The more you can share, the closer you can get; and the closer you can get, the more you can share. As intimacy grows, you tell more of the truth. In your Fifth Step, you will tell someone the whole truth at one time. You will tell them exactly what happened. Time after time we have had newcomers decide to hold something back in their Fifth Step. They didn't want to tell that one thing. Invariably these people get drunk because they don't prove to themselves that people will like them if they tell the whole truth. They keep the emptiness, loneliness, and isolation. The pain grows and sooner or later they relapse.

It is vitally important that you find out the truth about yourself. God created you in perfection. You are God's masterpiece. You were created in the image of God. God loves you and wants you to be happy. For some of you this will be difficult to hear, difficult to believe. How could God love you? Where was God when you needed God? If there is a God, where is God? These are the questions that you will seek the answers for in this program.

**Normal Development**

Today we are going to talk about normal development and how things go wrong for people who are chemically dependent. As infants, we can't see very well. Our eyes are developing and everything looks hazy. An infant knows only when it feels comfortable and uncomfortable. When it feels uncomfortable enough, it cries. It cries out in the only way it knows how. This cry is at such a pitch and timbre that parents cannot ignore it. Those of you who have heard the cry of an infant know what I'm talking about. The infant cries out into the haze, "Help me! help me!" It's the only thing the infant can do. Without someone coming to help, the infant will die.

*The Primary Caregiver*

But out of the haze, someone comes, and that someone meets our needs, and we feel comfortable again. In healthy homes, this someone always comes, at all hours of the day and night, and as the infant grows older, this someone has a particular sight, sound, taste, and smell. Later still, it has a name, Mother.

A great trust develops between mother and child. The child learns that whenever it cries out, mother will come. It happens time and time again, it happens every time, and the infant learns to trust in mother. She is always there.

*The Struggle for Independence*

As infants grow older, they begin to struggle for independence. They begin to do things for themselves. They reach out and grasp things. They learn language and they ask for things. In the second year, they learn the power of the word No. Mother can be all ready to go home, she can have her hands full of packages, she can be walking out the door, and we can say No. Oh, the power of that word! The whole world seems to stop and revolve around us. "No!" People get very upset with that word—it is very powerful.

*The Fear of Abandonment*

Somewhere between the ages of 3 to 5, and this depends on the maturity of the child, we learn a terrifying fact: Other people can also say no. This fact strikes terror into a child's heart. The child knows that they need other people for survival. What will happen if they cry out in the night and someone doesn't come? The child develops a new fear, the fear of abandonment. We never get over this fear. We carry it for the rest of our lives. It is the fear of life and death itself. When something goes wrong in our lives, this fear can come back, very intensely. Lovers and spouses panic when one attempts to leave the other. They fear that if that person leaves, they will die. You hear them say things like, "I can't live without her. I can't live without him."

*Learning the Rules*

Frightened, the child goes to the parents and searches out for an answer. "Mom, Dad, how can I be sure that when I cry out, you will always come?"

"These are the rules," the parents say. "These are the rules about how to be a good boy and a good girl. If you obey the rules, and you cry out, we will come. But if you are a bad boy, if you are a bad girl, if you break the rules, we may not come." As children we nod our head reverently; we want to live!

*The Development of Insecurity*

Now the parents hit us with a crippling blow, and from this blow, we will get another new feeling, insecurity. They don't tell us all the rules. The rules are too complicated, the rules keep changing. Sometimes things are against the rules and sometimes they are not. Sometimes we get punished for things and sometimes we do not get punished for the same things. We spend the rest of our lives trying to learn the rules. In every situation we are in, the rules are a little different. It is very complicated, and it causes a great deal of anxiety.

*The Peer Group* | As we move out of the home, and into the peer group, things are very different. The peer group does not love us just because we are a part of the family; the peer group loves us because we have a function. We are a good leader, or a good follower, we are funny, or we laugh, we are strong, or we are loyal. If we do not have a function in the group, we are rejected.

Little boys and little girls are very different by this age. Boys struggle for power, and girls struggle for connection. Boys work to control; girls work to cooperate. Boys work at being the one who can solve the problem, girls work toward who is the closest to whom. It's not that either of these personality styles is better or worse; they are just different. Both are necessary for healthy family roles.

If we have been told how wonderful we are, every day of our lives, we might be ready for school by the age of 6. In the best of circumstances, school is a struggle. It's a totally new situation, with a new set of rules. We are not rewarded for our individuality or our creativity, we are rewarded for our ability to cooperate. We are supposed to be quiet and stay still. It goes against everything that a child is, but we try to cooperate, we try to be quiet, we try to stay still. We remember that we don't want to be abandoned.

*Adolescence* | Adolescence is a time of great change. There is a huge hormone dam. It leaks, cracks, and finally breaks, releasing a flood of chemicals into our body. These hormones say one thing, "Mate." They say this loud and clear. We begin to mate in our dreams, in class, every waking moment. The opposite sex becomes exciting, irresistible, new. We try even harder than ever to fit in, because with all these changes going on, it is even more critical to be accepted. We struggle to fit in much more than we struggle for our individuality.

Society tells us to prepare to leave our parents who have been at the very core of our survival. We begin to question the morals and values of our parents. We begin to make decisions on our own. We prepare ourselves for the commitment of adulthood. We must know who and what we are. We try out many different things in an attempt to find ourselves.

For most chemically dependent persons, it is here, in early adolescence, that chemical use gets going. Here we first try chemicals and they make us feel good. Soon we begin to use chemicals to deal with our problems. Here is where our emotional development stops. If we treat our feelings with chemicals, we don't learn to use our feelings to solve problems. If we continue to use mind-altering chemicals, we do not have our real feelings any more. Most chemically dependent persons are emotionally stuck in adolescence. They still do not know how to use their feelings appropriately to solve problems.

*Adulthood* | The dividing line between adulthood and adolescence is the ability to make long-term commitments. Adults are emotionally stable and mature. They can commit to career, family, and home. They can build a nest, and rear healthy young. Adulthood should really be a long smooth ride. It is a gradual building of knowledge and skill. Financial problems fall to the wayside as we reach our full economic potential.

Somewhere in the sixties, the decision must be made, "Should I retire?" If you like your work, if it gives you joy, of course, keep working. If you don't like your work, retire and do something that you do enjoy; you deserve it.

In later life there will inevitably come a time of terminal illness. You will acquire a disease from which you will not recover. This is usually coronary artery disease or cancer, but it can be many others. If you are close to God, this is not such a scary time, you will have the hope of eternal life. If you do not know God, this time may be more difficult, but, in normal life, everyone dies.

We have discussed the normal life cycle, and we have seen where it usually goes wrong in chemical dependency. The illness can occur at any stage in life, but it usually gets started in adolescence. The moment we begin to use chemicals to excess, we cannot live a normal life, it is impossible. We cannot use our feelings, in real time, with real people, to solve life's real problems. In treatment you will learn the skills necessary for living a normal life. These are the tools of recovery. If you learn these skills, your life will stabilize, and you will ultimately live a normal life again.

## Physical Addiction and Recovery

This morning we are going to talk about physical changes that occur with chemical dependency. The cell is the basic building block of the body. It has a cell wall that protects the cell from harm, a nucleus, which is the brain of the cell, and it has a variety of other specialized parts with specialized functions, called *organelles*. The nucleus is made up of deoxyribonucleic acid, or DNA, and it decides how the cell is made, and how the cell works. It is the manager of the cell in the same way that the brain manages the body. The cell wall is an actively selective membrane that chooses what comes into and out of the cell.

## How Drugs Affect the Cell

Drugs pass through the cell wall in a variety of ways and influence how the cell operates. This is a very involved process, and we do not know exactly what each drug does. What we do know, however, is important, and you must understand some of this in your recovery program. Alcohol is a drug. One of its effects is that it dehydrates protoplasm. It sucks water out of the cell. This prevents the cell wall from operating properly. This happens in every cell in the body, but it has its most noticeable effect on the central nervous system. It suppresses higher cortical centers in the brain. This reduces people's normal ability to perceive the environ- ment. It tells the brain to go to sleep. This inability to perceive accurately makes us feel less inhibited. We lose the normal constraints the world puts on us. We miss the subtle cues. It makes us feel free.

The brain of the cell picks this up as a problem and changes things in the cell to correct the problem. Alcohol tells the brain to go to sleep. The cells tells the brain to wake up. At first these changes are transient chemical changes, subtle changes in metabolism, which will quickly return to normal after alcohol leaves the body. But if the alcohol keeps coming, the cell produces permanent changes in the cell wall. One way that it does this, is to make tunnels, or chloride channels, through the cell wall. This provides for easier transport of atoms across the cell wall. When more alcohol stays around, more of these chloride tunnels are needed.

*How Drugs Affect Behavior* | Now let's see what's happening to you behaviorally. You start drinking, and one beer gets you that feeling you are after. One beer is all you need, but sooner or later, the cell produces those changes and you need two beers to get that same feeling. In a few weeks, or months, or years, you are going to need three beers, and then four, and five, and six, and so on. The more beer you drink, the more the cells correct with those chloride channels. This is called tolerance. You need more and more of the drug to get the same effect. All chemically addicting drugs create this physiological pattern.

*Tolerance* | It is important for you to know that these changes in the cell may take years to develop, but once tolerance is there, it is there permanently. The cell never changes back completely to the way it was before. It never forgets. That is why you can never use drugs again. You have developed permanent changes in the cells in your body. If you were drinking a fifth a day, and you stay sober for 20 years, and you start drinking again, you will be drinking a fifth a day within 30 days. It took you years to develop tolerance, but this time it is there already. This will never change. You can recover completely from some of the psychological and social effects of this disease, but you can never recover from the physical changes that have taken place in your cells. Your cells never forget.

*Cross-Tolerance* | This is why cross-tolerance is such a problem. Alcohol, pot, sedatives, sleeping pills, all tell the brain to go to sleep and the cells counteract that drug in some of the same ways. If you develop a tolerance for one of these drugs, you will develop tolerance for them all. You can't leave treatment and say to yourself, "Well, I'm sure glad I got that alcohol problem licked, but I never had any problem with pot. I can have a little pot now and then." This would be disaster for you. Taking a little pot is like taking a little alcohol because of the cross-tolerance.

What we find in chemical dependency treatment is once you are addicted to one mood-altering chemical, you are addicted to them all. You have learned things physically, psychologically, and socially that will cross over to any other mood-altering chemical. If your drug of choice is whiskey, and you go out of here and smoke a little dope, you will be back to the whiskey very soon.

*Withdrawal* | The cells produce all of these short-term and long-term changes to counteract what the drug is doing, so guess what happens when the drug is removed? All of these cellular changes are still there, and the drug is gone. The cells produce wake-up signals to the brain, to counteract the go-to-sleep signals the alcohol produces, and all of a sudden, no alcohol. What happens is called acute alcohol withdrawal. The cells are screaming, "Wake up," and no alcohol is saying go to sleep. Acute withdrawal drives alcoholics to the liquor store every day. They go to sleep under the effects of alcohol, and in a few hours they wake up feeling nervous and restless. They can't sleep. Their stomach feels upset. They have a headache. Their hands shake. All these symptoms are withdrawal symptoms.

Some of you learned that what you needed was a drink or a Valium to get you back to sleep, but if you have that drink or that pill, the cycle starts all over again. Acute withdrawal is not fun. It produces the opposite effect of the drug you are using. If you were using a sedative drug, withdrawal will say, Wake up. If you were using a stimulant drug, the withdrawal symptoms will say, Go to sleep.

The length of acute withdrawal differs depending on the drug you were taking. With alcohol, withdrawal is usually over within a few days. With cannabis or certain of the benzodiazepines it can be weeks or even months. Once acute withdrawal is over, protracted withdrawal extends the problems for about 2 years. Protracted withdrawal is characterized by random mood swings, sleep problems, and generalized feelings of stress. These symptoms wax and wane over the next few months. Don't think you are crazy or think that anything is wrong, just recognize the symptoms for what they are (Geller, 1994).

The first 3 months out of treatment will be the hardest for you because of the extended withdrawal syndrome. This is where people tend to relapse, so do everything in your power to work a daily program of recovery in early sobriety. The daily program will put hurdles in the way of the first use.

*How We Learn*

Drug use is a habit. We get into the habit of drinking or using in certain situations or when having certain feelings. A habit is some movement or thought that is so practiced that it has developed a nice smooth pathway in the brain. Whenever we even randomly approach that area in the brain, we are very likely to take that pathway because it is so well traveled and easy to follow.

You have developed certain habits in your drinking or drug use. You may use when you celebrate, or when you feel angry, or when frightened or sad. You may always drink after work or always drink a certain kind of beer. These pathways in your brain are well developed. What treatment is all about is teaching you to get what you want by doing something else instead of using your old behavior. It is a process of learning new behaviors. If you want to feel less angry, for example, you will need to talk to someone about how you feel, and try to work the problem though. The second you realize that you are on one of your old pathways, you need to stop and change direction. Drinking and drug use are no longer an option for you. You need to find other methods for dealing with your problems.

## Alcoholics Anonymous

The idea behind Alcoholics Anonymous got started in 1935. Bill Wilson, one of the founders of AA, had gotten drunk again. He was at the end of his rope. He was afraid to go home; he was afraid he was going to kill himself. He hated himself. His spouse was still sticking by him, but he couldn't trust himself anymore. He had tried to quit drinking countless times, in countless ways, and he had always ended up drunk. Here he was, in the hospital again. He didn't know if he wanted to live or die, but he knew that he didn't want to live this way anymore. Medical science had given up on him as hopeless. He had no where to go—he was trapped.

*A Spiritual Awakening*

In his room alone, feeling totally powerless, he looked up toward heaven, and he cried out, "If there is a God, show me, give me some sign." At that moment Bill's room filled with a great white light. He felt incredibly filled with new hope and joy. "It was like standing on a mountain top with a strong clear wind blowing through me—but it was not a wind of the air," he said, "it was a wind of the Spirit." Bill felt like he had stepped into another world full of goodness and grace. There was a wonderful feeling of Presence that he had been seeking all of his life. He had never felt so complete, so satisfied, so loved. Bill Wilson had finally surrendered, and when he surrendered, God came into his life. Notice that God came into his life with such power and force that Bill never denied God again.

Bill never took another drink, but his spiritual awakening didn't fully resolve his problem. He still had a craving for alcohol. One day he passed a bar, and he felt himself being pulled into it. He thought that if he could just talk to another drunk, he might be able to pull himself back together. He got on the phone, and after making a few calls, finally found one Dr. Bob Smith. Dr. Bob was a hopeless alcoholic. He had destroyed his medical practice, and he was waiting to die. He reluctantly agreed to see Bill, but he had no hope that Bill could help him. Dr. Bob would have no nonsense, he had talked about his alcohol problem with the best, and now here was some other guy, a drunk, who was coming over to try to help him. He was in no mood for help.

*Two Alcoholics Talking to Each Other*

When Bill got there, Dr. Bob was surprised to learn that Bill wasn't there to keep him sober. "No," Bill said, "I'm not here to keep *you* sober, I'm here to keep *me* sober." Well, this was the new concept, one alcoholic talking to another to keep himself sober. Dr. Bob was going to give only Bill a few minutes, but they talked easily, and Bill stayed for hours. Dr. Bob began to open up and speak as frankly as Bill was doing. Having common experiences, they could speak to each other without shame. They talked about the helplessness and hopelessness they had been feeling, the feeling of total powerlessness. They talked about all of the problems that alcohol had caused them. Bill told him about the spiritual experience that he felt had saved him.

These two men became great friends and Alcoholics Anonymous was born. They began to meet with other alcoholics. They began to carry the program to others. Dr. Bob got drunk one more time, when he was away at a convention, but when he returned, he was more determined than ever to stay sober.

A bunch of drunks begins getting together to help each other stay sober. To everyone's amazement, it works. Hopeless cases begin to recover. Of course, the groups had their setbacks, but the way to recovery had been found. They wouldn't have the name Alcoholics Anonymous for 4 more years.

*The Big Book*

Bill dictated most of the first chapters to his secretary. He had considerable resistance when he came up with the Twelve Steps. Some of the members of the group were adamantly opposed to including so much God-talk in the program. They didn't want to scare drunks away with all the spiritual talk. Bill listened quietly, but he knew he was right. The only concession he made was to add the phrase God, "as we understood him." That made some members of the group feel more comfortable.

As the program developed and people began to stay sober, Bill was offered a job as the first alcohol counselor. A hospital wanted to incorporate the program and use it to help alcoholics. The group was opposed. They were afraid that it would make the program commercial, and this would destroy an essential element of the group. This time Bill agreed, and Alcoholics Anonymous remained a free self-supporting program.

Another problem was money. The group needed money to pay for expenses and to reach out to alcoholics who were still suffering. They went to John D. Rockefeller and he gave them 5,000 dollars. They had asked for 50,000, but Rockefeller felt that too much financial backing would weaken the program.

With the individual stories written by the new groups, Bill completed the *Big Book* in 1939. They ordered 5,000 copies to be printed. They didn't sell many until an article written by Jack Anderson appeared in the *Saturday Evening Post*. This gave Alcoholics Anonymous national exposure, and the mail began pouring in. Alcoholics Anonymous now has over one million members and it has meetings all over the world.

*The Twelve Steps* | The program is made up of Twelve Steps. You will hear them read at every meeting.

(1) We admitted we were powerless over alcohol that our lives had become unmanageable. (2) Came to believe that a Power greater than ourselves could restore us to sanity. (3) Made a decision to turn our will and our lives over to the care of God *as we understood Him*. (4) Made a searching and fearless moral inventory of ourselves. (5) Admitted to God, to ourselves, and another human being the exact nature of our wrongs. (6) Were entirely ready to have God remove all these defects of character. (7) Humbly asked him to remove our shortcomings. (8) Made a list of all persons we had harmed, and became willing to make amends to them all. (9) Made direct amends to such people whenever possible, except when to do so would injure them or others. (10) Continued to take personal inventory and when we were wrong promptly admitted it. (11) Sought through prayer and meditation to improve our conscious contact with God *as we understood Him*, praying only for His will for us and the power to carry that out. (12) Having had a spiritual awakening as a result of these steps, we tried to carry this message to alcoholics, and to practice these principles in all our affairs. (*Alcoholics Anonymous*, 1976, pp. 59-60)

Several slogans in AA will help you to reorganize your life and your thinking. Slogans such as, One day at a time, Easy does it, Keep it simple, Live and let live, and Let go and let God. These slogans have great meaning and they will help keep your program on track.

*Meetings* | Ideally, after treatment, you will attend a lot of AA or NA meetings. The more meetings you attend, the greater your chances of achieving a stable recovery. You need to ask someone further along in the program to be your sponsor. They will guide you though the steps, and they will be there for you in times of need.

You will find this program to be a healthy family. The regular meeting you attend will be called your home group. There is a stable set of rules. People will care about you. They will respond to how you feel. They will care for what you want. They will be there for you when you need them.

The choice is yours. We strongly recommend that you throw yourself into this program with all the enthusiasm and courage you can muster. Tell your group the truth. Don't hold back. Alcoholics Anonymous says, "Rarely have we seen a person fail who has thoroughly followed our path."

**Feelings**  | Most chemically dependent people have difficulty with their feelings. They do not know how to identify their feelings and don't know to use their feelings effectively. All feelings give us motivation; they give us specific energy and direction for movement. If you cannot use your feelings effectively, you can't adapt to the changes in your environment.

The reason chemically dependent persons don't use feelings appropriately is they learned not to trust their feelings. We learned that there was something wrong with our feelings. We learned this from watching people respond to us when we were having feelings. When we were children and we were feeling afraid, we heard, "There's nothing to be afraid of." When we were angry, we learned that we were bad. "There's nothing to be angry about," our parents said.

Look at what this does to the child. The child begins to think, "I am having feelings that I shouldn't be having; I am afraid when there is nothing to be afraid about; I am angry when there is nothing to be angry about." We believe our parents. We can reach only one conclusion: Something is wrong with us. I am not feeling right, or I'm having the wrong feeling at the wrong time.

We might be further confused when we get to school and are teased when we have feelings. The other kids tease us when we cry. They don't take us seriously when we are in love. We all know that feelings are one of the most basic things about us. It is one of the things that make us who we are. If there is something wrong with our feelings, there is something wrong with us. "Something is wrong with me," we think, "I can't trust myself."

Once we can't trust who we are, we have to become someone else. We begin to search for that person we want to be. We copy other people whom we respect. We imitate various roles to see if the role fits us. Whatever we do, we don't share our feelings—we have been taught not to do that. We keep our feelings more and more to ourselves until sometimes we don't know how we feel anymore. Boys aren't supposed to cry, so they get angry instead. Girls aren't supposed to get angry, so they cry when they are angry. More and more, we separate from ourselves. We become more isolated.

## Feelings Are Adaptive

Each feeling has a specific action attached to it. Fear gives us the energy to run away. Anger gives us the energy to fight. Acceptance gives us the energy to move closer. You may have more than one feeling at the same time, and this can be confusing, but if you break the feelings down into their basic units, you can always figure out what the feelings are telling you.

There are eight primary feelings: anger, acceptance, anticipation, joy, disgust, sadness, surprise, and fear. There are more complicated emotions, but they are only combinations of the basic eight. Jealousy for example, is when you feel sad, angry, and fearful, all at the same time. When you feel jealous, you have to break the feelings down into their smaller units. Each feeling has to be identified and dealt with. What exactly are you frightened of, and what can you do to relieve your fear? What exactly are you angry at, and what can you do with your anger to make the situation more tolerable? What makes you so sad, and what action can you take to help you feel more comfortable? As each of the feelings are addressed, you will have a more complete picture of the problem.

Remember, all feelings have movement attached. Fear moves you away from an offending stimulus. So does disgust. Sadness gives you the direction to recover the lost object. Anger gives you the direction to fight. Anticipation and surprise are orienting responses; they prepare your body for action. Joy and acceptance give you the direction to move closer and stay with the object that gives you those feelings.

You must learn how to identify your feelings and use your feelings to help you take action. It is a mistake to keep your feelings quiet. Sharing your feelings is an essential skill in interpersonal relationships. You cannot be close to someone if you don't know how each person feels. You don't have to act on all of your feelings, that wouldn't be wise, but you do have to process or deal with each feeling that is important to you.

*How to Be Assertive*

In treatment, we are going to learn the assertiveness formula. This is an excellent way of dealing with feelings appropriately. This is what we are going to say when we have an uncomfortable feeling.

I feel _____

When you _____

I would prefer it if _____

Start by describing your feelings, that will be one or more of the eight feelings we discussed. Then you describe the behavior of the other person that gave you that feeling. Exactly what did he do or say that made you feel uncomfortable? Then you tell him what you would prefer them to do.

Let's say your husband is an alcoholic and he is 2 hours late from work. You are scared and angry. He could be drunk again. He could have been involved in an accident. He could be having an affair. Just as your worry reaches its peak, and you begin to call the police, he comes home. Using the assertiveness formula, you would say, "I feel scared and angry when you come home late. I would prefer it if you would call me and let me know where you are." Now this statement gives him knowledge about how you are feeling, what he did to give you that feeling, and what he can do to improve things. This is good communication.

What if you feel that someone in your group is in denial and lying to herself? You might say something like this: "I feel sad when I hear you say you don't have a drinking problem. I would prefer it if you would try to see the truth about what you are doing to yourself."

In group you will have people reflect your feelings back to you. They aren't trying to hurt you; they are trying to get you to see the truth. They might tell you that they experience you as mad or sad when you don't really know how you feel. It is important to listen to your group members and try to see what they see. Maybe they can see a side of you that you can't see.

It is vitally important for you not to feel ashamed of your feelings. You can have your feelings whether or not you have a good reason for having them. They don't have to be logical and make sense to be important. You will learn how to trust your feelings in treatment. You will learn that all of your feelings are great wise counselors.

# Special Problems

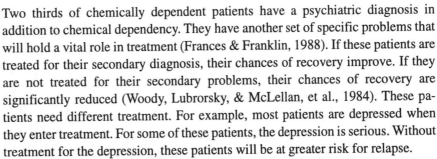

Two thirds of chemically dependent patients have a psychiatric diagnosis in addition to chemical dependency. They have another set of specific problems that will hold a vital role in treatment (Frances & Franklin, 1988). If these patients are treated for their secondary diagnosis, their chances of recovery improve. If they are not treated for their secondary problems, their chances of recovery are significantly reduced (Woody, Lubrorsky, & McLellan, et al., 1984). These patients need different treatment. For example, most patients are depressed when they enter treatment. For some of these patients, the depression is serious. Without treatment for the depression, these patients will be at greater risk for relapse.

One way of evaluating these clinical phenomena is to make a distinction between primary and secondary diagnoses. The disorder that occurred first is called primary, and the problem that appeared second is called secondary. When the first-appearing disorder is abuse of substances, it is highly likely (although not always true) that the secondary problems will improve rapidly (within days or weeks) once abstinence is achieved (Schuckit, 1994).

## The Psychiatric/ Psychological Assessment

All patients need to be carefully screened for psychiatric/psychological problems in the initial assessment process. This screening must be done by a psychiatrist or a psychologist with the special skills necessary for this examination. The assessment must include the following:

1. A systematic mental status examination with special emphasis on immediate recall and recent and remote memory.
2. A determination of current and past psychiatric/psychological abnormality.
3. A determination of the danger to self or others.
4. A neurological assessment, if indicated by the psychiatric/psychological assessment.

5. An evaluation of cognitive functioning, including any learning impairment that might influence treatment.

This assessment will signal for the staff problems that need further treatment. The psychologist/psychiatrist will flag for you serious psychopathology, but you still need to keep them informed if you feel something else is going on other than chemical dependency. You see the patients on a daily basis, and you are the most likely to know when things aren't going well. Sometimes more of the patients' abnormal behavior will become evident as they move through the treatment program.

## How to Develop the Treatment Plan

Once the patient is diagnosed with a secondary problem, the treatment team will develop a treatment plan. Sometimes you will not be formally involved in the treatment, the psychiatrist or psychologist may do it, but you will deal with the problem on some level, so you need special skills. If you ever feel over your head with a patient, you must inform the staff. You might need to refer the patient for further consultation. Do not strike out on your own with these patients; use the treatment team to guide you.

It would be beyond the scope of this book to cover all of the psychopathology that you will experience as a counselor, but we will discuss what you will see most often. You should familiarize yourself with the latest edition of the *Diagnostic and Statistical Manual of Mental Disorders* of the American Psychiatric Association. Keep this manual close to you for reference. It is not your job to diagnose these patients, but you should be alert for the major problems you will see and become familiar with methodologies to treat the problems.

All of the major psychiatric diseases, such as chemical dependency, have a biological component, a psychological component, and a social component. You must consider all three parts of the parts of the problem in developing a treatment plan.

Some psychiatric diseases require psychotropic medication. There is an old idea in AA/NA that all medications are bad. This is no longer appropriate. Many patients need their medication to survive. A certain type of depression, for example, is treated very well with antidepressant medication. If you deprive these patients of the treatment they need, some of them will die. Fifteen percent of people who have a serious depression may eventually kill themselves (Hirschfeld & Goodwin, 1988). The schizophrenic patient, and the patient with bipolar affective disorder, are other examples of persons that need their medication for normal functioning. Let the physician make this decision. Once the decision is made to treat the patient with medication, it is vital that you support this decision.

## The Depressed Patient

Depression by far the most common secondary diagnosis related to chemical dependency. Depression is a whole-body illness that involves the patient's body, mood, and thinking. It affects the way patients eat, sleep, the way they feel about themselves, and the way they think about things. There is a consistently high rate of depression in substance abusers (Dorus, Kennedy, Gibbons, & Raci, 1987; Hesselbrock, Meyer, & Kenner, 1985). Most chemically dependent individuals will come into treatment with some measurable degree of depression.

Excessive use of alcohol and other chemicals results in depressed mood. This depression can be organic, psychological, or interpersonal. You will first pick up depression in the mental status examination or in the psychological testing. A patient's depressed mood can range from mild to severe. The best way to measure the severity is to use a psychological instrument such as the Beck Depression Inventory (Appendix 31). A score under 10 indicates mild depression, 10 to 20 indicates moderate depression, and a score of above 20 indicates severe depression. Any depressive score above 10 should be followed up. The average Beck score of patients coming into inpatient treatment is 16.

The primary symptom of depression is the inability to experience pleasure. This is called *anhedonia*. Depression completely clouds patients' lives. Anhedonia is persistent and pervasive. Patients feel as if life is dead. The joy is gone. They feel sad or down most of the day almost every day. They sleep poorly; they undersleep or oversleep. Their appetite is off. They have a diminished ability to concentrate. They may feel helpless, hopeless, worthless, or excessively guilty. When people feel this bad, they may think that they would be better off dead. They may be suicidal.

*How to Assess Depression*

To assess depression, you will have the Beck score, the mental status examination, the history of the present problem, and the past history. All patients are asked: "Have you ever felt sad or down, most of the day almost every day, for more than 2 weeks?" If the answer to this question is yes, the patient needs to see someone on the staff experienced in depression. As the counselor, don't try to evaluate the extent of the depression yourself; it gets complicated and takes quite a bit of diagnostic skill. You should be familiar with the types of depression listed in the *Diagnostic and Statistical Manual* of the American Psychiatric Association. Some depressions are chronic and mild, and some can be acute and life-threatening.

*How to Treat Depression*

Depression can be treated by you if you work with the clinical team. Depression is treated in three ways: with antidepressant medication; with psychotherapy, such as behavior therapy or cognitive therapy; and with interpersonal therapy. If a pa- tient is placed on medication, you need to be supportive of this decision and encourage the patient to comply. In behavior therapy you will encourage patients to change their actions. For example, you will help them develop leisure-time activities that will increase their opportunity to experience joy. What they do will change how they feel. In cognitive therapy, you will help patients to correct their inaccurate thinking. In interpersonal therapy you will help them resolve interpersonal conflicts.

*Chemotherapy*

The biology of depression is centered around a chemical problem in the brain. Certain neurotransmitter systems, such as norepinephrine, dopamine, and serotonin, become deregulated or out of balance. This chemical problem can be corrected chemically, with medication. Four groups of antidepressant medications are commonly used in treating depression: selective serotonin reuptake inhibitors (SSRIs), tricyclics, monoamine oxidase inhibitors (MAOIs), and lithium. Lithium, carbamazepine, and valproic acid are the current treatments for manic-depressive illness, also called bipolar affective disorder. The doctor may have to try a variety of antidepressant medications or a combination of medications before finding the right one. Depression has strong genetic links, and certain genes predispose some people to manic or depressive episodes. Affective disorders can be caused by physical problems, psychological problems, or interpersonal problems, or it can occur without environmental precipitant. There is not always a psychological or a social cause of the disease, but it always has psychological and social effects that need treatment.

If the physician decides to put the patient on antidepressant medication, there will usually be a 3- to 6-week delay before the patient begins to feel better. You must encourage patients during this period. Keep telling them that it's going to get better. This encouragement will instill hope in the treatment and will increase patient compliance. There are side effects of antidepressants that the patient needs to discuss with the physician. Mostly these will be mild sedation and an overall drying effect experienced as dry mouth, urinary retention, and constipation. Some of the newer antidepressants can cause an increase in anxiety and loss of appetite. Be sure to chart any symptoms the patient reports and discuss them with the clinical team.

As it takes these drugs 3 to 6 weeks to work, you might not see the antidepressant take effect in every patient. Patients may respond only after they have left treatment. Once you see this change take place, however, you will be totally convinced. The dramatic effect that these drugs produce will win you over. They contribute in a major way to the treatment of depression.

Medication should never be the only treatment for depression. Studies have consistently shown that patients who undergo medication plus psychotherapy have a better prognosis (Beitman, Carlin, & Chiles, 1984; Conte, Putchik, & Wild, et al., 1986).

The two major psychological treatments for depression are behavior therapy and cognitive therapy. In the biopsychosocial interview, you will try to uncover any psychosocial stressors that may have precipitated the depression. Certain depressions are caused by specific environmental events, such as a death in the family, or divorce. If you can determine what caused or exacerbated the depression, you will have come a long way in knowing where to concentrate treatment.

*Behavior Therapy*  Behavior therapy for depression centers around teaching patients new skills and increasing positive reinforcers in the patient's environment. This increase in pleasure-oriented activity elevates mood. Studies have shown that depressed people don't do fun things. They tend to sit and feel helpless, hopeless, and depressed. Your behavioral intervention will increase the patients' activities. You will have them begin an exercise program, increase social interaction with treatment peers, and become more involved in games, sports, and hobbies. You must be specific in what you recommend, and you must make sure that the patient follows through with your recommendations.

Monitor depression with a weekly Beck Depression Inventory. You can give this test daily if necessary. As the patient gets better, the Beck score will drop. You want that score to drop to 10 or below before the patients leave the treatment center. If they level off for a few weeks at a score higher than 10, you will have to adjust the treatment plan.

A word about psychological testing is appropriate here. Testing will give you a general indication of what is going on. A test is not able to be absolutely certain about anything. The scores need to be considered in light of the total clinical picture. You need to trust your clinical judgment more than you trust a psychological test. If the tests show that the patient is not depressed, and you feel they are, you could be right. This is an issue that needs to be discussed with the clinical team. You will make more accurate judgments together.

An increase in goal-oriented behavior is essential to behavioral treatment of depression. Depressed persons have a difficult time doing anything, and they will need encouragement to set goals. If the person needs to increase their level of social interaction, you can get them to go through a communication exercise with one or two peers per day. You can get them to play pool or cards with someone once a day. The contracts are very helpful here, and most of these patients will need to work through the contracts with you or a treatment peer. Relaxation skills and stress-reduction skills will be important to some of these patients. Depressed patients may need to learn assertiveness skills. *Control Your Depression,* by Lewinsohn, Munoz, and Youngren, et al. (1978), is an excellent, highly structured, skill-training program for depression. You can work through this text with your patient and come up with specific behaviors for the patient to learn.

In groups, the depressed patients will need to be encouraged to talk in both individual and group sessions. They need to talk about how they feel and to detail what they are going to do to feel better. You can't let these patients ruminate about how bad they feel; they need to be encouraged to do something different. Have them go for a bike ride, a walk, play basketball, play pool, swim, talk to someone, call a friend, become involved in a hobby, listen to music, read pleasant material, breathe the clean air, pray, meditate, have something good to eat, listen to the sounds of nature, give a gift, help someone in the program, do a job until it's well done, take a hot bath, kick the leaves. You can have fun coming up with new ideas for them to try.

As the patients try these new fun behaviors, they will naturally begin to feel better. When they do, you need to reinforce them, and show them that it is what they are doing that is influencing how they feel. You must chart the new behaviors and the response of the patients. Place some quotations in the charts about what the patients say about their new behaviors.

*Cognitive Therapy*     Cognitive therapy concentrates on how a patient thinks. This therapy was developed by Albert Ellis (1962). It was further refined for depressed patients by Beck, et al. (1979). These researchers found that many depressed feelings come from negative self-talk. This tends to be inaccurate thinking, and it needs to be corrected. All patients who are depressed should read *Coping With Depression* by Beck and Greenberg (1974). This monograph explains cognitive therapy and will get the patient started.

Using the technique developed by Beck et al. (1979), the patients keep a daily record of their dysfunctional thinking. This is accomplished by having the patients write down each situation that makes them feel uncomfortable during the day. They need to be specific about this situation, exactly what happened that triggered the uncomfortable feelings. Then the patients make a list of each uncomfortable feeling they had following the situation. Did they feel fear, sadness, disgust, or anger? Then they rate the intensity of each feeling on a scale from 1, as little of that feeling as possible, to 100, as much of that feeling as possible. These numbers are called subjective units of distress. You are interested only in the negative feelings. Then the patients add up the scores: the total of the subjective units of distress they felt during the situation.

Now you help the patients determine what they were thinking between the situation and the negative feelings. Ask the patients what they were thinking and then be willing to make suggestions. Patients will not be able to come up with all of these thoughts by themselves, because the thinking was out of their awareness. The thoughts that you are after are negative, and they lead directly to uncomfortable feelings. Pull for as many of these negative thoughts as you can and write them all down. This is uncovering the automatic thinking that occurred between the situation and the uncomfortable feelings. It must be emphasized that patients don't try to think these thoughts—they are automatic, they come without conscious effort.

Once you have a list of the negative thoughts and feelings, have the patients go back and develop accurate thoughts. Go over what happened again and help the patients decide what they should have been thinking. What would have been an accurate judgment of that situation? Once you have a list of the accurate thoughts, re-rate each of the feelings based on an accurate evaluation of the situation. You will come up with new subjective units of distress based on accurate thoughts rather than inaccurate thoughts.

Patients will be amazed at how their inaccurate thinking directly causes their uncomfortable feelings. They need to keep actively involved in cognitive therapy the whole time they are in treatment. Each time they go though an uncomfortable situation, they need to keep a record of their thinking. In time, they will be able to catch themselves in inaccurate thinking, stop this thinking, and get their thinking accurate. Once patients are accurate, they will feel much better.

*An Example of Cognitive Therapy.* Let's go though an actual cognitive therapy session. In this session, the counselor uses the first time the patient hears about interpersonal group as the situation that caused uncomfortable feelings. The first time any patient hears about this group it creates quite a bit of anxiety. The patient is Kim, a 17-year-old female who is rather shy and avoidant. Her Beck depression score is 24, which puts her in the severely depressed range.

The counselor introduces the cognitive therapy session.

*Counselor:* Kim, I want you to begin to get accurate in your thinking. When you do this, you will feel more comfortable. What we are going to do now is go through an actual situation, and see if we can uncover some of your inaccurate thoughts. The first time you heard about interpersonal group, how did you feel?

*Kim:* Scared.

*Counselor:* How scared did you feel on a scale of from 1, as little scared as possible, to 100 as scared as possible?

*Kim:* I don't know.

*Counselor:* We're just going to guess. How scared do you think you were feeling on a scale of from 1 to 100?

*Kim:* (The patient pauses) About 85, I guess.

*Counselor:* Great, 85. How else were you feeling?

*Kim:* Oh, I don't know.

*Counselor:* Were you feeling angry?

*Kim:* No, I wasn't feeling angry.

*Counselor:* Were you feeling sad?

*Kim:* Yeah, I guess I was.

*Counselor:* How sad were you feeling, from 1, as little sad as possible, to 100 as much sad as possible?

*Kim:* About 60.

*Counselor:* Good. How else were you feeling?

(She does not respond.)

*Counselor:* Were you feeling surprised?

*Kim:* No.

*Counselor:* Were you feeling any anticipation?

*Kim:* No . . . I was feeling discouraged.

*Counselor:* How discouraged?

*Kim:* About 75.

*Counselor:* Good, now if we add all those negative feelings up, we get 230 subjective units of distress. When you hear about interpersonal group, you feel 230 units of uncomfortable feelings. Now, what were you thinking between hearing about interpersonal group and the feelings you felt. What thoughts ran through your mind?

*Kim:* I won't fit in.

*Counselor:* Great. What else were you thinking?

*Kim:* I'll be treated like an outcast.

*Counselor:* What else?

*Kim:* They will think I'm a psycho.

*Counselor:* Okay, what else?

*Kim:* They will get the idea that I'm not serious about treatment.

*Counselor:* What else were you thinking?

*Kim:* That's about it.

*Counselor:* Were you thinking, "They're not going to like me?"

*Kim:* Yeah, I was.

*Counselor:* Okay, let's put that down. Were you thinking, "I'll have to talk."

*Kim:* Yes.

*Counselor:* Were you thinking, "They'll make me talk about things I don't want to talk about."

*Kim:* Definitely.

*Counselor:* Any other thoughts?

*Kim:* They won't understand me.

*Counselor:* Good, now I have written down all of your automatic thoughts. It is important to recognize that these thoughts came to you automatically. You didn't try to think these thoughts; they came on their own. You will find that before you have negative feelings, you will always have rapid thoughts before the feelings. This is where you make assumptions or judgments about the situation. It's where you internally evaluate the situation and how it directly applies to you. Do you understand?

*Kim:* Yeah.

*Counselor:* Good. Now, we need to get accurate. Go back to the situation and think about it. You hear about interpersonal group. What is accurate thinking about that situation?

*Kim:* They might be able to help me in group.

*Counselor:* That's right, that's what they are there for. What else is accurate?

*Kim:* I won't have to talk if I don't want to.

*Counselor:* Good. What else is accurate?

*Kim:* I'll try to fit in. We all have problems in common.

*Counselor:* That's right. What else?

*Kim:* They'll try to make me feel like a part of the group.

*Counselor:* Yes. What else?

*Kim:* They have some of the same problems as I do.

*Counselor:* That's very true. What else?

*Kim:* That's all I can think of.

*Counselor:* How about, "They'll try to be supportive of me."

*Kim:* Yeah, that's true.

*Counselor:* How about, "If I want to get help, I should try to share as much as I can."

*Kim:* That's right.

*Counselor:* Okay, now let's go back and rate each of the negative feelings we rated before. You hear about interpersonal group, but this time you think accurately. You think, "They will try to make me feel like a part of the group. They might be able to help me. They will try to support me. They will try to understand me. I won't have to talk, but if I want help here, I should try to share as much of myself as I feel comfortable sharing." How much fear do you feel when you are thinking accurately.

*Kim:* About 20.

*Counselor:* How sad do you feel?

*Kim:* I don't feel any sadness.

*Counselor:* How discouraged?

*Kim:* 5.

*Counselor:* Great, now let's see. When you are thinking automatically and inaccurately, you score 230 units of distress. But when you stop and get accurate, you feel only 25 units of uncomfortable feelings. How do you feel about that?

*Kim:* That's amazing.

*Counselor:* Yes, it is. Many of these inaccurate thoughts come out of childhood. We judge situations automatically, as if our inaccurate thoughts are accurate. No wonder you were feeling bad about interpersonal group. You were thinking, "I won't fit in. I'll be treated like an outcast. They will think I'm psycho." What we are going to do over the next few weeks, Kim, is keep an account of each situation that makes you feel uncomfortable. Then we are going to uncover the inaccurate thinking that leads to your uncomfortable feelings. Then we are going to challenge these thoughts, and get accurate. You need to live in the real world. You can no longer live in the painful world of your inaccurate thinking. You need to commit yourself to reality.

In cognitive therapy, you can decrease the patient's negative feelings substantially if you get the patient accurate. You must make this therapy formal. Patients will not be able to do this therapy on their own. They will not be able to uncover their inaccurate thoughts, or to get accurate without your help. You will need to make suggestions. As the patients understand that they have been getting their depressed feelings from inaccurate thoughts, they will feel better and their depression will begin to lift.

As the patients bring in their dysfunctional thoughts, you will begin to see patterns in their thinking. Some of the same thoughts will come up over and over again. These thoughts give patients false information from which they make false assumptions. They collect the inaccurate thoughts and reach a conclusion based on false information. These conclusions must be challenged with accurate information. It is not uncommon for the patient to reach conclusions such as: I'm stupid, I'm ugly, I'm unworthy, No one will ever love me, I'm inadequate, Everyone is better than I am. They live their lives as if these false conclusions are true.

You will have some interesting therapy sessions with these patients; many of their false assumptions are held on to quite rigidly. You may have to get the support of the group to help convince patients that they are wrong. It is not uncommon for a strikingly beautiful person to think she is ugly. Many patients will fight to hold on to their inaccurate opinion of themselves.

Trust in you and in the group is important here. The patient will need to trust others to make accurate judgments. This is difficult, and the old ideas die hard, they seem to have a life of their own. With work, the patient will get more accurate. You should see the patient in cognitive therapy at least once a week. The more patients keep up on their thinking, the more rapidly they will improve.

*Interpersonal Therapy*    Interpersonal therapy for depression has been outlined by Klerman, Weissman, Rounsaville, and Chevron (1984). This therapy seeks to heal interpersonal problems that leave the patient feeling depressed. Many patients, for example, will come into treatment with an abnormal grief reaction. They have had a loss of a love object or self-esteem that they have not dealt with. Some patients are involved in interpersonal disputes. These unresolved conflicts leave the patient feeling lost and depressed. Some patients are in a role transition that they can't deal with. Some patients are impoverished; they have no socially reinforcing situation from which they can gain pleasure.

*Grief.* Patients in an abnormal grief reaction need to work through the grief process. Normal grief is much like depression, but it lifts without treatment within 2 to 4 months. The person gradually deals with the loss and moves on with life. Sometimes the person suffering a loss doesn't grieve until much later. This is a delayed grief reaction. They postpone the grief because they cannot deal with it at the time of its occurrence. A person with a delayed grief reaction will feel numb at the actual loss. It is only later that they begin to experience the pain.

Some patients will drink or use drugs that prevent them from feeling the pain. Grief can be unresolved for years. When patients come into treatment with a significant loss of a close family member or friend, you must consider how they handled the grief process. Did they work the death through, or do they still have grief work to do? Is the issue resolved, or is the patient still stuck in the grief process? Many persons who have had abortions have unresolved grief to work through.

Normal grief runs through a range of highly charged feeling states. The loss of a loved one leads to at least one year of disturbance. Three years of disturbance is not uncommon. Normal bereavement reactions include states of shame, guilt, personal fear of dying, and sadness. In normal grief, anger at the person who died, at the self, and at persons who are exempted from the tragedy are common. In pathological grief, the patient becomes frozen in one or more of these stages for weeks, months, or years (Karasu, 1989).

People in the unresolved grief process need to talk about their grief. To accept the reality of their loss they need to experience their pain. They need to talk about it in individual sessions and in group. They need to share the good and bad memories. They need to discuss the events prior to, during, and after the loss. They need to adjust more gradually to a new environment. This may include coming to terms with living alone, managing finances, learning to do the chores, facing an empty house, and changing social relationships. They need to begin to withdraw emotionally, reinvest in new relationships, and acquire new interests to substitute for the loss. They need to be reassured that they have a program full of people, which makes it impossible that they ever be lonely again. They need to see what they lost accurately, with all of the good and bad qualities. Someone who sees only the good things will not work through the grief.

These patients need to develop new relationships in the program. They need to be encouraged to increase their social interaction with treatment peers. Don't let them huddle up in your office bemoaning their fate. Get someone further along in the program to stick with them and keep them out with the patient population.

*Interpersonal Disputes.* Patients in interpersonal disputes will have to work toward resolving the interpersonal problem. In chemical dependency treatment, you will often see a spouse who is being rejected by their significant other. The drinking and drugging has taken its toll and the spouse has emotionally or physically left the relationship. Patients may come into treatment in a frantic attempt to save the relationship. They may feel hopeless and solely responsible for the problems.

Treatment begins with helping patients to identify the problem. Patients need to plan what they are going to do. What are all of the possible actions the patient can take regarding the problem? Patients will need to improve communication skills. They should work through the Relationships Skills Exercise (Appendix 12) and the Communication Skills Exercise (Appendix 14). They will need to practice these skills with their peers before they bring these skills into play in their current conflict. If possible, you need to meet with the patient and the significant other to work toward resolution.

At times, patients will only need to renegotiate a dispute with their significant other. This is the easiest conflict to resolve. First, you need a commitment from each party to work on the problem. At times there is an impasse, where one member of the couple is not willing to cooperate. You can't do much here, except encourage the patient to hope that in recovery this other person will change. Often a spouse needs to see recovery to know it is real. Many marriages reconnect after a few months or years of sobriety. The patient must understand that the other person has been devastated by the disease. It is the disease that is the problem. The best thing the patient can do now is get into a stable program of recovery and turn the situation over to the Higher Power. "God grant me the serenity to accept the things I cannot change, the courage to change the things I can, and the wisdom to know the difference."

*Suicide*
Most patients who are depressed consider suicide to relieve their pain. There is a 15% mean suicide rate in alcoholics (Talbott, Hales, & Yudofsky, 1988). Suicidal ideation begins with patients thinking that everyone would be better off if they were dead. Remember, the primary symptom of depression is the absence of pleasure. When all of life's pain remains and all of the pleasure leaves, it is logical for the patient to consider death. The incidence of suicide is about 20 times higher in drug abusers (Blumenthal, 1988). The patients who are suicide threats will move through three phases in increasing lethality:

1. They will have increasing suicidal thoughts.
2. They will plan their suicide.
3. They will carry out the plan.

Your job is to recognize the process and reestablish hope. All patients who are depressed need to hear that depression is an illness from which people recover. Depression is treatable and curable. The depression is not their fault. It is a sickness that happened to them. It is not a punishment.

On the Beck Depression Inventory, Question 2 assesses hopelessness, and Question 8 assesses suicidal ideation. Both of these questions answered positively should be taken seriously. The higher the score, the greater the risk.

During the mental status examination, all patients are formally assessed for suicidal risk, but you can also ask the suicidal questions anytime during treatment when you feel they may be important. The questions are as follows:

1. Have you ever wanted to go to sleep and not wake up? (If yes, tell me about that. What was going on?)
2. Have you ever thought about hurting yourself? (If yes, what was happening?)
3. If you were to hurt yourself, how would you do it? (If the patient has a suicide plan, write it down.)
4. If the above answer is yes, have you carried any of that plan out? (Carefully assess any actions the patient has taken to arrange for or commit suicide.)

These four questions accurately assess suicidal risk in escalating order of severity. Patients who have suicidal ideation, an active plan, and have carried any part of the plan out, should be transported to a psychiatric unit. These patients are in danger of hurting themselves and need more structure. A psychiatric facility has rooms and wards that are specifically designed to reduce the possibility of suicide.

Patients who are suicidal are usually afraid of themselves or they are resigned to their death. Each of these signs is an ominous indicator of serious intent.

Most patients who come in for chemical dependency treatment have thought about suicide but don't have an active plan. If they do have a plan, it is one that they worked out outside of the treatment center. A patient who has been actively considering suicide, and who has been considering a plan while in treatment needs to be transported. Do not leave these patients alone, not even for a second. Wait with the patient until you turn them over to the care of a professional.

Do not make decisions about suicidal patients by yourself. This is outside of your level of expertise. All of these patients need to be examined as soon as possible by an appropriate mental health professional. This covers you and your staff, and it will give you confidence in the decision reached.

Patients who are experiencing suicidal ideation with no plan can stay in treatment. They will need extra support and they will need to be watched more carefully than other patients. You do not want these patients isolating themselves, you want them to be with someone who is supporting and encouraging them. Patients need to feel that they are in a safe environment, and they need to be certain that the staff is going to respond to their needs. Once the patients begins to feel hope, their suicidal ideation will subside.

## The Angry Patient

Anger and resentment are poison for a chemically dependent person. "Resentment is the 'number one' offender. It destroys more alcoholics than anything else" (*Alcoholics Anonymous*, 1976, p. 64). It's not very far from that burning angry feeling to the chemicals. Anger has a lot of energy behind it. This angry energy is going to have to go somewhere, and it is important that it is directed positively, into the recovery program. Anger at the illness can be constructive.

Anger necessitates blame. Patients must believe that someone purposely did something wrong that ended up hurting them or the anger cannot continue. Each of these beliefs must be checked out for accuracy. The patient must stop and think before acting.

### How to Handle the Violent Patient

A patient who is actively violent does not belong in the normal chemical dependency treatment center. Like the actively suicidal patient, these patients belong in a more secure psychiatric facility. Psychiatric hospitals have the equipment and the staff to deal with violent patients. Most chemical dependency centers do not have this expertise. If your patients make overt attempts, acts, or threats of substantial bodily harm to themselves or another person, they should be transferred. Keep as many staff members with this patient as necessary to transport the patient safely. Do not hesitate to call the police. Apprise the officers carefully of your situation, and tell them to bring enough backup to manage the situation. Get an immediate consultation from your psychiatrist or psychologist and follow his or her orders carefully. The doctor can order chemical or mechanical restraints if this becomes necessary.

### How to Handle an Angry Patient

The patient who is feeling angry, or verbally acting angry, can usually be managed in your facility. It is rare for a patient to go through treatment without expressing anger. Most of your patients have unresolved anger issues. Chemically dependent persons tend to harbor deep anger and resentments. They boil and fume for years over some real or imagined slight. This all comes from the desire to be in control. "Each person is like an actor who wants to run the whole show; is forever trying to arrange the lights, the ballet, the scenery and the rest of the players in his own way" (*Alcoholics Anonymous,* 1976, pp. 60-61). When people don't do what the chemically dependent person wants them to, he or she is furious.

Treatment for the angry patient revolves around having them complete the Anger Management Exercise (Appendix 33), where the patient learns about the anger problem and learns specific skills to deal with angry feelings. Most people feel sadness and fear along with the anger. All of the feelings need to be expressed. Patients need to verbalize how they see the whole situation while you support them. Don't argue with an angry patient. Stay out of their reach and use a calm voice. Don't stand in the way of an exit. Let them rant and rave if they want to. Patients need to feel that they are important. If you listen to them, even when they are angry, it validates them as a person.

Angry patients are feeling afraid, and they will need a lot of reassurance. Patients often feel that their anger is so repulsive that they will be rejected for expressing it. You need to show them that their anger is friendly as long as it is used appropriately. Anger exists to help us to establish and maintain boundaries around ourselves. It keeps us from being violated. Anger is adaptive. People who cannot get angry will be have their boundaries violated.

Help the patient see that all anger comes from hurt. Anger is there to make the pain stop. First, something violates patients physically or emotionally, and then they get angry. If they learn to hold people accountable by expressing all of their feelings, they might not even get angry.

*Assertiveness Skills* | Patients do not have to act aggressively to show that they are angry. They need to be taught assertiveness skills. They need to see that assertiveness skills work and they bring people closer together. Aggressiveness, on the other hand, is controlling and it drive people away. The book *Your Perfect Right* by Alberti and Emmons (1988) is an excellent resource for you and your patients. If your patients need assertiveness training, they can read assigned parts of this book as homework. Assertiveness skills need to be practiced, over and over again, both in individual sessions, in role-playing, and in group.

*The Importance of Forgiveness* | Patients with an anger problem must learn how to forgive. They can use the Higher Power for this if they cannot forgive themselves. They want to be forgiven, and God will forgive them, as they learn to forgive others. "Forgive us our trespasses as we forgive those who trespass against us."

Forgiveness is difficult. Patients will never forget what happened, but they can understand the person that hurt them by understanding their own disease.

> We realized that the people who wronged us were perhaps spiritually sick. Though we did not like their symptoms and the way they disturbed us, they, like ourselves, were sick too. We asked God to help us show them the same tolerance, pity, and patience that we would cheerfully grant a sick friend. (*Alcoholics Anonymous,* 1976, p. 67)

All patients who are angry and resentful need to read the following passage from the Big Book:

And acceptance is the answer to *all* my problems today. When I am disturbed, it is because I find some person, place, thing, or situation—some fact of my life—unacceptable to me, and I can find no serenity until I accept that person, place, thing, or situation as being exactly the way it is supposed to be at this moment. Nothing, absolutely nothing happens in God's world by mistake. Until I could accept my alcoholism, I could not stay sober; unless I accept life completely on life's terms, I cannot be happy. I need to concentrate not so much on what needs to be changed in the world as on what needs to be changed in me and in my attitudes. (*Alcoholics Anonymous,* 1976, p. 449)

Have patients who are angry keep an anger diary. Take them through some cognitive therapy. Every time patients feel angry they should write the situation down and uncover their automatic thoughts. As these inaccurate thoughts are uncovered, patients will see why they have been so angry. They take the slightest look or word as an attack. They need to work through the impulse control exercise and begin to practice the assertiveness formula over and over again:

I feel _____

When you _____

I would prefer it if _____

## How to Teach Patients to Recognize Their Anger

These patients need to learn the specific changes in their body when they are getting angry. They need to learn how this feels. Do they feel a tightness in their chest? Does their face feel flushed? As early in the anger process as possible, they need to back out of the situation and use their new assertiveness skills. The initial response needs to be delayed until they can stop, think, and plan. This needs a lot of practice. Have them write down every time they use assertiveness skills and every time they slip back into aggressive behavior. You will be able to show them the damage they are doing to relationships with their old behavior. You will also show them how assertiveness skills bring people closer together.

## Disengagement

It will often help an angry patient to disengage from the current situation to be as detached as if the situation were happening to someone else. It is here that patients can step back from themselves and see themselves as if they are their own counselor.

"I'm feeling some anger."

"This is interesting."

"I need to check this out."

"What's going on with me right now?"

By stepping out of themselves and checking the anger out, patients will be more likely to get accurate and make better judgments. They can even laugh at themselves. They can recognize their anger, smile at themselves, and say, "That's a silly thing to do to myself." They can then take two deep breaths, breathing in slowly through the nose and out slowly through the mouth. As they exhale, they feel a warm wave of relaxation move down their body. Patients should practice this technique in your individual and group therapy sessions.

*Time-Out*  Patients who have a tendency to become verbally or physically violent must move away from an escalating situation as soon as possible. They must move away from the situation as far as necessary to recover their normal feelings. One useful technique to use if the anger happens in a family is to develop a "time-out" contract. This is a written contract between two or more people where they agree that either party can say at any time "Time-out." Once one person has said "Time-out," the other party can only say, "Okay, time-out." At this point, the couple separates and agrees to return in one hour to process further through the problem. When they are separated, it is important that they don't rehash the argument over again in their mind—they might come back more furious than when they left. When separated, it is important that they both tell themselves certain things to get their thinking more accurate (McKay, Rogers, & McKay, 1989):

1. No one is completely right or wrong.
2. It is okay to disagree.
3. The other person is not trying to hurt me, he (she) are trying to meet his (her) needs.
4. Do I need to call someone and talk about this? If I do, I need to do that right now.
5. I'll turn this situation over to my Higher Power.

The patient needs to keep a list of these statements along with several numbers of people to call with them at all times.

*How to Keep Your Cool as a Counselor*  It is not easy dealing with people who are angry. They may verbally abuse you, and you need to keep calm. The worst thing you can do is lose your temper. Anger from the counselor can do a lot of damage. Concentrate on feeling yourself relax. Feel your arms and legs become heavy. Focus on your breathing and breathe slowly. If you are getting angry, excuse yourself, take a few minutes outside of the room. Let someone else take over for a while. The best thing you can do for that patient is to remain calm and take good care of yourself.

## The Homicidal Patient

Patients who are experiencing homicidal ideation need to ventilate their feelings and then process through their options. They are not thinking clearly. They need help processing through their problem to a logical conclusion. It is not unusual for patients to feel like killing someone, even someone they love. You will find homicidal thoughts to be a common element in dealing with angry patients. Most patients are just blowing off steam, thinking about homicide, wanting the ultimate revenge.

*The Duty to Warn*  If the staff determines that a patient presents a serious danger of violence to another person, they have the obligation to protect the intended victim (*Tarasoff v. Regents of the University of California,* 1976). This is an unusual event, but it does happen, and it should be carefully discussed with the clinical staff. There is a delicate balance between duty to warn and confidentiality. Whenever you have a patient seriously threatening another person, it is necessary to staff the problem, and document the staff decision in the patient record. This patient may have to be transferred to a more secure facility, or the victim may have to be warned.

Persons who have homicidal ideation can usually be reasoned with if they can be guided to see the truth. What is really going to happen if they kill someone? They need to process through the whole idea, from beginning to end. Is killing someone taking good care of themselves? What good is going to come of homicide? Is murder going to do the world any good? Is it going to do them any good? What does God want from them? They will need to be encouraged to turn the situation over to the perfect judge, God.

Homicidal intent is assessed in escalating order of severity:

1. Have you ever thought about hurting anyone or anything like that? (If yes, who? Tell me what happened.)
2. If you were to hurt that person, how would you do it? (If the patient has a plan, write it down.)
3. Have you carried out any of that plan? (Get the details of the patient's behavior.)

Patients with homicidal ideation, with a plan, who have carried any part of that plan out, must be considered seriously homicidal. They must be watched. They must not be discharged or allowed to leave without being processed by the clinical staff. If patients were imminently harmful to others by overt attempts, acts, or threats within the last few hours, they may have to be detained against their will and transported to another facility. A psychiatrist, psychologist, physician, or police officer is necessary for this decision. Your job is to keep the appropriate personnel informed of the patient's condition. Let them take over the responsibility for the patient when they can.

## Personality

Personality is composed of two basic parts, temperament and character. *Temperament* is the general level of physiological responsivity to the environment. Some people are more sensitive to incoming stimulation. Some people seem dull and unresponsive. *Character* is what we learn about what to do and how to behave. It is shaped by the family and the social environment. Temperament and character are the primary elements in all personality disorders (Millon, 1981).

## What Is Personality?

Personality is the enduring way a person thinks, feels, and acts. Personality is stable, well learned, and resistive to change. Personality makes up the total person. It is the pattern of behavior that we all evolve as the style of our life, or how we adapt to our environment.

A *state* is a person's current condition. This is transient and flexible, and is easily manipulated by environmental stimulation. A person may feel sad, even depressed, by the loss of his car keys. Once the keys are found, the person immediately returns to his normal state of thinking, feeling, and acting.

A *trait* is a long-standing tendency to react in a particular way to a set of circumstances. A trait is fixed and resistant to change. This is how a person has acted for years. A person may feel frightened of social interaction. She fears doing something to embarrass or humiliate herself in a group. This tendency may be persistent.

Personality disorders are patterns of inflexible and maladaptive traits that cause significant impairment. These patterns are not time-limited; they are chronic. Personality disorders become evident by late adolescence and often last throughout life. The symptoms of personality disorder can be relieved. The patient can learn how to function better and more comfortably.

## The Antisocial Personality

■

### The Impulsive Temperament

You will see many antisocial personality disorders in your career. There is a higher incidence of this disorder in substance abusers (Khantzian & Treece, 1985; Weiss, Mirin, Griffin, & Michaels, 1988). This personality disorder has at its biological base the tendency to act impulsively. These patients have a diminished capacity to delay or inhibit action, particularly aggressive action (Siever & Davis, 1991; Siever, Llar, & Coccaro, 1985). These patients act too quickly on their feelings. They have a tendency to act before they think. They do not feel the same arousal levels that normal people feel, so they can push the limits further (Eysenck & Eysenck, 1976). These biological tendencies leave these individuals vulnerable to a variety of problems. When most people break the rules, they are afraid of getting caught. Antisocial persons do not feel this fear as much. They have difficulty anticipating the effects of their behavior and learning from the consequences of their past.

### A Disorder of Empathy

Antisocial patients do not feel normal empathy. They can break the rules of society to get their own way. They can openly defy authority and break the law without suffering much guilt or remorse. They do not feel at fault, and have a tendency to blame others. They lack insight and fail to learn from past experience. This is easy to understand. If they don't feel responsible for their actions, why should they change?

Antisocial patients begin to get into trouble with society by their early teens. They are in trouble at home, at school, and often with the police. As they grow older, they are unable to sustain work, and they fail to conform to the social norms with respect to lawful behavior. This is one of the most difficult disorders to treat. They can spend more time trying to outwit the staff than working through the program.

### How to Treat Antisocial Personality

Treatment for these patients revolves around teaching them the consequences of their behavior. They need to stop blaming others and accept the responsibility for their own actions. They must see how their choices lead directly to painful consequences. At every opportunity, the counselor needs to show them how their decisions and actions got them into trouble. They will love to argue the point so they can place the blame on someone else, but you are not going to allow them to do this. You are constantly going to direct them to see the truth.

You may hear these kinds of statements from a patient with an antisocial personality:

"I didn't know that was a rule."

"She didn't explain it properly to me."

"He did it. I didn't do it."

"I was just standing there. What are you looking at me for?"

These patients are used to lying their way out of everything. They need to keep a daily log of their honesty and work hard at learning from their behavior. Each time they do something wrong, take them aside and take them through the behavior chain. Cover the trigger, thoughts, feelings, actions, and consequences carefully. They need to see their patterns over and over again.

Working with the antisocial personality can be a frustrating experience, but these patients can do well in recovery. They will need a lot of structure in early sobriety. A halfway house or some other facility can be helpful in those first few months out of treatment.

These patients have little self-discipline and they have poor impulse control. They will all need to work though each of these problems in treatment. They need to stop, think, and plan before they act. This will be learned only with practice. They need to learn to stick to a task until it is completed. The contracts in treatment give them an opportunity to learn this new skill. They are notorious for procrastinating on their work or just doing barely enough to get by. The group will have to reject these poorly done contracts, and put up with the patient's anger, to show the patient what is required. Sobriety necessitates a long-standing commitment.

*How to Deal With a Rule Violation*

You need to be familiar with the rules of your facility. Antisocial atients will push the limits and they will argue that they are right. If they can find a way around a rule, they will break the rule. Rather than being totally negative, this provides the staff with an opportunity to intervene and teach the patient. The patients need to see what is causing their pain. The rules do not exist to keep them from having a good time; rules exist to keep them safe. They need to practice turning things over to their Higher Power rather than trying to manipulate everything.

If antisocial patients are caught breaking a rule, have them write a report on the incident and present it to the group. This is not intended to shame them but rather to help them see the consequences of their behavior. The group encourages and supports them in trying to bring their antisocial behaviors under control. The group and the counselor should constantly reinforce prosocial behavior.

Learning empathy and appropriate guilt is a difficult skill. The patient will do most of this work in group. When someone in the group is having a strong feeling the antisocial patients can be asked to relate to the feeling. Have they ever felt in a similar way? They try to match their experience with the feeling of the other person. If they can match the feelings, empathy will begin to develop.

When antisocial patients take advantage of someone in treatment (this is inevitable), they need to see the other person's pain. Take them through the behavior chain that revolved around the incident.

*Moral Development* | Moral development occurs in stages:

1. It's right as long as I can get away with it.
   (No rules)
2. It's right if it's within the law.
   (Rules outside of self)
3. It's right because I believe it's right.
   (Rules internalized)

The antisocial patient is stuck in the first stage of moral development. A spiritual program can do wonders for antisocial patients. If they can see that God is there and watching, they can begin to develop some external control.

Cognitive therapy is helpful with these patients but they must learn to be honest. Sometimes they will deny or hide what they are thinking to prevent reprisals. It is very important for these patients to know that you understand them and do not blame them for their antisocial thinking. Patients need to feel that they can share their antisocial thoughts and acts with you. Patients must never be shamed for their thinking. They are held accountable only for their actions.

It is very easy to get into a bad-guy role with antisocial patients. They may feel like you are pushing them around or being unnecessarily controlling. They want you to be the problem. That is why the rules and the consequences of breaking the rules needs to be very clear from the outset. Then when the patient breaks a rule, all you have to say is, "It's not me doing this to you, it's you doing this to yourself. You knew the rule and you broke it. There is a consequence for that. I hope that next time you will think before you act."

*How to Deal With the Family* | The family of an antisocial patient is usually in chronic distress. They need to be educated in how the patient manipulates them. Communication patterns need to be improved. The family must hold such patients accountable for their actions. This means allowing them to suffer the consequences. This means no more enabling.

Antisocial patients are not used to being loved and they are often suspicious of someone who tries to get close to them. They wonder what you are really after. They look for the hidden motive. Once they see you consistently act in their behalf, even when they are being difficult, they will begin to come around. The worst thing you can do with such patients is to get angry with them constantly. This is playing their game, and they know it better than you do. They are used to dealing with people's anger. They know just how to manipulate this situation, and they'll just blame you.

If you establish a good therapeutic alliance, there will come a time when the antisocial patient will want to please you. This gives you great power as a reinforcer. By carefully selecting when to give positive reinforcement, you can effectively shape the patient's behavior. A day without a violation of the rules should be soundly reinforced, perhaps by congratulating the patient in front of the staff or the patient population. A day without a lie is cause for celebration. The more positive attention you can give such patients for prosocial behavior, the further along they will be in their treatment program.

**The Borderline Patient**

The biological component of borderline personality disorder is a tendency to act impulsively plus affective instability. The affective instability is a rapidly changing affect, often overly reactive to emotional stimulation (Siever et al., 1985; Siever & Davis, 1991). These patients have marked shifts in their feelings when they encounter environmental stimuli, such as separation, criticism, or frustration. This emotional shift can be quick and extreme; it rarely lasts more than a few hours. It is common for the borderline patients to attempt to control these affective shifts with chemicals (Widiger & Frances, 1989). These patients grow up immature and unstable. They experience their feelings as being outside of their own control, controlled by environmental events. The environment becomes a major regulator of self-esteem and well-being. The boundaries between the patients and their environment become blurred (Siever et al., 1985).

*Interpersonal Relationships*

When borderline patients sense a supportive relationship with another person, a counselor, a staff, or a loved one, they feel uncomfortable. At first they adopt an engaging, clinging, overdependent style of relating. When the relationship is threatened, whether real or imagined, the patient shifts to angry manipulation. They may become self-destructive to regain control. The clinging dependency is rapidly replaced by devaluation of the goodness and worth of the other person (Gunderson & Zanarine, 1987).

Borderline patients will throw temper tantrums and will attempt to set one staff member against another. They tend to split people into all good or all bad. This split often occurs with the same person. At times, this person is the best, and at other times, the worst.

*Affective Dysregulation*

Borderline patients have extreme feeling shifts and they act impulsively on their feelings. They repeatedly become involved in self-destructive behaviors. They have chronic abandonment fears. They have a difficult time distinguishing who they are at any point in time. They usually have attempted to hurt themselves, and they tend to become involved in dangerous activities like shoplifting, sex, substance abuse, and reckless driving. They lack a life plan. They chronically feel empty and bored.

*How to Treat Borderline Patients*

Borderline patients bring all of this psychopathology into the treatment program. They can act out of control and they can be disruptive. You must provide a stable framework in which they can grow. They are emotionally immature and unstable. They will try your patience and push the limits of their relationship with you.

You must remain alert and active in their treatment. They need a lot of direction and input. They need to be confronted on their maladaptive behavior as soon as possible. Use the group if the patient is not under control. Patients need to identify the feelings and motivations behind their acting out. Often this comes as a shock to them. Self-destructive behavior will lose its savor if you draw the patient's attention to the consequences. They need to get real about what they are doing and what happens when they do it. They always seem to be in a mess, and they rarely feel the problem is their fault. They need to see how their behavior affects what happens.

*Setting Limits*

Treatment centers around setting limits, learning impulse control, and developing skills for dealing with feelings. The staff will have to keep up on this patient to make sure the patient doesn't set one staff member against another. Often patients will feel that one staff member is the enemy and someone else is their most trusted friend. Without staffing this patient, two staff members can end up in confrontation with each other. In such a situation, the staff needs to bring the patient in during staffing. Here everyone can get the same story at the same time.

*Dealing With Transference*    Transference and countertransference can be a real problem with these patients. They seem to have a way of creating strong feelings and relationships in the staff. You may end up feeling angry, guilty, or frustrated. You may feel helpless. At first these patients may see you as their savior and then their persecutor. It feels like an emotional roller coaster ride. It is common for some to see the patient as a poor little thing who just needs nurturing, and some of the staff to see the patient as an angry manipulator who needs limits. Consultation with other members of the staff is essential. This will keep you in balance. This is the patient's problem, not yours. Borderline patients can form overly intense relationships with their counselor. You need to carefully maintain your boundaries. Do not become overly involved. Don't do anything for the borderline patient that you wouldn't normally do for someone else.

*Coping With the Intense Feelings*    When borderline patients are feeling uncomfortable, they need to do something. They need a specific plan of action when they have strong feelings. They can exercise, talk to someone, turn it over to their Higher Power, become involved in something else, go to a meeting, read recovery material, and so on. They should not always talk to you when they are upset—this fosters dependency. It is notorious for borderlines to say they have to talk to you, right now! You need to teach them that they can't always come to you, and you can't always be there for them. They need to develop other coping skills.

Cognitive therapy is important. The patient needs to be able to see a person's good and bad qualities at the same time. When the patient is extremely angry at someone, help them see the person's positive characteristics. Borderlines would rather be joined in attacking someone, but you must encourage them to look for the good. They need to see themselves and others more realistically. Cognitive therapy will help them to uncover their unconscious thoughts and motivations. They need to see why they feel and act the way they do. What are they after? How can they get what they want more appropriately?

*Dealing With the Family*    Two family issues may be important with the borderline. The family may be overinvolved and need to let go, or they may have a history of abuse or neglect. Both of these issues need further counseling than you can provide in an inpatient program. This will need long-term psychotherapy. You can just help the family get started. The family must be referred to make sure they address the problems in continuing care. Borderline patients often have clinging dependency needs or extreme anger at their family members.

Everyone in the patient's family needs to be educated about the patient's diagnosis and become actively involved in treatment. They will be relieved to know that there is an illness called borderline personality disorder and to understand the signs and symptoms. Most family members will be amazed that other people have this disease.

Behaviorally, the patients need to work through the Impulse Control Exercise (Appendix 16), the Relationship Skills Exercise (Appendix 12), and the Communication Skills Exercise (Appendix 14). They need to practice these skills with their treatment peers. They need to rehearse and role-play problem situations in interpersonal group.

Borderline patients are a challenge for you and the staff. They take a lot of energy. It is important to remember that these patients have an illness; they did not ask for their disease, nor did they create it themselves. They are frantic for love and affection with no idea about how to get it. They should work through the Love, Trust, and Commitment Exercise (Appendix 10) to help them to understand exactly what love is. They need to practice establishing relationships without unrealistic expectations.

Patients will need to be referred to outpatient psychotherapy in continuing care. They may need the structure of a halfway house or some other long-term facility. Long-term involvement with AA/NA is very beneficial for these patients. They can learn to function reasonably well over the years.

## The Narcissistic Patient

Narcissistic patients can be difficult to deal with emotionally. They have a grandiose sense of their own self-importance. They feel as if they are the ruler of the Earth, and that everyone has to treat them as if they are special. They think they have special talents, beauty, power, or abilities. If you do not treat them in a special way, they get mad and reject you, destroying the therapeutic alliance. It is very difficult for them to hear the truth about themselves because they cannot tolerate criticism. They are excessively sensitive to having any flaw. When they are confronted with a problem they have, they tend to dissolve into shame and worthlessness. Then they become extremely angry and resentful, given over to what is called narcissistic rage. Narcissistic patients do not need to learn anything from you; they know everything already. They tell everyone else what to do.

These patients spend a lot of time with big plans and schemes for unlimited success or power. They want to rule over others rather than be one of the common people. They believe that they deserve to be treated special, due to their outstanding achievements, brilliance, beauty, or ability. They feel that only the special people of the world, those of a similar high caliber, can understand them. They think they should interact only with the beautiful people.

It is very easy to countertransfer with these patients and get angry, but if you do, you will destroy your therapeutic alliance, and they will think of you as inadequate. The best way to treat these patients is as if they really are the ruler. If you treat them as if they are the ruler, and you are the servant, you will come a long way toward getting them to listen. They often need to see that you are special too, with special powers and abilities—after all, only the greatest professional could help them. Once they see that you are wonderful, you can then show them that you have faults, you make some mistakes. If you can both agree that you are both wonderful, but both of you have made some mistakes, you have come a long way.

Give these patients the Narcissism Exercise (Appendix 34), which helps them learn about their narcissistic traits. The most important thing for narcissistic patients to do is get honest with themselves and others. After they do that, they need to turn their will and their lives over to the Higher Power. This is very difficult for them to do because they have been playing God for a long time.

Narcissistic patients grew up the king or queen of their household. They were in control. Their every whim was met. One of their primary caregivers was a servant doting on their every word, loving them, telling them that they were wonderful. The adults in the home used this child to build their own inadequate self-esteem. If my child is wonderful, then I am wonderful.

Narcissistic patients are interpersonally exploitative because they are interested only in their own needs. They are not capable of understanding how the other person feels. Their relationships start off in a blaze of glory but end in despair. A high relapse trigger for them is sex, and they often fall in love in treatment. They can become convinced that any new relationship, no matter how bad it may seem to others, is going to be ideal, wonderful. It's as if they are blind to the truth and make the same mistakes over and over again. They need love and attention so much that when they get it, they tend to idealize the other person, and this sets the relationship up to fail.

A narcissistic patient needs to spend time developing empathy for others. In group, when someone is having a feeling, have the narcissistic patient try to connect the other patient's feeling.

Most of the time, you will end up disappointing a narcissistic patient. You will not be empathic in the right way, in the right amount, or at the right time, and they will ultimately decide that you are not enough for them. It always ends up this way, every relationship. That is why the Higher Power concept is the only one what works. God is the one that can be enough. God is always available. God has all the power. God is smart enough. When you feel the patient's disappointment, carefully explain the ABCs of Alcoholics Anonymous:

A. That we were alcoholic and could not manage our own lives.
B. That probably no human power could have removed our alcoholism.
C. That God could and would if He were sought.

When narcissistic patients see that no one can meet their needs except God, things can change. It is to be hoped that they will begin a genuine search for their Higher Power.

## The Anxious Patient
■

Anxiety is a vague generalized fear. Some children are born with a nervous system that is more sensitive than others (Kagan, 1989; Kagan, Reznik, & Gibbon, 1987; Kagan, Reznik, & Snidman, 1987). This increased physiologic responsivity can heighten the sensation of unpleasant experience. These children have a low threshold for subjective fear and high arousal in anticipation of adverse consequences (Siever & Davis, 1991). Children with such heightened responses to the environment can become shy and inhibited. It takes less of an adverse experience to upset them (Rosenbaum, Biederman, Hirschfeld, Bolduc, & Chaloff, 1991).

Anxious patients are afraid but they are not sure why. These individuals are hypervigilant and tense. They look for the impending disaster. They feel the ax is falling. They feel a sense of dread and impending doom. Most of these patients are avoidant. They avoid social situations. They feel uncomfortable in groups and fear doing something that will humiliate them.

There is a high percentage of anxiety disorders in patients that end up abusing central nervous system depressants (Dorus et al., 1987; Hesselbrock et al., 1985). Patients attempt to reduce their anxious feelings with drugs that suppress central activity.

*How to Measure Anxiety*

Anxiety can be tested with a variety of psychological tests or rating scales similar to the Beck Depression Inventory (Beck, 1978). The test scores will help you determine the effectiveness of your treatment. The Self-Rating Anxiety Scale (Zung, 1971), the Hamilton Anxiety Rating Scale (Hamilton, 1959), or the State Trait Anxiety Inventory (Spelberger, 1983) can be used to measure anxiety. The tests are simple and can be given as often as necessary.

Multiple somatic complaints accompany anxiety. Patients may feel sweaty palms, a pounding heart, trembling, light-headed, dizzy, or numb. They may feel their life is threatened. They may think they are having a heart attack. The anxiety may go on for a few minutes, or it may last most of the day.

Certain nonaddictive medications can suppress or block certain forms of anxiety. Panic disorder is virtually eliminated with certain antidepressant medication. Feel relieved when the doctor orders medications for your patient. The physician can be trusted to treat the patient appropriately with medication.

Outside of the chemical dependency field, anxiety is often treated with benzodiazepines. These central nervous system depressants are contraindicated in chemically dependent persons because they can be highly addictive. Patients who come into chemical dependency treatment taking these drugs will have to be withdrawn.

*The Psychological Component of Anxiety*

The psychological part of anxiety disorders centers around an inaccurate perception of threat. This threat can be real or imagined, but it is exaggerated to the point that it interferes with normal functioning. To patients, all fears are real. The intensity of the fear prepares them to escape a dangerous situation. Patients can be immobilized by fear. They can freeze and be unable to move. This is no joke, and you will get nowhere pretending this patient has nothing to worry about. You must try to relate to, and understand, the intense fear the patient is feeling. Patients can be intensely afraid of spiders, even if there are no spiders. They can be terrified of a group, even if there is no logical reason to be afraid. These patients need gentle support and encouragement. They need to feel that someone understands them.

There are many forms of anxiety disorders and the feared objects are incredibly variable, but you can approach all anxiety in the same general way. You need to know the following things about the anxious patient:

1. What is the patient is afraid of?
2. Where does the fear seem to come from?
3. Is the fear accurate or inaccurate?
4. What can the patient do to reduce the fear?

Anxiety disorders are not character disorders. Patients with character disorders blame everyone else for everything; in anxiety disorders, the patients blame themselves for everything.

*How to Use Relaxation Techniques*

Anxious patients need to learn how to relax. They can't be anxious and relaxed at the same time; the two physiological states are incompatible. They will have to be taught how to relax using relaxation techniques. There are many relaxation tapes on the market. You can use relaxing music, sounds of nature, or imagery. Get a few tapes and have the patient listen to a relaxation exercise twice a day. You can take a patient through a relaxation exercise yourself by doing the following exercise.

Make sure you will not be interrupted. Have the patient sit or lie down in a quiet comfortable place. Read these words in a quiet slow voice.

> Close your eyes and pay attention to your breathing. Feel the cool air coming in and the warm air going out. As you focus your attention on your breathing, feel yourself beginning to relax. There is no right way or wrong way to do this exercise; there is just your way. Feel your self becoming calm. Your arms and legs are feeling more heavy. Inside of your mind, as completely as you can, in your own way, see ocean waves. Don't worry about how you are seeing these waves, just see them as completely as you can. Match the waves with your breathing. As the wave builds, you inhale, and as the wave washes ashore, you exhale. See yourself standing on an island, on a white sandy beach, looking at the waves. You are feeling at peace. With each breath and each wave you feel more relaxed. It is warm and you can feel the sunshine on your cheeks and on your arms. You are on an island. This is your island inside of your own mind. You are safe here. There is no one else on the island except you. There are palm trees on the island and lush green vegetation. There is a trail on the island, and you turn, and see yourself take that trail. You are not in a hurry. You have a plenty of time. You are walking slowly. There are flowers of every imaginable color and hue along the trail. You begin to walk up a hill, and as you walk up the hill, you become tired. Your arms and legs feel heavy. You come to a ridge that over looks a lush green valley filled with water-falls. You wander for as long as you like in this valley feeling at peace.

You can add any other relaxing scene to modify this exercise. When patients have been relaxing for 10 to 20 minutes, you need to bring them out of the state of relaxation. Say something like this:

> You walk out of the valley and down the trail. You walk back on the beach and watch the waves. They build and wash on the shore. You feel yourself becoming more awake and aware of yourself. You wiggle your toes and fingers. You feel yourself in this room and in your chair. Your eyelids begin to flicker. When you feel comfortable, open your eyes and become fully awake.

While patients are relaxed, you can give them some positive affirmations. They are a good person. They have talents. They have a Higher Power. They have people who support them. How they feel is important. They are going to take care of themselves. They are going to commit themselves to being honest. The patient should help you develop these positive self-statements. Use this exercise to build a more positive self-image.

*The Daily Log* | Patients will need to score the level of relaxation after each exercise from 1, as little as possible, to 100, as much as possible. They also need to keep log of their daily anxiety using the same scale. Patients score their general anxiety level at the end of each day. Patients should log any situation that caused or exacerbated their anxiety. This, plus the psychological testing, will give you a good idea of where the patient is in working through the program.

*Cognitive Therapy* | The patient needs to see you in individual sessions at least twice a week. You will take the anxious situations and go through the same cognitive therapy suggested for depression. Patients can be asked to read *Coping With Anxiety and Panic* by Beck and Emery (1979) or *Panic Attacks: How to Cope, How to Recover* by Greenberg and Beck (1987) to introduce them to the cognitive techniques. These pamphlets can be ordered from the Foundation for Cognitive Therapy, 133 South 36th Street, Room 602, Philadelphia, PA 19104.

Anxious patients often exaggerate the level of threat by inaccurately perceiving and judging the situation. They can do this in a lot of different ways. They may make any of the following cognitive distortions:

1. Catastrophize
   "I'm going to pass out."
   "I'm going crazy."
   "I'm losing control."

2. Exaggerate
   "This is the worst thing that could happen."
   "I fail at everything."
   "I'll make a fool of myself."

3. Ignore the positive
   "They hate me."
   "Nobody likes me."

Each of the patient's inaccurate thoughts needs to be challenged for accuracy. Patients will need to keep track of their automatic thinking while in treatment. You can't just do this for a few days; cognitive therapy takes weeks of concentrated effort.

If it is medically possible, patients need to exercise for 20 minutes once a day at a training heart rate (220 minus age times .75). They may have to build up to this level of fitness. The exercise will burn off excess stress hormones the patients are producing. They will be more relaxed for the 24 hours following the exercise.

Patients need to understand what triggers their anxiety and prepare for anxious moments with accurate thinking and relaxation techniques. They must learn that they can cope with anxiety using the tools of recovery. They are not going to die or go crazy from anxiety. They need to slow the anxiety cycle by stopping and thinking when they feel anxious. "What am I thinking? Is it accurate?" Then they replace negative thinking with positive thinking. At any time, they can use a relaxation technique to block the anxious symptoms.

*Panic Attacks* | If patients come to you when they are having a panic attack, you need to be calm and reassuring. Have them look at you and slow their breathing. Slow, deep breaths. Then begin one of your relaxation techniques to distract patients from their feelings. Tell them the anxiety will pass. You may want to take them on a walk and have them look at the scenery, at the blue sky, the clouds. You may have them contact their Higher Power and have the Higher Power begin to fill them with peace. Have them float in their anxiety and go with it. Reassure them that nothing bad is going to happen, that you are going to stay with them until they feel comfortable.

Patients will need to practice distracting themselves when feeling anxious. They can notice some fine details in the room or in the environment. They can look for styles of clothing or shoes. They can read something or estimate the cost of things. They need to develop a simple coping imagery, like a trip to the beach, to replace the fearful thoughts. The coping fantasy can be any relaxing situation where the patient feels comfortable and in control.

Anxious patients are usually easy to work with. They are frightened, but they are responsible individuals. They are willing to do almost anything to get better. These patients need a lot of love. It will be hard for them to accept your rewards—they often don't feel worth it—but you should give reinforcers lavishly. When they feel praised by their treatment peers, for their work in group, it is a triumph.

## The Psychotic Patient

Psychotic patients persistently evaluate reality mistakenly. They have disturbances in cognitive/perceptual organization. They are unable to perceive important incoming stimuli, process this information in relation to past experience, and select appropriate responses (Siever & Davis, 1991). This mistaken evaluation of experience results in tenacious false beliefs (Klein, Gittelman, Quitkin, & Rifkin, 1980). If you walked into a restaurant and a person turned around and looked at you, you wouldn't think much about it. But a psychotic patient might mistakenly evaluate this situation and think: "That person is after me." This mistaken evaluation has the force of reality and it results in distorted conclusions. "The mob sent that person to kill me."

*Hallucinations and Delusions* | Psychosis is characterized by hallucinations and delusions. *Hallucinations* are false perceptions. They can seem to come from any sense organ. Patients may hear voices, see visions, have a strange taste or smell, or feel something unusual on or under their skin. To the psychotic patient, these false perceptions are as real as reality itself.

*Delusions* are false beliefs that are intractable to logic. Patients may believe that they are being watched by someone, that they have strange or unusual powers, or that one of the organs in their body isn't operating properly. No rational argument will deter them from this irrational belief. Some patients have social or cultural beliefs that seem odd, but if these occur in a normal social context, they are not considered psychotic. For example, someone may believe that they have the power to read minds, but they have been trained culturally to believe this. *Psychosis* is a persistent mistaken perception of reality that is not accounted for by social indoctrination or normal life experiences.

All psychotic states are due to an abnormal condition of the brain. Chronic disorders, such as schizophrenia, schizoid personality disorder, and schizotypical personality disorder seem to result from a core vulnerability expressed in a relative detachment from the environment, often with defects in reality testing. This seems due to inherited neurointegrative dysfunction. These individuals do not develop normal interpersonal relationships; they lack empathy and a sense of connectedness. Their relationships are shallow and not satisfying (Siever et al., 1989).

Acute organic brain syndromes, including intoxication and withdrawal, can produce psychotic symptoms. Many other psychiatric conditions, such as schizophrenia and major depression, can create psychosis. Acute organic brain syndrome must be ruled out first because it can be life-threatening. Psychosis can be transient, as in some forms of acute alcohol withdrawal, or it can be chronic, as in some forms of schizophrenia.

## How to Treat the Psychotic Patient

In the psychotic patient, there is a mix of psychotic and real perception being evaluated. Your job is to respond to, and reinforce, the healthy side of the patient. Rarely will you respond to a psychotic statement, other than to reassure the patients, and point out reality to them. Even in the most florid psychotic states, patients have some hold on reality, and they do remember what happened. The environment of a patient having active hallucinations needs to be reduced to its lowest level of stimulation. A quiet room, without radio or TV, is best. Keep calm yourself, there is no reason for you to be afraid. A conversation with a psychotic patient might go something like this:

The patient, Mary, is lying in her bed, covers drawn up to her chest. She is looking at the walls with a freightened look on her face. The counselor walks over and sits in a chair beside the bed.

*Counselor:* How you doing, Mary?

*Mary:* Okay, I guess. . . . I keep seeing colors. The walls seem to be moving, like they're breathing.

*Counselor:* That's withdrawal, Mary. We're treating you for that. It will pass, just hang in there.

*Mary:* And I see spiders on the wall.

*Counselor:* I know that seems real to you, but the bugs are not real. They are coming from the withdrawal. There are no spiders on the wall.

*Mary:* But I see them.

*Counselor:* It seems real, doesn't it? Shows you how tricky the mind can be. You're going to be feeling a lot better soon. I'm proud of you for coming into treatment. That took a lot of courage.

*Mary:* Thanks.

*Counselor:* Can you tell me a little bit about your drinking?

The counselor didn't try to prove to the patient that there were no spiders. He just told the patient the truth and reassured her. Then he began to get some history of the patient's problems.

There may be patients who will have psychotic symptoms throughout treatment. These patients may need to be treated with antipsychotic medications that are the mainstay of the treatment for psychosis. The psychotic symptoms will probably gradually decrease in intensity over time. The hallucinations will go first, with the delusions gradually decreasing over the next several months. Some of the delusional material may be persistent, lasting for years or even the patient's entire life. Once these beliefs are set, they are very tenacious.

Don't allow psychotic symptoms to trouble the other patients. Psychotic patients are rarely dangerous. For the most part, you can ignore the symptoms in group. If they do come up, a frank explanation may be necessary. The other patients will understand as long as they know there is nothing to be frightened of. The group can be helpful in assisting the patient to test reality and to gain social skills.

Diseases such as schizophrenia or mania can be difficult to manage. Patients who are not in good control will need to be transferred to a more structured psychiatric facility. The psychotic patients that you work with will, for the most part, be having mild perceptual and thought disturbances. It is useless to argue with a patient about their delusional material. These beliefs are well defended and intractable. For the most part, you will reassure, support, and try to lead them through your program.

Many psychotic patients will have an unusual affect. The range of affect may be flat or they may have a general strange feel to them. They may have little or no motivation. You can help patients with flat affect to identify and use their feelings. Motivation can be improved by having the patient do many small tasks that can be separately reinforced. Don't set patients up to fail by asking them to do something that is too difficult for them.

These patients usually need social skills training. They may have to be taught how to sit, walk, talk, smile, and use eye contact. They may have to learn what is appropriate and what is not an appropriate conversation. They may need to practice communication skills and interpersonal relationship skills.

Patients who are chronically mentally ill will need help in becoming acquainted with community resources. They need to be referred to the appropriate agencies for follow-up. Social, vocational, and housing needs will all have to be appropriately addressed.

Insight-oriented therapy, or therapy that is highly confrontive, is contraindicated with these patients. If painful material is uncovered, the psychotic symptoms may worsen. With these patients it is best to stay with the here and now.

Patients will need to learn problem-solving skills in treatment, and they will need to practice these skills. They need to identify the problem, consider the options, plan their actions, and carry out the plan. Patients should check the problem later to see if their plan has been successful.

*The Family* | The family will have to meet with the staff to be educated about the patient's disease. The psychologist or psychiatrist should do this because they know more about the psychopathology. If you don't have anyone on staff who has this expertise, you may need to refer the patient to an outside agency. The family is important in preventing a relapse with these patients. Families that are emotionally unstable will increase the patient's chance of relapse (Brown, Monck, & Castain, 1962). The family needs to be educated to keep criticism and overinvolvement to a minimum.

The great healer in any good treatment program is love. You can actively care for and respond to these patients even though they make you feel a little uncomfortable. They are just people who have a difficult disorder. They need all of the love and encouragement that you can give them. It is incredibly rewarding to see these people improve.

## Acquired Immune Deficiency Syndrome (AIDS)

Some patients in need of treatment for chemical dependency will have Acquired Immunodeficiency Syndrome (AIDS), AIDS-Related Complex (ARC), or will test positive for HTLV-III antibodies. Needle sharing among intravenous drug users places them at high risk for contacting this disease. AIDS can affect the central nervous system, and it can affect thinking, feeling, and behavior, even in the absence of other symptoms (Gabel, Barnard, Norko, & O'Connell, 1986; Perry & Jacobsen, 1986). Patients with AIDS can develop a psychosis characterized by delusions, hallucinations, bizarre behavior, affective disturbances, and mild memory or cognitive impairment. The cause of this psychosis is yet to be established (Harris, Jeste, Gleghorn, & Sewell, 1991).

Approximately 30% of all AIDS cases are intravenous drug users. They are the second leading risk group for infection for transmission of the disease in the adult heterosexual population (Centers for Disease Control, 1990).

More than one third of AIDS patients develop symptoms of AIDS dementia complex. This organic brain disease may complicate the diagnosis and treatment of chemically dependent individuals because of the complicated cognitive, emotional, and behavioral changes that can occur. The course of AIDS-related dementia is variable. Early signs and symptoms may be subtle. AIDS dementia complex generally progresses to severe global impairment within months. Depression and psychosis are frequent complications (Perry & Jacobsen, 1986).

### High-Risk Patients

All high-risk patients—homosexuals, intravenous drug users, and sexual partners of high-risk individuals—should be routinely screened for HIV infection, particularly if they present with signs of organic or psychotic impairment, fever, or weight loss. Informed consent should be obtained before testing. Patients who are seropositive without active symptoms of AIDS can be safely taken through the program.

AIDS patients will have special issues revolving around their disease. Uncertainty of diagnosis, guilt about the previous lifestyle, fear of death, exposure of lifestyle, changes in self-esteem, and alienation from family and friends all can be important elements in treatment. The catastrophic nature of this illness will have to be dealt with on an individual basis. If possible, the patient needs to be referred to a facility that specifically deals with AIDS for continuing care.

The American Medical Society on Alcoholism and Other Drug Dependencies (AIDS and Chemical Dependency Committee, 1988) recommends that treatment be provided for these patients. Patients need to be assessed on a case-by-case basis and referred for follow-up by a physician familiar with AIDS. All staff members should be educated with the latest AIDS-related data. Patients with AIDS do *not* require isolation techniques any different from patients with active Hepatitis B. Hepatitis B precautions should be carefully followed. Caps, gloves, masks, and other kinds of protective wear are *not* necessary in routine contact, for example, blood pressure checks and group therapy. The principle of confidentiality is particularly important to protect these patients (AIDS and Chemical Dependency Committee, 1988).

## Patients With Low Intellectual Functioning

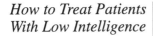

Patients with low intellectual functioning have defects in learning and in adaptive skills. Most of these patients will have below average to borderline intelligence. You will occasionally see someone in the mildly mentally retarded range. Intelligence below this is not amenable to the normal treatment program.

### *How to Treat Patients With Low Intelligence*

Some of these patients will need a specialized treatment plan. These patients have difficulty with abstract reasoning. Their program will have to be tangible and concrete. Many of them will have deficiencies in social skills that will need remediation.

*Abstract thought* is complicated. To have normal abstract thought, patients must easily shift from one aspect of a situation to another, keeping in mind simultaneous aspects of the situation. They must be able to grasp how the parts fit into a whole. They must be able to separate the parts, and put them back together again mentally. Patients with good abstract thought can plan ahead and think in complex symbols.

*Concrete thought* is immediate and tangible. It is set in the current situation without the ability to generalize to other situations. Use of complex symbols or the ability to see all of the parts is not possible. The ability to effectively plan and understand complicated issues is impaired.

### *Patients Who Can't Read*

Some of these patients cannot read or do the written exercises. Most of the reading material in the AA/NA program is written at a sixth-grade level. Patients with reading levels two or more grades below this are going to have difficulty. The psychologist can help you determine the extent of these problems and can give you advice on how to present the program. If patients can read a little, they should be encouraged to do so. The encouragement and praise they receive will more than offset minor problems.

If the patients cannot read, the program will have to be presented to them in oral form. They can watch videos and listen to AA/NA material on tape. Every treatment center has audiovisual material around for just such a purpose. Such patients will need more individual attention and additional support in group. Some of the group sessions will be over their head, and that's okay as long as they are getting the basic program. The program can be made simple enough for most anyone to follow.

You will have to do a lot of repeating with these patients, and you need to keep asking them to repeat what you said. This is the only way to be sure they understand. Many of these patients learn to be great head-nodders when they don't understand. If they can repeat the program to you, they are learning it. Give them a few key phrases to learn by heart. Check on them from time to time to see if they are learning the phrase and understanding what it means. "Don't drink. Go to meetings. Turn it over (to the Higher Power)."

These patients may need occupational rehabilitation in continuing care. They may qualify for locally supported programs. They may need a halfway house or other structured facility in continuing care. The Division of Vocational Rehabilitation is an excellent program for many of these patients.

*The Family*

The family of the person with low intelligence may not know of their loved one's disability. They will need to be informed about the patient's liabilities.

These patients can be some of the best AA/NA members. They can be fiercely loyal and consistent. They are often willing to do jobs that other members find distasteful. It is very reinforcing to watch them bond with the group and find a place for themselves.

## The Elderly Patient

Most counselors do not realize how prevalent addiction is among the elderly in the world. A recent study revealed that substance abuse was the third-ranked mental disorder in a large geriatric mental health population (Reifler, Raskind, & Kethley, 1982). The elderly are vulnerable to becoming addicted to a variety of over-the-counter drugs or their prescription medications, and they tend to take a variety of medications without proper medical supervision. Any medication or illicit drug tends to have more effect in the elderly than in a younger person. Drugs usually have one third more power in an older individual for a variety of physiological factors. There appears to be no age-related change in liver detoxification, but there is a decline in brain cells that results in higher concentration of alcohol and other substances. With normal aging, there is a decline in extracellular and intracellular fluid and an increase in body fat that result in a greater effect of many drugs on the central nervous system (Gambert, 1992).

Elderly patients have often outlived their psychosocial support system. Their spouse may have died, or be incapacitated, and the children may be unable to care for them. Loss of family and friends, coupled with retirement, loss of job, and self-esteem, may lead the elderly patient into a depressive state where substances can ease the pain. A study at the Mayo Clinic's inpatient alcohol unit found that 44% of elderly patients were compromised organically from chronic alcohol or drug use, but they went through treatment effectively and there was no difference in treatment outcome (Morse, 1994). Only 10% of elderly patients have a dementia that is serious enough to hamper their participation in a recovery program. Many patients suffer from mild cognitive defects, including impairment of orientation, concentration, short-term memory recall, or abstract thinking.

Atkinson and Kofed (1984) found a number of risk factors that contributed to the vulnerability of the elderly to substance abuse. Biological sensitivity to chemicals, loneliness, pain, insomnia, depression, and grief all were predisposing factors.

Symptoms of substance abuse are often overlooked in the elderly in medical settings, because they suffer from multiple pathological conditions. Changes in cognition or behavior may be blamed on an illness or on old age rather than on substance abuse.

For a variety of reasons, the elderly may start drinking heavily after they retire. They have more time on their hands and drinking or drug use can easily become a habit, using relatively small amounts of substances. It is most common for these patients to drink or use alone. Like any addict, there is a strong desire for patients to hide their use. This may be easy to do when they live alone and have no one to check on them periodically.

The good thing about recovery is it gives patients a new family. They do not have to live alone anymore. The patients can use their support group to reestablish social connections and develop new leisure activities. They develop a sense of belonging by helping other addicts, and this improves their self-worth. This gives elderly patients who are often ready to die a reason to live. Such patients have to know that their recovery group needs them. God trained them in addiction, they have grown wise over the years, and now they need to heal. They can do this by going to meetings and sharing their experience, strength, and hope. It might take a while before they realize this truth. The best way to have them learn it is to have them help someone in treatment. They can help someone go through detox or someone earlier in recovery. Once they see that their lives have meaning and worth for others, they are on the road to recovery.

## Patients With Early Childhood Trauma

Many chemically dependent patients have been raised in severely dysfunctional families, and some of them have been abused as children. For the most part, you need to leave severe early childhood trauma for treatment later in the recovery. The patients will need to maintain a stable recovery before they tackle the intense pain of these issues. To immerse themselves too deeply in the old trauma now is not appropriate.

If patients disclose abuse in individual sessions or in group, they need to be supported. They need to hear that it wasn't their fault. Little children are not responsible for what adults do. If the patient who discloses the abuse is an adolescent, the situation will have to be reported to the proper authorities. This is to protect the child from further harm. Do not do this without consulting with the clinical staff and carefully documenting it in the patient's record.

### How to Deal With Sexual Abuse

If the patient is stuck in treatment because of this pain, it will have to be addressed to relieve the pressure. This is a clinical decision. If patients are too vulnerable for this issue, they will feel anxious, and you will feel uneasy yourself. If you can, transfer this issue to the psychiatrist or psychologist. You may have to refer the patient to an outside mental health professional. Patients with posttraumatic stress disorder from childhood trauma will need to reexperience the trauma in a safe environment. They will need to tell their story many times. Detail is important. The story needs to include the events before, during, and after the trauma. Therapy begins with a safe relationship with the therapist.

A patient may decompensate when this material comes out. If the staff is loving and supportive, this shouldn't last long. The patient may experience feelings of derealization or depersonalization. This can be frightening to an unskilled counselor. If at any time you feel over your head, stop and get the help of someone more experienced.

Sexual abuse is not a topic for most groups. The material is too disturbing and explosive. These matters need to be addressed in individual sessions. Events such as rape and insults to self-esteem and security are particularly likely to cause long-term problems. The more extreme and long-lasting the trauma, the more likely the events are to cause psychological damage.

Such patients ultimately need to see the past event in a new context, and to attempt to forgive themselves and the offender. The patients are no longer children, and these things are unlikely to happen again. They now have power and control that they didn't have before. They will need to see themselves as competent and capable of handling stressful situations now. You can be a role model for them and help them develop skills for getting themselves out of trouble. "If that happened to you now, at your present age, what would you do?" The patients learn that they can take care of themselves.

People involved in traumatic events often become anxious when they have to deal with a similar situation in their current life situation. A spouse who was sexually abused as a child may feel frightened or numb when called on to perform sexually in her marriage. This patient may need some of the techniques you used with the anxious patient.

## Cognitive Therapy

Cognitive techniques are necessary to correct the negative self-talk of these patients. They often call themselves bad or evil in their own thinking. They think that no one will like them because they have been bad. This negative self-talk will have to be exchanged for positive affirmation.

Patients will need to develop trust. The Love, Trust, and Commitment Exercise (Appendix 10) is a good one for them to start with. First they need to reestablish a trusting relationship with themselves and then with you. This trust can ultimately be transferred to the group. Patients need to be encouraged to see their new support group as the healthy home they never had. The home group will be there for them when they need them. The group has a stable set of rules that don't change.

Patients need to learn interpersonal relationship skills and to practice these skills with their treatment peers. They need to work on honesty. The cocoon of individual therapy is important here, and patients must know that they can trust you. You need to be consistent and nonjudgmental. You need to be honest about how you feel about the abuse issues.

## How to Learn Forgiveness

As patients develop a good spiritual program, they need to try to forgive the perpetrator. By seeing the abuser as spiritually sick, they are relieved of some of the anger and the feeling of responsibility. When patients are ready, they can be encouraged to pray for the perpetrator. They can turn the judgment over to the perfect judge. God will judge all humankind. The judgment will be perfect because God sees into everyone's heart.

Small steps in trust will be beneficial with such patients. You may find them sharing their abuse with another patient who has had a similar experience. The Fifth Step is tremendously beneficial for these patients. If the step is done properly, they will feel relieved of the guilt and rage.

**Love in the
Treatment Center**

■

"I found out from another patient that he liked me. After that it preoccupied my mind. I jumped ahead and thought of marriage with this guy, and I didn't even know him. It was hard to concentrate on the lectures, or the steps, because I couldn't wait for us to have a break so I could be with him. He told me how violent he was, but that didn't faze me. I thought he was changing. The staff talked to me about it, and that started me to think, to realize it was wrong, but I needed to have a man in my life."

These thoughts and feelings are all too familiar. Two patients, in that fragile first few weeks of sobriety, have become romantically involved. These patients can lose the focus of treatment. They do not respond well to the interventions of the staff who are trying to get them to see the mistake they are making. They are in love and to them it is real. It is difficult for these patients to realize that what they are feeling is not love at all, that the intense feelings that they are experiencing are sexual. In their passion for each other they are confused; it feels like love, it feels like the real thing, it's heaven, it's the answer to what they have been looking for. They came into treatment feeling totally worthless and unimportant, and this other person has restored their sense of value. They have been made whole again. These patients do not realize that they are particularly vulnerable to such feelings in early sobriety. Feelings that were deadened by chemicals before treatment, are just beginning to blossom new and untested. Their whole treatment program is at stake.

One patient described the consequences of love in the treatment center like this:

"After treatment, we had sex right away and it all went downhill from there fast. He got too jealous. I was totally bending over backward for him, buying him cigarettes and pop. Even when I told him I only wanted to be friends, he wanted me back. He got drunk and threatened to kill me, so I went back with him for a while. I finally got the courage to tell him the truth. When he finally left, I felt so guilty."

*The Importance
of Unit Rules*

It is wise for treatment programs to develop a set of unit rules that discourage these relationships. The rule that only three or more patients may pair off together at any one time is a valuable one. Then if the staff sees two patients pairing off, they can intervene.

*How to Deal With
Patients in Love*

The first intervention attempted should be individual counseling with each patient. These sessions should focus on educating the patients about what love is and what it is not. Patients can explore these readings with you and use this opportunity to learn and grow in treatment. They must be helped to see the reality of the situation. With assistance, the situation can be seen accurately. Is this really the best time for romance? Is this the partner you want to spend the rest of your life with? What is his or her history? The patient and counselor must carefully collect all the evidence possible; they must get accurate information and explore all the options available. What's going on? Why? What do you hope to gain? What does it mean to you? Can you get your needs met another way? Do you see the danger? What is love? What are romance and sexual attraction? How do they differ? How are they alike?

The complexities of the feelings and motivations must be thoroughly explored. The dangers of this relationship, at this time, must be emphasized and addressed.

Disciplinary action may become necessary to prevent further problems. Considerable clinical skill is necessary here. Transference and countertransference issues may arise. Patients may resist your attempt to end a relationship that they see as beneficial. The staff must be sensitive to how in love these patients feel. Disapproving looks and derogatory comments will tend to intensify the feelings and draw the patients closer together.

The next intervention you may need is conjoint counseling. Here the relationship can be addressed with both parties at the same time. If the patients have separate counselors, both counselors should be involved in this session. The patients should be warned that they are placing each other's treatment at risk. It is not loving to risk someone else's sobriety. If the problem persists, it becomes an issue for group. Now everyone's treatment is threatened and the patient population needs to respond. If the group can't stop it, transfer of one patient to another facility, or dismissal from treatment, become viable options.

Love in the treatment center is a crisis that all patients can grow from. They can learn more about themselves. They can learn more about how to develop healthy relationships and the challenges that will confront them in sobriety. They must be encouraged to focus on their own recovery. They need to concentrate on loving themselves.

CHAPTER
TEN | # Adolescent Treatment

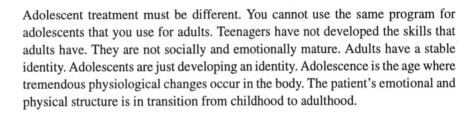

Adolescent treatment must be different. You cannot use the same program for adolescents that you use for adults. Teenagers have not developed the skills that adults have. They are not socially and emotionally mature. Adults have a stable identity. Adolescents are just developing an identity. Adolescence is the age where tremendous physiological changes occur in the body. The patient's emotional and physical structure is in transition from childhood to adulthood.

## The Normal Adolescent

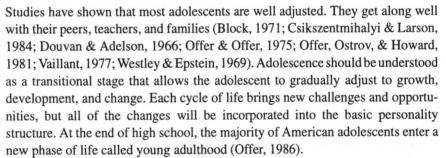

Studies have shown that most adolescents are well adjusted. They get along well with their peers, teachers, and families (Block, 1971; Csikszentmihalyi & Larson, 1984; Douvan & Adelson, 1966; Offer & Offer, 1975; Offer, Ostrov, & Howard, 1981; Vaillant, 1977; Westley & Epstein, 1969). Adolescence should be understood as a transitional stage that allows the adolescent to gradually adjust to growth, development, and change. Each cycle of life brings new challenges and opportunities, but all of the changes will be incorporated into the basic personality structure. At the end of high school, the majority of American adolescents enter a new phase of life called young adulthood (Offer, 1986).

Normal adolescents do not feel inferior to others. They do not feel that other people treat them badly. They feel relaxed. They believe that they can control themselves and they have confidence that they can handle novel situations. They feel proud of their body image and physical development. They feel strong and healthy. They have embraced the work ethic. They feel good when they do a good job. They are not afraid of their sexuality, and they like the recent changes in their bodies. They do not perceive any major problems between themselves and their parents. They are hopeful about the future, and they feel like they will be a success. They do not feel like they have major problems (Offer, 1986).

There are three alternative routes through normal adolescence. Twenty-three percent of adolescents develop continuously through adolescence, 35% show developmental spurts, alternating between periods of some conflict and turmoil, and 21% experience more severe turmoil (Offer & Offer, 1975).

These three groups have been labeled the continuous growth group, the surgent growth group, and the tumultuous growth group. The continuous group is characterized by excellent genetic and environmental backgrounds. They have strong egos, and are able to cope well with internal and external stimuli. They have mastered previous developmental stages without serious problems. They accept social norms and feel comfortable in society at large. The adolescents in the surgent growth group are different in that their genetic and environmental backgrounds are not as free of problems and traumas. Both of these groups are free of adolescent turmoil, and they make up 80% of the adolescent population (Offer, 1986).

*Ages 13 to 16*

The ages 13 to 16 bring an enormous change in physical and psychological development. Throughout adolescence, girls remain about 2 years ahead of boys in their level of maturity. Some adolescents bloom early, and some bloom late, each having a different psychological challenge. Early bloomers may be expected to perform with individuals of their size, whereas late bloomers suffer from the problems of self-esteem that result from looking more immature than their peers.

Adolescents of this age group experience a great deal of ambivalence and conflict and they often blame the outside world for their discomfort. As they struggle to develop their own identity, dependence on parents gives way to a new dependence on peers. Adolescents struggle to avoid dependence and may disparage their parents, devaluing past attachments. These early teens often find a new ego ideal that leads to idealization of sports figures or entertainers. Adolescents at this state are particularly vulnerable to people they would love to emulate.

The development of a self-concept is crucial at this stage. The adolescent must explore his or her own morals and values, questioning the accepted ways of society and family to gain a sense of self. They make up their own mind as to who they are and what they believe in. They must reassess the facts that were accepted during childhood, and accept, reject, or modify these societal norms as their own. The here-and-now thinking of earlier childhood gives way to a new capacity for abstract thought. These adolescents may spend long periods abstractly contemplating the "meaning of life" and "Who am I?"

*Ages 16 to 19*

In our culture, we expect a gradual development of independence and self-identity by the age of 19. The physical manifestations of approaching adulthood require numerous psychological adjustments, in particular the development of how one views self in relation to others. The vast majority of adolescents attain their adult size and physical characteristics by the age of 18, and the earlier differences between early and late bloomers are no longer evident. The process of abstract thinking changes along with physical development, becoming more complex and refined. Late adolescents are less bound by concrete thinking. A sense of time emerges where the individual can recognize the difference between past, present, and future. They can adopt a future orientation that leads to the capacity to delay gratification. The individual develops a sense of equality with adults.

Self-certainty and an internal structure develop while teens experiment with different roles. By age 19, most adolescents are considering occupational choices and have begun to develop intimate relationships (Weedman, 1992).

## The Chemically Dependent Adolescent

■

The tumultuous group of adolescents consists of 20% of the population. These adolescents come from family backgrounds that are not stable. There is often a history of mental illness in the family; the parents have marital conflicts; and the families have more economic difficulties. The moods of these adolescents are not stable and they are more prone to depression. They have significantly more psychiatric disturbances, and they do well only with the aid of intense psychotherapy. They do not grow out of it (Masterson & Costello, 1980; Offer, 1986). These figures parallel the percentage of mental illness found in adult populations (Freedman, 1984). It is in the tumultuous growth group that chemical dependency often develops.

In this country the average first use of mood-altering chemicals for boys is 11.9 years; for girls, 12.7 years (U.S. Department of Justice, 1983). Adolescents almost always use alcohol or drugs the first time under peer pressure. They want to be accepted and be a part of the group. Children are likely to model after the chemical use of their parents. Children with alcoholic parents are at greater risk of becoming chemically dependent (Spalt, 1979).

The adolescent who continues to use will increase drinking to a regular pattern (usually weekends). They may experiment with other drugs. They begin to use drugs to communicate, to relate, to belong. With regular drinking, tolerance develops. The adolescent needs more of the drug to get intoxicated. Emotional changes may first be noticed by the family. The adolescent may become irritable and more noncommunicative. They may begin to spend more time in their room. They may begin not caring for themselves or others. Polarization of parents and children begins to occur (Morrison & Smith, 1990).

As chemical dependency further develops, the adolescent can no longer trust themselves when using chemicals. The choice to use the drug is no longer available to them, they have to use to feel normal. The continued use of chemicals eliminates the ability to think logically and rationally (Suojanen, 1983). Rationalization, minimization, and denial cut the adolescent off from reality.

Chemically dependent adolescents gradually change their peer group to include drinking and drug-using friends. They begin to use chemicals to block out the pain. They use longer for the euphoric effect. They drink to escape pain. Blackouts and drinking alone are strong indicators of chemical dependency in the adolescent population. With the progression of the disease, family conflicts increase. The adolescent may run away, withdraw, or act out at home and at school. They withdraw from family and community activities. Problems with the police and school officials increase and become serious. The adolescent may become verbally abusive to parents and more rebellious toward authority figures. Life begins to center around alcohol or drugs. Daily use begins and the patient begins to use to maintain rather than to escape. Adolescents make attempts to cut back or quit but they are unable to stay clean and sober. Physical deterioration begins. Hiding and lying about drugs becomes more common. The adolescent feels more intensely isolated and alone. Concern is now openly expressed by parents, teachers, and even peers. Gradually the adolescent loses all self-esteem and depression begins. Persistent chemical use leads to incarceration, institutionalization, or death (Chatlos & Jaffe, 1994; Morrison & Smith, 1990).

Chemical dependency halts emotional development. To develop normally, a person must learn to use their feelings to give them energy and direction for problem solving. When feelings are consistently altered by alcohol or drugs, this is no longer possible. The major coping skill of the chemically dependent person is chemical use.

Adolescent chemical dependency can occur extremely quickly, within weeks, because the child's emotional development is immature. Adolescents don't have the internal structure to bring themselves and their lives under control. They cannot delay the onset of chemical dependency for years like adults can.

## The Adolescent Chemical Dependency Counselor

Working with adolescents can be some of the most rewarding work in the field. By making an early intervention in this person's life, you can save them years of misery. Adolescents can be frustrating, but to see someone blossom forth from a hurting child to someone who can laugh, is a wonderful thing to watch. Just being a part of their recovery will make you feel good about yourself.

Becoming an adolescent counselor is not for everybody. These patients have a lot of energy and the counselor has to tolerate a certain amount of disorder without feeling uncomfortable. The counselor must be able to withstand people challenging them face to face and toe to toe. The adolescent counselor has to have good impulse control. If you have a weak spot, these patients will find out what it is and use it against you. They are expert manipulators. It is normal for them to want to manipulate you and the system.

Adolescents almost never decide to come into treatment on their own. They are most often forced into treatment by someone else, their parents or the court. Most of their homes are extremely dysfunctional and many have chemically dependent parents. These patients come into treatment angry and resistant. Where most adults are ready to surrender, most adolescents are ready to fight. The staff must be willing to endure this initial resistance. Patients will gradually change their attitudes about chemicals as they process more of the facts.

Adolescents are not frightened by the physical consequences of chemical dependency like most adults are. It does little good to threaten them with talk about chemical dependency being a deadly disease. Adolescents need more time before they will listen to this information. They tend to think they are invincible to physical problems.

Adolescents are resistant to the initial part of the program and they need more structure in treatment. This allows the patient to learn self-discipline and social responsibility. A good way to add structure is to develop a system of levels, listed in Appendix 23, where patients move up in rank as they progress through the program. At each level change, they earn increased freedom and responsibility. A point system can be used in conjunction with the level system to increase the structure. In the point system, the patients earn points for working the program and lose points for resisting. Points can be given for a clean room, neat appearance, level of commitment, participation in group, completion of exercises, positive interaction with treatment peers, and so on. Whether you have a level system or a point system depends on your patient population. More rebellious adolescents will need more structure (Davidson & Seidman, 1974; Phillips, 1968).

## The Point System

With a point system, patients earn privileges as they accumulate points. They can earn telephone calls, soft drinks, free time, visits from guests, TV or radio time, snacks, and so forth. They lose points for breaking the rules. Each center needs to develop their own point or level system specific for their patient population. Each treatment center will be different and the systems will have to be constantly revised and updated. Various point systems, sometimes called token economies, have been developed for these purposes (Cohen & Filipczak, 1971; Phillips, 1968).

A level system is sufficient for most adolescent programs, but if you need more structure, a point system can be added (Herbert, 1982; Lynch & Ollendick, 1977; Wolf, Phillips, & Fixsen, 1975). In the point system, the patients earn points for each goal they complete during the day. Points can be given or taken away as the staff desires. For example, patients will be required to keep their rooms clean. They will be given points for completing this goal or lose points for failing to complete the goal. They can earn or lose 10 points per day for keeping a clean room. They can be scored on participation in group, or on commitment to treatment. If 10 behaviors are scored, patients can earn up to 100 points per day.

The staff must make sure that most reinforcers are positive. The patient turns in points for positive reinforcers, candy, TV time, or trips to the recreation room. The patient can earn greater privileges by saving points. A "fun" video, for example, might cost 75 points. A telephone call to a friend, 200 points. This teaches the patient self-discipline and how to delay gratification. Patients with serious conduct disorders need this kind of structure (Graziano & Mooney, 1984; Herbert, 1982; Ollendick & Cerny, 1981).

A point system adds structure because it gives the staff more controls over reinforcers. This tends to shape behavior more quickly. Token reinforcement programs for adolescent patients have existed for a long time and have a proven track record. If you want further information about such a point system, check the following references: Cohen, Filipczak, and Bis (1965); Davidson and Seidman (1974); and Phillips (1968).

## The Primary Elements in Adolescent Treatment

■

The most important thing that occurs in adolescent treatment is the change in perceptions, attitudes, and behaviors that revolve around addictive chemicals. The patients must come to realize that they have a problem, come to understand the problem, and develop tools of recovery. Adolescents must be habilitated rather than rehabilitated. They have never developed the skills necessary to live a normal, sober lifestyle. They need to learn these skills for the first time. They must stop using chemicals so they can grow and mature normally. Healthy role models are essential to this process. The staff on any adolescent unit must show the patients how to deal with problems. Patients further along in the program will also model coping skills. Patients must be shown how to treat each other with respect at all times.

### The Rules

Adolescents will constantly test the rules and each staff member. The staff must rigidly adhere to the rules of the treatment center. It is a manipulation for adolescents to try to get special privileges from you. If they can get you to bend a rule, even a little, they've got you right where they want you. Your rules don't mean anything if they can be manipulated.

### Communication Skills

Adolescents need to focus on developing communication skills. They need to practice identifying their feelings and sharing their feelings with their treatment peers. They must practice telling each other the truth. As they develop new skills, they can transfer this behavior to the family.

As open communication begins, the patients build trust. They usually transfer trust from the treatment peers, to the counselor, to the parents, in that order. Mutual respect is necessary and the patients must see that you are positive about the treatment. A positive attitude will take you a long way with these patients.

It is important for you to know that adolescents aren't acting out to hurt you personally. They are not mad at you; they are just mad at their lives. Most of their anger is transferred from the family and environment from which they came. If they act out, you must provide the structure of a consequence. Don't hesitate to give these consequences—they are learning tools. Explain to the adolescent that it's not you who is doing this to them—they are doing this to themselves. They knew the rule and they broke it.

It is normal for these adolescents to push the limits and break the rules. They will try to manipulate their environment just as they did at home and at school. This is all they know how to do. You can't blame them for using the old skills that have worked for them. Treatment will teach them what is wrong with the old skills and it will teach them new skills to get what they want more appropriately.

*Honesty* | Lying is a good example of an old behavior. Adolescents have learned how to lie to get their way. They lie to get out of trouble. They lie to get what they want. This works for them, at least to some degree, and the lying increases. As the lying grows, they feel more lonely and isolated. What they don't understand, and what they need to learn, is that lying and loneliness are directly connected; one causes the other. If you lie, you will be lonely. Most adolescents don't understand this, but they will learn it with education. Once they learn why they are telling the truth, they will be motivated to be honest.

Adolescents need to practice honesty. Just because they understand the principle doesn't mean the behavior changes. They must practice it over and over again. They need to experience the natural rewards that come when they use a new skill. As the patient sets up natural reinforcers, the behavior will ultimately become automatic.

*Exercise* | Adolescents need a challenging exercise program. They need to exercise at a training heart rate at least once a day. They need to be actively involved in sports and other athletic events. Weight training and jogging are excellent accompaniments to any program. These are exercises where the adolescents can see their gains and feel good about it.

*Fun in Sobriety* | Adolescents need to learn how to have fun in sobriety. One of the things that they are worried about is they won't be fun if they stop using drugs and alcohol. They don't want to be boring to their friends. They need to see that they can feel good without chemicals. The only way to do this is to take the patients out on recreational activities and have them experience first hand that they can still enjoy themselves. Trips to the zoo, an amusement park, a dance, a movie, a pizza or ice cream parlor, a video arcade, all can be used to show the adolescents that they can still have fun in sobriety.

*The Reinforcers* | Adolescents are very concerned about how they look and how they get along with others socially. If you are searching for a reinforcer, you can always hook into one of these. Adolescents want to be loved, desperately, no matter what they say. These children are starving for genuine love, compassion, help, attention, encouragement, and praise. They need someone to listen to them, and they need a chance to prove what they can do. Most of these patients feel like a failure in the real world, and they are mad about it. They are mad at themselves and they are mad at everyone else. They have felt overwhelmed by their dysfunctional home situation. Many of these children come from homes of severe abuse and neglect. They have been beaten down by society and many of them have given up. You will see these patients flourish in an environment of love. You will see the real child blossom forth. It is a beautiful thing to watch.

*Spirituality* | Adolescents have more difficulty with spirituality than adults. Most of them still have their health, and they are not as ready to surrender. They need to be shown that there is a God, and God is there for them. This takes a spiritual program of action rather than of words. You need to seek a clergy person with particular skills in working with adolescents. The patients should trust this person and not feel intimidated by them. The patients need to explore spirituality actively in spirituality group. The best way to hook adolescents into God is to have them directly experience God's presence. This is done using the imagery exercise we previously discussed.

Some of the adolescents will resist God but they cannot deny their own experience. Some of these patients have been involved in Satanism and it takes a great deal of skill to get them to a place where they can be open to a Higher Power. The best therapist here is often another peer. Peers have a way of trusting each other about this sensitive issue. Adolescents will explore spirituality if they don't feel like they will be shamed by their peers. A peer further along in the program is an excellent model.

*Group Therapy* | Group therapy with adolescents is different. The level of sharing at first is more shallow. Adolescents are inexperienced with their deeper feelings. They don't have the skills necessary to share openly. They feel just as deeply as adults, but most of them have never practiced communicating their feelings. Early attempts to share feel clumsy and awkward and the adolescent fears being humiliated in group. Once older members of the group begin sharing, the way is paved for new members. Role-playing works well for adolescents. They do not feel as vulnerable when playing a role. They can role-play drug refusal situations or parent-child conflicts.

Adolescents need to be active in group. If they are not talking, they need to be doing something else that is constructive to treatment. You can hold denial court, for example, for those patients who remain in denial. This is an active group, the adolescents enjoy and benefit from the experience. In denial court, the patients divide up and play the roles of defense attorney, prosecuting attorney, judge, and jury. The patient who is in denial is called to the stand and is examined and cross-examined by the attorneys. The patient tries to prove to the court that he or she is not chemically dependent. The group holds a trial and reaches a verdict.

The patients can act out the thoughts that exist inside of someone's head at certain decision points. One patient can pretend to be the illness, while another pretends to be the healthy side. The two sides try to get the adolescent in question to behave in certain ways. The three—the illness, the healthy side, and the person—can be placed in a variety of situations to see how all sides respond. Use your creativity and come up with group exercises. What you are after is active participation by all of the group members. Once the group starts talking, let them go, with only occasional guidance from time to time. The best treatment will be between the patients further along in the program and those just coming in. Once they get the hang of it, the adolescents will enjoy group. It draws them closer together. They feel supported, listened to, and understood. They lose that sense of separateness that has haunted them all their lives.

*Peer Pressure*

Peer pressure is vitally important to adolescents, and they can easily be swayed to use drugs by their peer group. Peer pressure comes in two forms: being in a social situation where chemicals are available, and being actively encouraged to use chemicals by a friend. The adolescents need to spend a lot of time role-playing drug refusal exercises. They need to practice exactly how are they going to say no. Most of the adolescents will need to work through the Peer Pressure Exercise (Appendix 24). Sometimes the adolescents will attempt to gang up on the staff because of something that happens between a staff member and a patient. In one way, this is a good sign because the group begins to function together. This process should be encouraged, and the staff should listen carefully to the complaint. Try to compromise and reach a decision that is agreed on by all. The center's rules must not be broken or manipulated in the process, but the situation can be explored to determine exactly what happened and who is responsible. This can be a difficult process, but once the whole truth comes out, it will be clear where the patients or the staff went wrong. Everyone makes mistakes and Step Ten says, "when we were wrong we promptly admitted it" (*Alcoholics Anonymous,* 1976, p. 59). This goes for the staff as well as for the patients. It is a great learning experience for the patients to see the staff struggle to be fair and impartial. It's not easy.

*Continuing Education*

Continuing education is necessary for adolescents, even those who have dropped out of school. They should have a thorough educational assessment, including an examination of school records, and psychological testing. From these data, the school teacher develops an individual plan for educating the patient. Some patients will need intensive remedial work, and some can continue regular, assigned schoolwork. School is an excellent opportunity to develop self-discipline. Patients need to determine what they want from further education, and they need to help develop a plan for reaching their goals. Do not allow patients to slough off school because they are dropouts. Quitting is old behavior. All adolescents need continuing education.

*Continuing Care*

Continuing care is essential for adolescent patients. They do not have the internal structure necessary to stick to a recovery program on their own. Just going to meetings is not enough. Adolescents need to move from an inpatient program into an extensive aftercare program. This will necessitate the patients' coming in for aftercare as often as needed to keep them in stable recovery. The content of the aftercare program must be individualized. Some patients will need a daily aftercare program; most will need at least three aftercare sessions per week. The aftercare program should continue to teach the tools of recovery plus show the patients that they can have fun in sobriety. The group needs to go on outings and do fun things together. They can attend things like concerts, zoo, park, games, dances, and so on. This establishes a new peer group and solidifies recovery.

*The Parents' Support Group*

As the adolescent is going through treatment, the parents attend at least two groups per week; again, this is individualized and based on the needs of the family. All parents attend a parents' support group, and a weekly conjoint session with the patient. The parents' support group encourages the parents, supports them emotionally, and teaches them the tools of recovery. This is a twelve-step group. The family concentrates on working the steps, developing healthy communication skills, and learning a behavior program to follow in aftercare.

*The Behavioral Contract*

The Behavioral Contract (Appendix 25) is the primary method by which the patient and the family hold each other accountable for their actions. The contract is necessary to show the patient and the family that they can function together in an atmosphere of mutual support. A point system will be necessary for more seriously disturbed adolescents. All parents need to be taught behavioral contracting and the point system.

Using the approach of Alexander and Parsons (1973), the parents negotiate a behavior contract with their adolescent. The contracts are jointly developed by the patient, the counselor, and the family. The family is taught how to negotiate future contracts on their own. The benefit of behavioral contracting has been widely confirmed by a variety of studies (Alexander, 1974; Sanders & Glynn, 1981; Wells & Forehand, 1981, 1984).

If the adolescent is a more serious behavior problem, the parents will need to develop a point system. All parents will need intensive training and practice in this procedure before the child comes home. The training is divided into three phases. In the first phase, the parents are taught basic social learning concepts (Patterson, 1977; Patterson & Guillion, 1976). In the second phase, they are taught how to define, track, and record deviant and prosocial behaviors. In the third phase, they learn how to develop a point system where the adolescent earns or loses points contingent on positive and negative behaviors. Points are exchanged *daily* for rewards previously selected by the child. The parents are taught to use positive social reinforcers (smiles, pats on the back, and so on) for appropriate behaviors and time-out procedures for inappropriate behavior. The counselor must work closely with the parents, particularly early on following discharge. Daily phone calls may be necessary to make sure the parents are following the program. The parents and the patient need to attend aftercare for at least 6 months following treatment. Some will attend for years, depending on their specific needs.

*Phases of Adolescent Treatment*

Adolescent treatment seems to go in phases. When the adolescents come into treatment, most of them are angry. This may be expressed overtly or covertly. They may be overly aggressive toward the staff or they may be quiet and sulk. This defiant period is a good indication that the patients have been out of control. They are attempting to use old skills to bring order to a new situation.

In a week or two, the adolescents will begin to comply with the staff, but they still have not begun to internalize the program. They have learned how to get along in treatment, but they don't think they have a problem, and they are planning to go back to their old behavior when they leave treatment.

As the adolescents begin to feel the genuine love of the staff and the group, they begin to take a real look at themselves. They see the negative consequences of their chemical use. They realize that they don't want to go on living like that. This is positive movement and it depends primarily on trusting others. Many of these patients have never trusted anyone, but as they open up to the group and continue to be accepted, they soften. When they behave at their worst and the staff still sticks with them, a light comes on. The adolescents, who came into treatment defiant and trusting no one, begin to reach out to others. They feel loved and understood for the first time in their lives.

As trust develops, denial becomes more evident. The patients begin to see the truth. They are encouraged to transfer this trust of the group, to trust of their new AA/NA group. Many adolescent patients hate group when they come into treatment, but in time, they like it. It's the only time in their lives when people have dealt with real feelings. The patients are encouraged to see their new AA/NA group as a healthy family. In this family, the patient can grow and develop normally. The goal is to stay involved with AA or NA for life.

CHAPTR
ELEVEN

# The Family Program

The purpose of the family program is to begin to heal the many wounds caused by chemical dependency and to improve the patient's recovery environment. A family system that has been altered by chemical dependency may reinforce addiction. Frequently, it is a family crisis that brings the patient into treatment, and including the family in the treatment program increases the chances that the patient will engage in treatment.

You should carefully evaluate the patient's social system and move it toward being supportive of recovery. If anyone in the family needs long-term intervention, it is your job to refer him or her to the appropriate professionals.

If the family is not supportive, you intervene with education and counseling to change the attitudes and behaviors that will make the patient's recovery more difficult. It should be obvious that patients will do better in recovery when they are supported by their family.

Each primary relationship needs to be examined carefully. You should send each significant person the Family Questionnaire (Appendix 26). This will give you a good idea of how the family members are functioning and explores what they think about the patient and his or her chemical dependency.

By the end of the family program, you should know how each person is functioning and how the family is functioning as a unit. You need to gather enough data to show you how the family is coping with its environment. Many families will need financial aid or therapy of some sort in continuing care.

**The First Contact**

The patient's family should be contacted within the first few hours of the patient's admission. Once you have met the patient, you need to meet the family, either in person or over the phone. You need to speak to them and light a spark of hope about recovery. The family will be relieved to have the patient in treatment but they will feel frightened that treatment won't work. Don't give them unrealistic expectations, but reassure them that the patient is safe and has a new opportunity

173

to recover. The family members should be immediately encouraged to begin attending Al-Anon meetings. Give them a list of meetings in their area and stress that they need some support right now. The best place to feel understood is with people who are in recovery.

## How to Handle Early AMA Risk

The family must be warned that the patient may attempt to leave treatment early against the advice of the staff. It is not uncommon for the patient to want to go home after the first few hours in treatment.

You want to reduce the possibility that patients will call the family and have someone come and pick them up. You need to make it clear that this is very common, and it is to be expected in early recovery. It is not a matter of concern as long as it is handled properly. Tell the family to say a firm no, along with some gentle encouragement. That is usually enough to keep the patient in treatment. If the patient is a serious AMA (Against Medical Advice) risk, you may have to plan an in-house intervention with the family. Some patients come into treatment not yet ready to surrender to the disease.

The family may have a lot to tell you over the phone, but you want them to save this information for the forms you will be sending them. The first contact with them is to reduce fear and to support their decision for treatment. The forms take the history of the problem and give the family members an opportunity to provide input into the treatment process.

## The Family Process

No one can grow up in an alcoholic family, or live in one, without its changing them. People in a chemically dependent home live in a whirlwind. They grasp at anything that will help them to regain control. Their environment has been totally out of control for a long time. They don't know what is going to happen next. They can't predict anything or trust anyone. They desire, more than anything, to achieve stability in the family.

### Codependency

A codependent person is obsessed with controlling the person that is out of control (Beattie, 1987; Weinhold & Weinhold, 1989). Chemical dependency adversely affects everyone in the home. Codependents, adult children of alcoholics, children of alcoholics, are some of the names given to these suffering persons.

These people have been seriously damaged by chemical dependency. They have learned to live in a chemically dependent world, and this takes certain maladaptive skills. They learn to stuff their feelings, never ask for what they want, and to keep secrets. They focus their lives totally on the chemically dependent person. They don't have time for themselves and their own needs.

Codependents are as blinded and reality-distorted as the chemically dependent person. They do not think about their own problems because their own problems are too painful. They would rather think about someone else. Their whole lives revolve around the sick person. Codependents become so obsessed with helping and controlling the other person that they lose the ability to think. They cannot see reality. Over the years, in what would be an unbearable situation for most, they have developed an incredible tolerance for neglect and abuse. They keep thinking that if they just do enough, if they figure it out, everything will work out.

*Guilt* | Often family members feel incredible guilt. They think that they are at fault. The chemically dependent person keeps denying responsibility, and someone must be held accountable, so the family members often take the blame. The spouse may feel that everything would be okay if he or she could be the right kind of a husband or wife.

These people attempt to control their out-of-control environment in any way they can think of. They whine, wheedle, threaten, cry, moan, seek counseling (for themselves), manipulate, and lie. Each attempt at control works, to some degree, and it is kept tucked away in the behavioral repertoire to be used later.

The wife might start calling her husband to make sure he got to work. She feels responsible that he get to work on time, and her anxiety builds as the time approaches for him to be there. The little boy of the family may try to do extra good in school in hopes that the drinking or drug use will stop. The child is anxious because he feels a direct relationship between his grades and the family problems. Family members will go to incredible lengths to control the chemical dependency. They pour out bottles, they threaten using friends, they scold, argue, cry, get depressed, get anxious, go to church, talk to the boss, make excuses. They chase drinking or using friends away from the house. They talk to the family physician or their clergy person trying to get support.

*Loss of Control* | As more and more energy is expended in trying to control someone else, the family loses contact with themselves. They become so involved in the addicted person that they forget who they are. They do not know what they want. They do not know how they feel. They cannot ask for what they want. They cannot share how they feel. This leaves their interpersonal relationships unstable and unfulfilled. They cannot use their real feelings to solve problems; therefore, their problems escalate until they are out of control. They are on a treadmill, frantically trying to keep the family together.

*Shame* | Codependency is deeply rooted in the feeling of shame. The family members feel that something is wrong with them. The family is in such a mess because they aren't doing enough, they aren't working hard enough or long enough. If they could just figure this whole thing out, things would be better. They are battered and beaten. They keep trying but they keep failing. They can never keep up with the increasing nightmare.

*Caretaking* | Family members of addicted persons learn to be caretakers. They are obsessed with taking care of the chemically dependent person. In their frantic attempt to take care of someone else, they lose contact with their own needs. In group they will be able to tell you how the chemically dependent person is feeling, but they will be unable to tell you how they are feeling. Their whole life is caught up in taking care of the other person. This happens to divert the family member from feeling the pain in their lives. In the groups, you must redirect the family member to stop concentrating on the other person and to explore his or her own pain.

*Enabling* | The family will have a long history of making excuses for the chemically dependent person. They have been protecting the addicted individual from facing the severity of the problem. They help the addicted individual get out of trouble. They will all lie because they are ashamed of the reality of their family life.

Children will lie to friends, the spouse will call the boss, the father or mother will make excuses, the siblings will pretend that nothing is wrong. Enabling is the major way the family protects itself from the reality of the situation. If they don't enable, they fear their world will collapse. The truth is, they are living with an addictive individual, their lives are out of control, but they keep the family from falling into disaster by shoring up the situation.

Family members must realize that they have kept the illness alive by protecting the chemically dependent individual from the reality of his or her behavior. By constantly getting that person out of trouble, they keep the addicted individual from learning the truth. To protect themselves, family members allowed the illness to go unchecked. They fed into the denial of the disease.

*Inability to Know Feelings* | People in chemically dependent homes are so separated from reality that they don't know how they feel. Their feelings have been suppressed for so long that all they feel is a numbness. They have let go of the pain and live in a life full of false beliefs. They have learned to keep their feelings hidden because they feared that if they expressed themselves, the drug addict would punish them. It is not unusual to find a family who has been subjected to incredible abuse thinking they feel relatively fine.

*Inability to Know Wants* | These family members do not know what they want. Their lives are centered around the chemically dependent individual. They only know what the addict wants; that is the focus of their attention. Most family members are trying to hold on to their sanity, and to keep themselves and the family from going under. They have no time for the superficial wishes and wants of normal people. They only have vague hopes that everything can be better. They are so used to the broken promises that they don't listen anymore.

*Lack of Trust* | These people have learned to trust no one. They learned that the people they trusted ultimately abandoned them. Therefore, they lie to everyone, parents, friends, brothers, sisters, neighbors, and fellow employees. They tell no one the secret. They never trust that they will be safe and comfortable again. They have had their dreams shattered so often that they are afraid to dream anymore.

*People Pleasing* | Family members of chemically dependent persons learn to be people pleasers. They will do anything to prevent someone from feeling bad. This comes from the attempt to be responsible for other people's pain. If someone is hurting, they feel anxious. The pain is their fault, and they have to do something about it. They feel that their wants and wishes are always secondary to the needs of someone else. They get to the point where they feel guilty when they get anything; someone else may be deprived.

*Feelings of Worthlessness* | These individuals feel worthless. They feel that no one cares about how they feel or about what they want. They feel profoundly inadequate and unlovable. They feel rejected by others. They do not feel that they have a fair chance in life, and somehow they feel that this is fair since it is all their fault anyway. This wouldn't be happening to them if they were a better person. This is all they deserve. This is the best they can get.

*Dependency* | Codependent persons do not trust their own decisions. They feel incapable of dealing with life. Something always goes wrong with their plans. The very thought of leaving the addicted individual terrifies them. They cling to the person. The more they try to control things, the more things slip out of control. They develop a profound sense of inadequacy and indecisiveness that keeps them locked into an intolerable situation.

*Poor Communication Skills* | These family members have poor communication skills. They learned a long time ago the credo of the chemically dependent family: Don't talk and don't feel. These individuals don't talk to their friends or family. They are cut off from everyone. They feel afraid of open communication. If they talked openly, the truth might come out, and the family would be destroyed. They constantly tell other people what they think others want to hear rather than what they themselves really think or feel.

**How to Treat Family Members**

Before reading this section, read the Codependency Exercise (Appendix 27). The exercise will show you basically what the family members need to work on in treatment. It must be emphasized, that each family, and each family member, must be treated individually. No one intervention works for everyone. They will need individually developed treatment plans. No two families are the same.

The first thing the family needs is support. They need to feel listened to and understood. They need to be encouraged to share the reality of their lives. They need to feel like they are in a safe, loving place, where people care about how they feel and will respond to what they want. They are not used to being cared for; they are used to caring for someone else. Some of them will resist any attempt of yours to help them. "I'm fine," they will say. They want you to help their loved one, not them. They have identified that person as the "sick" one.

In treatment, the family will need to realize that they, too, have a problem. Each member of the family will work through the Codependency Exercise. This should open their eyes to what they have been doing that is maladaptive. This exercise gives basic information about codependency and helps family members identify the problems they are having.

These individuals have been living in an addicted world and they are suffering, whether they realize it or not. They have learned skills to survive that are inappropriate for normal living. They will need to examine exactly what they are doing wrong and learn how to do it another way. They need to practice the tools of recovery in the family groups and with the patient.

Many families, or family members, will have to be referred to outside agencies for continuing therapy. They have severe marital and family problems that need further treatment. It is your job to refer them to an appropriate therapist.

The family member needs to understand that they are powerlessness over the disease and their life has been unmanageable. If they think they can still control things, they may try to work the patient's program for them, and that is a setup for relapse. The family members need to admit to the patient that they have a problem, to identify the problem, to understand the problem, and to learn what they are going to do differently.

Some family members come into the program ready to blame the patient for everything. This isn't going to do anybody any good. Chemical dependency is a family disease, everyone is affected, and everyone needs to bear some responsibility. All need to keep the focus on what they can do to make things better. All of the eight core feelings (See Appendix 11) need to be explored. Don't let the family get by with sharing only the feelings they feel comfortable with.

Don't think that you can handle all of the family problems in treatment. All you can do is start them off in the right direction and give them some practice in the tools of recovery. You will see the family members in conjoint sessions. In these sessions, try to get the family members to share the whole truth with each other. If a family member withholds truth or lies, the illness will have a foothold and, just like a cancer, it will grow until it ends in relapse.

All members of the family need to write a letter to the patient stating exactly how they feel and what they want. The patient does the same thing for each family member. The family will read each other these letters in the conjoint sessions. It is from these letters, and from the questionnaires, that you will get a good idea of what needs to be worked on in the conjoint sessions. Only with the whole truth can you help the family move closer to a healthy lifestyle.

The only truth that can be withheld is something that will injure someone. Use your best judgment here. Alcoholics Anonymous says "Made direct amends to such people wherever possible, except when to do so would injure them or others (*Alcoholics Anonymous,* 1976, p. 59). Sometimes a truth is too painful or harmful to the patient or to others to disclose.

After the family member has been involved in the family program long enough to break through initial resistance, they should each be given the Codependency Exercise to complete at home. The family member will then read their answers to the group. As the family members do this, they will begin to bond together, understanding how chemical dependency has affected them.

## The Family Program Schedule

■

The family program in most facilities lasts for one week. This gives the family members enough time to get started in their own recovery. The family group meets separately from the patients for the first few sessions. The family members are oriented into the program and hear several lectures. They learn about the disease concept of chemical dependency, how it affects families, and codependency. The family members need to hear people talk about their problems rather than keep them secret.

The family program members need to share their experience, strength, and hope with each other. A family group, without the patients, should meet at least once a day. Here each member needs to tell his or her story in brief autobiographical form. This helps remove the intense shame and guilt he or she has been feeling. The counselor should continue to educate the family members about chemical dependency and codependency in the groups. The family members need to see how the tools of recovery offer better solutions to their problems.

Many times family members are so beaten up by the disease that it is difficult for them to share. If you wait and extend the silence, they will begin talking. They really want to talk. They have been closed up for a long time, and they long for closeness. These people are people pleasers and they will want to please you. They feel uncomfortable and anxious in extended silence. If you ask a question and remain quiet, someone will get the idea and start sharing. Once the ice is broken, it will become easier for others.

The group needs to be introduced to the Al-Anon program, and should attend an Al-Anon group once a day throughout the family week. It is essential that the family members bond with their new Al-Anon group as quickly as possible. This will happen only with regular attendance at meetings. They should each receive a copy of *One Day at a Time in Al-Anon* or *Alateen: A Day at a Time*. They should be encouraged to begin daily meditation. These books and other literature can be ordered from Al-Anon Family Group Headquarters, Inc., P.O. Box 862, Midtown Station, New York, NY 10018-0862. Samples of literature should be on display in the family program meeting area.

As the family group shares, they will feel understood and supported by the group. Most groups begin to bond after a day or two. Many tears will be shed as they hear each other's stories. Once the group of family members has bonded, the patients can be brought into the group. This must not be done until the family members are supporting each other. The patients have bonded in treatment, and they are supporting each other. The family needs a similar support system. The groups with families and the chemically dependent patients in them will be able to address the problems more fully.

## How to Work With the Family in Group

You can't solve each family problem in these groups. You need to concentrate on the process. Help the family members gain support from each other and eliminate dysfunctional communication skills. You should have each person share and work toward group acceptance. This is the first time in years that these people have had anyone listen to them.

You should not let one family member interrupt, manipulate, or speak for another. You must explain how these techniques are used for control. With group support and encouragement, the patients and their family members will have the opportunity to express themselves fully. Quiet family members, who have been intimidated at home, will find new strength from the group. This group work prepares the family members to flow smoothly into continuing care.

Family members are encouraged to keep a daily journal during the family program. They write down at the end of the day the important things they learned. They write down how they did that day and make plans for what changes they need to make tomorrow. This is their daily inventory. What do they need to do next? How can they be more actively involved in uncovering the truth? This log can be shared periodically in group.

The family members will need to learn and practice healthy communication skills and healthy interpersonal relationship skills. They can work through each of the exercises, just like the patients did. You will develop a mini treatment plan for each family. What does this family need, specifically? The family members need to identify that they have a problem, understand the problem, and learn skills to deal with the problem. They must see that they have problems, or they will not continue to go to aftercare and support groups.

**The Conjoint Session**

Once the family has practiced the tools of recovery for a few days, you will begin to see the family in conjoint sessions. This is where you meet with the family members, and work out a specific recovery plan. You may want to meet with the spouse more regularly, but you need at least one session with the whole family. They all need to hear the plan of recovery and to understand their responsibility. They need to know exactly what they are expected to do. This is a family disease, and everyone will have to do things differently.

In the conjoint sessions, the family members will read the letters they have written. They will share how they feel, and will ask for what they want from each other. They need to understand that they are developing a program of recovery. They are responsible for acting in a manner that is conducive to recovery. All of the problems are not going to be solved right away. First, they each must enter into a personal recovery program. They need to take it one day at a time. They are not going to address all of the problems immediately.

You will occasionally get resistance from the family. Some family members are not willing to cooperate. Some of them are chemically dependent, or they are not interested in recovery. Some individuals have an investment in keeping the patient sick. If the sick person gets well, the family member may fear that their role in the family will be threatened. These people only want to show the family that they are in recovery; they really want things to stay the same. The family needs to see the truth about this dynamic, and the problem needs to be worked through. The person who wants the patient to remain sick cannot see that everyone will be better off in recovery. They are trying to meet their own needs inappropriately. Once they see the truth, you will see these family members turn around. If they continue to deny that this problem even exists, they will continue to be a detriment to recovery.

At the end of the family program, there will be a short grieving process where the family members say good-bye to each other. For the first time in their lives, they have felt unconditionally loved. They don't want to leave this warm supportive atmosphere. If you have encouraged them to seek this support in their outside Al-Anon meetings, this will not be overly difficult, but some pain will be involved. They need to transfer this good feeling to their new support group. All of the family members will need continuing care, and some of them will need further counseling or treatment. This must be arraigned before the family goes home.

To see the family members come into the family program frightened and sad and to see them go out with new hope is a very rewarding experience. The family members will never forget the major role you played in their lives.

CHAPTER
TWELVE | # The Clinical Staff

The staff of any treatment center is the life blood of treatment. A good staff can provide effective treatment anywhere. The clinical staff should have a great deal of respect for each individual member of the staff and should listen carefully to each other. No one staff member is more important than another—all are essential for the recovery program.

A good staff is fun. They enjoy working together and supporting each other in the war against chemical dependency. A good staff laughs a lot. Sometimes you have to laugh to keep the full impact of the disease from getting you down.

Everyone has input into the patient's treatment plan, but each has his or her own area of specialization. Professional boundaries are important and should be respected and guarded. To question another person's skills or decisions when you don't know what these skills are, is silly. If you stay within your own boundaries, the boundaries of the chemical dependency counselor, you will be a lot better off, you will feel better, and you will give better quality treatment. Each person on the staff is an expert in his or her chosen field. Since the staff members are all licensed by their respective boards, you have to assume that they know what they are doing.

**The Physician**

The medical doctor is in charge of all treatment, and has the most training in the total disease process. A physician completes a bachelor's degree in premedicine, 3 or 4 years of advanced medical training, and at least 1 year of internship. Many physicians go on to specialize in one or more areas of medicine. Physicians can have a specialty in addiction, called *addictionology*.

All patients must have a complete medical history and physical examination given by the physician. If you have any questions about any type of physical disease or medical treatment, this is the person to rely on. It is important to establish a professional working relationship with the physician. They are a wealth of information. Do not be intimidated by professionals with advanced degrees, they are just people like you, fallible and human.

The physician will be in close contact with you, particularly if your patient has a medical condition that requires treatment. Close consultation with the physician will prevent you from assuming that behavior caused by an organic disease is a psychological problem.

The physician is in charge of any medication order. If you feel your patient needs pharmacological treatment, you need to tell the physician or nurse. Once you have discussed this issue carefully with the medical staff, your job is over. The physician will examine the patient and make a determination based on clinical judgment. Do not argue with the physician or the nurse about what they are doing, they know more about it than you do. Trust them to do their job.

## The Psychologist/ Psychiatrist

All treatment centers should have a consulting psychologist or psychiatrist. The psychologist/psychiatrist has advanced training in the diagnosis and treatment of mental disorders. A psychiatrist is a medical doctor with 3 years of residency in psychiatry. A psychologist has at least 4 years of graduate training beyond a bachelor's and a master's degree.

Two thirds of chemically dependent patients have a concomitant psychiatric diagnosis (Frances & Franklin, 1988). They have problems such as depression, anxiety, personality disorders, in conjunction with their chemical dependency. Patients will not do well in recovery unless these disorders are treated effectively (Talbott et al., 1988; Woody et al., 1984). It is important to have a professional in your center who can deal with these coexisting problems.

The Joint Commission on Accreditation of American Hospitals requires that all patients in inpatient treatment receive a psychiatric/psychological evaluation. This examination includes a mental status examination, a determination of current and past psychiatric/psychological abnormality, a determination of the degree of danger to self or others, and a brief neuropsychological assessment. It is from this examination that you will learn about any secondary diagnosis and will develop a treatment plan. The psychiatrist or psychologist will tell you what to do. Follow their directions as precisely as you can. Use these professionals as valuable information sources. They understand the development of personality and the forces that motivate behavior. If you are confused by a patient, talk the situation over carefully with them.

## The Nurse

There are two types of nurses, registered nurses and licensed practical nurses. Registered nurses complete a registered nurse's degree from an accredited institution. Most go on for a bachelor's degree. Licensed practical nurses complete a 1-year vocational-technical program in nursing.

Nurses are frontline medical personnel. They take responsibility for the patient in the absence of the physician. In an inpatient setting, they are usually available 24 hours a day. There is a tendency in some centers for some conflict between the nursing staff and the counseling staff. This is a boundary issue and it is a big mistake for all concerned. A good clinical staff has little of these turf battles. They should know, and feel comfortable with, their unique functions in the treatment setting.

Nurses are second in command in medical treatment. Only a physician has more authority. The physician writes the orders and the nurse carries them out. In many facilities, standing orders allow the nurse to make certain medical decisions. This is necessary to reduce response time and to prevent the physician from being called every time every decision is made. If the nurse tells you to do something, carry out this order as if it came from the physician.

Nurses will listen to you and will help you. You will find them to be very supportive. They tend to be caring people who are willing to go the extra mile to provide good-quality care. They are used to charting and are usually wonderfully self-disciplined.

## The Clinical Director

Clinical directors have the primary responsibility for making sure that the clinical team provides good treatment. They hire the professional staff and develop and implement the treatment program. Clinical directors have advanced training and experience in treating chemical dependency. They make sure the team is working well together and is accomplishing its goals. They decide who does what, when, how, and with whom. They direct the treatment program. This person has administrative experience. They usually do not see many patients themselves since they are working with the staff. All program and policy changes go through the clinical director.

## The Clinical Supervisor

Clinical supervisors are chemical dependency counselors with several years of experience in counseling and supervision. Their primary responsibility is to supervise the counseling staff. They will do some hands-on work with the patients and will sit in on some of your groups. They make up the work schedule and will see the counselor for supervision. This is a person that you should use often. He or she is meant to be your mentor. A clinical supervisor will set a good example of how to take a patient through treatment effectively. If you have any questions about treatment planning, charting, or therapy, this is the first person to ask. You should receive continuing education from the supervisory personnel. If you feel that you have any weak points in your training, ask them for in-service training sessions to build your expertise.

The clinical supervisor will be going over your charts to be sure you are treating the patient according to JCAHO standards. The Joint Commission on Accreditation of Healthcare Organizations (JCAHO) requires specific standards of care to be met before they will allow a facility to receive accreditation. You can order a copy of the standards by contacting the Joint Commission on Accreditation of Healthcare Organizations, 875 North Michigan Avenue, Chicago, IL 60611.

## The Chemical Dependency Counselor

Chemical dependency counselors must meet state standards set by a certification board. They take specialized college courses and work at least one year in a treatment setting under a qualified supervisor. In most states they have to pass a national examination and are certified by the state. Counselors must show competency in 12 core function areas: screening, intake, orientation, assessment, treatment planning, counseling, case management, crisis intervention, client education, referral, reports and record keeping, and consultation. Many counselors are involved in their own recovery program, but many are not—it doesn't seem to matter. It is the on-the-job training in addictions and personal experience that gives the addictions counselor his or her unique professional character. They are excellent health care professionals.

## The Rehabilitation Technician or Aid

The rehabilitation technician, sometimes called the aid or orderly, is usually someone with no formal training in chemical dependency. Sometimes they are people who are getting their degrees in chemical dependency and need experience. This person does a variety of work assigned by supervisory personnel. They will be working with the patients, sometimes individually and sometimes in groups. They work under the direct supervision of the counseling staff. It is your responsibility to help them to function effectively around the patient population.

There is often some conflict about how far these people should go in treating patients. For the most part, the care they offer should be highly structured and supervised by someone on the clinical staff. You will find that much of the real work in treatment is offered by these individuals. You must see to it that they offer quality care. The only way to do this is to listen to them, talk to them, and educate them. They may be in recovery and know the AA/NA program well, but you can still improve their skills by extending yourself.

## The Activities Coordinator

Activities coordinators are in charge of getting the patients involved in constructive leisure time activities. They will be doing an activities assessment to see what the patients are doing for entertainment, play, or fun. They will develop an exercise program for each patient. Most chemical dependency patients have lost the capacity to have fun in sobriety. They need to be encouraged to develop healthy recreational activities and hobbies. They need to learn how to have fun while clean and sober. It is important that you encourage your patients to become active in pleasure-oriented activities in recovery. The patients who enjoy sobriety will be more likely to stay sober. One of the most important things patients can do in their recovery program is establish regular exercise habits. All patients should be encouraged to exercise on a daily basis.

## Clinical Staffing

The clinical staff makes up the treatment team. The staff usually meets once a day to discuss the patient's current status. Once a week the staff meets for a more formal clinical staffing. Here the patients will be discussed in more detail and each problem on the problem list will be evaluated.

The staff must be constantly kept informed about how the patient is doing in treatment. In these meetings, treatment plans will be updated. A multidisciplinary staff can much more effectively take a patient through treatment; more expertise comes into play and several heads are better than one.

Clinical staffing is your opportunity to discuss your patients with the whole team. You can get advice and help from everyone at the same time. The patients are reassessed throughout treatment to determine current clinical problems, needs, and response to treatment. The assessment includes major changes in the patient, family, or life events that might complicate or alter treatment. A patient might learn that his wife is divorcing him, or he is being prosecuted for a crime. Someone in the patient's immediate family might die or become ill. All changes in treatment need to be documented in the patient record.

The atmosphere of clinical staffing is a professional one. The principle matter of concern is the patient. You must assume that all members of the professional staff are willing and able to help. The staff should be very supportive of each other. Treating chemical dependency is emotionally draining and everyone will occasionally make mistakes. The atmosphere in clinical staffing should be one of mutual respect. You should enjoy clinical staff meetings. They should be educational and they should help you develop your professional skills.

*How to Present a Patient* | You will present each of your patients to the clinical staff and will discuss how treatment is generally going. If you have any questions, now is the time to ask them. The first time you present a patient you need to be through. As the patient remains in treatment, you need to just cover the pertinent issues. An outline for case presentation is handy to use your first few times. The outline might look something like this:

*Outline for Case Presentation*

1. Identifying data
2. Present illness
3. Past history
4. Family history
5. Social history
6. Medical history
7. Mental status examination
8. Most likely diagnosis
9. Formulation
   a. Predisposing factors
   b. Psychosocial stressors
   c. Stress that precipitated treatment
10. Further assessment you propose
11. Treatment plan
12. Prognosis

Your presentation should sound something like this:

Mr. Roberts is a 43-year-old black male who just got his third DWI. He has been drinking heavily for the past 20 years. He is divorced with two children. He lives alone. He came to treatment after spending the night in jail. He is working on his chemical use history and problem assessment form. He is doing well around the unit so far. He is in good physical health except for some mild withdrawal. He seems to be getting along well with his treatment peers. In group, he did admit to a drinking problem. I think he is committed to treatment. He says he doesn't want to go on living this way anymore. I talked to his oldest son this morning and the family is supportive of treatment. He is in some withdrawal, but he seems to be handling that okay. He needs to take the Minnesota Multiphasic Personality Inventory (MMPI) and to visit with the psychologist to rule out other psychiatric disorders. He is somewhat depressed. I have diagnosed him with alcohol dependence, severe. He will be working through the steps and we will probably address his depression depending on the psychologist's report.

The case presentation globally advises the treatment team of the patient's condition and describes how the patient is doing in treatment. After the primary counselor presents the patient, each member of the treatment team can comment. The physician or the nursing staff may have something to share about withdrawal or medical condition the patient is being treated for. The dietitian may make a report on the patient's diet. The recreational therapist may have a comment on how the patient has been using his or her leisure time. The other counselors may have something to say about what they see. The primary counselor collates this material and enters the staff's input in the patient record. These progress notes don't have to be very long, but they do have to show that the treatment team is reassessing the patient and changing the treatment plan where necessary.

## Team Building

A good staff is constantly building up the team. They are actively encouraging to each other and reinforcing each other's work. When you see someone do a good job you say so. "You did a good job with Mark this morning. I was impressed with how you handled yourself." These are very reinforcing to fellow staff members. Often the staff puts so much energy into the patients that they forget that they have needs too. This is emotionally difficult work and everyone needs support. A good team knows this. They go out of their way to treat each other well.

New members of the team are welcomed and are assisted in adjusting to the flow of treatment. Every treatment center is different and new staff need orientation on both an intellectual and an emotional level. A good team constantly talks each other up, to insiders and to outsiders; they never talk someone on the staff down. You can share the truth about someone without damaging their reputation. A good staff communicates well together. They share openly how they feel and what they think. They work together as a group. If a personal problem develops between members of the staff, this problem is handled by a supervisor.

A good staff never gossips about each other. This is one of the most harmful things you can do in any staff organization. Gossip will cause a team to fail. Everyone's life outside of the center should be private. Unless they decide to confide in you, keep out of the issue. Do not spread damaging rumors about anyone. A good way to check yourself is to refuse to repeat anything unless you have okayed it with the person you are talking about.

A good staff member gets support, not treatment, from their fellow staff members. It is a mistake for someone in recovery to think that they no longer need their AA/NA meetings because they have the support of the clinical team. The clinical staff does not exist to treat you, they exist to treat the patients. If you want to see someone on the staff for a brief consultation about a problem, that's fine, but keep it short. Don't be afraid to seek outside help for your problems. Your mental and physical health directly affects your job performance. If your problems are bogging you down, you can't be effective. Becoming involved in a good program of recovery will make you a better counselor and a better person. One of the best ways to learn about good therapy is to go to a good therapist. Make sure that this therapist is highly qualified in the field.

A good clinical staff does not subgroup against each other. This is where a smaller group of staff members gets together and talks about the other members. This is very common, and it is a disaster for the clinical team. If you are having problems with a staff member, first go to that staff member and try to work the issue through. If you are unable to resolve the problem, go to your supervisor and get them to help you. If you and the supervisor can't handle the problem, then it needs to be addressed before the clinical staff as a whole. Don't let problems fester. The only way to resolve problems is to get everyone together and have them share how they feel. Any problem can be solved in an atmosphere of love and truth. The staff needs to practice what they preach to the patients.

The following guidelines are excellent for maintaining productive staff interaction:

*Commitment to Coworkers* | As your coworker with a shared goal of providing excellent care to our patients, I commit myself to the following:

1. I will accept responsibility for establishing and maintaining healthy interpersonal relationships with you and every member of this staff. I will talk to you promptly if I am having a problem with you. The only time I will discuss it with another person is when I need advice or help in deciding how to communicate to you appropriately.

2. I will establish and maintain a relationship of functional trust with you and every member of this staff. My relationships with each of you will be equally respectful, regardless of job titles or levels of educational preparation.

3. I will not engage in the "3 Bs" (bickering, backbiting, and bitching) and will ask you not to do as well.

4. I will not complain about another team member, and ask you not to do as well. If I hear you doing so, I will ask you to talk to that person.

5. I will accept you as you are today, forgiving past problems and ask you to do the same with me.

6. I will be committed to finding solutions to problems, rather than complaining about them, and ask you to do the same.

7. I will affirm your contribution to quality patient care.

8. I will remember that neither of us is perfect, and that human errors are opportunities, not for shame or guilt, but for forgiveness and growth (Manthey, 1991).

*Boundaries* | Everyone on the clinical team needs to know and respect each other's professional boundaries. You need to know what each person's function is in treatment. Once you know that a part of treatment is not in your area of expertise, stay out of that area. Everyone on the staff wants to hear what you think; that is helpful, but don't concern yourself with patient care outside your area of specialization. You are a chemical dependency counselor, not a physician or a nurse. You should not concern yourself with who gets aspirin. Many counselors spend long hours worrying about whether or not their patients are being properly treated by the medical staff. If you worry that your medical staff is inadequate, work somewhere else. Never accept a job in an institution that gives substandard care. Once you decide to accept a position, act as if your staff is the greatest. Be grateful for all the good work they are doing.

Most staff problems are attitude problems, and attitudes can change. You need to keep a positive attitude about you and your coworkers. This will go a long way in making your day more pleasant and enjoyable. If you see your attitude slipping, talk about this with your supervisor. Check your own life. How are you doing? Many times a negative attitude flags personal problems that need to be addressed outside of the treatment center.

## Staff-Patient Problems

The staff and the patients will constantly have problems with each other. It is the nature of transference and countertransference that there will be conflict. As the patient's maladaptive attitudes and behaviors come into play, the staff can teach new methods of dealing with problems.

Never agree that a patient has been treated unfairly by a staff member until you first talk with the staff member. Patients will attempt to use you in a manipulative way against someone else. You must not subgroup with patients against staff. This decreases the effectiveness of the entire staff. You must prevent patients from using their old manipulative skills. If a patient is having a problem with a staff member, arrange for the staff member and the patient to meet to see if they can resolve the issue together. You are teaching the patients something dysfunctional; if they have a problem with someone, they have to go to that person to resolve the issue.

Certain patients will try to split the staff against each other. This is common for borderline and antisocial patients. This must be resolved by the staff as a whole. The patient usually attempts this by telling different staff members different things. The only way to stop this manipulation is to call everyone together at the same time. This way the patient can't continue to manipulate. Any other means of trying to solve this problem will not work because the lies will continue to operate. Once everyone gets together you will have a more accurate picture of what the problem is and how to resolve it.

## When a Patient Doesn't Like a Counselor

Sometime a patient will want to change counselors. Such patients need to share how they feel with their current counselor. Something may be going wrong with the therapeutic alliance. This matter needs to be discussed with the counselor and the patient who are having the problem. It should be rare for a patient to change primary counselors while in treatment. Most of these problems revolve around lack of trust, and this is a common problem for chemically dependent persons.

Many staff-patient problems result from miscommunication. It is common for two people to misinterpret each other's behavior. Only by bringing the parties together, and having them check out their interpretations, will the problem be resolved. Each person needs to ask about, and listen to, the other person's thoughts and feelings.

Some patients will want their counselor to do too much. It's a if they want the counselor to do all the work for them. When the counselor balks at this, the patient feels resentful. Such patients need to accept responsibility for their own behavior. They can't count on someone else to work the program for them; they must work it for themselves.

Patients who are having a problem with a staff member may need more time in individual sessions. They need to get their thinking accurate. Trust issues are of paramount importance in recovery. Trust is essential for the development of a good therapeutic alliance. If patients are having trust problems with the staff, you can bet that they have this same problem outside the treatment setting. They may need to track their lack of trust to earlier situations, perhaps in childhood. Things that happened early in life can convince patients that they trust no one. Keep asking them if they ever felt these feelings at an earlier time in their life. These situations will have to be explored in depth and worked through. The patients need to see that the situation has changed. They are not in the original situation anymore. They are in a new situation that demands a new level of trust. What is it about the new situation that leaves them to feel that they can't trust? What is the most rational decision for them to make? Trust issues must be resolved for them to move forward in treatment. They will remain stuck until they can trust someone. Once they trust one person, they can transfer the trust to someone else, to the group, and then to the Higher Power.

## When a Patient Complains About a Rule

Many staff-patient problems revolve around rule violations. Patients will say that they didn't break the rule, and they may have a very good story to tell about the situation. You must support other members of the staff in the consequences they give out. If you don't, that staff member will be unable to discipline the patients. If the patients learn that the rules can be manipulated, all of the rules become meaningless. Bring all members involved in the situation together and talk the issue through. In very rare instances, the person who leveled the consequence may remove the consequence or change it to something more appropriate. This should be done only by the person who leveled the consequence.

No chemically dependent person wants to obey the rules, but the rules exist to protect them from harm. Once they understand that the rules are for them, rather than against them, they will be more likely to obey the rules. Patients who are breaking the rules need to see how this tendency feeds into their chemical dependency. If they learn how to follow the rules, particularly the rules of AA/NA, this is recovery.

## The Work Environment

A treatment center should be a fun place to work. People who come into recovery at their worst are at their best in a few short weeks. This is an extremely rewarding environment. It is a place full of great joy. Real love abounds in good treatment centers. Patients and staff alike enjoy their day. If you do not genuinely enjoy your work, you are at the wrong treatment center or you are in the wrong business. Chemically dependent persons are a lot of fun to work with. They laugh and have a good time. They have been the life of the party. The staff can learn how to have fun at work. If the staff members work together and love each other, they can grow from work.

Good treatment must be done in an atmosphere of love and trust. The staff must support each other through the good times and the bad times. The old saying applies: When the going gets tough, the tough get going. Even in periods of stress, the well-functioning staff pulls together and works it out. Humor often saves the day and a genuine caring for each other smooths the rough spots. Remember, you are in this field not only for your patients but for yourself. You are actively involved in your own individual growth.

CHAPTER
THIRTEEN

# Discharge Summary and Aftercare

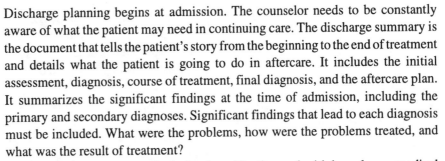

Discharge planning begins at admission. The counselor needs to be constantly aware of what the patient may need in continuing care. The discharge summary is the document that tells the patient's story from the beginning to the end of treatment and details what the patient is going to do in aftercare. It includes the initial assessment, diagnosis, course of treatment, final diagnosis, and the aftercare plan. It summarizes the significant findings at the time of admission, including the primary and secondary diagnoses. Significant findings that lead to each diagnosis must be included. What were the problems, how were the problems treated, and what was the result of treatment?

The course of treatment includes detoxification and withdrawal, any medical treatment, and all treatment provided by the clinical team. You will follow each problem on the problem list, detailing what the problem is, and how the problem was treated. You will discuss how the treatment affected the problem. Make sure you concentrate on behaviors. Include any changes in the treatment plan and the reasons for those changes and the family's response to treatment.

The final assessment of the patients' current condition must include how they are functioning at discharge, compared to how they were functioning before treatment and during treatment. The changes in feelings, thoughts, and behaviors should be detailed. The aftercare plan should be laid out, and the patients must agree to follow the aftercare plan. If the patient needs to see someone for further treatment in continuing care, this person must be named in the discharge summary. If the patient is on any medication at discharge, this medication should be listed and a follow-up plan for continuing or discontinuing this medication.

All patients must meet the discharge criteria developed by the American Society of Addiction Medicine (1996).

**Outpatient Discharge Criteria**

For adult and adolescent outpatient discharge, the patient must meet one of the following conditions:

I. The patient is assessed, postadmission, as not having met the *DSM* criteria for a substance use disorder.

II. The patient must meet at least one of the following criteria:
1. All of the following:
   a. Patient is not intoxicated or in withdrawal.
   b. Patient does not manifest symptoms of protracted withdrawal syndrome.
   c. Patient does not meet any of the Level I continued stay criteria.
2. One of the following:
   a. Patient's medical problems, if any, have diminished or stabilized to the point that they can be managed through outpatient appointments.
   b. A biomedical condition is interfering with treatment and requires treatment at another setting.
3. Patient's emotional behavioral problems have diminished or stabilized to the point that he or she can be managed through outpatient appointments.
4. One of the following:
   a. The patient's awareness and acceptance of an addiction problem and commitment to recovery are sufficient to expect maintenance of a self-directed recovery plan as evidenced by the following:
      (i) The patient is able to recognize the severity of his or her relationship with alcohol or drugs.
      (ii) The patient has an understanding of his or her self-defeating relationship with drugs or alcohol.
      (iii) The patient is applying the essential skills necessary to maintain sobriety in a self-help fellowship and/with further post-treatment care.
   b. The patient has consistently failed to achieve treatment goals and no further progress is likely to be made.
5. One of the following:
   a. Patient's therapeutic gains that address cravings and relapse issues have been learned and internalized.
   b. The patient is experiencing an exacerbation in drug-seeking behavior or craving that necessitates treatment in a more intense treatment setting.
6. One of the following:
   a. The patient's social system and significant others are supportive of recovery to the point that the patient can be expected to adhere to a self-directed treatment plan.
   b. The patient is functioning adequately in assessed deficiencies in life areas of work, social functioning, or primary relationships.
   c. The patient's social system remains nonsupportive or has deteriorated, and the patient is at risk for relapse. The patient needs placement in a higher level of care to prevent relapse.

**Inpatient Discharge Criteria**

■

Adults and adolescents in inpatient treatment are ready for discharge if they do not meet the *DSM* criteria for substance use disorder or when they meet the specifications in one of the following six dimensions.

I.  One of the following:
    1. Patient is not intoxicated or in withdrawal or the symptoms have diminished to the point that the patient can be managed in a less intense level of care.
    2. The patient has protracted withdrawal symptoms that no longer require 24-hour monitoring.
    3. The patient meets criteria for a more intensive level of treatment.

II. One of the following:
    1. The patient's biomedical problems, if any, have diminished or stabilized to the extent that daily availability of a 24-hour medical staff is no longer necessary.
    2. There is a biomedical condition that needs treatment in another setting.

III. One of the following:
    1. The patient's emotional/behavioral problems have diminished or stabilized to the point that a 24-hour-a-day staff is no longer necessary.
    2. An emotional/behavioral problem exists that needs treatment in another setting.

IV. One of the following:
    1. The patient's awareness and acceptance of an addiction problem and commitment to treatment are sufficient to expect compliance in a less intensive setting as evidenced by the following:
        a. The patient is able to recognize the severity of his or her addictive problem.
        b. The patient understands his or her self-defeating relationship with alcohol and other drugs and understands the triggers that lead to use.
        c. The patient accepts continued care and has participated in the development of an aftercare plan.
        d. The patient does not meet any of the Level III continuing care dimensions.
    2. The patient has consistently failed to meet treatment goals, even with changes in the treatment plan, and no further progress is expected.

V. One of the following:
    1. The patient is capable of following and completing a continuing care plan and the patient is not at substantial risk for relapse.
    2. The patient is not committed to continuing care and has achieved the maximum benefit from all attempts to have the patient see that they need an aftercare plan.

VI. One of the following:
1. Problem aspects of the patient's social and interpersonal environment are responding to treatment and the environment is now supportive enough to transfer the patient to a less intense level of care.
2. The social and interpersonal environment has not changed or has deteriorated, but the patient has learned skills necessary to cope with the situation or has secured an alternative environment.
3. The social environment has deteriorated and the patient has not learned the skills necessary to cope. An extended care environment has been secured but the patient is unwilling to be transferred.

*How to Develop a Discharge Summary*

The discharge summary must be entered into the patient record within 15 days following discharge. It must summarize the following things about the patient's treatment:

1. The significant findings of the clinical staff. These include the problem list and the initial primary and secondary diagnosis.
2. The course of treatment through each identified problem.
3. The final assessment of the patient's current condition.
4. The recommendations and arrangements for further treatment and aftercare.
5. The final primary and secondary diagnosis.

The aftercare plan details how the patient is going to continue treatment after leaving the treatment center. All patients will have an aftercare plan that will list the specific arrangements for continuing care.

Each patient will need an AA/NA contact person. It is this person's job to see to it that the patient gets to the new AA/NA group and is introduced around. The contact person stays close to the patient until the patient chooses a sponsor. You will want to build up your AA contact list carefully over the years and get the other counselors to help you. Try to match the patient and the contact person carefully. Some patients will need someone who is hard and pushy, and some will need just the opposite. The AA/NA contact is an important link from you to the new group. They will keep you informed if anything goes wrong.

The aftercare plan is developed in accordance with the patient's identified needs at the time of discharge. The plan is developed with the full participation of the patient. They must agree to abide by the aftercare plan. It is no use developing a great aftercare plan if the patient has no intention of following it.

Patients will need a variety of care following treatment, and you need to find the least restrictive environment for the patient. Each of the following methods of continuing treatment needs to be considered in developing an aftercare plan:

1. *Inpatient treatment:* If the patient's recovery is still shaky, and they have serious medical or psychological problems, they may need further inpatient care.

2. *Halfway house:* Some patients will need the structure of a halfway house to help them to stay clean and sober. These patients will not function well on their own. They may have poor social skills or they may need someone else to be in control of their environment. A good halfway house will structure the patient's day

and will usually have AA/NA meetings at the house. Everyone eats together and shares the responsibilities of cooking and cleaning. This is a good alternative for many patients who are shaky in early recovery. If you feel uncomfortable about your patient's ability to maintain a recovery program, this is something you should encourage.

*3. Outpatient treatment:* Some patients need further treatment, but they can handle that treatment in an outpatient setting. Outpatient programs usually offer 1 to 3 days of structured treatment per week. The patients come in and move through an individualized outpatient program. This is much like inpatient treatment, but it's not nearly as intensive or as structured. These patients must be able to stay abstinent between appointments.

*4. Aftercare:* All patients who come through treatment will need an extended care program to make sure the patients are following through with their recovery plan. This program will need to be scheduled at least once a week for at least 3 months. Ideally, programs should offer aftercare as long as it is necessary. It's not unusual for patients to stay in aftercare for a year or longer.

The Personal Recovery Plan (Appendix 28) describes the patient's goals in recovery. It is another treatment plan developed with the patient's input. If they still have problems that need to be addressed in continuing care, each of these problems will need a treatment plan. You cannot send a patient out of treatment with an unstable psychiatric or family problem without making arrangements for the patient to receive treatment for this problem.

*The Discharge Summary*

You have collected the data necessary and you are ready to do your discharge summary. You have the patient's record before you. Remember, this is a summary: You don't have to put in everything, just the significant findings, and the course of treatment. You will keep the personal recovery plan in the chart and give a copy to the patient to take home. A sample discharge summary is given in Appendix 29.

After you have completed the discharge summary, write a letter to each of the people to whom you are referring the patient. These letters are important to maintain good communication between your facility and the other professionals in the community. You will need to telephone each of these professionals and tell each one about the patient. You may want to send them each a copy of the discharge summary.

The patient's employers may request an exit interview. You should call the employers and let them know that the patient is getting out of treatment and tell them how the patient is doing. Employers are an important referral source for your facility, and they have an interest in the patient's recovery.

*Saying Good-bye*

When patients walk down that hallway for the last time, they are going to have mixed feelings. Probably for the first time in their life they have had a group of people consistently act in their behalf. They will not want to leave a good program. They will be feeling some fear of what's going to happen on the outside. For the first time in weeks, they are going to be on their own. It will be easy to get back to the old self-destructive behaviors, and they should know this. Alcohol and drugs will be easily accessible. They don't know if they are going to make it. It's a long walk out that front door.

You need to be smiling and offering the patient encouragement all the way. Tell them that you're available to them if they have difficulty. Explain that you want to see them at the alumni functions your center will be sponsoring. Tell them that they can make it, and tell them you have faith in them. Tell them that no matter what happens out there, you care for them. You will be there for them if they need you. If they have trouble, they can call you or come back to the treatment center. Most of all, you need to give the patients a hug. You have walked with them through one of the most difficult and rewarding periods of their lives.

<table>
<tr>
<td>CHAPTER<br>FOURTEEN</td>
<td># The Drugs</td>
</tr>
</table>

All psychoactive drugs of abuse alter feelings, thoughts, and behavior. They directly affect the brain and the central nervous system (CNS). The specific actions of these drugs are highly complex. Feelings are altered when the drugs affect neurotransmitters and intercellular communications that seek a balance between excitatory and inhibitory functions. Every organism is driven toward establishing a balance between these two systems that is called homeostasis.

It is widely believed by many experts in the field that the level of drug use in the United States is the highest in the industrialized world. More than one half of American youth try an illicit drug before they finish high school. An estimated 14.5 million Americans used a drug illegally in the month prior to being surveyed in the 1988 National Household Survey on Drug Abuse. The number of people admitted to emergency rooms following cocaine use increased four times over the 5-year period between 1985 and 1989 (Adams, Blanken, Ferguson, & Kopstein, 1990).

Specific drug action depends on the route of administration, the dose, the presence or absence of other drugs, and the clinical state of the individual. Generally, psychoactive drugs can be classified by their primary action on the central nervous system (Gilman, Goodman, & Gilman, 1980).

**CNS Depressants**

The central nervous system's depressants depress excitable nervous tissue at all levels of the brain and nervous system. The CNS depressants include all sleeping medications, anti-anxiety drugs (also called minor tranquilizers), opium derivatives, cannabis, and the inhalants (Schuckit, 1984).

**CNS Stimulants**

The central nervous system stimulants achieve their effect by the stimulation of nervous tissue through blocking the actions of inhibitory cells or the release of transmitter substances from the cells, or by the direct action of the drugs themselves. These drugs include all of the amphetamines and cocaine. Nicotine and caffeine also stimulate nervous tissue but to a much less degree (Schuckit, 1984).

## The Hallucinogens

The effect of these drugs is the production of an altered perception, thought, or feeling that cannot be experienced otherwise except in dreams. The hallucinations are usually of a visual nature. These drugs have no known medical usefulness. Lysergic acid diethylamide (LSD) is the most common hallucinogen currently found on the street (Jaffe, 1980).

## The Reinforcing Properties of Drugs

Drugs of abuse are powerful reinforcers. Animals quickly learn to self-administer most of these drugs for their rewarding properties. Animals will press a lever over 4,000 times to get a single injection of cocaine. They will continue to self-administer for weeks, alternating between self-imposed abstinence and drug administration. These animals generally die of drug toxicity and lack of food; they would rather use drugs than eat.

When given continuous access to drugs of abuse, animals show patterns of self-administration strikingly similar to human users of the same drug. These drugs are strongly reinforcing, even in the absence of physical dependence (Thompson & Pickens, 1970; Woods & Carney, 1977).

## Tolerance and Dependence

Tolerance and physical dependence develop after chronic administration of any one of a wide variety of mood-altering substances. With increasing tolerance, the individual needs more of the drug to get the same effect. Tolerance and dependency develop as the nerve cells chemically and structurally counteract the drug's psychoactive effects. Tolerance is a complex generalized phenomenon that involves many independent physiological and behavioral mechanisms. It leaves the chemically dependent individual physiologically and psychologically craving the drug. The individual becomes obsessed with obtaining the drug for a sense of well-being. Chemically dependent persons become inflexible in their behavior toward the drug despite adverse consequences. The intensity of this felt "need" or dependence may vary from a mild craving to an intense, overwhelming obsession. At severe levels, the individual becomes totally preoccupied with the drug (Kalant et al., 1978; Wilcox, Gonzales, & Erickson, 1994).

Physical dependence is characterized by withdrawal symptoms. Withdrawal develops in an addicted individual when the drug is discontinued too quickly. Physical dependence occurs throughout the entire nervous system (Smith, 1977). Withdrawal symptoms are a rebound effect in the physiological systems modified by the drug. For example, alcohol depresses the CNS, while withdrawal stimulates the CNS. In studying the effects of withdrawal, look for the opposite effect that the drug was used for initially. Amphetamine is used to stimulate, to give energy, so amphetamine withdrawal causes depression and a lack of energy. The time required to produce physical dependence can vary. Withdrawal symptoms can develop in a day with large quantities of CNS depressants (Alexander, 1951). For most drug users, development of physical dependence is gradual, occurring over weeks, months, or years of chronic administration.

**Cross-Tolerance**

The ability of one drug to suppress withdrawal symptoms created by another is referred to as cross-dependence or cross-tolerance. Cross-tolerance may partially or completely remove symptoms of withdrawal. All drugs of abuse cause intoxication and induce a psychological dependency. The individual is self-administering the drug to change their level of consciousness or to increase psychological comfort (Schuckit, 1984).

**Alcohol**

No one knows when alcohol was first produced. If any watery mixture of vegetable sugars or starches is allowed to stand long enough in a warm temperature, alcohol will make itself. Nature alone cannot produce anything stronger than 14% alcohol, but by distillation, the percentage can be increased to 93% (Kinney & Leaton, 1987).

Alcohol is the most used and abused psychoactive chemical in the United States (U.S. Department of Health and Human Services, 1984). Approximately 30% of the general population are abstainers, 10% are heavy drinkers, and 5% to 10% are problem drinkers (Warheit, 1985). Ninety-two percent of children use before they leave high school, and 36% have consumed more than five drinks at one time in the last 30 days (Centers for Disease Control, 1991a). It is estimated that 200,000 deaths per year are alcohol related (U.S. Department of Health and Human Services, 1984).

The early detection of alcohol abuse and dependency is complicated by the denial that is found in the individual, the family, and in society. Long-term alcohol dependence has profound effects on personality, mood, cognitive functioning, and a variety of physiological problems involving virtually all organ systems. The interaction of alcohol and other drugs may lead to fatal overdoses (Frances & Franklin, 1988).

Alcoholism is the result of a complex interaction of biological vulnerability and environmental factors. Environmental factors such as childhood experience, parental attitudes, social policies, and culture strongly affect vulnerability to alcoholism. Genetic variables significantly influence the disease. There is probably no personality style that is predictive of alcoholism (Goodwin, 1985; Vaillant, 1984).

*Alcohol-Induced*
*Organic Mental*
*Disorders*

*Alcohol Intoxication*

Alcohol intoxication is the most frequent induced organic mental disorder. It is time limited and may occur with varying amounts of ingested alcohol. Intoxicated individuals exhibit maladaptive behavioral changes due to recent ingestion. These changes may include aggressiveness, impaired judgment, impaired attention, irritability, euphoria, depression, emotional liability, and other manifestations of impaired social functioning. Although alcohol is basically a central nervous system depressant, its initial effects disinhibit the individual. Early in intoxication the person may feel stimulated with an exaggerated sense of well-being. With further use, the person may slow down and become depressed, withdrawn, and dull. They may lose consciousness (American Psychiatric Association [APA], 1987; Woodward, 1994).

*Alcohol-Induced Amnestic Disorder (Blackouts)*

A blackout or alcohol-induced amnestic disorder is a period of amnesia during periods of intoxication. The person may seem fully conscious and normal when observed by others, but they are unable to remember what happened or what they did while intoxicated. The disorder may last for a few seconds or for days. The severity and duration of alcoholism correlate with the occurrence of these blackouts (Goodwin, Crane, & Guze, 1969).

*Wernicke-Korsakoff Syndrome*

Wernicke-Korsakoff syndrome begins with a sudden change in organic functioning. Patients become ataxic, with a wide-based, unsteady gait. They may be unable to walk without support. They are mentally confused and are unable to transfer memory from short-term memory to long-term memory. Patients may be disoriented, listless, inattentive, and indifferent to the environment. Questions directed to them may go unanswered, or they may fall asleep while being examined. The etiology of this syndrome involves a thiamine deficiency due to dietary, genetic, or medical factors. All patients with compromised mental functioning or a deficit in memory need to be examined by the medical staff as soon as possible (Braunwald et al., 1987).

*Alcoholic Idiosyncratic Intoxication*

Alcoholic idiosyncratic intoxication is a marked behavior change, usually to aggressiveness, due to recent ingestion of small amounts of alcohol. There is usually amnesia for the period of intoxication. The behavior is unusual for the person when they are not drinking. The person may, with one drink, become belligerent, assaultive, or manifest other unusual behavior (APA, 1987).

*Alcohol Withdrawal*

Alcohol withdrawal symptoms relate to a relative drop in alcohol blood level. Withdrawal can occur when the individual is still drinking. The classic withdrawal symptom is a coarse, fast-frequency tremor observed when the patient's hand or tongue is extended. The tremor is made worse by motor activity or stress. The patient may experience nausea and vomiting, malaise, weakness, elevated pulse and blood pressure, anxiety, craving, depressed mood, irritability, transient hallucinations, headache, and insomnia. These symptoms follow several hours after cessation or reduction in alcohol intake and peak within 72 hours. They almost always disappear within 5 to 7 days of abstinence. The patient in alcohol withdrawal is treated with a cross-tolerant drug similar in pharmacological effects to alcohol, usually one of the benzodiazepines. This stabilizes the patient in a mild withdrawal syndrome (Schuckit, 1984).

*Alcohol Withdrawal Seizures*

Withdrawal seizures may occur 7 to 38 hours after the last alcohol use in chronic drinkers. The tendency to seizure peaks within 24 hours (Adams & Victor, 1981).

*Alcohol Withdrawal Delirium (Delirium Tremens)*

One third of patients with seizures go on to develop alcohol withdrawal delirium. This is characterized by confusion, disorientation, fluctuating or clouded sensorium, and perceptual disturbances (Adams & Victor, 1981). Typical symptoms include delusions, vivid hallucinations, agitation, insomnia, mild fever, and marked autonomic arousal. Patients frequently report visual hallucinations of insects, small animals, or other perceptual disturbances. The patient may be terrified. The delirium typically subsides after a few days but it can continue for weeks (Gessner, 1979).

*Alcohol Hallucinosis*     Alcohol hallucinosis is a syndrome in which hallucinations develop and persist shortly after cessation or reduction in alcohol ingestion in a person who is alcohol dependent. The hallucinations may be auditory or visual. The auditory hallucinations are usually voices or unformed sounds such as hissing or buzzing. The disorder may last several weeks or months. The patient with the chronic form of this disorder may have to be treated with antipsychotic medication (APA, 1987).

**Sedatives, Hypnotics, and Anxiolytics**

Benzodiazepines and barbiturates are useful medications with a potential for abuse and dependence. They are medically useful for a variety of symptoms such as insomnia and anxiety. Approximately 15% of the population use a benzodiazepine each year (Gottochalk, McGuire, & Haser, et al., 1979). Sixteen percent of patients abuse the sedatives that are prescribed by their physician (Richels, Case, & Downing, 1983). In 1977, 18% of young adults reported nonmedical use of sedatives (Abelson, Fishburne, & Cisin, 1977). No sharp line can be drawn between appropriate use, abuse, habituation, and addiction. Neither the patient nor the physician may recognize symptoms of dependence. Both may assume that the anxiety, tremulousness, and insomnia that develop when the drug is discontinued is a return of the original anxiety (Jaffe, 1980). Low-dose benzodiazepine dependence is very common today. Some of these patients have been on a succession of various benzodiazepines for years. When the medication is withdrawn, anxiety symptoms may increase for months. These patients must be followed by someone experienced in treating anxiety disorders. The therapist can work to reduce the anxiety symptoms while the patient is experiencing withdrawal (Burant, 1990; Geller, 1994; Juergens, 1994).

Diagnosis of sedative abuse may prove difficult. The abuse can start in the context of medical treatment for anxiety, medical disorders, or insomnia. Physical dependence can develop to low doses over several years or high doses over a few weeks (Dietch, 1983). Intoxication, withdrawal, withdrawal delirium, and amnestic disorder, are similar to those found with alcohol. Benzodiazepines have a much longer half-life, therefore withdrawal may not be evident until 7 to 10 days after cessation of use. These patients can have a protracted withdrawal that can last for months (Geller, 1994). Alcohol and opioid CNS depression may interact with sedative hypnotics and potentiate the depression. Adding small amounts of alcohol or opioids to the sedatives can quickly lead to overdose (Frances & Franklin, 1988). Treatment of sedative, hypnotic, or anxiolytic withdrawal is similar to that of alcohol withdrawal. A cross-tolerant sedative is administered to prevent severe withdrawal symptoms. This medication is gradually decreased until the patient is clear of the drug.

**Opioids**

In the late 1960s, the use of heroin increased in the United States. Once centered in large urban areas, use of heroin infiltrated smaller communities. Members of lower socioeconomic groups continue to be overrepresented in this patient population, but the use of heroin is now observed with greater frequency in affluent members of society. A survey in 1977 indicated that 2% to 3% of young adults had tried heroin at some time in their lives. During the peak period of heroin use

(1970-1973) there were more than 500,000 heroin addicts in the United States. The existence of opioid addiction among physicians, nurses, and health care professionals is many times higher than in any other group with a comparable educational background (Gilman, Goodman, & Gilman, 1980).

Rapid intravenous injection of an opioid produces a warm flushing of the skin and sensations in the lower abdomen described by addicts as similar to orgasm. This lasts for about 45 seconds and is known as the "kick" or "rush" (Jaffe, 1980). Tolerance to this high develops with repeated use. Physical signs of intoxication include constricted pupils, marked sedation, slurred speech, and impairment in attention and memory. Daily use over days or weeks will produce opioid withdrawal symptoms on cessation of use. The withdrawal symptoms are intense but generally not life-threatening. Withdrawal starts approximately 10 hours after the last dose (Frances & Franklin, 1988). Mild opioid withdrawal presents as a flulike syndrome with symptoms of anxiety, yawning, dysphoria, sweating, runny nose, tearing, pupillary dilation, goose bumps, and autonomic nervous system arousal. Severe symptoms include hot and cold flashes, deep muscle and joint pain, nausea, vomiting, diarrhea, abdominal pain, and fever. Protracted withdrawal may extend for months (Gold, 1994b; Kosten, Rounsaville, & Kleber, 1985).

The treatment of opioid addiction can be grouped into opioid maintenance with methadone versus abstinence approaches. Choice of the proper treatment depends on the patient's characteristics. The course of heroin addiction typically involves a 2- to 6-year interval between the start of regular heroin use and the seeking of treatment. The need to participate in criminal activity to procure the drug predisposes the addict to further social problems. Treatment takes total psychosocial rehabilitation.

Methadone programs substitute a long-acting methadone for short-acting heroin, and then gradually withdraw the methadone. They transfer the addiction from heroin to methadone. Methadone is administered to the patient orally at established methadone clinics. Although a mainstay of treatment, these programs reach only 20% to 25% of addicts, with program retention rates between 59% and 85% (Stimmel, Goldberg, & Rotkopf, 1977). Opioid detoxification should be slow to avoid relapse. The drug should be removed by as little as 10% per week. Total abstinence may be the only alternative for many patients.

## Cocaine and the Amphetamines

Moderate doses of the psychoactive stimulants produce an elevation in mood, a sense of increased energy and alertness, and decreased appetite. Task performance that has been impaired by boredom or fatigue improves. Some individuals may become anxious or irritable. Cocaine addicts describe the euphoric effects of cocaine in a way that is indistinguishable from that of amphetamine addicts. In the laboratory, subjects familiar with cocaine cannot distinguish between the two drugs when both are given intravenously (Fischman et al., 1976). Animals use the drugs in a similar fashion, and the toxic and withdrawal syndrome of the drugs is indistinguishable. There is a difference in the half-life of the drugs effects. Cocaine's effects tend to be brief, lasting a matter of minutes, while amphetamine effects last for hours (Griffith, Cavanaugh, Held, & Oates, 1972; Wesson & Smith, 1977).

The user of a psychoactive stimulant at first feels increased physical strength, mental capacity, and euphoria. They feel a decreased need for sleep or food. A sensation described as a "flash" or "rush" immediately follows intravenous administration. It is described as an intensely pleasurable experience similar to an orgasm. With time, tolerance develops, and more of the drug is necessary to produce the same effects. With continued use, toxic symptoms appear. These include gritting the teeth, undue suspiciousness, and a feeling of being watched. The user becomes fascinated with their thinking and the deeper meaning of things. Stereotypical, repetitious behavior is common. Individuals may become preoccupied with taking things apart and putting them back together. The mixture of another CNS depressant drug, such as an opioid (speedball) or alcohol, can be used to decrease irritable side effects. The patient often becomes addicted to both drugs (Wesson & Smith, 1977).

*Pattern of Use* | Stimulants may be injected or taken intranasally every few minutes to every few hours around the clock for several days. Such a "speed run" usually lasts until the individual has exhausted the drug supply or is too paranoid or disorganized to continue. Stopping administration is followed within a few hours by deep sleep. On arising, the individual feels hungry and lethargic. Some are depressed. Cocaine is inhaled, smoked, or injected intravenously. Cocaine users who try to maintain the euphoric state will ingest the drug every 30 to 40 minutes (Wesson & Smith, 1977). Animals given free access to stimulants develop weight loss and self-mutilation, and succumb to death within 2 weeks (Jaffe, 1980). Given a choice between food and cocaine, monkeys consistently choose cocaine (Aigner & Balster, 1978).

A toxic psychosis may develop after weeks or months of continued stimulant use. A fully developed toxic syndrome is characterized by vivid visual, auditory, and tactile hallucinations. There are paranoid delusions with a clear sensorium (Griffith et al., 1972). Unless the individual continues to use the drug, these psychotic symptoms usually clear within a week. The hallucinations are the first symptom to disappear (Jaffe, 1980). Craving for the drug, prolonged sleep, general fatigue, lassitude, and depression commonly follow abrupt cessation of chronic use (Post, Kotin, & Goodwin, 1974).

The National Institute on Drug Abuse estimated that between 25 to 40 million Americans tried cocaine by 1986 (National Institute on Drug Abuse, 1986). Adolescent cocaine abuse leads to more rapid and severe consequences than for adults. The time from first use to addiction is reduced from 4 years in adults to 1½ years in adolescents (Washton, Gold, & Potash, 1984). Cocaine's price has dramatically decreased to the point that it costs as little as 5 dollars to get high. In the mid-1980s, the distribution of the ready-to-smoke freebase cocaine known as "crack" spread nationwide (Featherly & Hill, 1989). With the potent freebased form, there is an almost instantaneous euphoric high that is extremely desirable (Frances & Franklin, 1988). Cocaine's half-life is less than 90 minutes, and the euphoric effect lasts for only 15 to 30 minutes (Jaffe, 1980).

*The Cocaine Abstinent Syndrome* | The cocaine abstinent syndrome has three phases. Phase 1 is the crash, where the subjects report depression, anhedonia, insomnia, anxiety, irritability, and intense cocaine craving. These symptoms can last up to 3 days. In Phase 2, low-level cocaine craving continues, with irritability, anxiety, and decreased capacity to experience pleasure. Over several days the negative consequences of cocaine use fade, the person feels more normal and the craving for cocaine increases, especially in the context of environmental cues. The third phase consists of several weeks of milder episodic craving triggered by environmental stimuli. Many patients will appear to have a major depression shortly after cessation of cocaine or amphetamine use. These patients may become suicidal. Most of these symptoms will clear, but some symptoms, such as sadness and lethargy, can last for months (Gawin & Kleber, 1986a; Schuckit, 1984).

The treatments for stimulant rehabilitation are similar to the treatment of alcoholism. The euphoria that stimulants offer needs to be replaced by more adaptive achievements. Stimulant intoxication can be managed with the benzodiazepines or propranolol. Amphetamine or cocaine psychosis may have to be treated with antipsychotic medication. Patients in psychosis need to be kept in a quiet place, supported, and reassured. Antidepressants such as desipramine may ease the withdrawal syndrome (Gawin & Kleber, 1986b).

## Phencyclidine (PCP)

Phencyclidine (PCP) is an anesthetic initially manufactured for animal surgery. For a short time it was used as a general anesthetic for humans. Street use of PCP became widespread in the 1970s, when it was introduced as a drug to be smoked or snorted (Jaffe, 1980). Phencyclidine is still epidemic in certain eastern American cities (Caracci, Megone, & Dornbush, 1983).

In humans, small doses of PCP produce a subjective sense of intoxication, with staggering gait, slurred speech, and numbness of the extremities. The user may experience changes in body image and disorganized thought, drowsiness, and apathy. There may be hostile or bizarre behavior. Amnesia for the episode may occur. With increasing doses, stupor or coma may occur, although the eyes may remain open (Domino, 1978). Animals will self-administer PCP for its reinforcing properties (Balster & Chait, 1978). Psychoactive effects of PCP generally begin within 5 minutes and plateau in 30 minutes. In contrast to the use of hallucinogens, use of PCP may lead to long-term neurological damage (Davis, 1982).

Few drugs are able to produce as wide a range of subjective effects as PCP. Among the effects that users like are increased sensitivity to external stimuli, stimulation, mood elevation, and a sense of intoxication (Carroll & Comer, 1994). Other effects, seen as unwanted, are perceptual disturbances, restlessness, disorientation, and anxiety. Smoking marijuana cigarettes laced with PCP is the most common form of administration (Frances & Franklin, 1988). Phencyclidine produces several organic mental disorders, including intoxication, delirium, delusional mood, and flashback disorders (APA, 1987). Acute adverse reactions to this drug generally require medication to control symptoms. Benzodiazepines are usually the drug of choice, but antipsychotics may become necessary.

## Hallucinogens

No sharp line divides the psychedelics from other psychoactive drugs that cause hallucinations. Anticholinergics, bromides, antimalarials, opioid antagonists, cocaine, amphetamines, and corticosteroids can produce illusions and hallucinations, delusions, paranoid ideation, and other alterations in mood and thought similar to psychosis. What seems to distinguish the psychedelic drugs from the others is the unique characteristic to produce states of altered perception that cannot be experienced except in dreams (Carroll & Comer, 1994; Jaffe, 1980).

The psychedelic most available in the United States is lysergic acid diethylamide (LSD). The psychedelic psilocybin has long been used in religious ceremonies by Southwest American Indians. In 1982, 21% of 18- to 25-year-olds had tried a psychedelic at least once (Miller, 1983). Thankfully, the use of this drug is on the decline.

Hallucinogens are not reinforcing to animals, and in humans, use is infrequent. Using more than 20 times is considered chronic abuse. Hallucinogens produce a variety of organic brain syndromes, including hallucinogen hallucinosis, delusional disorder, mood disorder, and flashback disorder (APA, 1987). Flashbacks may occur in as many as 25% of users (Naditch & Fenwick, 1977). Chronic delusional and psychotic reactions, and rarely schizophrenoform states, have been reported in some psychedelic users (Vardy & Kay, 1983).

*The Psychedelic State*

During the psychedelic state, there is an increased awareness of sensory input often accompanied by a sense of clarity. There is a diminished ability to control what is experienced. The user experiences unusual and vivid sensory sensations. Hallucinations are primarily visual. Colors may be heard or sounds seen. Frank auditory hallucinations are rare. Time seems to be altered. Frequently, the user feels like a casual observer of the self. The environment may be experienced as novel, often beautiful and harmonious. The attention of the user is turned inward. The slightest sensation may take on profound meaning. Commonly, there is a diminished ability to differentiate the boundaries of objects and the self. There may be a sense of union with the universe. The state begins to clear after about 12 hours (Freedman, 1968). Generally, intoxicated patients can be talked down without sedation. They need to be placed in a quiet environment free of excess stimulation. Occasionally a sedative may be necessary to calm the patient (Frances & Franklin, 1988).

**Cannabis**

Cannabis is an India hemp plant that has been used for medicinal purposes for centuries. Marijuana is a varying mixture of the plant's leaves, seeds, stems, and flowering tops. The psychoactive ingredient in cannabis is Delta-9-tetrahydro-cannabinol (THC). Hashish consists of the plant's dried resin, and it contains a higher percentage of THC (Turner, 1980).

Marijuana remains the most commonly used illegal drug in the United States. According to the 1988 National Household Survey, an estimated 66 million Americans had tried marijuana at least once in their lifetime (Adams et al., 1990). Surveys reveal that 31% of teenagers, 40% of young adults, and 10% of older adults have tried marijuana. It is generally acknowledged that marijuana use among adolescents peaked in the 1970s. Daily users of marijuana dropped from 10.2% in 1978 to 5% in 1984 (Centers for Disease Control, 1991a; Frances & Franklin, 1988).

Cannabis produces effects on mood, memory, motor coordination, cognitive ability, sensorium, time sense, and self-perception. Peak intoxication with smoking generally occurs within 10 to 30 minutes. Most commonly, there is an increased sense of well-being or euphoria, accompanied by feelings of relaxation and sleepiness. Where subjects can interact, there is less sleepiness and there is often spontaneous laughter (Hollister, 1986; Jones, 1971). Physical signs of use include red eyes, strong odor, dilated pupils, and increased pulse rate. With higher doses, short-term memory is impaired, and there develops a difficulty in carrying out actions requiring multiple mental tasks. This leads to a tendency to confuse past, present, and future. Depersonalization develops with a strange sense of unreality about the self (Melges, Tinklenberg, Hollister, & Gillespie, 1970). Balance and stability of stance are affected even at low-doses (Evans et al., 1973). Performance of simple motor skills and reaction times are relatively unimpaired until high doses are reached (Hollister, 1986; Jones, 1971).

Marijuana smokers frequently report an increase in hunger, dry mouth and throat, increased vivid visual imagery, and a keener sense of hearing. Subtle visual and auditory stimuli may take on new meaning (Clopton, Janowsky, Clopin, Judd, & Huey, 1979). Higher doses can produce frank hallucinations, delusions, and paranoid feelings. Thinking becomes confused and disorganized; depersonalization and altered time sense increase. Anxiety to the point of panic may replace euphoria. With high enough doses, the patient presents with a toxic psychosis with hallucinations, depersonalization, and loss of insight. This syndrome can occur acutely or after months of use (Chopra & Smith, 1974; Nahas, 1973; Thacore & Shukla, 1976).

Chronic smoking of marijuana and hashish has long been associated with bronchitis and asthma. Smoking affects pulmonary functioning even in young people. The tar produced by marijuana is more carcinogenic than that produced by tobacco (Secretary of Health, Education, and Welfare, 1977). Subjects using marijuana chronically exhibit apathy, dullness, and impairment of judgment, concentration, and memory. They lose interest in personal appearance, hygiene, and diet. These effects have been observed in young users who regularly smoke a few marihuana cigarettes a day. These chronic effects take months to clear after cessation of use (Jaffe, 1980; Tennant & Grossbeck, 1972).

The pharmacological effects of marihuana begin within minutes after smoking. Effects may persist for 3 to 5 hours. THC and its metabolites can be found in the urine for several days or weeks after a single administration. THC is highly lipid soluble and its metabolites tend to accumulate in the fat cells. They have a half-life of approximately 50 hours (Hollister, 1986; Secretary of Health, Education, and Welfare, 1977). Tolerance and dependence develops to marijuana, and abrupt cessation after chronic use is followed by headache, mild irritability, restlessness, nervousness, decreased appetite, weight loss, and insomnia. Tremor and increased body temperature may occur (Gold, 1994a; Jones, Bennowitz, & Bachman, 1976; Wikler, 1976). As the withdrawal symptoms tend to be mild, detoxification is usually not necessary (Francis & Franklin, 1988).

## Inhalants

Inhalants include substances with diverse chemical structures used to produce a state of intoxication. Gasoline, airplane glue, aerosol (spray paints), lighter fluid, fingernail polish, typewriter correction fluid, a variety of cleaning solvents, amyl and butyl nitrate, and nitrous oxide. Hydrocarbons are the most active ingredients in these substances. In 1980, 10% of 12- to 17-year-olds reported using inhalants at least once (Francis & Franklin, 1988).

Several methods are used to inhale the intoxicating vapors. Most commonly, a rag soaked with the substance is applied to the mouth and nose and the vapors are breathed. The individual may place the substance in a paper or a plastic bag and the gases inhaled. The substance can also be inhaled directly from containers or sprayed into the mouth or nose (APA, 1987).

Dependent individuals may use inhalants several times per week, often on weekends and after school. They are sometimes used by young children, 9 to 13 years of age. These children usually use with a group of friends who are likely to use alcohol and marijuana as well as the inhalant. Older adolescents and young adults who have inhalant dependence are likely to have used a wide variety of substances (APA, 1987).

While high doses of these agents produce CNS depression, low doses produce an increase of CNS activity and a brief period of intoxication. Intoxication can last from a few minutes to 2 hours. Impaired judgment, poor insight, violence, and psychosis may occur during the intoxicated period. Inhalants are easily and cheaply acquired, and they can be attractive to children who cannot drink legally. Animals will self-administer inhalants as a reinforcement. There is a strong cross-tolerance between inhalants and the CNS depressants. Studies of inhalers have found indications of long-lasting brain damage (Cohen, 1979; Sharp & Brehm, 1977; Sharp & Carroll, 1978). Long-term damage to the bone marrow, kidneys, liver, and brain have also been reported (Francis & Franklin, 1988). There have been a number of deaths among inhalant abusers, the deaths are attributable to respiratory depression or cardiac arrhythmia. These deaths often appear to be accidental (King, Smialick, & Troutman, 1985).

**Nicotine**

The crews who accompanied Columbus to the New World were the first Europeans to observe the smoking of tobacco. They brought the leaves and the practice of smoking back to Europe. Tobacco addiction is the number one preventable health problem in the United States. Approximately 50 million Americans currently smoke tobacco (Centers for Disease Control, 1991b). Cigarettes are responsible for more than 434,000 deaths each year in the United States (Centers for Disease Control, 1988). About 4,000 different compounds are generated by the burning of tobacco, but tobacco's main psychoactive ingredient is nicotine. Nicotine produces a euphoric effect and has reinforcing properties similar to cocaine and the opioids (Henningfield, 1984). Tolerance to some of the effects of nicotine quickly develops, but even the chronic smoker continues to exhibit an increase in pulse and blood pressure after smoking as little as two cigarettes. Nicotine has a distinct withdrawal syndrome characterized by craving for tobacco, irritability, anxiety, difficulty concentrating, restlessness, increased appetite, and increased sleep disturbance (Hughes & Hatsukami, 1986; Surgeon General, 1979).

Tobacco addiction has many similar properties to opioid addiction. The use of tobacco is usually an addictive form of behavior (Frances & Franklin, 1988). Tobacco produces a calming euphoric effect, particularly on chronic users. Nicotine in cigarette smoke is suspended on minute particles of tar and it is quickly absorbed from the lungs with the efficiency of intravenous administration. The compound reaches the brain within 8 seconds after inhalation. The half-life for elimination of nicotine is 30 to 60 minutes (Surgeon General, 1979).

Chronic use of tobacco is causally linked to a variety of serious diseases ranging from coronary artery disease to lung cancer. The likelihood of developing one of these diseases increases with the degree of exposure that is measured by the number of cigarettes per day. Cigarette-smoking men have 70% higher death rates than nonsmokers. Smoking in women is increasing along with smoking-related diseases. Smoking is responsible for an estimated 350,000 premature deaths each year in the United States (Braunwald et al., 1987).

It is estimated that 42 million Americans have stopped smoking. Approximately 30% of smokers make an attempt to quit smoking each year. Eight percent of these attempts succeed. More than 90% of successful quitters do so on their own without participating in an organized cessation program. Smokers who quit "cold turkey" are more likely to remain abstinent than those who gradually decrease their daily consumption of cigarettes, switch to cigarettes with lower tar or nicotine, or use special filters or holders. Quit attempts are nearly twice as likely to occur among smokers who receive nonsmoking advice from a physician. Heavily addicted smokers (more than 25 cigarettes per day) are more likely to participate in an organized cessation program (Pierce, Fiore, Novotny, Hatziandreu, & Davis, 1989).

As addiction specialists, all counselors need to advise their patients against smoking and help them quit. Smokers can and do quit. All smokers should consult with the staff physician for nonsmoking advice. Self-help material can be presented to the patients who request more information and a pharmacological alternative, such as gum containing nicotine or a nicotine patch, can be substituted to ease withdrawal. Formal smoking cessation programs, such as the American Lung Association's "Freedom From Smoking" clinic, may be beneficial for heavier smokers (Glynn, 1990). The twelve steps can be useful in giving a smoker support in their attempt to quit. Some patients will want to quit smoking while in treatment. This should be encouraged and supported.

## Polysubstances

Few drug abusers abuse only one drug. There is a strong correlation between misuse of heroin and alcohol problems, abusers of stimulants frequently use depressants to cut irritable side effects, and alcoholics are at a higher risk to abuse other depressants and stimulants (Schuckit, 1984).

In Western society, youths begin drug use with caffeine, nicotine, and alcohol. If they go on to use other drugs, the next drug of choice will most likely be marijuana, followed by one of the hallucinogens, depressants, or stimulants. These drugs are taken at first on an experimental basis; they are reinforcing and lead to few serious consequences. Marijuana is seen as a step on the road to the use of other substances. Once the illegal barrier is crossed, it becomes easier to take a second and a third drug (Gould & Keeber, 1974; Kandel, 1978).

The effects of a drug may be either increased or decreased by adding an additional drug. Depressants taken together may potentiate the effect of either drug taken alone. Depressants and stimulants taken together may decrease the level of side effects encountered when one of the drugs is used alone. Marijuana has been shown to potentiate the effects of alcohol, and may increase the likelihood of a flashback from hallucinogen use (Schuckit, 1984). Over half of the patients presenting to a polydrug clinic report the use of three or more substances (Cook, Hostetter, & Ramsay, 1975; Fisher, Halikas, & Baker, 1975).

The most common multiple-drug withdrawal syndromes are those seen following concomitant use of multiple depressants or depressants and stimulants. Depressants produce the most severe and life-threatening withdrawal symptoms. When depressants and stimulants are used together, the withdrawal syndrome more closely follows the clinical picture of depressant withdrawal, but it probably includes greater levels of sadness, paranoia, and lethargy (Shuckit, 1984).

## Treatment Outcome

The Treatment Outcome Prospective Study (TOPS) is the largest and most comprehensive study of drug abuse treatment ever completed. It collected data on over 10,000 patients admitted for chemical dependency treatment nationwide. The patients were in 37 different programs that varied from methadone maintenance, to residential, to outpatient treatment. The major finding was that treatment works. Drug abuse is significantly reduced after treatment, and the amount of decrease is greater in patients who remain in treatment longer. Patients needed to remain in treatment at least 6 months before significant impact on drug abuse was achieved. Associated problem behavior decreased (e.g., criminal behavior, family problems, suicidal thoughts). This study found that drug addiction is a chronically relapsing condition usually requiring prolonged or repeated treatment (Hubbard et al., 1989).

The overwhelming weight of evidence from a large number of outcome studies and epidemiologic studies indicates that treatment contributes significantly to positive behavior change in chemically dependent patients (Anglin & Hser, 1990; Gerstein & Harwood, 1990; Hoffmann, 1994; Hubbard, 1992; Sisk, Hatziandreu, & Hughes, 1990).

The National Institute of Medicine's Committee for the Study and Treatment and Rehabilitation Services for Alcoholism and Alcohol Abuse (Committee for the Study and Treatment, 1990), as well as many individual reviewers, Anglin and Hser (1990), Sisk et al. (1990), and Hubbard and DesJarlais (1991), have concluded that chemical dependency treatment changes patients for the better, and other studies confirm that the benefits of these changes considerably outweigh the costs of treatment (Hubbard, 1992).

Follow-up studies of proprietary programs reviewed by the National Institute of Medicine (1989) find abstinence rates between 40% and 60% in the first year after treatment. Similar results were found in studies of state programs and private programs (Hoffman & Harrison, 1987; Hubbard & Anderson, 1988; National Institute of Medicine, 1989).

Comprehensive Assessment and Treatment Outcome Research (CATOR) is the largest independent evaluation service for the chemically dependent field in the United States. Since 1980, CATOR has collected data on over 50,000 adults and 10,000 adolescents who have entered treatment programs. CATOR finds that there are large differences in the clinical characteristics of patients admitted to inpatient verses outpatient programs. Cocaine dependence is much higher in the inpatient group; marijuana and stimulant dependence is also higher. Half of the inpatients are dependent on illicit drugs, whereas only one third of the outpatients were so addicted. Almost 20% of inpatients admit to using at least two drugs other than alcohol on a weekly basis; only 8% of the outpatients admit to such heavy use. Recent ingestion is more common in the inpatient population, with 44% using alcohol or drugs within the last 24 hours before admission, contrasted with 23% of the outpatients.

Detailed analysis of the CATOR research has encouraging words for chemical dependency counselors. Patients who complete treatment, whether outpatient or inpatient, have a 50% chance of staying clean and sober for the year following treatment. If they complete treatment and attend AA/NA once a week for the next year, they have a 70% chance of staying sober. If they complete treatment and attend one AA/NA meeting and one aftercare session per week, they have a 90% chance of remaining sober for the next year. These are fantastic results—90% of the patients can stay sober if they complete treatment and attend AA/NA and aftercare on a regular basis (Hoffmann, 1991, 1994).

# The Good Counselor

CHAPTER
FIFTEEN

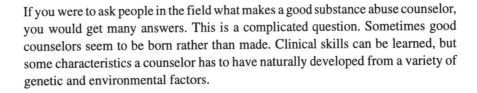

If you were to ask people in the field what makes a good substance abuse counselor, you would get many answers. This is a complicated question. Sometimes good counselors seem to be born rather than made. Clinical skills can be learned, but some characteristics a counselor has to have naturally developed from a variety of genetic and environmental factors.

**Being Loving**

Good counselors are first of all loving. They are interested in and actively involved in other people's interpersonal growth. They care about how people feel and they care about what they want. They feel this not only at work but in their social life as well. They instinctively feel that their patients have great worth. They help their patients to grow by gently guiding them. They don't hammer their patients, for hurting their patients would deeply hurt them as well. They do not constantly confront patients with their faults; rather, they praise them for their strengths. They build on the patient's strengths rather than concentrating on their weaknesses. They focus their attention on helping their patients grow in the way that they want to grow. They never push their own values and moral beliefs on their patients. They constantly encourage patients to see truth about themselves and others. They want them to be fully themselves and to reach for their full potential.

*Loving Counselors Enjoy Their Work*

Loving counselors do not feel burdened by their work. They feel their work is a great privilege. It is an honor to have someone share the intimate details of their life with you. By loving others in this program, the counselors will have love turned back on them. They will feel loved and important. Thomas Merton said that "happiness is unselfishly giving to others." Loving counselors give freely of themselves and expect nothing in return.

211

*Loving Counselors Don't Become Overly Involved*

Loving counselors don't become overly involved with their patients, because to do so would not be loving, it would be self-serving. To be loving you have to have a healthy personal lifestyle. You have to be reasonably comfortable with who you are, where you are, what you do, and who you are with. If you have unmet needs, these will be a obstacle to your becoming a good counselor. It's not that you have to be completely problem free, no one ever is, but you have to have a strong support system within yourself and outside of the treatment center. You have to be able to meet your own needs. If you ever think that patients can meet your needs, you are in for trouble. Counselors who are in the field to heal their own problems will feel angry and frustrated. Patients are too sick to help you; they need to concentrate on their own recovery.

*Loving Counselors Don't Lie*

Loving counselors never lie. Love necessitates action in truth. Without truth, love cannot survive. It is never loving to lie. You can tell a patient that you don't want to talk about an issue, but you should never make up a story, even if you think it is for the patient's own good. It is never in the patient's good interest to lie. Lies cut the patient off from reality.

*Loving Counselors Are Gentle*

Loving counselors are gentle and kind. They are sensitive to the patient's pain. To cause unnecessary pain is inexcusable. The truth may also cause the patient some pain, but without the truth the patient will never recover. Good counselors can give consequences because they know it's for the patient's own good.

Being gentle means that you encourage the patient to see the truth. Never yell or call people names. You may get angry, that's normal, but try to use your anger appropriately. Patients can have a very difficult time dealing with their counselor's anger. It can permanently damage the therapeutic relationship. It is useful when you are angry to be angry at the illness rather than at the patients. If the patients understand this, they can join you in feeling angry at the disease. It may hurt them some to give them a consequence, but it will feel good in the long run. You are doing the right thing for them by helping them to learn from their maladaptive behavior.

*Good Counselors Love Themselves*

Good counselors love themselves. They nourish themselves. They cultivate stable, loving relationships with family and friends. They spend quality time alone. If they are in recovery, they work a daily program. Through prayer and meditation they seek a conscious contact with the God as they understand him. Good counselors don't overwork and they don't become overly involved. When they leave work, they don't bring the problems home.

**Sensitivity**

A good counselor must be sensitive to other people's feelings. This seems to be an inborn trait: Some people have this sensitivity naturally, and some people don't. Some sensitivity can be learned, but the sensitivity a counselor needs can't be—you need a hypersensitive autonomic nervous system for this. To be sensitive, you need to feel other people's pain almost as if it is your pain. When they hurt, you hurt; and when they feel joy, you feel joy. This is called empathy. With empathy you perceive, feel, and understand the other person's experience.

*The Sixth Sense*

The more sensitive you are, the better a counselor you are going to be. Your sensitivity will enable you to know where a patient is emotionally. This gives you accurate information about the patient's motivation. Patients may not know how they feel; they may be cut off from their feelings. In a sense, you need to be ahead of the patients. You will feel the feeling as they are feeling it, but you will feel it before they have processed it. There will be those few seconds when you know where they are going. You know, because that sixth sense of yours has picked it up. Remember, feelings give us energy and direction for movement. If you know how someone feels, you can predict what they are going to do.

You can learn sensitivity to some degree by trial and error. Constantly ask patients how they are feeling to check yourself. Most patients will correct you if you are wrong. As you reflect their feelings and they correct you, you will develop greater sensitivity. This skill will develop and become more accurate over the years. As you learn what people want and how they feel, you will be able to help them move forward more quickly. You will make mistakes, but you will learn many things about people. You will learn that no one really wants to do a bad thing. They do bad things because they see the good in it. If you understand this, you will be able to understand your patients. Child abuse can occur simply because the parent wanted the child to be quiet. They didn't want to hurt the child for the joy of seeing someone in pain.

Your supersensitivity will help you to know what motivates the patient. Borderline patients or schizophrenic patients are very difficult to understand unless you understand how they are feeling and what they are thinking. These are patients that you have to explore until you understand how they perceive the world.

*Good Counselors Don't Become Overemotional*

A few counselors seem to be overly sensitive. They become overemotional. This is countertransference. These are the counselors who weep openly with most clients and at family sessions. They encourage patients to call them at home, anytime. They call the patients after they leave treatment just to see how they are doing. They encourage patients to drop by their house. These counselors have a need to be liked and they are transferring their need to the patient. Some of these counselors have unresolved psychological problems that are driving them. Their desire to help, people-please, and care take of others is out of control. These counselors get hurt, frustrated, and angry because they learn that patients don't want a friend—they want a counselor. Many of these people burn out and finally leave the profession. They never seek the professional help they need to get their work in prospective.

You can't be too sensitive if you use your sensitivity correctly. This supersensitivity will give you accurate direction. You will be able to say the right thing at the right time. You will know just know what to say. You will know what you would want to hear. Best of all, this supersensitivity will give you great timing. You will be able to say the right thing at the right time. This is almost a magical experience. It will happen to you more and more as you grow in your counseling career.

**Active Listener**

■

Good counselors listen. They know when to be quiet and focus on what the patient is saying. They are interested in how the patient perceives things. They want to know what the patient is thinking and feeling. They desire to become a part of the patient's world. Counselors who are good listeners will have patients tell them that they are good. The patient feels understood.

*Good Counselors Don't Talk Too Much*

A common mistake of inexperienced counselors is to talk too much. If they recorded themselves in group or in individual sessions, they would realize that they do most of the talking. They think that they have a lot to say and patients have a lot to learn, so why not just teach them? Counseling with these individuals is more like going to a lecture. Good counselors ask a lot of questions and listen carefully for the answer. They are attentive to the patients' verbal and nonverbal behavior. If they see patients saying one thing with their words and another thing with their behavior, they believe the behavior.

An active listener will reflect how the patient is feeling and wait for feedback. Even with supersensitivity, you never know perfectly what another person is experiencing. You have to ask and listen. Nothing helps a patient feel more understood than to be listened to attentively. As you focus your attention on patients, they feel important, they feel that someone cares for them and knows them. Active listening takes a lot of energy, it is not easy. You have to listen with every fiber of your being. If you don't listen, your patient will never feel loved. Counselors with poor listening skills hear their patients say, "You don't understand me." Good counselors very rarely hear these words. If patients don't feel understood, they will be frustrated, and their treatment will suffer, the therapeutic alliance will be shaky, and the patients will not trust. To trust you, the patient must feel known.

## Boundaries

■

Good counselors knows their boundaries. They know who they are as a person, and they will not allow other people to violate them. You will have patients in treatment that will try to threaten you or throw their weight around. You will use the group with these patients to give you the support you need. Angry patients are using the only skill they know how to use. It's your job to teach them how to get what they want some other way.

You must know your professional boundaries and not cross them. You must use only techniques you have learned by professional training and experience. You should never use a technique if you have only heard about it. Watch a skilled person use the technique a few times. Then have them watch you. Use only the skills that you have been trained to use. You must be able to demonstrate, through professional education and experience, that you know what you are doing.

If you feel comfortable with yourself and your training, it is a relief to let the rest of the staff do their own thing. You don't have to question their skills. The professional staff organization will accept that responsibility. You can relax and enjoy your role as the counselor. That's plenty of work. You don't have to do everyone's job, just your own.

Boundaries include keeping your relationships with your clients professional. A good counselor never takes advantage of their relationship with a patient. They never act on romantic feelings or become involved in business dealings with their clients. If you do these things, it will be confusing to you and your patient. Your patients are in a vulnerable situation; you are their confidant, their hero. If you use this relationship for your own gain, you are going to hurt somebody. The relationship with your patients is special—don't take advantage of them.

**Patience**

A good counselor is patient. They treat the chemically dependent person at that person's own pace. They know that different patients come into treatment with different levels of readiness for treatment. Some patients are ready to disclose the truth very fast, the first day, and some patients will be reluctant to share the truth. It never helps to threaten or push a patient to disclose information. All you can do is to give the patient the opportunity to share in a loving environment. You teach the patient the consequences of not sharing. If patients understand, and they see unconditional positive regard, they will share. If they can't share with you, they can share in their Fifth Step. If they can't share the truth there, encourage them to share at a later date. You can't make people talk. If you try, you will be in trouble. People will see you as abusive and harmful. Your job is to provide a loving atmosphere where people want to talk.

You need to give patients the chance to grow at their own rate. You must take them through treatment at a pace that they can follow and understand. They must recognize the severity of their illness, understand their self-defeating relationship with substances, and apply the tools of recovery. They must see their new behaviors work.

Some patients will not do written work well, or they will not get things if they read them. Learning disabilities can handicap patients. These patients have to be treated differently. If you try to push them to do something that they can't do, you will fail. Many people have physical, emotional, or social roadblocks to learning. You must recognize when a patient is struggling and intervene as soon as possible. You must do something differently to make the program more understandable.

**Interpersonal Relationship Skills**

Good counselors have good interpersonal relationship skills. They are good communicators. They tell people how they feel and what they think. They do not keep their feelings to themselves. They use their feelings appropriately to help them solve problems. They are trustworthy and reliable. If they tell the patient they are going to do something, they do it. They are there for the patient when they are needed. If the patient asks for help, the counselor stops what they are doing and focuses on the patient. This may take only a few minutes. If the discussion is going to take longer, you can make an appointment to see the patient later.

Good counselors never manipulate to get their way. They never say one thing and mean another. They never plot against or plan against a patient or against a member of the professional staff. Manipulation necessitates lies, and treatment is a program of rigorous honesty. A good counselor will not become involved in dishonest communication.

A good counselor is assertive, not aggressive. They don't use the power of their position or their personality to make the patient do something. They share their feelings with the patient and are frank about what they want. If the patient has broken the rules and consequences are required, they are leveled without excessive guilt or remorse. The good counselor never attacks, assaults, abuses, yells, screams, chastises, torments, scolds, assails, batters, shames, berates, condemns, lays into, insults, tongue-lashes, intimidates, threatens, terrorizes, forces, violates, oppresses, sneaks, defames, or belittles. They treat the patient the way they would want to be treated.

Good counselors sense when a patient is transferring energy from a previous relationship to the therapeutic relationship. They help the patient to understand

and work through the transference. They always keep the patient informed about what they are thinking and how they are feeling. The patient never feels left in the dark.

Good counselors treat the patient with honor and respect. They feel it is a privilege to work with each person, no matter who they are. If they have a patient whom they cannot work with, they refer the patient to someone else. They care about how the patient feels and about what they want. They want to help the patient feel comfortable.

Good counselors are constantly reinforcing. They are fun to be around. They enjoy life. They like giving people praise. They look for things to reinforce. These counselors try to see the good in everything. They are always reaching for the positive. They praise people for the little things. They notice when someone does something right and they point it out. Good counselors are rarely punitive; they don't like to punish. When they are giving good things to others, they feel the best about themselves.

## Sound Code of Ethics

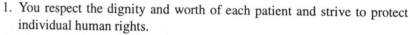

Good counselors have a good code of ethics. This is what you need to do to maintain the highest ethical principles.

1. You respect the dignity and worth of each patient and strive to protect individual human rights.
2. You are committed to patients understanding themselves and reaching their full potential.
3. You protect the welfare of those who seek your services as a professional.
4. You do not permit your skills to be misused.
5. You accept the responsibility for the consequences of your actions. When you are wrong, you promptly admit it.
6. You make sure that your services are used appropriately.
7. You avoid relationships that may create a conflict of interest.
8. You try to prevent distortion or misuse of your findings.
9. You present material objectively, fully, and accurately.
10. You know that in your work you bear a heavy responsibility because your recommendations and actions may alter the lives of others.
11. You accurately represent your competence, education, training, and experience.
12. You recognize the need for continuing education and are open to new procedures and changes.
13. You recognize the differences among people of different races, sexes, cultures, creeds, ethnic backgrounds, and socioeconomic status, and when necessary are willing to obtain special training in how to deal effectively with such persons.
14. If you use assessment tools, you are responsible for knowing the reliability and validity of such instruments.
15. You recognize that personal problems may interfere with your professional effectiveness. You refrain from becoming engaged in an activity where your personal problems may have influence. If you have serious problems, you have a responsibility to seek appropriate professional assistance.

16. You obey the law.
17. You do not condone practices that you perceive as being inhumane or unjust.
18. When announcing professional services, you do not make claims that cannot be demonstrated by sound research.
19. You present yourself accurately, avoiding misrepresentation of yourself or your findings.
20. You respect the confidentiality of all information obtained within the context of your work.
21. You reveal such information only with the written permission of the patient or the patient's legal representative, except when the patient is a clear danger to self or others.
22. Where appropriate, you inform the patient of the legal limits of confidentiality.
23. Information obtained in professional relationships is discussed only for professional purposes and only with persons clearly concerned with the case.
24. You ensure that appropriate provisions are made for maintaining confidentiality in the storage and disposal of the patient record.
25. You recognize your own needs and are cognizant of your potential to influence clients and subordinates.
26. You make every effort to avoid relationships that could impair your professional judgment or increase the risk of exploitation. This includes, but is not limited to, treatment of employees, close friends, or relatives.
27. Sexual intimacies with patients are unethical.
28. You make arrangements for payment of services that safeguard the best interest of your client.
29. You terminate your services when it is reasonably clear that the patient is not benefiting.
30. You understand the areas of your competence and make full use of other professionals that will serve the best interest of your patient.
31. You cooperate fully with other professionals.
32. If a person is receiving a similar service from another professional, you carefully consider that relationship, and proceed cautiously, protecting the other professional and the patient.
33. If you employ or supervise other professionals or professionals in training, you accept the obligation to facilitate the professional development of these individuals. You provide appropriate working conditions, timely evaluations, constructive consultation, and continuing education.
34. You do not exploit your professional relationships with patients, supervisees, students, or employees sexually or otherwise. You do not condone nor participate in any form of sexual harassment.
35. When you know of ethical violation by another counselor, if it seems appropriate, you bring this violation to the attention of the counselor. If this behavior is not corrected you bring the information to the appropriate local, state, or national board.

Are you a good counselor? I hope so. If you are, you have chosen a field that will give you indescribable joy. You will see people at their worst and at their best.

You will see them crying, and you will see them laughing. You will help people to change for the better. You will be there to help put broken families back together. You will see in the eyes of your patients the love and appreciation that they will feel for you. You will experience a deep love for others. You will learn to appreciate people for their uniqueness. You will savor the fact that no two people are the same. You will travel with men and women who are addicted as they struggle toward new hope and a new life. Their hope is in you, because you are the chemical dependency counselor.

# List of Appendixes

1. Cognitive Capacity Screening Examination
2. Short Michigan Alcoholism Screening Test (SMAST)
3. CAGE Questionnaire
4. DSM-IV Psychoactive Substance Use Disorder
5. Clinical Institute Withdrawal Assessment of Alcohol Scale
6. Narcotic Withdrawal Scale
7. Sample Biopsychosocial
8. Chemical Use History
9. Honesty
10. Love, Trust, and Commitment
11. Feelings
12. Relationship Skills
13. Addictive Relationships
14. Communication Skills
15. Self-Discipline
16. Impulse Control
17. Relapse Prevention
18. Step One
19. Step Two
20. Step Three
21. Step Four
22. Step Five
23. Adolescent Unit Level System
24. Peer Pressure
25. The Behavioral Contract
26. Family Questionnaire

27. Codependency
28. Personal Recovery Plan
29. Sample Discharge Summary
30. Stress Management
31. The Beck Depression Inventory
32. Biopsychosocial Assessment
33. Anger Management
34. Narcissism

# Appendix 1

## Cognitive Capacity Screening Examination

Examiner _____   Date _____

*Instructions:*   Check items answered correctly. Write incorrect or unusual answers in the space provided. If necessary, urge the patient once to complete task.

*Introduction to patient:*   "I would like to ask you a few questions. Some you will find very easy and others may be very hard. Just do your best."

1. What day of the week is this? _____
2. What month? _____
3. What day of the month? _____
4. What year? _____
5. What place is this?_____
6. Repeat the numbers 8 7 2. _____
7. Say them backward. _____
8. Repeat these numbers: 6 3 7 1 _____
9. Listen to these numbers: 6 9 4.  Count 1 through 10 out loud, then repeat 6 9 4.
   (Help if needed. Then use numbers 5 7 3.)

   _____
10. Listen to these numbers: 8 1 4 3. Count 1 through 10 out loud, then repeat 8 1 4 3. _____
11. Beginning with Sunday, say the days of the week backward. _____
12. 9 plus 3 is _____
13. Add 6 (to the previous answer or to 12). _____
14. Take away 5 (from 18). _____

   Repeat these words after me and remember them, I will ask for them later: *hat, car, tree, twenty-six.*

15. The opposite of fast is slow. The opposite of up is _____
16. The opposite of large is _____
17. The opposite of hard is _____
18. An orange and a banana are both fruits. Red and blue are both _____
19. A penny and a dime are both _____
20. What are those words I asked you to Remember? (*hat*) _____
21. (*car*) _____
22. (*tree*) _____
23. (*twenty-six*) _____
24. Take away 7 from 100, then take away 7 from what is left and keep going: 100 minus seven is _____
25. Minus 7 _____
26. Minus 7 (Write down the answer; check correct subtraction of 7.) _____
27. Minus 7 _____
28. Minus 7 _____
29. Minus 7 _____
30. Minus 7 _____

   Total Correct  _____

Patient was:

Cooperative _____

Uncooperative _____

Depressed _____

Lethargic _____

Other _____

If the patient's score is less than 20, the existence of diminished cognitive capacity is present. Therefore, an organic mental syndrome should be suspected and the medical staff notified.

_____

Reproduced, with permission, from J. W. Jacobs, M. R. Bernhard, A. Delgado, et al. (1977). Screening for organic mental syndromes in the medically ill, *Annuals of Internal Medicine 86,* 40-46.

# Appendix 2
## Short Michigan Alcoholism Screening Test (SMAST)

1. Do you feel you are a normal drinker? (By *normal* we mean you drink less than or as much as most other people?) (No)
2. Does your wife, husband, a parent, or other near relative ever worry or complain about your drinking? (Yes)
3. Do you ever feel guilty about your drinking? (Yes)
4. Do friends or relatives think you are a normal drinker? (No)
5. Are you able to stop drinking when you want to? (No)
6. Have you ever attended a meeting of Alcoholics Anonymous? (Yes)
7. Has drinking ever created problems between you and your wife, husband, a parent or other near relative? (Yes)
8. Have you ever gotten into trouble at work because of your drinking? (Yes)
9. Have you ever neglected your obligations, your family, or your work for 2 or more days in a row because you were drinking? (Yes)
10. Have you ever gone to anyone for help about your drinking? (Yes)
11. Have you ever been in a hospital because of drinking? (Yes)
12. Have you ever been arrested for drunken driving, driving while intoxicated, or driving under the influence of alcoholic beverages? (Yes)
13. Have you ever been arrested, even for a few hours, because of other drunken behavior? (Yes)

Answers related to alcoholism are given in parentheses after each question. Three or more of these answers indicate probable alcoholism; two answers indicate the possibility of alcoholism; less than two answers indicate that alcoholism is not likely.

Reprinted with permission from the *Journal of Studies on Alcohol, 36*, 117-126 (1975). Copyright by Journal Studies on Alcohol, Inc., Rutgers Center of Alcohol Studies, New Brunswick, NJ 08903.

# Appendix 3
## CAGE Questionnaire

1. Have you ever felt you ought to **C**ut down on your drinking?
2. Have people **A**nnoyed you by criticizing your drinking?
3. Have you ever felt bad or **G**uilty about your drinking?
4. Have you ever had a drink first thing in the morning (**E**ye opener) to steady your nerves or to get rid of a hangover?

Two or more affirmative answers indicate probable alcoholism. Any single affirmative answer flags further evaluation.

---

Reprinted with permission from the *Journal of the American Medical Association 252,* 1905-1907 (1984). Copyright 1984, American Medical Association, 515 North State Street, Chicago, IL 60610.

# Appendix 4

## DSM-IV Psychoactive Substance Use Disorder

I.  Diagnostic Criteria for Psychoactive Substance Abuse

    A.  A maladaptive pattern of substance use leading to clinically significant impairment or distress, as manifested by one (or more) of the following occurring within a 12-month period:

        1.  Recurrent substance use resulting in a failure to fulfill major role obligations at work, school, or home (e.g., repeated absences or poor work performance related to substance use; substance-related absences, suspensions, or expulsions from school; neglect of children or household)

        2.  Recurrent use in situations in which it is physically hazardous (e.g., driving while intoxicated or operating a machine when impaired by substance use)

        3.  Recurrent substance-related legal problems (e.g., arrests of substance-related disorderly conduct)

        4.  Continued use despite knowledge of having a persistent or recurrent social or interpersonal problems caused or exacerbated by the effects of the substance (e.g., arguments with spouse about consequences of intoxication, physical fights)

    B.  Never met the criteria for Psychoactive Substance Dependence for this substance.

II.  Diagnostic Criteria for Psychoactive Substance Abuse Dependence

    A maladaptive pattern of substance use, leading to clinically significant impairment or distress, as manifested by three (or more) of the following, occurring at any time in the same 12-month period:

    A.  Tolerance, as defined by either of the following:

        1.  A need for markedly increased amounts of the substance to achieve intoxication or desired effect.

        2.  Markedly diminished effect with continued use of the same amount of the substance.

    B.  Withdrawal, as manifested by either of the following:

        1.  Characteristic withdrawal syndrome of the substance.

        2.  The same (or a closely related) substance is taken to relieve or avoid withdrawal symptoms.

    C.  Substance often taken in larger amounts or over a longer period than was intended.

    D.  There is a persistent desire or unsuccessful efforts to cut down or control substance use.

    E.  A great deal of time spent in activities necessary to get the substance (e.g., visiting multiple doctors or driving long distances), use the substance (e.g., chain smoking), or recover from its effects.

    F.  Important social, occupational, or recreational activities given up or reduced because of substance use.

    G.  The substance use is continued despite knowledge of having a persistent or recurrent social, psychological, or physical problem that is likely to have been caused or exacerbated by the use of the substance (e.g., keeps using heroin despite family arguments about it, cocaine-induced depression, or having an ulcer made worse by drinking).

*Specify if:*
*With Physiological Dependence: evidence of tolerance or withdrawal.*
*Without Physiological Dependence: no evidence of tolerance or withdrawal.*

---

Used with permission, *Diagnostic and Statistical Manual of Mental Disorders* (4th ed., 1994), American Psychiatric Association, Washington, DC.

# *Appendix 5*

## *Clinical Institute Withdrawal Assessment of Alcohol Scale*

Patient _____ Date _____ Time _____

Pulse or heart rate taken for one minute _____

Blood pressure _____ / _____

---

Nausea and Vomiting

    Ask "Do you feel sick to your stomach? Have you vomited?"

    Observation:

    0  no nausea and no vomiting

    1  mild nausea with no vomiting

    2

    3

    4  intermittent nausea with dry heaves

    5

    6

    7  constant nausea, frequent dry heaves and vomiting

---

Tremor

    Arms extended and fingers spread apart.

    Observation:

    0  no tremor

    1  not visible but can be felt fingertip to fingertip

    2

    3

    4  moderate, with patient's arms extended

    5

    6

    7  severe, even with arms not extended

---

## Proximal Sweats

Observation:

0  no sweat visible

1  barely perceptible sweating, palms moist

2

3

4  beads of sweat obvious on forehead

5

6

7  drenching sweats

---

## Anxiety

Ask "Do you feel nervous?"

Observation:

0  no anxiety, at ease

1  mildly anxious

2

3

4  moderately anxious or guarded, so anxiety is inferred

5

6

7  equivalent to acute panic states, as seen in severe delirium or acute schizophrenic reactions

---

## Agitation

Observation:

0  normal activity

1  somewhat more than normal activity

2

3

4  moderately fidgety and restless

5

6

7  paces back and forth during most of the interview, or constantly thrashes about

---

## Tactile Disturbances

Ask "Have you had any itching, pins-and-needles sensations, burning, numbness, or do you feel bugs crawling on or under your skin?"

Observation:

0 none

1 very mild itching, pins and needles, burning, or numbness

2 mild itching, pins and needles, burning, or numbness

3 moderate itching, pins and needles, burning, or numbness

4 moderately severe hallucinations

5 severe hallucinations

6 extremely severe hallucinations

7 continuous hallucinations

## Auditory Disturbances

Ask "Are you more aware of sounds around you? Are they harsh? Do they frighten you? Are you hearing anything that is disturbing to you? Are you hearing things you know are not there?"

Observation:

0 not present

1 very mild harshness or ability to frighten

2 mild harshness or ability to frighten

3 moderate harshness or ability to frighten

4 moderately severe hallucinations

5 severe hallucinations

6 extremely severe hallucinations

7 continuous hallucinations

## Visual Disturbances

Ask "Does the light appear to be too bright? Is the color different? Does it hurt your eyes? Are you seeing anything that is disturbing to you? Are you seeing things that you know are not there?"

Observation:

0 not present

1 very mild sensitivity

2 mild sensitivity

3 moderate sensitivity

4 moderately severe hallucinations

5 severe hallucinations

6 extremely severe hallucinations

7 continuous hallucinations

## Headache, Fullness in Head

Ask "Does your head feel different? Does it feel like there is a band around your head?" Do not rate dizziness or lightheadedness. Otherwise, rate severity.

0 not present

1 very mild

2 mild

3 moderate

4 moderately severe

5 severe

6 very severe

7 extremely severe

## Orientation and Clouding of Sensorium

Ask "What day is this? Where are you? Who am I?"

0 oriented and can do serial additions

1 cannot do serial additions or is uncertain about date

2 disoriented for date by no more than 2 calendar days

3 disoriented for date by more than 2 calendar days

4 disoriented for place and/or person

Total score _____

Rater's initials _____

Maximum possible score 67

A score greater than 25 indicates severe withdrawal (impending DTs). If score is less than 10 after two 8-hour reviews, monitoring can stop. If scores are above 20, the patient should be assessed hourly until the symptoms are under control.

# Appendix 6
## Narcotic Withdrawal Scale

There are four major stages in narcotics withdrawal:

Grade I:  Lacrimation (teary eyes)
   Rhinorrhea (runny nose)
   Diaphoresis (sweating)
   Yawning
   Restlessness
   Insomnia (difficulty sleeping)

Grade II:  Dilated pupils
   Piloerection (goose bumps on skin)
   Muscle twitching
   Myalgia (muscle pain)
   Arthralgia (joint pain)
   Abdominal pain

Grade III:  Tachycardia (pulse or heart rate over 100)
   Hypertension (high blood pressure)
   Tachypnea (rapid breathing)
   Fever
   Anorexia (loss of appetite)
   Nausea
   Extreme restlessness

Grade IV:  Diarrhea
   Vomiting
   Dehydration
   Hyperglycemia (high blood sugar)
   Hypotension (low blood pressure)
   Curled-up position

---

Used with permission, J. M. Fultz & E. C. Senay (1975), Guidelines for the management of hospitalized narcotics addicts, *Annuals of Internal Medicine 82,* 815-818.

# Appendix 7
## Sample Biopsychosocial

DATE: 6-2-91

PATIENT NAME:  Patty Jean Robbins

DEMOGRAPHIC DATA:  This is a 28-year-old single white female. She is childless. She lives by herself in Watertown, South Dakota. She has lived in Watertown for the past 5 years. She has a high school education. She is employed as a beautician at The Cut Above.

CHIEF COMPLAINT:  "I couldn't go on drinking the way I was."

HISTORY OF THE PRESENT ILLNESS:  This patient's father died when she was an infant. She was raised by an overly demanding alcoholic mother. Her mother had strict rules and made the patient work hard to keep the house clean. The patient never made an emotional connection with her mother. "I grew up feeling left out, abandoned, lost, and alone. I think I was loved, but I wasn't shown it." In school she continued to feel isolated from her peers. She began drinking in her early teens. In high school the patient didn't date a lot, but when she did, she fell immediately in love. She began a series of addictive relationships with men. In these relationships she was able to experience the affection she had always longed for. The patient was "devastated" when her boyfriends would go out with someone else. She would frantically "keep grasping" to hold on to the relationship. After high school the patient began an affair with a married man. This man was demonstrative in his affection, and this fooled the patient into thinking that he "really loved me." The patient was unable to disengage from this relationship even though he was married and emotionally and physically abusive. The patient's drinking began increasing. Her tolerance to alcohol increased. She had blackouts. The patient began to use Valium for sleep. Her dose of Valium has more than doubled. She is currently drinking at least a six-pack of beer and taking 30 milligrams of Valium every night. The patient is currently suffering from acute alcohol and anxiolytic withdrawal. Her withdrawal will probably be protracted since she has been on Valium for 5 years. In withdrawal she reports she feels restless and is sleeping poorly. The patient has few assertiveness skills and can be excessively dependent. She enjoys men who are powerful and controlling. The patient has few healthy relationship skills and she is dishonest. The patient is accepting of treatment and has a strong desire to get help for her chemical dependency.

PAST HISTORY:  This patient was born in Livingston, South Dakota, on June 28, 1963. She reports a normal birth and normal developmental milestones. She was raised with her mother and two younger sisters. Her father died when she was too young to know him. Her ethnic heritage is Irish. She describes her home of origin as "I didn't like it. I felt alone." In grade school, "I was timid, not very outgoing." In high school, "I was scared to relate." The patient denies ever serving in the military. Her occupational history includes a 5-year stint as a secretary. She has held her current job as a beautician for 10 years. She is happily employed. The patient is heterosexual. She has a complex history of addictive relationships with men who have been abusive both verbally and physically. The patient is currently involved with a new boyfriend. She has been seeing him for the past few months. She reports that this relationship is going well. Her friends and family support her coming into treatment. Spiritually, the patient believes in God. She was raised in the Lutheran church. She attends church regularly. She denies any legal difficulties. For strengths, the patient identifies, "I'm caring. I get along with people real well. I think I'm intelligent." For weaknesses, the patient states, "I have a drinking problem." For leisure activities the patient enjoys biking and jogging. Her leisure activities have only been mildly affected by her chemical use.

MEDICAL HISTORY:
- Illnesses: Measles, mumps, chicken pox
- Hospitalizations: None
- Allergies: None
- Medications at present: The patient is taking 5 milligrams of Valium three times a day for withdrawal

FAMILY HISTORY:
- Father: Age of death, "in his twenties." Cause of death, unknown. The patient does not remember her father.
- Mother: Age 53, in good health. History of alcoholism. Described as "quiet, demanding."
- Other relatives with significant psychopathology: None

MENTAL STATUS: This is a tall, thin, 28-year-old white female. She has short curly light brown hair and blue eyes. She has a broad smile and a freckled face. She was dressed in white jeans and a white sweatshirt. Her sensorium was clear. She was oriented to person, place, and time. Her attitude toward the examiner was cooperative, friendly, and pleasant. Her motor behavior was mildly restless. The patient fidgeted in her chair. She made good eye contact. Her speech was spontaneous and without errors. Her affect was mildly anxious. Her range of affect was within normal limits. Her mood was mildly anxious. Her thought processes were productive and goal directed. Suicidal ideation was denied. Homicidal ideation was denied. Disorders of perception were denied. Delusions were denied. Obsessions and compulsions were denied. The patient exhibited an above average level of intellectual functioning. She could concentrate well. Her immediate, recent, and remote memories were intact. She exhibited fair impulse control. Her judgment was fair. She is insightful about her alcohol problem and is in minimal denial about her drinking. She is in greater denial about her problem with Valium.

## DIAGNOSTIC SUMMARY

DATE: 6-10-91

PATIENT NAME: Patty Jean Robins

This is a 28-year-old single white female. She is childless. She lives by herself in Watertown, South Dakota. She has lived in Watertown for the past 5 years. She has a high school education. She is currently employed as a beautician at The Cut Above. She comes to treatment with a chief complaint of a drinking problem. The patient's father died when she was an infant. She was raised by an emotionally distant alcoholic mother. Patty grew up feeling a profound sense of abandonment. All her life she has felt empty and lost. She could gain her mother's approval only by being a hard worker. In grade school the patient was timid and shy. In high school she began a series of addictive relationships with men. Patty gets love and sex mixed up. She is starved for attention and affection. She is vulnerable to manipulation. She had an affair with a married man. Her relationships with men have been dysfunctional and abusive. The patient has few assertiveness skills. She cannot ask people for what she wants or share how she feels. She is dishonest. She lies to get what she wants. Patty began drinking in her early teens. After high school her drinking began to increase. Her tolerance to alcohol increased. She has had multiple blackouts and suffered withdrawal symptoms. She is drinking at least a six-pack of beer per day. Patty has been taking Valium for sleep for the last 5 years. She has increased her tolerance to Valium and has more than doubled her bedtime dose. The patient is currently experiencing symptoms of alcohol and Valium withdrawal. She has been anemic for the last several years. She is being treated with vitamins. She has cold symptoms and is taking aspirin and an antihistamine. She has a history of arthritis but exhibits no current symptoms. She has a history of a heart murmur. The patient is highly motivated for treatment and her relapse potential is low. She is psychologically minded and is opening up well in group. She shows minimal resistance to treatment. Her current recovery environment is poor. She has no social support system except for her boyfriend of the last 2 months. The psychological testing shows that Patty is emotionally unstable and manipulative. She will break the rules of society to get her own way. She will openly defy authority. She is suffering from mild depressive symptoms and she is experiencing significant daily anxiety. These symptoms seem to relate directly to the patient's chemical dependency.

Diagnosis

Axis I: 303.90 Alcohol dependence
304.10 Anxiolytic dependence
291.80 Alcohol withdrawal
292.00 Anxiolytic withdrawal
Axis II: V 71.09 No diagnosis axis II
Axis III: Anemia, mild cold symptoms.
Axis IV: Severity of psychosocial stressors, personal illness, severity, 3, moderate.
Axis V: Current global assessment of functioning: 50.
Highest global assessment of functioning past year: 70.

Problem List and Recommendations

Problem 1: Extended withdrawal from alcohol and Valium as evidenced by autonomic arousal and elevated vital signs.

Problem 2: Inability to maintain sobriety outside a structured program of recovery as evidenced by patient has tried to quit using chemicals many times unsuccessfully.

Problem 3: Anemia as evidenced by a chronic history of low red-cell counts.

Problem 4: Upper respiratory infection as evidenced by sore throat and rhinitis.

Problem 5: Fear of rejection and abandonment as evidenced by patient feeling abandoned by both her mother and father and now clinging to relationships even when abusive.

Problem 6: Poor relationship skills as evidenced by patient not sharing the truth about how she feels or asking for what she wants, leaving her unable to establish and maintain intimate relationships.

Problem 7: Dishonesty as evidenced by patient's chronically lying about her chemical use history.

Problem 8: Poor assertiveness skills as evidenced by patient allowing other people to make important decisions for her inhibiting her from developing a self-directed program of recovery.

## TREATMENT PLAN

Problem 1: Inability to maintain sobriety outside a structured program of recovery. As evidenced by:
Repeated unsuccessful attempts to remain abstinent, increased tolerance and withdrawal symptoms.

*Goal A:* Acquire the skills necessary to achieve and maintain a sober lifestyle.

Objective 1: Patty will discuss three times she unsuccessfully attempted to stop drug and alcohol use with her counselor by 6-15-91.

Objective 2: Patty will verbalize her powerlessness and unmanageability in group by 6-15-91.

Objective 3: Patty will verbalize her understanding of her chemical dependency with her group by 6-15-91.

Objective 4: Patty will share her understanding of how to use Step Two in recovery with her counselor by 6-20-91.

Objective 5: Patty will log her meditation daily and will discuss how she plans to use the Third Step in sobriety with her clergy person by 6-25-91.

Objective 6: Patty will develop a relapse prevention plan by 6-30-91.

Objective 7: Patty will develop an aftercare plan with her counselor by 7-5-91.

Problem 5: Chronic fear of abandonment as evidenced by fear of losing all interpersonal relationships.

*Goal B:* To alleviate the fear of abandonment by connecting the patient to her Higher Power and her AA/NA support group.

Objective 1: In one-to-one counseling Patty will share her feelings of abandonment by her parents and how this relates to her chemical dependency by 6-15-91.

Objective 2: Patty will share her feelings of fear, loneliness, and isolation with her group by 6-20-91.

Objective 3: Patty will discuss her fear that the group will abandon her and receive feedback from the group by 6-25-91.

Objective 4: In one-to-one counseling, the patient will discuss accepting her AA/NA group as her new support system by 6-28-91.

Objective 5: Patty will write a letter to her father and mother telling them how she felt as a child. She will share this letter with her counselor and in group by 6-20-91.

Problem 6: Poor interpersonal relationship skills as evidenced by inability to share emotions and wants.

Goal C: To develop healthy interpersonal relationship skills.

Objective 1: Patty will verbalize an identification of her problem with relationships with her counselor by 6-15-91.

Objective 2: Patty will ask five treatment peers for something she wants and share with them how she feels, keeping a log of each conversation and sharing this with her counselor by 6-15-91

Objective 3: Patty will complete the Addictive Relationships Exercise and share her understanding of the differences in addictive and healthy relationships with her counselor by 6-20-91.

Objective 4: Patty will use and log 10 "I feel" statements a day until the end of treatment. She will share her daily feeling log with her counselor weekly.

Objective 5: Patty will discuss her normal and addictive relationships with her group by 6-30-91.

Problem 7: Dishonesty as evidenced by chronic lying about chemical use.

Goal D: Develop a program of recovery based on rigorous honesty.

Objective 1: Patty will complete the Honesty Exercise and verbalize in group 10 times that she was dishonest about her chemical use by 6-15-91.

Objective 2: Patty will discuss in group how her alcohol use contributed to her dishonesty by 6-20-91.

Objective 3: Patty will keep a daily log of the times she lies in treatment and will share this log with her counselor weekly.

Objective 4: Patty will give a 20-minute speech to her group about why it is important to be honest in recovery.

Objective 5: In a conjoint session with her mother, Patty will share her Chemical Use History.

Objective 6: Patty will discuss how dishonesty separated her from her Higher Power with the clergy by 6-20-91.

Problem 8: Poor assertiveness skills as evidenced by being too passive, allowing other people to make important decisions.

Goal E: To develop assertiveness skills.

Objective 1: In group, Patty will verbalize an identification of her problem of being passive and directly relate her passivity to her chemical use by 6-20-91.

Objective 2: Patty will verbalize an understanding of how her passive behaviors lead directly to increased chemical use with her group by 6-15-91.

Objective 3: Patty will practice the assertiveness formula with two treatment peers per day, keeping a daily log of each interaction by 6-20-91.

Objective 4: Patty will have weekly individual sessions with her counselor where she role-plays assertiveness situations.

# Appendix 8

## Chemical Use History
### Robert R. Perkinson, Ph.D.

This exercise will help you become more aware of how chemicals have affected your life and the lives of those around you. Using alcohol or any other mood-altering substance will be considered chemical use. Answer the questions as completely as you can. It is time to get completely honest with yourself. Write down exactly what happened.

1. How old were you when you had your first drink? Describe what happened and how you felt.

2. List all of the drugs you have ever used and the age you first used each drug.

3. What are your drug-using habits? Where do you use? With whom? Under what circumstances?

4. Was there ever a period in your life when you used too much or too often? Explain.

5. Has using chemicals ever caused a problem for you? Describe the problem or problems?

6. When you were using, did you find that you used more or for a longer period of time than you had originally intended? Give some examples.

7. Do you have to use more of the chemical now to get the same effect? How much more than when you first started?

8. Did you ever try to cut down on your use? Why did you try to cut down and what happened to your attempt?

9. What did you do to cut down? Did you change your beverage? Limit the amount? "I'll only have three tonight." Restrict your use to a certain time of day? "I'll only drink after 5 o'clock."

10. Did you ever stop completely? What happened? Why did you start again?

11. Did you spend a lot of time intoxicated or hung over?

12. Did you ever use while doing something dangerous like driving a car? Give some examples.

13. Were you ever so high or hung over that you missed work or school? Give some examples.

14. Did you ever miss family events or recreation because you were high or hung over? Give a few examples.

15. Did your use ever cause family problems? Give some examples.

16. Did you ever feel annoyed when someone talked to you about your drinking or use of drugs? Who was this person and what did they say? Give some examples.

17. Did you ever feel bad or guilty about your use? Give some examples.

18. Did using ever cause you any psychological problems like being depressed? Explain what happened.

19. Did using ever cause you any physical problems or make a physical problem worse? Give a few examples.

20. Did you ever have a blackout? How old were you when you had your first blackout? Give some examples of blackouts.

21. Did you ever get sick because you got too intoxicated? Give some examples.

22. Did you ever have a really bad hangover? Give some examples about how you felt.

23. Did you ever get the shakes or suffer withdrawal symptoms when you quit using? Describe what happened to you when you stopped using your drug of choice.

24. Did you ever use chemicals to avoid symptoms of withdrawal? Give some examples of when you used a substance to control withdrawal symptoms.

25. Have you ever sought help for your drug problem? When? Whom did you see? Did the treatment help you? How?

26. Why do you continue to use? Give five reasons.

27. Why do you want to stop using? Give 10 reasons.

28. Has alcohol or drug use ever affected your reputation? Describe what happened and how you felt.

29. Describe the feelings of guilt you have about your use. How do you feel about yourself now?

30. How has using affected you financially? Give a few examples of how you wasted money in your addiction.

31. Has your ambition decreased due to your use? Give an example.

32. Has your addiction changed how you feel about yourself? How have your feeing changed?

33. Are you as self-confident as you were before? Explain.

34. Describe the reasons why you want treatment now.

35. List all of the chemicals you have used in the past 6 months.

36. List how often and in what amounts you have used each chemical in the past 6 months.

37. List the life events that have been affected by your chemical use (school, marriage, job, children).

38. Have you ever had legal problems because of your use? List each problem.

39. Have you ever lost a job because of your use? Describe what happened.

40. Do you want treatment for your chemical problem? List a few reasons why.

# Appendix 9

## *Honesty*
### Robert R. Perkinson, Ph.D.

This exercise helps you to get honest with yourself. In recovery it is essential to tell the truth. As you will hear at every AA/NA meeting, this is a program of rigorous honesty. "Those who do not recover are people who cannot or will not completely give themselves to this simple program, usually men and women who are constitutionally incapable of being honest with themselves" (*Alcoholics Anonymous,* 1976, p. 58).

Why is it so important to be honest? Because dishonesty to self and others distorts reality. "Rigorous honesty is the most important tool in learning to live for today" (*Narcotics Anonymous,* 1988 p. 92). You will never solve problems if you lie. You need to live in the facts. In sobriety you must commit yourself to reality. This means accepting everything that is real.

People who are chemically dependent think that they cannot tell the truth. If they do, they feel they will be rejected. The facts are exactly the opposite: Unless you tell the truth, no one can accept you. People have to know you to accept you. If you keep secrets, you will never feel known or loved. An old AA saying states, "We are only as sick as our secrets." If you keep secrets from people, you will never be close to them.

You can't be a practicing alcoholic or drug addict without lying to yourself. You must lie, and believe the lies, or the illness cannot operate. All the lies are attempts to protect you from the truth. If you had known the truth, you would have known that you were sick and needed treatment. This would have been frightening, so you kept the truth from yourself and from others. "Let's face it; when we were using, we were not honest with ourselves" (*Narcotics Anonymous,* 1988, p. 27).

There are many ways you lied to yourself. This exercise will teach you exactly how you distorted reality and it will start you toward a program of honesty. Answer each of the following questions as completely as you can.

1. *Denial:* Telling yourself or others, "I don't have a problem." Write down a few examples of when you used this technique to avoid dealing with the truth.


2. *Minimizing:* Making the problem smaller than it really was. You may have told yourself, or someone else, that your problem was not that bad. You may have told someone that you had a couple of beers, when you really had six. Write down a few examples of when you distorted reality by making it seem smaller than it actually was.


3. *Hostility:* Becoming angry or making threats when someone confronted you about your chemical use. Give a few examples.


4. *Rationalization:* Making an excuse. "I had a hard day. Things are bad. My relationship is bad. My financial situation is bad." Give a few examples of when you thought you had a good reason to use chemicals.


5. *Blaming:* Shifting the responsibility to someone else. "The police were out to get me. My wife is overreacting." Give an example of when you blamed someone else for a problem you caused.

6. *Intellectualizing:* Overanalyzing and thinking about a problem to avoid doing something about it. "Sure, I drink some, but everyone I know drinks. I read this article, and it said that this is a drinking culture." Give an example of how you use intellectual data and statistics to justify your use.


7. *Diversion:* Bringing up another topic of conversation to avoid the issue. Give an example.


8. Make a list of five lies you told to someone close to you about your drinking or drug use.

    1. _____
    2. _____
    3. _____
    4. _____
    5. _____

9. Make a list of five lies you told yourself about your drug problem.

    1. _____
    2. _____
    3. _____
    4. _____
    5. _____

10. Make a list of 10 people you have lied to.

    1. _____
    2. _____
    3. _____
    4. _____
    5. _____
    6. _____
    7. _____
    8. _____
    9. _____
    10. _____

11. How do you feel about your lying? Describe how you feel about yourself when you lie.


12. What do you think will change in your life if you begin to tell the truth?


13. How do you use lies in other areas of your life?


14. When are you the most likely to lie? Is it when you've been drinking or using chemicals?

15. Why do you lie? What does it get you? Give five reasons.

   1. _____
   2. _____
   3. _____
   4. _____
   5. _____

16. Common lies of chemical dependency are listed below. Give a personal example of each. Be honest with yourself.

   A. Breaking promises:

   B. Pretending to be sober when you're intoxicated:

   C. Blackouts: Pretending you remember when you don't:

   D. Minimizing use: Telling someone you drink no more than others:

   E. Telling yourself you were in control when you weren't:

   F. Telling someone you rarely get high:

   G. Hiding morning drinking:

   H. Hiding your supply:

   I. Substituting alcohol for food and telling someone you weren't hungry:

   J. Saying you had the flu when you were really hung over or sick from using:

   K. Having someone else call in to work to say you are too sick to come to work:

   L. Pretending not to care about your drug problem:

People who are chemically dependent lie to avoid facing the truth. Lying makes them feel more comfortable, but in the long run, they end up feeling isolated and alone. Recovery demands living in the truth. "I am an alcoholic. My life is unmanageable. I am powerless over alcohol. I need help. I can't do this alone." All of these are honest statements from someone who is living in reality.

You will either get real, and live in the real world, or you will live in a fantasy world of your own creation. If you get honest, you will begin to solve real problems. You will be accepted for who you are.

Wake up tomorrow morning and promise yourself that you are going to be honest all day. Write down in a diary when you are tempted to lie. Watch your feelings when you lie. How does it feel? How do you feel about yourself? Write it all down. Keep a dairy for 5 days and share it with your group. Tell them how it feels to be honest.

Take a piece of paper and write the word *TRUTH* on it and tape it on your bathroom mirror. Commit yourself to rigorous honesty. You deserve to live a life filled with love and truth. You never need to lie again.

# Appendix 10

## Love, Trust, and Commitment
### Robert R. Perkinson, Ph.D.

It seems that going through life we should be taught a few simple things about relationships. After all, we have a relationship first with ourselves, and then, if we so choose, with others. How can we trust ourselves? How can we trust others? When are we committed? When do we love? This exercise will start you thinking about these essential parts of a relationship. Use this exercise to ask yourself some important questions.

## THE FIRST RELATIONSHIP

Infants learn about love, trust, and commitment from their primary caregiver; this is usually the mother. When the infant cries out, someone comes and addresses its needs. The baby can't see very well, so this something comes out of a haze, seemingly out of nowhere. Whenever the baby cries, this something comes. It comes every time, and a great trust develops between infant and mother. As the child grows older, it becomes aware that this something has a particular sight, smell, sound, taste, and feel; soon it has a name, Mother.

Somewhere in childhood, the child learns that mother doesn't have to come, she chooses to come. Why does she come? Why, at all hours of the day or night, does she choose to come? She comes because she is bonded with her child. Her child's pain is her pain, her child's joy is her joy. She cannot ignore her child's pain because when her child hurts she hurts. In this bonding or joining of mother and child, there is love, trust, and commitment. "Mother will always be there for me." The child knows this. Their very life depends on it.

It is from this first relationship that we learn what to expect from all of our other relationships. We expect relationships to have certain core characteristics. If the relationships are healthy, they will have as essential building blocks love, trust, and commitment.

## TRUST

How do you know that you can trust yourself? What are you going to do to prove to yourself that you are trustworthy? First, you will need to develop consistency of action in your own behalf. If you act consistently in a manner that is in your best interest, you have gone a long way in learning how to trust yourself. You must be consistent even when times get rough. You need to learn that no matter what, you are going to do things that are good for yourself. You are trustworthy to someone else when you consistently act in that person's interest.

## COMMITMENT

Commitment means you are faithful and loyal for an extended period of time. It means that on a daily basis, you can count on yourself to follow through. You have plans to be good to yourself, and you are going to stick with these plans. You are going to, day by day, hammer away at the things you want. You are not going to give up. These same elements apply when you commit yourself to someone else.

## LOVE

A good definition of *love* is that love is the interest in, and the active involvement in, a person's individual growth. Love for someone else needs trust and commitment, but it needs something more—it needs empathy. You must feel the other person's feelings as if they are your own. Empathy is the feeling you share with another. It is being on the same wavelength. I feel your feelings. When you feel sad, I feel sad. When you feel joy, I feel joy. To help you is to help myself. To love you is to love myself.

Perhaps somewhere along the way you have lost the ability to experience normal relationships. Maybe you never developed a trustworthy, committed, loving relationship with your primary caregiver. It could be that you never really felt accepted the way you needed to be. Children need a lot of encouragement when they try things, and a lot of praise. This makes them feel accepted, cherished, and loved. If you take a child and sit on her or his bed every day of their life, and tell him or her how wonderful they are, maybe by the time the child is 6 years old, he or she will be ready for school. Children need a lot of encouragement to develop a sense of self-worth.

## HOW TO BE LOVING TO YOURSELF

To be loving to yourself, you must give yourself a lot of encouragement and a lot of praise. If you missed this as a child, your challenge is to reinforce yourself. Treat yourself the way you wanted to be treated. Be your own mother and your own father. Give yourself all the love you wanted.

Imagine for a moment that you are a very young child with a fragile, impressionable mind. Write down 10 things you would need to see from your parents.

1. _____
2. _____
3. _____
4. _____
5. _____
6. _____
7. _____
8. _____
9. _____
10. _____

Only you know what you need. It is up to you to give to yourself everything you wanted. Give to yourself all of the love you need.

## RELATIONSHIP WITH SELF

List the things you need to see from yourself that will prove that you can be trusted to act in your own best interests.

_____
_____
_____
_____

List the things you need to see from yourself that will show that you are committed to your own growth. This is a day-by-day commitment.

_____
_____
_____
_____

List the things you will need to see from yourself that will show you that you love yourself.

_____

_____

_____

_____

## How to Find Out the Good Things About Yourself

List the things about yourself that you feel good about or are proud of. Start with physical appearance. What are some of your good physical qualities? List as many as you can think of. Start with your hair, and move downward to the tips of your toes. Admire the color, size, shape, feel, smell, sound, whatever you can think of. Don't let the old stinking thinking keep you feeling bad about yourself. Get accurate.

Physical Appearance: What do you like about how you look?

1. _____
2. _____
3. _____
4. _____
5. _____
6. _____
7. _____
8. _____
9. _____
10. _____

Personality: List all of the personality characteristics that you like and admire about yourself. What do people seem to like about you? What do you like about yourself?

1. _____
2. _____
3. _____
4. _____
5. _____
6. _____
7. _____
8. _____
9. _____
10. _____

You need a lot of encouragement and praise. Now you have a lot of accurate things to say to yourself that make you feel good about yourself.

Things you enjoy: List the things you enjoy doing. How do you play? What do you do for fun or entertainment? What would you like to start doing?

1. _____
2. _____
3. _____
4. _____
5. _____
6. _____
7. _____
8. _____
9. _____
10. _____

People you enjoy: List some of the people you enjoy being around. Write down what makes them feel special to you.

1. _____
2. _____
3. _____
4. _____
5. _____
6. _____
7. _____
8. _____
9. _____
10. _____

Take a long look at what you have written. See how wonderful you really are.

## Say Good Things to Yourself

Now you have all these good things to say to yourself. Start with 10 things and write them down on note cards. Carry these cards with you and read them to yourself periodically through the day. Look at yourself in the mirror and say these things to yourself. Practice until you have these 10 memorized, then take 10 more. Constantly bombard yourself with positive self-talk. When you find yourself speaking harshly to yourself, stop and self-correct, get out the cards if you have to, but don't continue to treat yourself poorly.

## Do Good Things for Yourself

You are saying good things to yourself. That's healing and treating yourself well. Now what can you do for yourself to-day that's really special? Maybe take a long hot bath, or go for a relaxing walk. Could you spend some time with a friend you enjoy? How about getting some ice cream, or just reading and taking a nap? Come up with a few special things to do for yourself today. Write each of these things down and do them. When you are doing these things, think of why you are doing them, because you are a person of great worth. Do this every day. Before you get up in the morning, commit yourself to treating yourself well, then get up and get busy, enjoy life, feel the pleasure of being alive. You deserve it!

## RELATIONSHIPS WITH OTHERS

You have some things that you want from a partner, a friend, a lover. It is your responsibility to ask for what you want. Be specific, and give them a lot of encouragement when they try to give these things to you. You know the secret: Be reinforcing, give encouragement, shower people with praise—it's contagious. If you give more often, you will get more often. Happiness is created when we unselfishly give to others.

### How to Find Out If a Relationship Is Good for You

What are the things you need to see from someone that will show you that they are trustworthy, committed, and loving to you?

1. _____
2. _____
3. _____
4. _____
5. _____
6. _____
7. _____
8. _____
9. _____
10. _____

### How to Get What You Want in a Relationship

If you have a friend or partner, you must ask them for what you want. They can't guess what you want or need, you must tell them. Remember, give them a lot back when they give you something. Ask them what they want, and do your best to give it to them. As you give to this other person, you will feel good about yourself and you will get more of your needs met in return. The more you give, the more you will get.

After completing this exercise, you should be treating yourself well. You should know what you need to see from yourself, and from others, to make you feel good. You have learned that you directly influence how you feel. You are not helpless before others or before your environment. You can love yourself. You are special. You are worth it. Others can love you. You can love others. You can feel whole, healthy, and complete. You have all the skills you need.

# Appendix 11

## *Feelings*
### Robert R. Perkinson, Ph.D.

Chemically dependent persons have a difficult time with their feelings. They have never learned how to use their feelings appropriately. They have been chemically altering their feelings for years. They don't know how they feel, and they don't know what to do when they do feel. Many chemically dependent people were shamed for having normal feelings when they were children. When they were afraid, they were told that there was nothing to be afraid of. When they were angry, they were told there was nothing to be angry about. A child who is taught these things learns that their feelings can't be trusted. They learn that there is something wrong with their feelings. This exercise will help you to identify your feelings and use your feelings appropriately.

## THE PURPOSE OF FEELINGS

Feelings or emotions are physiological states that motivate action. Each feeling gives you specific energy and direction for movement. This is how problems are solved. First there is a situation that triggers thought. The thoughts create feelings, which motivate action. This is how all problems are solved. A person becomes involved in a problem, thinks about the problem, has feelings generated by the thoughts, acts on the feelings, and eventually resolves the issue.

## THE CORE FEELINGS

There are only a few core feelings. More complicated feelings are various combinations of the primary ones. Plutchic (1980) studied feelings and found that there were eight primary emotions:

1. Joy
2. Acceptance
3. Anticipation
4. Surprise
5. Fear
6. Anger
7. Disgust
8. Sadness

Each of these feelings gives us specific energy and direction for movement. We need to discuss each feeling carefully and have you learn specifically what each feeling is like. Then you can recognize when the feeling occurs and you will know what the feeling is telling you to do. You need practice in experiencing the subtle physiological changes that differentiate each feeling from the other.

### Joy

Joy is that feeling we experience when we reach a goal we have been striving for. The harder we have been working for the goal, and the more important the goal is to us, the more joy we feel. List five times when you felt joy in your life. As you write each situation down, take a moment to reexperience the feeling you had at that moment in your life. Feel the situation as if you were actually there.

1. _____
2. _____
3. _____
4. _____
5. _____

Joy gives us the energy and direction to celebrate and enjoy. It directs us to seek more of whatever is giving us this pleasure.

## Acceptance

Acceptance is the feeling you get when someone likes you or approves of you. List five times in your life when you felt accepted. Allow yourself to feel the feeling as you remember the situation.

1. _____
2. _____
3. _____
4. _____
5. _____

The feeling of acceptance gives you the energy and direction to stay involved with the person or group that is accepting. It is a feeling that bonds people together.

## Anticipation

Anticipation is the feeling we get when we prepare ourselves for change. It mobilizes us for something new. We can anticipate something good or bad. List five times when you felt an intense sense of anticipation. Reexperience the feeling.

1. _____
2. _____
3. _____
4. _____
5. _____

Anticipation gives us the energy and direction to mobilize ourselves for change. We prepare ourselves for something exciting.

## Surprise

Surprise is the feeling we get when something unexpected happens. Surprise give us the energy to orient ourselves to a new situation. List five times when you felt surprised. Feel the feeling you felt each time

1. _____
2. _____
3. _____
4. _____
5. _____

Surprise mobilizes your body to take in the new situation as quickly as possible. The brain is very quickly deciding how to respond.

## Fear

Fear is the feeling we have when something is perceived as dangerous. List five times when you felt fear. Allow yourself to feel the feeling generated by each situation.

1. _____
2. _____
3. _____
4. _____
5. _____

Fear gives us the energy and direction to withdraw or escape from a dangerous situation. It mobilizes us to get away from the offending stimuli.

## Anger

Anger is the feeling we have when we are violated. This violation may be real or imagined. List five times when you were angry. Feel the anger you felt in each situation. Concentrate on the physical changes that occur when you get angry.

1. _____
2. _____
3. _____
4. _____
5. _____

Anger gives us the energy and direction to fight. It helps us to reestablish the boundaries around ourselves. Anger is necessary to prevent people from violating us.

## Disgust

Disgust is the emotion we feel when something repels us: We loathe it; it is repugnant. List five times when something disgusted you. Allow yourself to reexperience the feeling.

1. _____
2. _____
3. _____
4. _____
5. _____

Disgust gives us the energy and direction to withdraw from the offending stimulation. We need to move away from the object that repels us.

Sadness

Sadness is the feeling we get when we have lost something. We can lose a love object or self-esteem. List five times when you felt sad. Feel the sad feeling. Sense the subtle physiological changes that occur when you feel sad.

1. _____

2. _____

3. _____

4. _____

5. _____

Sadness gives us the energy and direction to recover the lost object. If we are unable to recover the object, the sadness can deepen. Sadness can immobilize an organism so healing can begin to take place. The organism does not move or do new things. It stays still and recovers from the loss.

## HOW TO USE FEELINGS APPROPRIATELY

Feelings can be used appropriately or inappropriately. They can be based on accurate or inaccurate information. They can lead to adaptive behavior or maladaptive behavior. It is important to know how you feel and what to do when you have a feeling. Feelings will help you to solve problems. Unless you are using your feelings appropriately, you will never be able to solve problems well.

When you feel, you will be experiencing one or more of the eight primary feelings. Jealousy is feeling fearful, angry, and sad, all at the same time. Each feeling needs to be addressed for full resolution of the problem.

If you feel confused, you are feeling many feelings at the same time. Some of these feelings may be in conflict with each other, and you may be torn about what to do. When confused, you must separate each feeling and examine it carefully. What is each feeling telling you to do? What is the most rational thing to do?

When you have a feeling, you must decide how to act. The feeling is motivating you to take action. Feelings need to flow naturally and spontaneously into adaptive action. The actions must be appropriate to the situation. To fight every time you are angry is not appropriate. Most of the time it is necessary to stop and think before you act. You want to use your feelings. When you are having an intense feeling, always ask yourself two questions:

1. What is the best thing I can do for myself?
2. What is the best thing I can do for the others?

For the most part, you must practice thinking and planning before you act. Plan carefully how you are going to act when you have each feeling, and practice these actions until they flow naturally.

Your feelings are important. They are great wise counselors that need to be listened to. You don't need to hide from your feelings—you need to listen and learn.

# Appendix 12

## *Relationship Skills*
### Robert R. Perkinson, Ph.D.

Certain skills are necessary to establish and maintain close interpersonal relationships. The skills seem simple, but some of them can take great courage. Love is not a feeling. It is an action. We must love in action and in truth. To love someone you must be actively involved in that other person's individual growth. Love is not self-oriented; it is other-oriented. There is also the love that you show yourself; this is when you are involved in your own growth.

### HOW TO LOVE

The first skill is love. Love is an action. You are interested in and actively involved in the other person's individual growth. You are there for that other person when they need your help. You respond to how they feel and what they want. You tell the truth all the time. You are willing to spend your time and energy being involved in the other person's well-being.

List three times when you were not there for someone when they needed you. Then list what you could have done, or should have done, to help them at that moment.

1. _____
2. _____
3. _____
4. _____
5. _____

List five times when you lied to someone you loved. Love cannot exist where there are lies.

1. _____
2. _____
3. _____
4. _____
5. _____

### HOW TO COMMIT YOURSELF

The second skill is commitment. You must commit yourself, on a daily basis, to work on building the relationship. This means you work to provide a safe atmosphere where the relationship can grow. This is an atmosphere full of love and trust. You dedicate yourself to the relationship. You must take the time necessary to nourish yourself, the other person, and the relationship. You consistently ask yourself what you can do for the other person and then you do it. Now make a plan. What are you going to do to make your relationships grow?

1. _____
2. _____
3. _____
4. _____
5. _____

## HOW TO BE ENCOURAGING

The third skill is you must be encouraging. You must encourage the other person to reach their full potential in life. This takes a lot of reinforcement and praise. No one needs to be punished and criticized—this dampens the spirit and weakens interpersonal bonds. People need soothing, encouraging words. They need to know that you have faith in them, that you trust them, that you will help them to grow. People need their good points praised. They need to hear what they are doing right. Encourage five people today. Write their name and the situation down below. Watch their reaction and make a note of how you feel.

1. _____
2. _____
3. _____
4. _____
5. _____

## HOW TO SHARE

The fourth skill is the skill of sharing. You must practice sharing how you feel and what you think. You must ask for what you want. You cannot keep these things to yourself. The relationship will falter if you withhold the truth. As children, we are taught that asking for what we want is selfish, but it's not selfish in a loving relationship, it's necessary. Happiness is unselfishly giving to others. How can your partner give to you if you don't tell them what you want? How can they be encouraged to grow and change unless you hold them accountable for their actions? If you keep your feelings and wants to yourself, your relationship will not work. Your partner cannot guess what you want, she (he) is not capable of that. List 10 important things you want from your relationships and decide how you are going to ask for these things.

1. _____
2. _____
3. _____
4. _____
5. _____
6. _____
7. _____
8. _____
9. _____
10. _____

Now list the feelings you have difficulty sharing with your partner. What feelings do you tend to keep inside?

1. _____
2. _____
3. _____
4. _____
5. _____

Make yourself a promise: "The next time I have a sharing time with someone, I am going to share how I feel and think. I am going to ask for what I want."

## HOW TO COMPROMISE

The fifth skill is compromise. No one is going to get exactly what they want in a relationship. You have to create an atmosphere of give and take. You must be willing to respond to how the other person feels and what the other person wants. Always ask yourself what you would want if you were in the other person's position. Compromise creates an atmosphere of fairness and equality. List five areas in your life where you have stubbornly wanted to have things your own way. What are you going to do to be more flexible in those situations?

1. _____
2. _____
3. _____
4. _____
5. _____

## HOW TO SHOW RESPECT

The sixth skill is to establish a relationship filled with respect. This means you show others that they are important to you. You do things that make them feel special. You care for how they feel and for what they want. They matter to you. They count. You don't treat them poorly; you love them too much for that. You want them to be happy. When they feel happy, you feel happy. List five ways you can show someone they are special and important to you.

1. _____
2. _____
3. _____
4. _____
5. _____

These relationship skills need practice. They will not come easily. You need to work at telling the truth all the time. You need to practice being encouraging. You need to practice sharing how you feel and asking for what you want. You need to develop the skill of commitment. You will struggle when you compromise. You need to work at showing someone that they are important.

Keep a log every day for the next week. Detail how you did on each skill and watch for the other person's reaction. Look carefully at how the other person's response changes. How you feel about yourself?

## THE DAILY PLAN

1. Encourage someone today.
   a. Write the situation down. Exactly what happened?
   b. How did the person feel when you encouraged them?
   c. How did you feel?

2. Ask for something you want.
   a. How did it work?
   b. Did you get what you wanted?
   c. How did you feel about asking?
   d. How did the other person respond?

3. Share your feelings.
   a. What was the situation?
   b. How did you feel about yourself?
   c. What response did you get?

4. Tell someone he or she is important to you.
   a. How did you feel about doing this?
   b. How did the other person feel?

5. Evaluate yourself on honesty.
   a. Did you lie or withhold truth today?
   b. How do you feel about what you did?

6. Help someone and watch his or her reaction.
   a. How did the person respond?
   b. How did you feel?

7. Give something to someone without expecting anything in return.
   a. How did you feel about yourself?
   b. How was your gift accepted?

8. Compromise with someone.
   a. How did you feel?
   b. How did the other person feel?
   c. What was the result of your compromise?

The more you practice these skills, the more proficient you will become. If you hit all of the skills accurately, your relationships will be stable. If you leave one skill out, your relationships will be shaky and you will feel frightened. These skills are just like riding a bike: The first few times you try to use some of them, they feel awkward and clumsy and you may feel frightened of getting hurt, but with practice, they will get easy and you will be able to relax and enjoy yourself.

# Appendix 13

## Addictive Relationships
### Robert R. Perkinson, Ph.D.

Relationships are our greatest challenge. Even the best relationships have periods of intense strain. It takes hard work to get along consistently. You have to be willing to give and to think of the other person's needs first. This is not easy. Chemically dependent persons are often just as addicted to their partner as they are to their drug of choice. Sometimes that "love" feeling is the drug. This shouldn't surprise you. Sexual feelings are created by powerful chemicals in the body called *hormones*. These chemicals can be just as addictive as any drug, and they can be just as destructive.

Addictive relationships are very different from normal ones. You need to be able to tell which is which. For stability and happiness, you want to get in and stay in a healthy relationship. You want to get out of or treat an addictive one.

## THE CYCLE OF ADDICTIVE RELATIONSHIPS

The addictive relationship begins with strong feelings. These feelings may fool you because most of us are taught that these feelings are love. They are not love; they are sexual feelings. These first feelings are extremely powerful and they draw you, seemingly irresistibly, toward that other person. These are the "love at first sight" feelings, but don't be fooled; it's not love. We can feel these feelings for a movie star or even someone's picture. In an addictive relationship, you see someone across a crowded room. Your eyes are drawn to them. You can't stop looking at them. You feel a freight train roar in your chest. Sexual acting out occurs quickly because these feelings are so powerful. Within a short period of time, you may be experiencing the greatest sex of your life.

The juice continues to be sweet, so sweet that you will do anything to keep it. Here's where addictive relationships begin to get sick. You are so thrilled and enchanted with your new love that you begin to lie to keep the relationship going. You say things you don't mean and do things you don't want to do. You just want to keep the juices flowing. This can be subtle, but it is the clearest difference between addictive and normal relationships. In addictive relationships you lie. In normal relationships you tell the truth.

People have an instinctive way of knowing when someone is being dishonest with them. It might take them a while to catch on, but lies begin to show. Fear begins to build. This feels uncomfortable, and the partners begin to test each other to check for the truth. Jealousy rears its head, and the partners begin to accuse others of being dishonest and unfaithful. They may begin to suspiciously keep track of each other. Where were you? Who were you with? What did you do? Over and over again, the accusations fly back and forth. All of this craziness gets its fuel from the lies. That's the problem. There are lies to uncover, and both people feel it.

Sooner or later there is an explosion. The fear, jealousy, and accusations reach a fever pitch and the relationship shatters. There is a violent argument. This is usually verbally abusive and possibly physically abusive. The feelings are so intense, the pleasure and the pain, that things explode. There is usually screaming and name-calling. Demands are made as the couple tries to reestablish their individual boundaries and resolve the aching fear pounding in their chest. Words like, "Get out! I never want to see you again!" are screamed at each other.

After the explosion, there is a short cooling-off period, and then we are back to the juice. It's make-up time. The sex is just as good as it was before, maybe even better. "How could we have fought? We love each other so much. What could we have been thinking about? This is the real thing. It feels so good."

This vicious cycle repeats itself over and over again. There is incredible pain in addictive relationships. You constantly feel desperately in love, scared, and angry. It feels like a roller coaster out of control. The intensity of the feelings, and the lies, are the primary factors that keep this sick relationship going. Round and round, in the agony and the ecstasy.

## NORMAL RELATIONSHIPS

Normal relationships begin when you meet someone who interests you as a friend. There is no intense sexual desire at first, you just want to spend time together because you enjoy each other's company. There is no reason to lie, so you tell each other the truth.

Sharing the truth, you gradually draw closer together. The intimacy begins to grow. The more you share, the closer you get, and the closer you get, the more you share.

There is a genuine concern for each other. This relationship is based on trust and friendship. There is no reason to be afraid. In this safe atmosphere, surrounded by real love, the sexual feelings come and romance begins.

## LOVE

Love is an action. It is not a feeling. We must love in action and in truth. Love is the active involvement in someone's individual growth. If you love yourself, you will actively participate in your own growth. Similarly, if you love someone else, you will be actively involved in their growth. Listen at what the Bible says about love. This is from I Corinthians 13:4-7:

> Love is patient, love is kind. It does not envy, it does not boast, it is not proud. It is not rude, it is not self-seeking, it is not easily angered, it keeps no record of wrongs. Love does not delight in evil but rejoices with the truth. It always protects, always trusts, always hopes, always perseveres.

It's time to find out where you are in your relationship. Is this relationship addictive or normal? Take out a piece of paper and at the top of it write LIES. Now list all of the lies that you can think of that exist in the relationship. Start with the big lies, like infidelity, and work down from there. You will immediately get the idea if there are major lies in your relationship. A normal relationship cannot exist on a foundation of lies. Such a relationship will falter, crumble, and fail.

Get another piece of paper and label it FEAR. Write down some things you are afraid of in your relationship. Are you afraid of infidelity? Why? Do you have any information that your partner has been unfaithful? If you do, what is it? Strong fears of infidelity are one of the core components in addictive relationships. These fears can be based on good evidence or be completely groundless. It doesn't matter what causes the fear, it's the fear itself that is the damaging factor. Are you verbally or physically afraid of your partner? Abusive relationships are extremely damaging. Abusive relationships need treatment. Verbal and physical abuse are very common in addictive relationships.

Label another piece of paper FIGHTS. Here describe three major fights you have had with your partner. Pick the worst ones you can remember. What were the fights about? How did they progress? Were the problems resolved or did you tend to fight about the same things over and over again? How do you fight? What words are said? How do each of you act when you are very angry?

The next page will deal with LOVE. Does your partner consistently care about how you feel? Do they change what they do because of how you feel? Are they interested in and involved in what you want? Are they committed to your individual growth? Some partners are so caught up in their own needs that they will not become involved in their partner's needs. Such people may be incapable of love.

Now go over this information with your counselor or group. Do you feel you are involved in an addictive relationship? If you are, you must do one of two things: You must get out of the relationship entirely or get treatment. Both people must go to treatment. If you continue on the way you are going, you are in for more misery. You now know what love is and what a normal relationship is like. You deserve a relationship filled with love. Don't settle for less.

# Appendix 14

## *Communication Skills*
### Robert R. Perkinson, Ph.D.

In developing good communication skills you need to learn how to listen and how to share. You need to understand where the other person is coming from and you need the ability to express yourself clearly. People communicate with words and with actions. Tears or an angry voice can say a lot. You need to be sensitive to both verbal and nonverbal behavior.

## EMPATHY

Empathy is the ability to put yourself in other people's shoes. You understand how they feel. You are on the same wavelength. To develop empathy, you practice paraphrasing what the other person has said until you get the communication correct. The other person needs to be encouraged to correct your mistakes until you have the message correct.

Repeat what the person said, as exactly as you can, the verbal and the nonverbal message. Continue to repeat the message until the person agrees you have it right. This may take a few tries, but you will get better as you practice. Include the verbal and the nonverbal parts of the message. You may have to ask questions as you go along. Try to be genuine, not sarcastic or punitive. Act as a mirror, reflecting exactly what the other person is saying, and how they are feeling. Practice getting the total communication correct. As time goes on, you will need to ask for clarification less, only when you are unsure of certain parts of the communication.

## VALIDATION

Others have a right to their opinion, and their opinion should always be important to you. This is an essential element in healthy communication. Others need to know that you value them and that you will try to understand them. People need to be validated often, particularly when they disagree with you. Everything a person says is not wrong. Find the areas that the two of you agree on and emphasize those areas. Always pick out the things you have in common and bring out those points for discussion.

## HOW TO USE THE "I FEEL" STATEMENT

Practice beginning many of your communications with "I feel." You may not know what is right or wrong in a given situation, but you always know how you feel. Start with your feelings, and then fill in what you think is creating those feelings. If you are feeling confused, you are having many feelings at the same time. Try to break the feelings down and address each one separately. The "I feel" statement prevents you from concentrating on the other person. Communications that begin with "you" can be accusatory and punitive. Instead of pointing out what the other person is doing, concentrate on how you feel and what you think.

## BE POSITIVE

Always try to find something positive to say to the other person. Even when you are disagreeing, you need to show them that you are going to be reinforcing. This shows the other person that you respect them and care about them. Be genuine in your compliments; don't say something that isn't true. Continue to be positive throughout your communications with others. Being positive is contagious: The more you look at the bright side of things, the better things actually become. A positive attitude can go a long way in improving communications skills. People like being around someone who is positive. It gives them a lift, and they will want to be around you again.

## HOW TO USE PHYSICAL PROXIMITY

One of the most important elements in whether a person will like you or not is physical proximity. People that you are around more often are more likely to be attracted to you. When you are talking with someone, stand or sit at a comfortable distance from them. In the United States, this a little more than an arm's length apart. In other countries, this can be different, so you must be up on the social norms. Don't have a piece of furniture or something else between you as you communicate; this increases interpersonal distance. Be conscious of how the other person is feeling. If they seem uncomfortable, back up a little.

## HOW TO USE TOUCH

Touch is a very powerful communication tool. It is hard to act angry at someone you are touching. Touch increases intimacy and decreases fear. It shows the other person that you value them and the relationship. You can often touch someone during a conversation. Try to find that opportunity and take it. Even a simple touch on the arm is a powerful message that says, I care.

## HOW TO USE EYE CONTACT

Good communication requires good eye contact. If you don't look at the other person, you will miss a good deal of what they are saying. Eye contact is a lot like touch—it shows the person that you are interested. It also shows them that they are important enough to warrant your full attention.

## BE REINFORCING

Compliment the other person. Say something nice. Tell him how much you appreciate them. Try to be patient and kind. Give the person your full attention. Try to understand his point of view. Dress appropriately and take good care of your appearance and personal hygiene. All of this makes you a reinforcing person.

## HOW TO PRACTICE COMMUNICATION SKILLS

Find two people and ask them to do the following exercise with you. Watch each of the communication skills in action as you go through the exercise. All of the information disclosed during your conversation should be kept confidential. Each person should have the opportunity to respond to each statement before continuing on to the next item.

Sit close to each other and make eye contact before you speak. Read the first part of the sentence and fill in the rest with your own words.

1. My name is . . .
2. My current hometown is . . .
3. My marital status is . . .
4. My occupation is . . .
5. The reason I am here is . . .
6. Right now I am feeling . . .

## DEVELOPING EMPATHY

1. When I think about the future, I see myself . . .
2. The second person repeats what the first person said until the first person agrees that she has been heard correctly.
3. When I am in a new group . . .
4. The second person repeats what the first person said until the first person agrees that he has been heard correctly.
5. When I enter a room full of people, I usually feel . . .
6. The second person repeats.
7. When I am feeling anxious in a new situation I usually . . .
8. For the rest of the exercise, the second person will repeat or question only if they don't understand the communication.
9. In groups I feel the most comfortable when . . .
10. When I am confused, I . . .
11. I am happiest when . . .
12. The thing that turns me on the most is . . .
13. Right now I am feeling . . .
14. The thing that concerns me the most is . . .
15. When I am rejected, I usually . . .
16. I feel loved when . . .
17. A forceful person makes me feel . . .
18. When I break the rules . . .
19. The thing that turns me off the most is . . .
20. Toward you right now, I feel . . .
21. When I feel lonely, I usually . . .
22. Make a listening check. Have the second person repeat the last communication. "What I hear you saying is . . . "
23. I am rebellious when . . .
24. Take a few minutes to discuss the exercise so far. How do you feel you are doing? Is the level of sharing deep enough? How can you improve the level of sharing? Are you getting to know each other?
25. The emotion I find the most difficult to control is . . .
26. My most frequent daydreams are about . . .
27. My weakest point is . . .
28. I love . . .
29. When I feel jealous, I . . .
30. I am afraid of . . .
31. I believe in . . .
32. I am the most ashamed of . . .
33. Right now I am most afraid to discuss . . .
34. Reach out and touch the person on the arm.
35. When I touched you, I felt . . .

Take some time to evaluate each other's communication skills. Talk about what you did well and what you need to work on. Ask for help in developing your skills. Discuss one or two other issues together (politics, religion, sports, work, family).

# Appendix 15

## Self-Discipline
### Robert R. Perkinson, Ph.D.

Life is full of problems that need to be solved. We can reach our full potential in life only when we meet our problems head on, accept responsibility for them, and work toward resolution. Problems cause us to feel pain. This pain is not bad. It is good. It is a motivation for change. It gives us energy and direction for action. We can solve problems only if we learn how to endure this pain. If we always seek immediate pain relief, we will never stretch ourselves and grow. If we can learn how to delay the instant pleasure, we can get higher-quality and more enduring pleasure later. To get an *A* on an English test next week, we have to study this week. Studying hurts. We must learn how to endure the pain of work to get what we want later. This is the pathway to excellence.

## DELAYED GRATIFICATION

Self-discipline requires training and practice. Work doesn't feel good—if it did it would be called play. Work is the expenditure of energy. When we expend energy, things change.

We all want to be a champion, but to be a champion, we have to work. Professional athletes train every day. It's the only way to excel. They can't win a race every day, but they can train for the race every day. They must constantly keep in excellent physical and mental condition. They must be so practiced in their sport that they do things automatically. So it is with us, to do something well, we must practice, and we must learn how set long-term goals.

Take a piece of paper and write down some things you wanted in your life that you didn't get because you didn't work hard enough. Perhaps you wanted to go to college or get a certain job. Did you want a particular car or a certain house? Did you want to go out with someone special? Did you want to play a musical instrument? Find five things that you wanted that you didn't get. Write those down and take a long look at each of them.

1. _____
2. _____
3. _____
4. _____
5. _____

What would it have taken for you to achieve each of these goals? What work needed to be done that you didn't do? Nothing reasonable is out of your grasp if you work hard enough. Write down the steps you needed to take to achieve that goal. Spend time thinking about exactly what needed to be done, and think about why you didn't do it.

Suppose you wanted to be a mechanic. The first thing you would need is training. You need the skills of a mechanic. Where would you get those? You could start with the yellow pages, or call an employment service and ask. Now this is work, and nobody likes it. You have to move, expend energy. It's not fun. It hurts. But you want the job as a mechanic, and you will have to work to get it. It will happen one step at a time, not all at once. You can't just wish it to be true. You need to be patient. You need to go through the pain first.

Okay, suppose you look in the yellow pages and find a mechanics school. Now you have to get an application, fill it out, and mail it in. This is getting to be hard work; it's not fun, but it will pay off. You will not get what you want if you don't work for it. If you quit, you will get nothing, so don't quit. Keep trying. Stay committed to what you want. You deserve the best. Don't settle for less.

267

## THE IMPULSIVE TEMPERAMENT

Some people have a harder time with discipline because they have an impulsive temperament. They are born needing only a little of a feeling to initiate action. For example, they don't need to feel much anger before they act angry. Are you that kind of a person? Do you anger easily and act angry quickly? Do you do things impulsively that you feel sorry for later? The impulsive person responds too quickly to their feelings. This can be a problem because they don't naturally stop and think a problem through. These individuals do not solve problems well, and they tend to have poor self-discipline.

What would you do if you came home and saw the person you love making love with someone else?

"I'd kill them," you might say.

This is a typical impulsive response. It went immediately from feeling to action. Now stop and think about it. What good is it going to do you to kill two people? Is this going to really help you? Are you going to feel better? Is your problem solved? You may get transient relief, yes, but what is the long-term consequence? The result of a double homicide will be years of imprisonment. You will experience pain for a long time. If you are a person with an impulsive temperament, you need to learn how to endure feelings before you act. You need to stop, think, and plan before you act. Until you do this, you will be helpless to circumstances.

These new skills don't come easily, they take practice. When you feel a feeling, particularly an intense one, stop and think the problems through, consider your options, plan your response, and then act. For the next week, keep a log of five situations that give you strong feelings. Write down the situation and the thoughts and feelings you had during the situation. Did you respond appropriately or did you act impulsively? Learn from your mistakes. Practice.

## RULES

Rules do not exist to deny you pleasure. They exist to protect you from pain. If you break the rules, you will hurt—it's as simple as that. Consistently obeying the rules takes self-discipline. You must decide that the rules are for your own good. The legislature didn't make the speed laws to deny you the pleasure of driving fast. They made the rules to keep you safe.

Many of us who have a difficult time with self-discipline were raised in homes where the rules were inconsistent. This is confusing to a child. Sometimes our parents would enforce the rules, and sometimes they wouldn't. Sometimes we would get punished, even abusively punished, and sometimes we would get no punishment at all. Sometimes our parents would do the same things they told us not to do. They would tell us not to hit others, for example, and then they would hit us. This teaches a child that rules aren't important.

A person without rules is a person with no self-respect. Only when we respect ourselves do we set limits on what we will and will not do. Children know that people who love them set limits for them. There is no one more unhappy than a child with no rules. They are allowed to be the ruler of the home. This monarch of the house will demand more and more until they make themselves miserable. Are you important enough to keep safe? If you are, you need rules.

Get a piece of paper and write down some rules you have broken. For example, write down three times when you lied, or three times when you stole. Write the situation down as completely as you can. You had some good reasons for doing those things, didn't you? Why did you do it? What good came out of it?

1. _____
2. _____
3. _____

Now write down the consequences of breaking each of those rules. How did you feel about yourself? How did you feel about the other people? What happened?

1. _____
2. _____
3. _____

Now, look at each situation and ask yourself this question: "Did breaking this rule help me grow and reach my full potential as a person? Did I honor myself, others, and God?" You will find that breaking rules results in pain, your pain. Take lying for example. We lie to avoid getting into trouble. Now this works in the short run, but in the long run, it is interpersonal disaster. We want people to love us. If we lie, people don't know us, so they can't love us. In the long run, if you lie, you will be lonely and you will hurt.

To love you must be self-disciplined. Love is an action, not a feeling. Love is work. Love takes time, energy, and commitment. To do unto others as you would have them do unto you is not always easy, but you will not experience joy unless you love like this. To love, you must be consistent. If you are selfish, if you always come first, you will hurt, you will be deprived of the joy of giving unselfishly to others.

Many parents love without discipline. They don't take time with their children, and they don't solve problems with their children. It is important for children to see their parents hurt with them when they have a problem. The family feels the pain together, and they buckle down to solve the problem together. In healthy homes, the family has confidence that if they work together, they can solve the problem.

## HOW TO SOLVE PROBLEMS

Life is an endless puzzle of problems that need to be solved. Problem solving is challenging, necessary, and fun. It needs to be practiced enough times so that it gets to be automatic. Get a piece of paper and write down a problem of yours, and we will go through the problem-solving steps together.

1. First, write the problem down. What is the problem exactly? How do you feel about it? What do you want to see happen?

2. Then make a list of options. What are all of the possible ways you can deal with this problem? Get input from others you trust. Ask other people to give you alternatives of action. You will be surprised. Other people will come up with good ideas you didn't have.

3. Now consider each option carefully and decide which choice will help you to grow into the person you want to be. If people are involved, remember to treat them the way you would want to be treated.

4. Put the option you have chosen into action.

5. Evaluate the effect of your action on the original problem. This gives you information about how to solve future problems.

Problem → Options → Decision → Action → Evaluation

Work through several problems with your counselor or your group. Get in the habit of writing the problem down and getting advice on options.

## RESPONSIBILITY

To solve a problem effectively, you must accept that problem as your problem. If you blame the problem on something else, you are helpless. It's easy to feel this way, but it's self-defeating. "I would be okay if they would just leave me alone," is a common cry in treatment. This is the cry of someone who is defeated by life. Blaming other people for your problems is never effective. There is always something you can do to make things better. You have great power and influence over your own life. If you sit and do nothing, nothing will change.

Take a piece of paper and write down five times when you got into trouble. Maybe you were arrested or got into trouble at home or at school.

1. _____
2. _____
3. _____
4. _____
5. _____

Think about your choices that lead to this problem. What did you do that ended you up in trouble? Think about all of the choices you made along the way that led to the problem. Don't blame anyone else, just look at your own behavior. Get your counselor and group to help you. If you look closely, you will see that a series of choices, your choices, led to these events. Accidents happen, yes, but most of what happens to you is a result of your choices. Think of how scary the world would be if some other person had the power to make you happy or unhappy. No one has that power but you.

Think of yourself as a gift to the world. There has never been anyone like you. There will never be anyone like you. You owe the world only one thing, to be different. Only you can do this. Only you can be responsible for what you do. You will change the course of history because you were here. Maybe you will change things for the good, maybe for the bad, maybe you will change things a little, maybe a lot, but you will definitely change things. Things will be different because you were here. You have a great responsibility to be yourself.

# Appendix 16

## Impulse Control
### Robert R. Perkinson, Ph.D.

You have problems controlling your impulses if you act too quickly on your feelings. You constantly suffer negative consequences because you act without careful thought. If you had stopped to think, you wouldn't have gotten in all that trouble. Maybe you ended up in jail, or struck someone you cared for, or just got drunk. This set of exercises is for those people who lose control over their behavior. It outlines the skills necessary to overcome problems with impulse control.

The first thing you have to understand is that you are held accountable in our society only for what you do. You are not held accountable for what you think or for how you feel. Your movements are what count. That's what people see. That's how people judge you. You can think about robbing a bank all day long and you won't get arrested. But if you rob a bank, you have committed a crime and you might be in big trouble. To control your impulses, you must learn to control your movements.

## HOW TO UNDERSTAND YOUR FEELINGS

To control your impulses you need to understand your feelings. Feelings are impulses, and feelings motivate action. They are a powerful force. They direct behavior. Each feeling is connected to a specific activity. Let's examine several feelings and the actions they stimulate. There are only a few basic feelings; fear, anger, sadness, and joy are a few of them. Fear motivates you to run, anger to fight, sadness to recover a lost object. Examine each feeling and the movement to which it is attached. Learn that each feeling motivates a specific action, and learn what each feeling is and the action it initiates.

## HOW TO DEVELOP GOALS

Now it's time to take a close look at exactly what you want to change. Remembering that behavior is movement, take a piece of paper and detail exactly what you want to do differently. For example, someone who physically abuses their spouse or kids would want to write down something like this:

"I want to stop hitting my spouse and children."

Study each of your goals. Is it reasonable that you can attain these goals? Make sure the goal is written in behavioral terms. It needs to be a movement you can see, hear, or feel.

Now that you have the specific behavior you want to change, we can look at exactly how you are going to change.

## THE BEHAVIOR CHAIN

Behavior can be analyzed by studying the behavior chain. This chain starts with a stimulus or trigger that initiates a thought, the thought initiates a feeling and the feeling motivates action. All behavior results in a consequence. This consequence may be positive or negative. The behavior chain looks like this:

Trigger → Thought → Feeling → Behavior → Consequence

There are many points along a behavior chain where you can do things differently. Look at it this way: If you are on a train that is going to Kansas and you stay on that train, you are going to end up in Kansas. Likewise, if you initiate an old behavior chain and continue on that chain, you're going to end up with the same consequence. Now maybe that behavior got you in a lot of trouble, and maybe you don't want to repeat the behavior again. Next time, you want to do something different. The key word here is *doing*. You have to do something different if things are going to change.

## Trigger

Let's take a close look at the behavior chain and see where you can change. Behavior will surface under certain situations or triggers. Marlatt and Gordon (1985) grouped relapse triggers into several categories. The first trigger is negative emotions. Often old behavior returns when we are experiencing negative feelings, particularly anger and frustration. You may return to the old behavior under social pressure or when you are in an interpersonal conflict. You may go back to that old behavior when feeling good. Let's list the high-risk situations and spend some time on each one.

1. Negative feelings
2. Social pressure
3. Interpersonal conflict
4. Positive feelings

### Negative Feelings

Start by getting out a clean piece of paper and at the top of the page write the heading, "Negative Feelings." Under this heading, write all the negative feelings you can think of that lead to the behavior you want to change. Maybe you lapse into the old behavior when angry, bored, lonely, happy, embarrassed, frustrated, irritable, or excited. Write down the feelings that seem to precede the action you want to change.

### Social Pressure

Make another heading, "Social Pressure," and list all the social situations in which you are likely to lapse into the old behavior. Remember that social pressure can be direct, as when someone actively encourages you to act in the old way, or indirect, as in a social situation where the behavior might normally occur. Maybe you will be more likely to get back to the old behavior when you are with certain friends, or at certain places or events. Write down every social situation in which you feel you will be vulnerable.

### Interpersonal Conflict

Interpersonal conflict comes next. Start with that heading and under it write every situation you can think of where a conflict with someone else leads to the behavior you want to change. Try to include the total situation, such as, Who said what and how? What happened? When did you lose control? What preceded your behavior?

### Positive Feelings

Now write "Positive Feelings" as a heading, and list the times when you acted in that old way when feeling good, to celebrate, to increase the good feeling. Detail the situations and carefully study what you were after, the feelings you wanted to enhance.

## Thoughts

We'll analyze thoughts next. These get a little tricky, so pay careful attention to them. Aaron Beck et al. (1979) developed cognitive therapy for depression. David Burns (1980) further developed this technique. Many thoughts are very quick, so quick that they occur out of your awareness. These thoughts are called automatic thoughts because they don't come from anything you try to think—you think them automatically.

Take another piece of paper and at the top write a situation where you lost control. Write the specific situation in as much detail as you can. Now explore how you were feeling in that situation. Remember the eight primary feelings: anger, acceptance, joy, sadness, anticipation, fear, surprise, and disgust. Write each feeling down and score the intensity of the feeling on a scale of 1 to 100, 1 = as little of the feeling as possible, 100 = as much of the feeling as possible.

Let's take an example: Frank came home and his spouse angrily asked him where he had been. He was late coming home from work. Frank felt hurt at an intensity of 45, angry at 90, and frightened at 75.

Now it's your turn, you have the situation, and all the feelings you had during that situation. You have scored how intensely you were feeling each feeling. Now, carefully process with your counselor what you were thinking between the situation and the feelings. This will take some time, so take it slow. Try to think of all the thoughts that came to mind between the event and the feelings. Let's see how Frank did. "My wife asked me where I had been. I thought the following: Here we go again; she's mad; she thinks I've been drinking again; she's always mad at me; she never trusts me; she doesn't love me; she has never loved me."

Make as long a list of these thoughts as you can. You will be surprised at how many thoughts you can have in a short period of time. Next, look at the thoughts and check them out for accuracy. Which thoughts are accurate, which are inaccurate? Frank decided his spouse was mad, that she was worried that he had been drinking again. Those thoughts were accurate, but she wasn't always mad at him, and she trusted him plenty of times. She does love him, and she has loved him for a long time. So the other thoughts were inaccurate.

Now, with your counselor or your group, discover which thoughts are accurate and which are inaccurate. On another sheet, write down the situation again. Write only the accurate thoughts you were having and then score all the feelings you had listed on the previous page.

Frank did it this way:

> My wife asked me where I had been. She was frightened that I had been drinking again, and a little angry just at the thought of it. She is very concerned for me. She loves me very much and she is afraid for my health. That doesn't hurt me at all so I'd put the hurt at 0. It still makes me a little mad but much less so, I would put that at 20. That doesn't scare me at all, so I would rate the fear at 0.

Now, add up your scores on each sheet, coming up with a total score of all the feelings when you were thinking inaccurately and when you were thinking accurately. This is Frank's sheet.

|  | Inaccurate Thinking | Accurate Thinking |
|---|---|---|
| Hurt | 45 | 0 |
| Angry | 90 | 20 |
| Fear | 75 | 0 |
| Total | 210 | 20 |

You can now see what we are after. Many of your thoughts are automatic, inaccurate, and lead to uncomfortable feelings. Some of these feelings are unnecessary because they are inaccurate assessments of reality. Obviously, if you see a situation inaccurately, you will react inaccurately. If you develop the skill of stopping and assessing the situation accurately, you will feel more comfortable, and you will be able to deal with the situation with more precision and skill.

For the next few days, keep a running account of any situation that makes you feel uncomfortable, and do this exercise again. After a few days, you will notice patterns in your thinking. You will see that you think the same inaccurate thoughts in many different situations. These are thoughts that need to be challenged in treatment. Address them carefully with your group and your counselor, and begin to watch out for them. When they resurface, stop and correct yourself. Try to keep your thinking accurate.

## Feelings

All feelings are friendly, even the painful ones. They help us adapt to our environment and give us energy and direction for action. The skill necessary for dealing with feelings appropriately is to learn exactly what coping skills to use when having a particular feeling. Feelings should not be ignored—they should be acted on. Which action to take is the skill you want to learn. You need to spend some time with a few feelings and learn coping skills for dealing with these feelings. Then you must practice the new skills until they become automatic. You can't just learn what to do, you must practice the actual behavior until it becomes second nature. This will take a lot of time and practice. Don't try to do this perfectly—just make progress.

### Anger

Anger gives chemically dependent persons more problems than any other feeling. You can relapse into old behavior when you feel angry and frustrated. Anger gives you the energy and direction to fight. Anger is good, and fighting is good, as long as the actions are appropriate. The problem comes in when we fight all the time or at inappropriate times.

Anger is friendly—it needs to be listened to and expressed. You need to learn how to use your anger assertively rather than aggressively. Much of this work is taken from *Your Perfect Right*, an assertiveness guide by Alberti and Emmons (1986). They found that verbal and physical aggression is rarely necessary, and even harmful. Acting on your anger assertively is a much more effective means of getting what you want. Here is an assertiveness formula that you should memorize and practice until it becomes automatic.

I feel _____

When you _____

I would prefer it if _____

When you feel angry with people, you start by describing how you feel. Then, in behavioral terms, describe what they did that led to your feelings. Then, again in behavioral terms, tell them what you want them to do.

Let's try it in a situation to show how the assertiveness formula works.

### The Aggressive Response

Bob comes home from work one hour late. Barbara, his spouse, is hurt and angry.
   Barbara:   Where have you been! You're such an incredible jerk!

How is Bob going to be feeling: attacked, hurt, angry, defensive? He might retaliate and say:
   Bob:   What a nag! You're always mad at me!

### The Assertive Response

   Barbara:   I feel hurt and angry when you're late. I would prefer it if you would call me and tell me when you're not going to be on time.

The assertiveness formula gives other persons accurate information that they can use to remedy the situation. They know what they did, and they know what to do differently.

Try the assertiveness formula at least two times today. After each use, write the situation down and how it turned out. Notice the feelings you have. If you are like most people, you will feel much more in control of your feelings. You will also get more of what you want. This will lead to less anger.

### Fear

Fear is another difficult feeling for people. Fear motivates us to run or withdraw from a dangerous situation. Fear is friendly. Withdrawal is friendly, and it can be adaptive, but it can also be inappropriate. It is important to think accurately, and consider the consequences before you withdraw. What are the pros and cons of withdrawing from the situation? It is not appropriate to run from all of your problems, even if they are scary. If you did, you wouldn't solve many of them.

You must learn to stand your ground, even in a painful situation. This way you can work a problem through to resolution. If you find that you are always running away, you must find other coping skills to use when you feel frightened. The same assertiveness formula works here. "I feel . . . , when you . . . , I would prefer it if . . . ," works as well with fear as it does with anger. If people know you are frightened, they will often respond positively to your fear. It even helps to share your fear with someone who is not involved with the immediate situation. Remember, share your feelings. This is a major coping skill. It can be used with all feelings.

## Behavior

By now you know that using the right behavior at the right time is the real secret to success when dealing with impulse control problems. It's the movements, the behavior, that people are responsible for, so you must practice not moving quickly. You have to delay action until you have time to think and plan. Some people have to back away from the situation entirely to give themselves the time to think. They may have to go for a walk, a run, or a drive. They may have to leave the house or the place of conflict, and give themselves some space.

You know yourself best, and you know beforehand when you are about to lose control. You must practice catching this increase in your feelings, before you lose control. At this point, you must move away from the situation. You cannot stay there and hope to achieve control, that is too dangerous. Don't worry—you are going to come back to the problem, the situation is going to be addressed, but you need some time away from the problem.

If you stay in a situation where you have lost control, you are playing with fire. Don't do that to yourself.

Exactly what coping skills to use in a particular situation will take some planning. This planning must take place before the situation, and it must be practiced until it becomes automatic.

Get out another piece of paper and write down the situation you are having difficulty with. Now brainstorm with your counselor and your group: What else could you do in that situation? Barbara is trying to control her tendency to hit her children. She made this plan when she feels angry with them again.

When I'm getting angry I'm going to do the following:

1. Recognize my anger.
2. Step back from the situation as far as necessary to feel the anger go down and then:
   a. Go in another room.
   b. Go for a walk.
   c. Go for a drive.
   d. Go to mother's house.
   e. Go talk to a friend next door.
   f. Call my sponsor.
3. When I'm thinking clearly, I will plan my response. I may have to do this with someone I trust.
4. Come back to my children and try my plan.
5. If I get too angry again, I will go back and repeat the whole procedure.

## Consequence

It is important to take a careful look at the consequences of your behavior. You will learn from your actions only if you see clearly what happens when you act in a certain manner. On another piece of paper, write briefly what happened each time you lost control of your actions. Under each situation, write down the negative consequences that resulted from that loss of control. This must be done in great detail. Take a lot of time and think. Don't blame anyone else for what happened; concentrate on your own actions. Use every situation you can think of. The more clearly you can see the negative consequences of your behavior, the more you will tell yourself never to act that way again. You can learn from your behavior, if you stop, think, and plan before you act.

We have looked carefully at the behavior you want to change. We have studied the trigger, thought, feeling, behavior, and consequence. Now let's go over what you are going to do when you are in a high-risk situation. What is your plan when you feel impulsively? First, think of the word *stop*.

S = Stop:  Stop and commit yourself to a rational response.

T = Think:
  1. What is the situation?
  2. What is at stake?
  3. Get your thinking accurate.


O = Options:
  1. What are the options?
  2. What are the pros and cons of each option?
  3. Choose the best option.


P = Plan:
  1. Carry out the plan.

With your counselor and group, work through the situations and feelings with which you are having the most difficulty. If you are having a difficult time with anger, discuss your anger carefully in individual sessions and in group. Come up with specific coping skills to deal with each feeling. Exactly what you are going to do. List options available to you and carry them in your pocket or purse. Now practice, practice, practice. When you lapse into the old behavior, don't give up, use the lapse as an education. What happened? What coping skill could you have used? How can you do things differently next time? You can do this. You no longer have to be a slave to your impulses. You can change your behavior. You have all the necessary skills.

# Appendix 17

## Relapse Prevention
### Robert R. Perkinson, Ph.D.

There is some bad news about relapse and some good news. The bad news is many patients have problems with relapse in early sobriety. About two thirds of patients coming out of addiction programs relapse within 3 months of leaving treatment (Hunt et al., 1971). The good news is most people that go through treatment ultimately achieve a stable recovery (Frances, Bucky, & Alexopolos, 1984). Relapse doesn't have to happen to you, and even if it does, you can do something about it. Relapse prevention is a daily program that can prevent relapse. It can also stop a slip from becoming a disaster. This relapse prevention exercise has been developed using a combination of the models of Gorski and Miller (1986) and Marlatt and Gordon (1985). This exercise uses both the disease concept model in combination with a behavioral approach.

## RELAPSE IS A PROCESS

Relapse is a process that begins long before you use drugs or alcohol. Certain symptoms precede the first use of chemicals. This relapse prevention exercise teaches how to identify and control these symptoms before they lead to actual drug or alcohol use. If you allow these symptoms to go on without acting on them, serious problems will result.

## THE RELAPSE WARNING SIGNS

All relapse begins with warning signs that will signal for you that you are in trouble. If you do not recognize these signs, you will decompensate and finally use chemicals. All of the signs are a reaction to stress, and they are a reemergence of the disease. They are a means by which your body and mind are telling you that you are in trouble. Gorski and Miller (1982) recognized 37 warning signs in patients who had relapsed. You may not have all of these symptoms, but you will have some of them long before you actually use chemicals. You must determine which symptoms are the most characteristic of you, and you must come up with coping skills for dealing with each symptom.

Listed below are the 37 warning symptoms. Circle the ones that you have experienced before you used drugs or alcohol.

1. Apprehension about well-being
2. Denial
3. Adamant commitment to sobriety
4. Compulsive attempts to impose sobriety on others
5. Defensiveness
6. Compulsive behavior
7. Impulsive behavior
8. Loneliness
9. Tunnel vision
10. Minor depression
11. Loss of constructive planning
12. Plans begin to fail
13. Idle daydreaming and wishful thinking
14. Feeling nothing can be solved
15. Immature wish to be happy
16. Periods of confusion

17. Irritation with friends
18. Easily angered
19. Irregular eating habits
20. Listlessness
21. Irregular sleeping habits
22. Progressive loss of daily structure
23. Periods of deep depression
24. Irregular attendance at meetings
25. Development of an "I don't care" attitude
26. Open rejection of help
27. Dissatisfaction with life
28. Feelings of powerlessness and helplessness
29. Self-pity
30. Thoughts of social use
31. Conscious lying
32. Complete loss of self-confidence
33. Unreasonable resentments
34. Discontinuing all treatment
35. Overwhelming loneliness, frustration, anger, and tension
36. Start of controlled using
37. Loss of control

## WHAT TO DO WHEN YOU EXPERIENCE A WARNING SIGN

When you recognize any of the above symptoms, you need to take action. Make a list of the coping skills you can use when you experience a symptom that is common for you. This will happen. You will have problems in recovery. Your task is to take affirmative action. Remember, a symptom is a danger signal. You are in trouble. Make a list of what you are going to do. Are you going to call your sponsor, go to a meeting, call your counselor, call someone in AA/NA, tell someone, exercise, read the Big Book, pray, become involved in an activity you enjoy, turn it over to your Higher Power or your group, go into treatment. Detail several plans of action.

Plan 1. _____
Plan 2. _____
Plan 3. _____
Plan 4. _____
Plan 5. _____
Plan 6. _____
Plan 7. _____
Plan 8. _____
Plan 9. _____
Plan 10. _____

You need to check each warning symptom daily in your personal inventory. You also need to have other people check you daily. You will not always pick up the symptoms in yourself. You may be denying the problem again. Your spouse, sponsor, or a fellow AA/NA member can warn you when they feel you may be in trouble. Listen to these people. If they tell you they sense a problem, take action. You may need professional help in working the problem through. Don't hesitate in calling and asking for help. Anything is better than relapsing. If you overreact to a warning sign, you are not going to be in trouble, but if you underreact you may be headed for real problems. Chemical dependency is a deadly disease. Your life is at stake.

## THE HIGH-RISK SITUATIONS

Marlatt and Gordon (1985) found that relapse is more likely to occur in certain situations. These situations can trigger relapse. They found that people relapsed when faced with life situations that they couldn't cope with except by using chemicals. Your job in treatment is to develop coping skills for dealing with each high-risk situation.

### Negative Emotions

Thirty-five percent of people who relapse, relapse when feeling a negative feeling that they can't cope with. Most felt angry or frustrated, but some felt anxious, bored, lonely, or depressed. Almost any negative feeling can lead to relapse if you don't learn how to cope with the feeling. Feelings motivate you to take action. You must act to solve any problem.

Circle any of the following feelings that seem to lead you to use chemicals.

| | | | | |
|---|---|---|---|---|
| 1. Lonely | 11. Envious | 21. Selfish | 31. Scared | 41. Irritated |
| 2. Angry | 12. Exhausted | 22. Restless | 32. Spiteful | 42. Overwhelmed |
| 3. Rejected | 13. Bored | 23. Weak | 33. Sorrowful | 43. Panicked |
| 4. Empty | 14. Anxious | 24. Sorrowful | 34. Helpless | 44. Trapped |
| 5. Annoyed | 15. Ashamed | 25. Greedy | 35. Neglected | 45. Unsure |
| 6. Sad | 16. Bitter | 26. Aggravated | 36. Grieving | 46. Intimidated |
| 7. Exasperated | 17. Burdened | 27. Enervated | 37. Confused | 47. Distraught |
| 8. Betrayed | 18. Foolish | 28. Miserable | 38. Crushed | 48. Uneasy |
| 9. Cheated | 19. Jealous | 29. Unloved | 39. Discontented | 49. Guilty |
| 10. Frustrated | 20. Left out | 30. Worried | 40. Restless | 50. Threatened |

*Develop a Plan to Deal With Negative Emotions*

These are just a few of the feeling words; add more if you need to. Develop coping skills for dealing with each feeling that makes you vulnerable to relapse. Exactly what are you going to do when you have this feeling? Detail your specific plan of action. Some options are: Talk to my sponsor. Call a friend in the program. Go to a meeting. Call my counselor. Read some recovery material. Turn it over to my Higher Power. Get some exercise. For each feeling, develop a specific plan of action.

Feeling _____

    Plan 1. _____

    Plan 2. _____

    Plan 3. _____

Feeling _____

    Plan 1. _____

    Plan 2. _____

    Plan 3. _____

Feeling  _____

    Plan 1. _____

    Plan 2. _____

    Plan 3. _____

Continue to fill these feeling forms out until you have all the feelings that give you trouble, and you have coping skills for dealing with each feeling.

## Social Pressure

Twenty percent of people relapse in a social situation. Social pressure can be direct, as when someone directly encourages you to use chemicals, or it can be indirect, as in a social situation where people are using. Both of these situations can trigger intense craving and this can lead to relapse. Over 60% of alcoholics relapse in a bar.

Certain friends are more likely to encourage you to use chemicals. These people don't want to hurt you—they want you to relax and have a good time. They want their old friend back. They don't understand the nature of your disease. Perhaps they are chemically dependent themselves and are in denial.

### High-Risk Friends

Make a list of the friends who might encourage you to use drugs or alcohol.

1. _____

2. _____

3. _____

4. _____

5. _____

What are you going to do when they offer you drugs? What are you going to say? In group, set up a situation where the whole group encourages you to use chemicals. Look carefully at how you feel when they are encouraging you. Look at what you say. Have them help you develop appropriate ways to say no.

### High-Risk Social Situations

Certain social situations will trigger craving. These are the situations where you have used chemicals in the past. Certain bars or restaurants, a particular part of town, certain music, athletic events, parties, weddings, family get-togethers. All of these situations can trigger intense cravings. Make a list of five social situations where you will be vulnerable to relapse.

1. _____

2. _____

3. _____

4. _____

5. _____

In early sobriety, you will need to avoid these situations and friends. To put yourself in a high-risk situation is asking for trouble. If you have to attend a function where there will be people using chemicals, take someone with you who is in the program. Take someone with you who will support you in your sobriety. Make sure that you have a way home. You don't have to stay and torture yourself. You can leave if you feel uncomfortable. Avoid all situations where your sobriety feels shaky.

## Interpersonal Conflict

Sixteen percent of people relapse when in a conflict with another person. They have a problem with someone and they have no idea how to cope with the problem. The stress of the problem builds and leads to drinking or using drugs. This conflict usually happens with someone that you are closely involved with, wife, husband, children, parents, siblings, friends, or boss.

You can have a serious problem with anyone, even strangers, so you must have a plan for dealing with interpersonal conflict. You will develop specific skills in treatment that will help you communicate even when you are under stress.

You need to learn and practice the following interpersonal skills repeatedly.

1. Tell the truth all the time.
2. Share how you feel.
3. Ask for what you want.
4. Find some truth in what the other person is saying.
5. Be willing to compromise.

If you can stay in the conflict and work it out, that's great, but if you can't, you have to leave the situation and get help. You may have to go for a walk, a run, or a drive. You might need to cool down. You must stop the conflict. You can't continue to try to deal with a situation that you feel is too much for you. Don't feel bad about this, interpersonal relationships are the hardest challenge we face. Carry a card with you that lists the people you can contact. You may want to call your sponsor, minister, counselor, fellow AA/NA member, friend, family member, doctor, or anyone else who may support you.

In an interpersonal conflict you will fear abandonment. You need to get accurate and reassure yourself that you have many people who still care about you. Remember that your Higher Power cares about you. God created you and loves you perfectly. Remember the other people in your life who love you. This is one of the main reasons for talking with others. When they listen to you, they give you the feeling that you are loved.

If you still feel afraid or angry, get with someone you trust and stay with that person until you feel safe. Do not struggle out there all by yourself! Every member of AA or NA will understand how you are feeling. We have all had these problems. We have all felt lost, helpless, hopeless, and angry.

Make an emergency card that includes all of the people you can call if you are having difficulty. Write their phone numbers down and carry this card with you at all times. Show this card to your counselor. Practice asking someone for help in treatment once each day. Write the situation down and show it to your counselor. Get into the habit of asking for help. When you get out of treatment, call someone every day just to stay in touch, and keep the lines of communication open. Get used to it. Don't wait to ask for help at the last minute, this makes asking more difficult.

## Positive Feelings

Twelve percent of people relapse when they are feeling positive emotions. Think of all the times you used drugs and alcohol to celebrate. That has gotten to be such a habit, that when something good happens, you will immediately think about using. You need to be ready when you feel like a winner. This may be at a wedding, birth, promotion, or any event where you feel good. How are you going to celebrate without drugs and alcohol? Make a celebration plan. You may have to take someone with you to a celebration, particularly in early recovery.

Positive feelings can also work when you are by yourself. A beautiful spring day can be enough to get you thinking about drinking or using. You need an action plan for when these thoughts pass through your mind. You must immediately get accurate and get real. In recovery we are committed to reality. Don't sit there and recall how wonderful you will feel if you get high—tell yourself the truth. Think about all the pain that chemical dependency has caused you. If you toy with positive feelings, you will ultimately use chemicals.

Circle the positive feelings that may make you vulnerable to relapse.

| | | | | |
|---|---|---|---|---|
| 1. Affectionate | 11. Joyful | 21. Lazy | 31. Silly | 41. Ecstatic |
| 2. Bold | 12. Free | 22. Loving | 32. Vivacious | 42. Upbeat |
| 3. Brave | 13. Glad | 23. Peaceful | 33. Adequate | 43. Splendid |
| 4. Calm | 14. Gleeful | 24. Pleasant | 34. Efficient | 44. Yearning |
| 5. Capable | 15. Happy | 25. Pleased | 35. Successful | 45. Blissful |
| 6. Cheerful | 16. Honored | 26. Sexy | 36. Accomplished | 46. Excited |
| 7. Confident | 17. Horny | 27. Wonderful | 37. Hopeful | 47. Exhilarated |
| 8. Delightful | 18. Infatuated | 28. Cool | 38. Cheery | 48. Proud |
| 9. Desire | 19. Inspired | 29. Relaxed | 39. Elated | 49. Aroused |
| 10. Enchanted | 20. Kinky | 30. Reverent | 40. Merry | 50. Festive |

*A Plan to Cope With Positive Feelings*

These are the feelings that may make you vulnerable to relapse. You must be careful when you are feeling good. Make an action plan for dealing with each positive emotion that makes you vulnerable to using chemicals.

Feeling _____

    Plan 1. _____

    Plan 2. _____

    Plan 3. _____

Feeling _____

    Plan 1. _____

    Plan 2. _____

    Plan 3. _____

Feeling _____

    Plan 1. _____

    Plan 2. _____

    Plan 3. _____

Continue this planning until you develop a plan for each of the positive feelings that make you vulnerable.

## TEST PERSONAL CONTROL

Five percent of people relapse to test if they can use chemicals again. They fool themselves into thinking that they might be able to use normally. This time they will use only a little. This time they will be able to control themselves. People who fool themselves this way are in for big trouble. From the first use, most people are in full-blown relapse within 30 days.

Testing personal control begins with inaccurate thinking. It takes you back to Step One. You need to think accurately. You are powerless over mood-altering chemicals. If you use, you will lose—it's as simple as that. You are physiologically, psychologically, and socially addicted to mood-altering chemicals. The cells in your body won't suddenly change, no matter how long you are clean and sober. You are chemically dependent in your cells. This will never change.

## HOW TO SEE THROUGH THE FIRST USE

You need to look at how the illness part of yourself will try to convince you that you are not chemically dependent. The illness will flash on the screen of your consciousness all the good things that drugs and alcohol did for you. Make a list of these things. In the first column, marked Early Use, write down some of the good things you were getting out of using chemicals. Why were you using? What good came out of it? Did it make you feel social, smart, pretty, intelligent, brave, popular, desirable, relaxed, sexy? Did it help you sleep? Did it make you feel confident? Did it help you to forget your problems? Make a long list. These are the good things you were getting when you first started using. This is why you were using.

*Early Use*

1. _____
2. _____
3. _____
4. _____
5. _____
6. _____
7. _____
8. _____
9. _____
10. _____

*Late Use*

1. _____
2. _____
3. _____
4. _____
5. _____
6. _____
7. _____
8 _____
9. _____
10. _____

Now go back and place in the second column, marked Late Use. How you were doing in that area once you became chemically dependent? How were you doing in that same area right before you came into treatment? Did you still feel social or did you feel alone? Did you still feel intelligent or did you feel stupid? You will find that a great change has taken place. The very things that you were using for in early use, you get the opposite of in late use. If you were drinking for sleep, you couldn't sleep. If you were using to be more popular, you felt more isolated and alone. If you were using to feel brave, you were feeling more afraid. This is a major characteristic of chemical dependency.

Take a long look at both of these lists and think about how the illness is going to try to work inside of your thinking. The addicted part of yourself will present to you all of the good things you got in early use. This is how the disease will encourage you to use. But you must see through the first use to the consequences that are dead ahead.

Look at that second list. You must see the misery that is coming if you use chemicals. For most people who relapse, there are only a few days of controlled use before loss of control sets in. There are usually only a few hours or days before all the bad stuff begins to click back into place. Relapse is terrible. It is the most intense misery that you can imagine.

## LAPSE AND RELAPSE

A *lapse* is the use of any mood-altering chemical. This is called a *slip*. A *relapse* is continuing to use the chemical until the full biological, psychological, and social disease is present. All of the complex biological, psychological, and social components of the disease become evident very quickly.

## THE SLIP PLAN

You must have a plan in case you slip. It is foolish to think that you will never have a problem again. You must plan what you are going to do if you have problems. Hunt et al. (1971), in a study of recovering addicts, found that 33% of patients lapsed within 2 weeks of leaving treatment. Sixty percent lapsed within 3 months. At the end of 8 months, 63% had used. At the end of 12 months, 67% had used.

The worst thing you can do when you have a slip is to think that you have completely failed in recovery. This is inaccurate thinking. You are not a total failure. You haven't lost everything, you have made a mistake, and you need to learn from it. You let some part of your program go, and you are paying for it. You need to examine exactly what happened and get back into recovery.

A slip is an emergency. It is a matter of life or death. You must take immediate action to prevent the slip from becoming a full relapse. You must call someone in the program, preferably your sponsor, and tell them what happened. You need to examine carefully why you slipped. You cannot use drugs and alcohol and the tools of recovery at the same time. Something went wrong. You didn't use your new skills. You must make a plan of action to recover from your slip. You cannot do this by yourself because you are in denial. You don't know the whole truth. If you did, you wouldn't have relapsed.

Call your sponsor or a professional counselor and have them develop a new treatment plan for you. You may need to attend more meetings. You may need to see a counselor. You may need outpatient treatment. You may need inpatient treatment. You have to get honest with yourself. You need to develop a plan and follow it. You need someone else to agree to keep an eye on you for a while. Do not try to do this alone. What we cannot do alone, we can do together.

## THE BEHAVIOR CHAIN

All behavior occurs in a certain sequence. First, there is the TRIGGER. This is the external event that starts the behavioral sequence. After the trigger, there comes THINKING. Much of this thinking is very fast and you will not consciously pick it up unless you stop and think about it. The thoughts trigger FEELINGS, which give you energy and direction for action. Next come the BEHAVIOR or the action initiated by the trigger. Lastly, there are always CONSEQUENCES for any action.

Diagramed, the behavior chain looks like this:

Trigger → Thinking → Feeling → Behavior → Consequence

Let's go through a behavioral sequence and see how it works. On the way home from work, Bob, a recovering alcoholic, passes the local bar (this is the trigger). He thinks, "I've had a hard day. I need a couple of beers to unwind" (the trigger initiates thinking). Bob craves a beer (the thinking initiates feeling). Bob turns into the bar and begins drinking (the feeling initiates behavior). Bob relapses (the behavior has a consequence.)

Let's work through another example. It's eleven o'clock at night and Bob is not asleep (trigger). He thinks, "I'll never get to sleep tonight unless I have a few drinks" (thinking). He feels an increase in his anxiety about not sleeping (feelings). He gets up and drinks a few drinks (behavior). He gets drunk and wakes up hung over and unable to work the next morning (consequence).

### How to Cope With Triggers

At every point along the behavior chain, you can work on preventing relapse. First you need to examine your triggers carefully. What environmental events lead you to using chemicals? We went over some of these when we examined high-risk situations. Determine what people, places, or things make you vulnerable to relapse. Stay away from these triggers as much as possible. If a trigger occurs, use your new coping skills.

Don't let the trigger initiate old behavior. Stop and think. Don't let your thinking get out of control. Challenge your thinking and get accurate about what's real. Let's look at some common inaccurate thoughts.

1. It's not going to hurt.
2. No one's going to know.
3. I need to relax.
4. I'm just going to have a couple.

5. I've had a hard day.
6. My friends want me to drink.
7. I never had a problem with pot.
8. It's the only way I can sleep.
9. I can do anything I want to.
10. I'm lonely.

All of these inaccurate thoughts can be used to fuel the craving that leads to relapse. You must stop and challenge your thinking until you are thinking accurately. You must replace inaccurate thoughts with accurate ones. You are chemically dependent. If you drink or use drugs, you will die. That is the truth. Think through the first drink. Get honest with yourself.

## HOW TO COPE WITH CRAVING

If you think inaccurately, you will begin craving. This is the powerful feeling that drives compulsive drug use. Craving is like an ocean wave—it will build and then wash over you. Craving doesn't last long if you move away from your drug of choice. If you move closer to the drug, the craving will increase until you are compelled to use. Immediately on feeling a desire to use, think this thought:

"That is no longer an option for me."

Now, drinking and using drugs are no longer an option. What are your options? You are in trouble. You are craving. What are you going to do to prevent relapse? You must move away from your drug of choice. Perhaps you need to call your sponsor, go to a meeting, turn it over to your Higher Power, call the AA/NA hotline, call the treatment center, call your counselor, go for a walk, run, visit someone. You must do something else other than thinking about chemicals. Don't sit there and ponder using—you will lose that debate. This illness is called the great debater. If you leave it unchecked, it will seduce you into using chemicals.

Remember, the illness must lie to work. You must uncover the lie as quickly as possible and get back to the truth. You must take the appropriate action necessary to maintain your sobriety.

## DEVELOP A DAILY RELAPSE PREVENTION PROGRAM

If you work a daily program of recovery, your chances of success greatly increase. You need to evaluate your recovery daily and keep a log. This is your daily inventory.

1. Assess all relapse warning signs.
    a. What symptoms did I see in myself today?
    b. What am I going to do about them?

2. Assess love of self.
    a. What did I do to love myself today?
    b. What am I going to do tomorrow?

3. Assess love of others.
    a. What did I do to love others today?
    b. What am I going to do tomorrow?

4. Assess love of God.

    a. What did I do to love God today?

    b. What am I going to do tomorrow?

5. Assess sleep pattern.

    How am I sleeping?

6. Assess exercise.

    Am I getting enough exercise?

7. Assess nutrition.

    Am I eating right?

8. Review total recovery program.

    a. How am I doing in recovery?

    b. What is the next step in my recovery program?

9. Read the 24-Hour-a-Day Book.

10. Make conscious contact with God.

    a. Pray and meditate for a few minutes.

    b. Relax completely.

Fill out this inventory every day following treatment and keep a journal on how you are doing. You will be amazed as you read back over your journal from time to time. You will be surprised at how much you have grown.

Make a list of 10 reasons why you want to stay clean and sober.

1. _____
2. _____
3. _____
4. _____
5. _____
6. _____
7. _____
8. _____
9. _____
10. _____

Never forget these reasons. Read this list often and carry a copy with you. If you are struggling in sobriety, take it out and read it to yourself. You are important. No one has to live a life of misery. You can recover and live a clean and sober life.

# Appendix 18

## Step One
### Robert R. Perkinson, Ph.D.

*We admitted we were powerless over alcohol—that our lives had become unmanageable.*

*Alcoholics Anonymous* (1976)

Before beginning this exercise, read Step One in the *Twelve Steps and Twelve Traditions* (AA, 1981).

No one likes to admit defeat. Our mind rebels at the very thought that we have lost control. We are big, strong, intelligent, and capable. How can it be that we are powerless? How can it be that our lives are unmanageable? This exercise will help you to sort through your life and to make some important decisions. Answer each question that applies to you as completely as you can. This is an opportunity for you to get accurate. You need to see the truth about yourself.

Let's pretend for a moment that you are the commander of a nuclear missile silo. You are in charge of a 10-megaton bomb. If you'll think about it, this is exactly the kind of control you want over your life. You want to be in control of your thinking, feeling, and behavior. You want to be in control all of the time, not just some of the time. If you do something by accident, or do something foolishly, you may kill a lot of people. You never want to be out of control of your behavior, not even for a second.

People who are powerless over alcohol or drugs will occasionally be under the influence of the chemical when they are doing something physically hazardous. They may be intoxicated or hung over when they are at work, or using dangerous equipment, or driving. About 25,000 Americans are killed each year driving while intoxicated. If you have ever done anything like this, you have been out of control. You have risked your own life and the lives of others. Surely, you can't drive better when you are intoxicated than when you are sober. Now it is time to get honest with yourself.

### POWERLESSNESS

1. Have you ever been intoxicated when you were doing something dangerous? For example, have you ever driven a car when you were using? Give some examples.

   _____

   _____

   _____

2. Did you think that you were placing your life and the lives of others in jeopardy? What were you thinking?

   _____

   _____

   _____

3. Whose lives did you risk? Make a list of those people you endangered.

   _____

   _____

   _____

4. How do you feel about what you did?

_____

_____

_____

People who are powerless will occasionally do things while intoxicated or hung over that they feel bad or guilty about later. They may act foolishly at a party, or act out sexually, or get angry, or say things they don't mean. Have you ever done anything while intoxicated that you felt guilty or bad about later? Make a list of the things that made you feel the most uncomfortable.

1. _____

2. _____

3. _____

4. _____

5. _____

People who are powerless will gradually lose respect for themselves. They will have difficulty trusting themselves. In what ways have you lost respect for yourself due to drug or alcohol use?

1. _____

2. _____

3. _____

People who are powerless will do things that they don't remember doing. If you drink enough or use enough drugs, you can't remember things properly. You may have people come up to you after a party and tell you something you did that you don't remember doing. You may wake up and not know where you are. You may not remember how you got home. This is a blackout and they are very scary. You could have done anything. Most blackouts last a few minutes, but some can go on for hours or days.

1. Describe any blackouts you have had.

_____

_____

_____

2. How does it feel to know that you did something that you don't remember?

_____

_____

_____

3. Think for a minute of what you could have done. You could have done anything and you wouldn't have known it.

People who are powerless cannot keep promises they make to themselves or others. They promise that they will cut down on their drinking and they don't. They promise they won't use and they do. They promise to be home, to be at work, to be at the Cub Scout meeting, to go to school, but they don't make it. They can't always do what they want to do because sometimes they are too intoxicated or hung over. They disappoint themselves and they lose trust in themselves. Other people lose trust in them. They can count on themselves some of the time, but they can't count on themselves all of the time.

1.  Did you ever promise yourself that you would cut down your drug or alcohol use?

      Yes _____    No _____

2.  What happened to these promises?

      _____
      _____
      _____

3.  Did you ever promise yourself that you would quit entirely?

      Yes _____    No _____

4.  What happened to your promise?

      _____
      _____
      _____

5.  Did you ever make a promise to someone that you didn't keep because you were intoxicated or hung over? Give a few examples.

      _____
      _____
      _____

6.  Are you reliable when you are intoxicated?

      Yes _____    No _____

People who are powerless have accidents. They fall down, or have a car accident, when they are intoxicated. Evidence proves that drugs profoundly affect thinking, coordination, and reaction time. Have you ever had an accident while intoxicated? Describe each accident.

   _____
   _____
   _____
   _____

People who are powerless lose control of their behavior. They do things that they wouldn't normally do when clean and sober. They may get in a fight. They may hit or yell at someone they love, their spouse, child, parent, or friend. They can say things that they don't mean.

Have you ever gotten in a fight when you were intoxicated? Describe each instance.

   _____
   _____
   _____
   _____

People who are powerless say things they don't mean. They may say sexual or angry things that they feel bad about later. We may not remember everything we said, but the other person does remember. Have you ever said something you didn't mean while intoxicated? What did you say? What did you do?

_____
_____
_____
_____
_____

People are powerless when they have feelings that they can't deal with. They may drink or use drugs because they feel frightened, angry, or sad. They medicate their feelings. Have you ever used drugs to cover up your feelings? Give a few examples.

_____
_____
_____

What feelings do you have difficulty dealing with?

_____
_____
_____

People are powerless when they are not safe. What convinces you that you can no longer use drugs or alcohol safely?

_____
_____
_____

People are powerless when they know that they should do something, but they can't do it. They may make a great effort, but they just can't seem to finish what they started out to do.

1. Could you cut down on your drug or alcohol use every time you wanted to and for as long as you wanted?

   Yes _____ No _____

2. Did being intoxicated or hung over ever keep you from doing something at home that you thought you should do? Give some examples.

_____
_____
_____

3. Did being intoxicated or hung over ever keep you from going to work? Give some examples.

_____
_____
_____

4. Did you ever lose a job because of your drinking or drug use? Write down what happened.

_____

_____

_____

People are powerless when other people have to warn them that they are in trouble. You may have felt like you were fine, but people close to you noticed something was wrong. It was probably difficult for them to put their finger on just what was wrong, but they were worried about you. It is difficult to confront someone when they are wrong, so people avoid it until they can't stand the behavior anymore. When addicts are confronted with their behavior, they feel annoyed and irritated. They want to be left alone with the lies that they are telling themselves. Has anyone ever talked to you about your drinking or drug use? Who was this? How did you feel?

_____

_____

_____

People are powerless when they don't know the truth about themselves. Addicts lie to themselves about how much they are drinking or using. They lie to themselves about how often they use. They lie to themselves about their problems, even when the problems are obvious. They blame others for their problems. Some common lies they tell themselves are the following:

"I can quit anytime I want to."

"I only had a couple."

"The police were out to get me."

"I only use when I need it."

"Everybody does it."

"I was drinking, but I wasn't drunk."

"Anybody can get arrested for drunk driving."

"My friends won't like me if I don't use."

"I never have problems when I drink beer."

"I won't drink until after 5 o'clock."

"From now on, I'll only smoke pot."

"I'm going to cut down to five pills a day."

Addicts continue to lie to themselves to the very end. They hold on to their delusional thinking and they believe that their lies are the truth. They deliberately lie to those close to them. They hide their use. They make their problems seem smaller than they actually are. They make excuses for why they are using. They refuse to see the truth.

1. Have you ever lied to yourself about your chemical use? List some of the lies you told yourself.

_____
_____
_____
_____

2. List the ways you tried to convince yourself that you didn't have a problem.

_____
_____
_____
_____

3. List some of the ways you tried to convince others that you didn't have a problem.

_____
_____
_____
_____

## UNMANAGEABILITY

Image that you are the manager of a large corporation. You are responsible for how everything runs. If you are not a good manager, your business will fail. You must carefully plan everything and carry out those plans well. You must be alert. You must know exactly where you are and where you are going. These are the skills you need to manage you life effectively.

Chemically dependent persons are not good managers. They keep losing control. Their plans fall though. They cannot devise and stick to things long enough to see a solution. They are lying to themselves, so they don't know where they are, and they are too confused to decide where they want to go next. Their feelings are being medicated, so they can't use their feelings to give them energy and direction for problem solving. Problems don't get solved; they escalate.

You don't have to be a bad manager all of the time to be a bad manager; it's worse to be a bad manager some of the time. It's totally confusing. For most chemically dependent persons, they have flurries of productive activity where they work too much, they work themselves to the bone, they overwork, and then they let things slide. It's like being on a roller coaster. Sometimes things are in control; sometimes things are out of control. It's up and down, and they can never predict which way things are going to be tomorrow.

People's lives are unmanageable when they have plans fall apart because they were too intoxicated or hung over to complete them.

Make a list of the plans you failed to complete because of your chemical use.

_____
_____
_____
_____

People's lives are unmanageable when they cannot manage their finances consistently.

1.  List any money problems you are having.

_____

_____

_____    _____

2.  Is any of this trouble the result of your chemical dependency? Explain how chemicals have contributed to the problems.

_____

_____

_____

People's lives are unmanageable when they cannot trust their own judgment.

Have you ever been so intoxicated that you didn't know what was happening? Explain.

_____

_____

_____

Did you ever lie to yourself about your chemical use? Explain how your lies contributed your being unable to manage your life.

_____

_____

_____

Have you ever made a decision while intoxicated that you were sorry about later? Explain.

_____

_____

_____

People's lives are unmanageable if they can't work or play normally. Addicts miss work and recreational activities because of their drug use. They make excuses, but the real reason they missed these events was that they were too intoxicated or hung over.

Have you ever missed work because you were too intoxicated or hung over? List the times.

_____

_____

_____

Have you ever missed recreational or family activities because you were too drunk or hung over? List the times.

_____

_____

_____

People's lives are unmanageable if they are in trouble with other people or society. Chemically dependent persons will break the rules to get their own way. They have problems with authority.

Have you ever been in legal trouble when you were drinking or using drugs? Explain the legal problems you have had.

_____

_____

_____

Have you ever had problems with your parents because of your drinking or using drugs? Explain.

_____

_____

_____

Have you ever had problems in school because of your chemical use? Explain.

_____

_____

_____

People's lives are unmanageable if they cannot consistently achieve their goals. Chemically dependent people reach out for what they want, but something keeps getting in the way. It doesn't seem fair. They keep falling short of their goals. Finally, they give up completely. They may have had the goal of going to school, getting a better job, improving the family problems, getting in good physical condition, or going on a diet. No matter what the goals are, something keeps going wrong. The chemically dependent person will always try to blame someone else, but they cannot work hard enough, long enough, to reach their goal. Alcoholics and drug addicts are good starters but they are poor finishers.

List the goals that you had for yourself that you didn't achieve.

_____

_____

_____

People's lives are unmanageable if they cannot use their feelings appropriately. Feelings give us energy and direction for problem solving. Chemically dependent persons medicate their feelings with drugs or alcohol. The substance gives them a different feeling, a chemically induced feeling. The chemically dependent person becomes very confused about how they feel.

What feelings have you tried to alter with the use of chemicals?

_____

_____

_____

What feelings are created by your drug of choice? How do you feel when you are intoxicated or hung over?

_____

_____

_____

People's lives are unmanageable if they violate their own rules, if they violate their own moral values. Chemically dependent persons compromise their values to continue using chemicals. They have the value not to lie, but they lie anyway. They have the value not to steal, but they steal anyway. They have the value to be loyal to their spouse or friends, but when they are intoxicated or hung over, they do not remain loyal. Their values and morals fall away, one by one. They end up doing things that they do not believe in. They know they are doing wrong, but they do it anyway.

Did you ever lie to cover up your chemical use? How did you feel about yourself?

_____

_____

_____

_____

_____

Did you ever steal to get your drugs? Explain what you did and how you felt about yourself later.

_____

_____

_____

Did you ever break the law when intoxicated? What did you do?

_____

_____

_____

Did you ever hit someone you loved while intoxicated or hung over? Explain.

_____

_____

_____

Did you treat yourself poorly by refusing to stop drinking or using drugs? Explain how you were feeling about yourself.

_____

_____

_____

Did you stop going to church? How did this make feel about yourself?

_____

_____

_____

People's lives are unmanageable when they continue to do something that gives them problems. Chemicals create physical problems, headaches, ulcers, nausea, vomiting, cirrhosis, and many other physical problems. Even if the chemically dependent person is aware of a physical problem caused by chemicals, they keep on using anyway.

Chemicals cause psychological problems. They can make people feel depressed, fearful, anxious, or overly angry. Even if an alcoholic or drug addict is aware of these symptoms, they will continue to use.

Chemicals create relationship problems. They cause family problems such as family fights and verbal and physical abuse. They are the cause of interpersonal conflict at work, with family, and with friends. The chemically dependent person withdraws and becomes more isolated and alone. Even if the chemically dependent person believes that the problems are caused by the alcohol or drugs, they continue to use.

Did you have any persistent physical problems that were caused by your chemical use? Describe the problems.

_____

_____

_____

Did you have any persistent psychological problems, such as depression, that were caused by your chemical use? Describe the problems.

_____

_____

_____

Did you have a persistent interpersonal conflict that was exacerbated by your chemical use? Describe this problem.

_____

_____

_____

You must have good reasons to work toward a clean and sober lifestyle. Look over this exercise and list 10 reasons why you want to continue to remain clean and sober.

1. _____

2. _____

3. _____

4. _____

5. _____

6. _____

7. _____

8. _____

9. _____

10. _____

After completing this exercise, take a long look at yourself.

1. Have there been times when you were powerless over drugs or alcohol?

    Yes _____  No _____

2. Have there been times when your life was unmanageable?

    Yes _____  No _____

"We admitted that we were powerless over alcohol—that our lives had become unmanageable" (*Alcoholics Anonymous,* 1976 p. 59).

# Appendix 19

## Step Two
### Robert R. Perkinson, Ph.D.

*Came to believe that a Power greater than ourselves could restore us to sanity.*

*Alcoholics Anonymous* (1976)

Before beginning this exercise, read Step Two in the *Twelve Steps and Twelve Traditions* (AA, 1981).

In Step One, you admitted that you were powerless over drugs or alcohol and that your life was unmanageable. In Step Two, you need to see the insanity of your disease and to seek a Power greater than yourself. If you are powerless, you need power. If your life is unmanageable, you need a manager. Step Two will help you to decide who that manager will be.

Most alcoholics and drug addicts who see the words "restore to sanity" revolt. They think that they may have a drinking or a drug problem, but they don't feel like they have a mental illness. They don't think that they have been insane.

In Alcoholics and Narcotics Anonymous, the word *sanity* means being of sound mind. Someone with a sound mind knows what is real and they know how to adapt to reality. A sound mind feels stable, safe, and secure. People who are insane cannot see reality; they are unable to adapt. A person doesn't have to have all of reality distorted to be in trouble. If you miss some reality, you will ultimately get lost. It takes only one wrong turn to end up in the ditch.

Going through life is like going on a long journey. You have a map given to you by your parents. The map shows the way to be happy. If you make some wrong turns along the way, you will end up unhappy. This is what happens in chemical dependency. Searching for happiness, we make wrong turns. We find out that our map is defective. Even if we followed our map to perfection, we would be still lost. What we need is a new map.

Alcoholics and Narcotics Anonymous gives us this new map. It puts up 12 signposts to show the way. If you follow this map, as millions of people have, you will find the joy and happiness you have been seeking. You have reached and passed the first signpost, Step One. You have decided that your life is powerless and your life is unmanageable. Now you need a new power source. You need to find someone else who can manage your life.

This program is a spiritual program and it directs you toward a spiritual answer to your problems. It is not a religious program. *Spirituality* is the intimate relationship you have with yourself and how you relate to everything else. *Religion* is an organized system of faith and worship. Everyone has spirituality but not everyone has religion.

You need to explore three relationships very carefully in Step Two: the relationship with yourself, others, and a Higher Power. This Higher Power can be any Higher Power of your choice. If you do not have a Higher Power, don't worry. Most of us started that way. Just be willing to consider that there is a power greater than you in the universe.

To explore these relationships, you need to see the truth about yourself. If you see the truth, you can find the way. First you must decide if you were insane. Did you have a sound mind or not? Let's look at this issue carefully.

People are insane when they cannot remember what they did. They have memory problems. They don't have to have memory problems all of the time, just some of the time. People who abuse chemicals may not remember what happened to them when they were intoxicated.

List any blackouts or memory problems you have had while drinking or using drugs.

_____

_____

_____

People who are insane lose control over their behavior. They do things when they are intoxicated that they would never do when they were sober.

List three times when you lost control over your behavior when intoxicated.

_____

_____

_____

List three times when you could not control your drinking or drug use.

_____

_____

_____

People who are insane consider self-destruction.

Did you ever consider hurting yourself when you were intoxicated or hung over?

Yes _____ No _____ Describe what happened.

_____

_____

_____

People who are insane feel emotionally unstable.

Have you ever thought you were going crazy?

Yes _____ No _____ Describe this time.

_____

_____

_____

Have you felt emotionally unstable recently?

Yes _____ No _____ Describe how you have been feeling.

_____

_____

_____

People who are insane are so confused they cannot get their life in order. They may frantically try to fix things, but problems stay out of control.

List some personal, family, work, or school problems that you have not been able to control.

_____

_____

_____

People who are insane cannot see the truth about what's happening to them. People who are chemically dependent hide their drinking and drug use from themselves and from others. They minimize, rationalize, and deny that there are problems.

Do you feel you have been completely honest with yourself?

Yes _____ No _____

List some of the lies you told yourself.

_____

_____

_____

People who are insane cut themselves off from healthy relationships. You may find you don't communicate with your spouse as well. You may not see your friends as often. More and more of your life centers around alcohol or drugs.

List three people you have cut yourself off from.

_____

_____

_____

As your drinking and drug use increased, did you go to church less often?

Yes _____ No _____

List any relationships you have damaged in your drinking and drug use.

_____

_____

_____

People who are insane cannot deal with their feelings. Alcoholics and drug addicts cannot deal with their feelings. They don't like how they feel so they medicate their feelings. They may drink or use drugs to feel less afraid or sad. They may drink to feel more powerful or more friendly.

List the feelings that you drank or use drugs to change.

_____

_____

_____

Now look back over your responses. Get out your Step One Exercise and read through it. Look at the truth about yourself. Look carefully at how you were thinking, feeling, and behaving when you were drinking or using drugs. Make a decision. Do you think you had a sound mind? If you were unsound, at least some of the time, you were insane. If you believe this to be true, say this to yourself: "I am powerless. My life is unmanageable. My mind is unsound. I have been insane."

## A POWER GREATER THAN OURSELVES

Consider a power greater than yourself. What exists in the world that has greater power than you do? A river, the wind, the universe, the sun?

List five things that have greater power than you do.

1. _____
2. _____
3. _____
4. _____
5. _____

The first Higher Power you need to consider is the power of the group. The group is more powerful than you are. Ten hands are more powerful than two. Two heads are better than one. Alcoholics and Narcotics Anonymous operates in groups. The group works like a family. The group process is founded in love and trust. The members shares their experience, strength, and hope in an attempt to help themselves and others. There is an atmosphere of anonymity. What you hear in group is confidential.

The group acts as a mirror reflecting you to yourself. They will help you to discover the truth about who and what you are. You have been deceiving yourself for a long time. The group will help you to uncover the lies. You will come to understand the old AA saying, "What we cannot do alone, we can do together." In group, you will have greater power over the disease because the group will see the whole truth better than you can.

You weren't lying to hurt yourself, you were lying to protect yourself. In the process of building your lies, you cut yourself off from reality. This is how chemical dependency works. You cannot recover from addiction by yourself, you need power coming from somewhere else. Begin by trusting your group. Keep an open mind.

You need to share in your group. The more you share the closer you will get, and the more trust you will develop. If you take risks, you will reap the reward. You don't have to tell the group everything, but you need to share as much as you can. The group can help you straighten out your thinking and restore you to sanity.

Many chemically dependent persons are afraid of a Higher Power. They feel a Higher Power will punish them or treat them like their father did. They may fear losing control. List some of the fears you have about a Higher Power.

_____
_____
_____
_____
_____

Some chemically dependent persons have difficulty trusting anyone. They have been so hurt by others that they don't want to take the chance of being hurt again. What has happened in your life that makes it difficult for you to trust?

_____
_____
_____
_____
_____

What are some of the things you will need to see from a Higher Power that will show you that the Higher Power can be trusted?

_____

_____

_____

_____

_____

Who was the most trustworthy person you ever knew?

Name _____

How did this person treat you?

_____

_____

_____

_____

What do you hope to gain by accepting a Higher Power?

_____

_____

_____

Alcoholics Anonymous wants you to come to believe in a Power greater than yourself. You can accept any Higher Power that you feel can restore you to sanity. Your group, nature, your counselor, your sponsor, all can be used to give you this restoration. You must pick this Higher Power carefully. We suggest that you use Alcoholics or Narcotics Anonymous as your Higher Power for now. Here is a group of millions of people who are recovering. They have found the way. Ultimately this program will direct you toward God, a God of your own understanding. "That we were alcoholic and could not manage our own lives. That probably no human power could have removed our alcoholism. That God could and would if He were sought" (*Alcoholics Anonymous,* 1976, p. 60).

Millions of chemically dependent persons have recovered because they were willing to reach out for God. Alcoholics Anonymous makes it clear that nothing else will remove the obsession to use chemicals. Some of us have so glorified our own lives that we have shut God out. Now is your opportunity. You are at a major turning point. You can begin to open your heart and let God in, or you can keep God out. God tells us that all who seek will find.

Remember, this is the beginning of a new life. To be new you have to do things differently. All the program is asking you to do is be open to the possibility that there is a power greater than yourself. Alcoholics Anonymous does not demand that you believe in anything. The twelve steps are but suggestions. You do not have to swallow all of this now, but you need to be open. Most recovering persons take the Second Step a piece at a time.

First you need to learn how to trust yourself. You must learn how to consistently treat yourself well. What do you need to see from yourself that will show you that you are trustworthy?

_____

_____

_____

_____

_____

Then you need to begin to trust your group. See if they act consistently in your interest. They won't always tell you what you want to hear—no real friend would do that. They will give you the opportunity and the encouragement to grow. What will you need to see from your group that will show you that they are trustworthy?

_____

_____

_____

_____

Every person has a unique spiritual journey. No one can start this journey with a closed mind. What is it going to take from God to show you that God exists?

_____

_____

_____

_____

Step Two does not mean that we believe in God as God is presented in any religion. Remember that religion is an organized system of worship that is made by human beings. Worship is just a means of assigning worth to something. Many people have been so turned off by religion that the idea of God is unacceptable. Describe the religious environment of your childhood. What was it like? What did you learn about God?

_____

_____

_____

_____

How did these early experiences influence the beliefs you have today?

_____

_____

_____

_____

What experiences have caused you to doubt God?

_____

_____

_____

_____

Your willingness is essential to your recovery. Give some examples of your willingness to trust in a Higher Power of your choice. What are you willing to do?

_____

_____

_____

_____

Describe your current religious beliefs.

_____
_____
_____
_____

Explain the God of your understanding.

_____
_____
_____
_____

List five reasons why a Higher Power will be good for you.

1. _____
2. _____
3. _____
4. _____
5. _____

If you asked the people in your AA/NA group to describe God, you would get a variety of answers. Each person has his or her own understanding of God. It is this unique understanding that allows God to work individually for each of us. God comes to each of us differently.

Through the ages there have been two philosophical arguments against there being a God.

1. If there is a God, where is He? Why doesn't God make Himself more knowable?
2. If there is a God, and God is all good, how come bad things happen?

To understand these questions, you must understand what God is like, and what God is doing. God created you to love. That is the only reason that you exist. God did not need you; God has no needs. God wants a loving relationship with you. God desires the most intimate friendship possible, that is why God lives inside of your thinking.

God knows that love necessitates freedom. God created you and gave you the freedom to make your own decisions. You can do things that God doesn't want you to do. If God placed his face in the sky or was so obvious that everyone worshipped Him, no one would have a free choice. This is why God exists in a gentle whisper inside of your thoughts. You have to stop and listen to hear God. It is incredibly easy to keep God out, and it is incredibly easy to let God in. When you were abusing yourself, God was there encouraging you to love yourself. When you were lying to others and treating others poorly, God was there, encouraging you to love others. God has loved you from the beginning.

It is difficult to deny God, because God exists inside of you. To deny God is to deny an essential part of yourself. We all know instinctively what is right and what is wrong. We do not have to be taught these things. The rules are the same across every culture and group. No matter where you were raised, or how you were raised, the laws are the same. Everyone knows these moral laws. We know not to lie or steal. We know that we should help others. We know that we should love ourselves.

Bad things happen because God allows free will. People hurt each other when they make their own choices independent of God's will. They can break God's law, and when this happens, there is great suffering. You have probably done some things you are ashamed of. You never would have felt this shame if you had followed God's plan.

"Where was God when I needed God?!" many people cry. "Where was God when all those bad things were happening to me?!" Well, the answer to that question is, God was right there, loving you, encouraging you to see the truth. God never promises that life is not going to hurt. God promises that He is there, loving you all the time.

Don't be discouraged if you doubt God. Your doubt about God is not bad, it is good. It means you think and reason. You shouldn't blindly accept things without proof, that would be foolish. What you must know is this: Only God can overcome your doubt. There is nothing you can do to make doubt go away, you can only trust that if you seek God, God will find you. Once God finds you, your doubt will be removed. Only by swimming in the sea of doubt can you learn how to swim with strong strokes. This is how your faith gets strong. No one is asking you to accept God blindly. Follow your AA/NA group. They know the way. Be willing to seek God. Open your heart and your mind in every way you know how. Seek God as you understand Him. Ask your clergyperson or your counselor for some reading. Go at your own rate. Follow God in your own way. Before long you will find a peace that will surpass your understanding. This is the peace that we serenity.

"Came to believe that a Power greater than ourselves could restore us to sanity" (*Alcoholics Anonymous,* 1976, p. 59).

# *Appendix 20*

## *Step Three*
### Robert R. Perkinson, Ph.D.

*Made a decision to turn our will and our lives over to the care of God as we understood Him.*

*Alcoholics Anonymous* (1976)

Before beginning this exercise, read Step Three in *The Twelve Steps and Twelve Traditions* (AA, 1981).

You have come a long way in the program and you can feel proud of yourself. You have decided that you are powerless over mood-altering chemicals and your life is unmanageable. You have decided that a Higher Power of some sort can restore you to sanity. In Step Three you will reach toward God, the God of your own understanding. You will consider using God as your Higher Power. This is the miracle that you have been searching for. It is the major focus of the AA/NA program. This is a spiritual program that directs you toward the ultimate in truth. It is important that you be open to the possibility that there is a God. It is vital that you give this concept room to blossom and grow. The Big Book says, "That probably no human power could have relieved our alcoholism. That God could and would if He were sought" (*Alcoholics Anonymous*, 1976, p. 60).

Step Three should not confuse you. It calls for a decision to correct your character defects under spiritual supervision. You must make an honest effort to change your life.

The program of Alcoholics Anonymous is a spiritual program. About the Big Book it states, "It's main object is to enable you to find a Power greater than yourself that will solve your problem" (*Alcoholics Anonymous*, 1976, p. 45). Alcoholics and Narcotics Anonymous clearly states that the God of your understanding is the answer. If you are willing to seek God, you will find God; that is God's promise.

## UNDERSTANDING THE MORAL LAW

All spirituality has, at its core, what is already inside of you. You don't have to look very far for God. Your Higher Power lives inside of you. Inside of all of us there is inherent goodness. In all cultures, and in all lands, this goodness is expressed in what we call the moral law. The law demands love in action and in truth. It is simply stated as follows: Love God all you can, love others all you can, love yourself all you can. This law is very powerful. If some stranger were drowning in a pool next to you, this internal law would motivate you to help. Instinctively, you would feel driven to help, even if it put your own life at risk. The moral law is so important that it transcends our instinct for survival. You would try to save that drowning person even at your own risk. This moral law is exactly the same everywhere, in every culture. It exists inside of everyone. It is written on your heart. Even among thieves, honesty is valued.

When we survey religious thought, we come up with many different ideas about God, and how to worship God, but if we look at the saints of the various religions, they are living practically indistinguishable lives. They are all doing the same things with their life. They don't lie, cheat, or steal, they believe in giving to others before they give to themselves, and they try not to be envious of others. To believe in your Higher Power, you must believe that this good exists inside of you. You must also believe that there is more of this goodness at work outside of you. If you don't believe in a living, breathing God at this point, don't worry—every one of us has started where you are.

All people have a basic problem: We break the moral law, even if we believe in it. This fact means that something is wrong with us. We are incapable of following the moral law like we want to. Even though we would think it unfair for someone to lie to us, occasionally we lie to someone else. If we see someone dressed in clothes that they look terrible in, we might tell them they look good. This is a lie, and we wouldn't want other people lying to us like that. In this, and in other situations, we don't obey the very moral law that we know is good. We might even stand there and watch that person drown.

You must ask yourself several questions: Where did we get this moral law? How did these laws of behavior get started? Did they just evolve? The program of AA/NA believes that these good laws comes from something good and that there is more of this good at work in the universe. People in the program believe that people can communicate with this good, and they call this good, God.

We do not know everything about the Higher Power. Much of God remains a mystery. If we look at science, we find the same thing—most of science is a mystery. We know very little about the primary elements of science, such as gravity, but we can make judgments about these elements using our experience. No one has ever seen an electron, but we are sure it exists because we have some experience of it. It is the same thing with the Higher Power, we can know that there is a Power greater than ourselves if we have some experience of this Power. Both science and spirituality necessitate faith, a faith based on experience.

There emerges in people, as naturally as the ability to love or hate, the ability to experience God. The experience cannot be taught—it is already there and must be awakened. It is primal, already planted, awaiting growth. God is experienced as a force that is alive. This force is above, and more capable than human beings. God is so good, pure, and perfect, that God obeys the moral law all the time. The experience of the Higher Power brings with it a feeling of great power and energy. This can be both attractive and frightening, but mainly, you will find that God is loving. God has contacted humankind through the ages and has said, "I am. I exist."

Instinctively people know that if they can get more of this goodness, they will have a better life. Spirituality must be practical. It must make your life better or you will discard it. If you open yourself up to the spiritual part of the program, you will immediately feel better.

God knows that if you follow the law of love, you will be happy. God makes love known to all people. It is born in everyone. The consequence for breaking the law is separation from God. This separation is experienced as deep emotional pain. We feel isolated, empty, frightened, and lonely.

God tells us that God is hungry for your love. God desires a deep personal relationship with you. All people have a similar instinctive hunger for God. By reading this exercise you can begin to develop your relationship with God. You will find true joy here if you try. Without some sort of a Higher Power, your recovery will be more difficult. A Higher Power can relieve your chemical dependency problem as nothing else can. Many people achieve stable recovery without calling their Higher Power "God"; that is certainly possible. There are many wonderful atheists and agnostics in our program, but the AA/NA way is to reach for some sort of a God of your own understanding.

You can change things in your life, you really can. You do not have to drown in despair any longer. No matter who you are, God loves you. God is willing to help you. Perhaps God has been waiting for you for a long time. Think of how wonderful it is. There is a God. God created you. God loves you. God wants you to be happy. Open yourself up to this experience.

## THE KEY TO STEP THREE

The key to working Step Three is willingness, the willingness to turn your life over to the care of God as you understand God. This is difficult for many of us because we think we are in control. We are completely fooled by this delusion. We feel like we know the right thing to do. We feel that everything would be fine if others would just do things our way. This leads us to deep feelings of resentment and self-pity. People wouldn't cooperate with our plan. No matter how hard we tried to control everything, things kept getting out of control. Sometimes, the harder we worked, the worse things got.

You are not in control, and you have never been in control. Your Higher Power is in control. God is the only one that knows about everything. God created you and the universe. Chemically dependent persons, in many ways, have been trying to be God. We have wanted the universe to revolve around us. "Above everything, we alcoholics must be rid of this selfishness" (*Alcoholics Anonymous,* 1976, p. 62).

## HOW TO TURN IT OVER

To arrest chemical dependency, you have to stop playing God and let your Higher Power take control. If you sincerely want this and you try, it is easy. Go to a quiet place and talk to your Higher Power about your chemical dependency. Say something like this, "God, I am lost. I can't do this anymore. I turn this situation over to you." Watch how you feel when you say this prayer. The next time you have a problem, stop and turn the problem over to your Higher Power. Say something like this: "God, I can't deal with this problem, you deal with it." See what happens.

As you ask for God's will to be done, you will find the right direction. God knows the way for you. If you follow your Higher Power, you will never be lost again. God will encourage you to see the truth and then God will leave the choice up to you. You can always decide. God wants you to be free. God wants you to make all of your own decisions, but God wants to have input into your decisions. Your Higher Power wants to show you the way. If you try to find the way yourself you will be constantly lost. God promises us that if we will follow His plan, God will see to it that we receive all of the desires of our heart. God knows exactly what you need.

Step Three offers no compromise. It calls for a decision. Exactly how we surrender and turn things over is not the point. The important thing is that you be willing to try. Can you see that it is necessary to give up your self-centeredness? Do you feel it is time to turn things over to a Power greater than yourself?

List the things you have to gain by turning your will and your life over to a Higher Power.

1. _____
2. _____
3. _____
4. _____
5. _____

Why do you need to turn things over?

1. _____
2. _____
3. _____
4. _____
5. _____

We should not confuse organized religion with spirituality. In Step Two you learned that spirituality deals with your relationship with yourself, others, and God. Religion is an organized system of faith and worship. It is person-made, not God-made. It is our way of interpreting God's plan. Religion can be very confusing, and it can even drive people away from God. Are old religious ideas keeping you from God? If so, how?

_____
_____
_____
_____

A great barrier to your finding God may be impatience. You may want to find God right now. You must understand that your spiritual growth is set by God and not by you. You will grow spiritually when God feels that you are ready. Remember, we are turning this whole thing over. Each person has his or her own unique spiritual journey. Each person must have their own individual path. Spiritual growth, not perfection, is your goal. All you can do is seek the God of your understanding. When God knows that you are ready, God will find you. Total surrender is necessary. If you are holding back, you need to let go absolutely. Faith, willingness, and prayer will overcome all the obstacles. Don't worry about your doubt, just keep seeking, in every way you know how.

List 10 ways you can seek God. Ask your friends or counselor to help you.

1. _____
2. _____
3. _____
4. _____
5. _____
6. _____
7. _____
8. _____
9. _____
10. _____

What does the saying, "Let go and let God," mean to you?

_____
_____
_____
_____

What are some ways you can put Step Three to work in your life?

_____
_____
_____
_____

What things in your life do you still want to control?

_____
_____
_____
_____

How can these things be handled better by turning them over to your Higher Power?

_____
_____
_____
_____

List five ways you allowed chemicals to be the God in your life.

1. _____
2. _____
3. _____
4. _____
5. _____

How did your chemical use separate you from God?

_____
_____
_____
_____
_____

What changes have you noticed in yourself since you entered the program?

_____
_____
_____
_____
_____

Of these changes, which of them occurred because you listened to someone else other than yourself?

_____
_____
_____
_____
_____

Make a list of the things that are holding you back from turning things over.

_____
_____
_____
_____
_____

How do you see God caring for you?

_____
_____
_____
_____
_____

How do you understand God now?

_____
_____
_____
_____
_____

## HOW TO PRAY

Pray by reading the Step Three prayer once each day for one week. Say the words carefully out loud, and listen to yourself as you speak. Feel God's presence with you, and when you are ready, begin to talk to God. Make prayer a dialogue, not a monologue. Talk to God and then listen for God's answer to come to you inside of your thinking.

> God I offer myself to Thee—to build with me and to do with me as Thou wilt. Relieve me of the bondage of self, that I may better do Thy will. Take away my difficulties, that victory over them may bear witness to those I would help of Thy Power, Thy Love, and Thy Way of Life. May I do Thy will always! (*Alcoholics Anonymous*, 1976, p. 63)

Listen for God in others. God may speak to you through them. Look for God's actions in the group, in the weather, in nature. Read the Bible and seek God through your reading. Ask your counselor or your clergyperson for some suggestions.

## HOW TO MEDITATE

Take time to meditate each day. Sit in a quiet place for about 10 to 20 minutes and pay attention to your breathing. Ask God to come into your thinking, then ask God a question: "God, what is the next step in my relationship with you?". Don't be nervous if there is only silence for a while. Listen for God's message for you. Write down any words or images that come into your mind. Keep a log of each meditation for one week.

Day 1. _____
_____
_____

Day 2. _____
_____
_____

Day 3. _____
_____
_____

Day 4. _____
_____
_____

Day 5. _____
_____
_____

Day 6. _____
_____
_____

Day 7. _____
_____
_____

Write down your spiritual plan. What are you going to do on a daily basis to help your spiritual program grow?

_____

_____

_____

_____

_____

Trust that if you are seeking God, God will find you. No matter who you are, no matter where you are, God loves you more than you can imagine. You are God's perfect child, created in God's image. God has great plans for you.

"Made a decision to turn our will and our lives over to the care of God *as we understood Him*" (*Alcoholics Anonymous,* 1976, p. 59).

# Appendix 21

## Step Four
### Robert R. Perkinson, Ph.D.

*Made a searching and fearless moral inventory of ourselves.*

*Alcoholics Anonymous* (1976)

Before beginning this exercise, read Step Four in *The Twelve Steps and Twelve Traditions* (AA, 1981).

You are doing well in the program. You have admitted your powerlessness over chemicals, and you have found a Higher Power that can restore you to sanity. Now you must take an inventory of yourself. You must know exactly what resources you have available, and you must examine the nature of your wrongs. You need to be detailed about the good things about you and the bad things about you. Only by taking this inventory will you know exactly where you are. Then you can decide where you are going.

Much of this step was developed by Lynn Carroll in his years at Hazelden and Keystone. In taking this inventory you must be detailed and specific. It's the only way to see the complete impact of your disease. A part of the truth might be, "I told lies to my children." The complete truth might be, "I told my children that I had cancer. They were terrified and cried for a long time." These two statements would be very different. Only the second statement tells the exact nature of the wrong, and the patient felt the full impact of the disclosure. You can see how important it is to put the whole truth before you at one time. The truth that will set you free.

The Fourth Step is a long autobiography of yourself. You should write it carefully. Read this exercise before you start and underline things that pertain to you. You will want to come back and cover each of these issues in detail as you write it down. If the problem doesn't relate to you, leave it blank. Examine exactly what you did wrong. Look for your mistakes even though the situation wasn't totally your fault. Try to disregard what the other person did and concentrate on yourself. In time you will realize that the person who hurt you was spiritually sick. You need to ask your Higher Power to help you forgive that person, to show that person the same understanding that you would want for yourself. You can pray that person finds out the truth about themselves.

Review your natural desires carefully and think about how you acted on them. You will see that some of them became the Higher Power in your life. Sex, food, money, relaxation, relationships, sleep, power, influence, all can become the major focus of our lives. The pursuit of these desires can take total control and can become the center of our existence.

Review your sexuality as you move through the inventory. Did you ever use someone else selfishly? Did you ever lie to get what you wanted? Did you coerce or force someone into doing something she or he didn't want to do? Who did you hurt and exactly what did you do?

In working through the inventory, you will experience some pain. You will feel angry, sad, afraid, ashamed, embarrassed, guilty, and lonely. The Fourth Step is a grieving process. As you see clearly your wrongs, you may feel that no one will ever love you again, but remember, God created you in perfection. You are God's masterpiece, God's work of art. There is nothing wrong with you, you just made some mistakes.

Now let's take a basic look at right and wrong. We will cover the following areas:

## THE TEN COMMANDMENTS

These are the rules that God made to keep you from hurting. If you break these rules you will experience pain. These are taken from the New International Version of the Bible. Mark the commandments that you have broken.

1. "You shall have no other gods before me."

   Did God come first in your life? Did you seek and follow God's will all times?

2. "You shall not make for yourself an idol in the form of anything in heaven above or on the earth beneath or in the waters below."

   What were your idols, money, fame, position, alcohol, drugs, sex, power, relationships?

3. "You shall not misuse the name of the Lord your God, for the Lord will not hold anyone guiltless who misuses his name."

   Have you been profane? Have you honored God with your language?

4. "Remember the Sabbath day by keeping it holy."

   Have you always set aside a day to improve your relationship with God?

5. "Honor your father and your mother, so that you may live long in the land the Lord your God is giving you."

   Have you loved, honored, and respected your parents?

6. "You shall not murder."

   Do you have unresolved hate, anger, and resentments?

7. "You shall not commit adultery."

   Were you ever guilty of adulterous acts or thoughts?

8. "You shall not steal."

   Have you ever cheated, misrepresented, made pressure deals, had bad debts?

9. "You shall not give false testimony against your neighbor."

   Have you ever been guilty of slander or spreading gossip?

10. "You shall not covet your neighbor's house."

    Have you ever wanted something that belongs to someone else, felt envious, or overly competitive?

## SEVEN WAYS TO GET LOST

*1. Pride.* Egotistical vanity, too great an admiration of yourself. Pride makes you your own law, moral judge, and your own higher power. Pride produces criticism, backbiting, slander, barbed words, and character assassinations that elevate your own ego. Pride makes you condemn as fools those who criticize you. Pride gives you excuses. It produces the following:

a.  Boasting or self glorification
b.  Love of publicity
c.  Hypocrisy—pretending to be better than you are
d.  Hardheadedness—refusal to give up your will
e.  Discord—resenting any who crosses you
f.  Quarrelsomeness—quarreling whenever another challenges your wishes
g.  Disobedience—refusal to submit your will to the will of superiors or to God

*2. Greed.* Perversion of man's right to own things. Do you desire wealth such as money or other things as an end in itself rather than as a means to an end, such as taking care of the soul and body? In acquiring wealth in any form, do you disregard the rights of others? Are you dishonest, and if so, to what degree and in what fashion? Do you give an honest day's work for an honest day's pay? How do you use what you have? Are you stingy with your family? Do you love money and possessions for these things in themselves? How excessive is your love of luxury? How do you preserve your wealth or increase it? Do you stoop to such devices as fraud or perjury or dishonesty or sharp practices in dealing with others? Do you try to fool yourself in these regards? Do you call stinginess "thrift"? Do you call questionable business practices "big business" or "drive"? Do you call unreasonable hoarding "security"? If you presently have no money and little other wealth, how and by what practice will you go about getting it later? Will you do almost anything to attain these things and kid yourself by giving your methods innocent names?

*3. Lust.* Inordinate love and desires of the pleasures of the flesh. Are you guilty of lust in any of its forms? Do you tell yourself that improper or undue indulgence in sexual activities is required? Do you treat people as objects of your desire rather than as God's perfect creation? Do you use pornography or think unhealthy sexual thoughts? Do you treat other people sexually the way you want to be treated?

*4. Envy.* Sadness at another person's good fortune. How envious are you? Do you dislike seeing others happy or successful as though they had taken from you? Do you resent those smarter than you are? Do you ever criticize the good done by others because you secretly wish you had done it yourself for the honor or the prestige to be gained? Are you ever envious enough to try to lower another person's reputation by starting or engaging in gossip about them? Being envious includes calling religious people "hypocrites" because they go to church and try to be religiously good even though subject to human failings. Do you depreciate the well-bred person by saying or feeling that he puts on airs? Do you ever accuse the educated or wise or learned of being highbrow because you envy their advantages? Do you genuinely love other people or do you find them distasteful, because you envy them?

*5. Anger.* A violent desire to punish others. Do you ever fly into rages of temper, become revengeful, entertain urges to "get even" or an "I won't let him get away with it" attitude? Do you ever resort to violence, ever clench your fists, or stomp about in a temper flare-up? Are you touchy, unduly sensitive to the smallest slight? Do you ever murmur or grumble even in small matters? Do you ignore the fact that anger prevents development of personality and halts spiritual progress? Do you realize at all times that anger disrupts mental poise and often ruins good judgment? Do you permit anger to rule you when you know it blinds you to the rights of others? How can you excuse even small tantrums of temper when anger destroys the spirit of recollection that you need for compliance with the inspirations of God? Do you permit yourself to become angry when others are weak and become angry with you? Can you hope to entertain the serene spirit of God within your soul when you are often beset by angry flare ups of even minor importance?

*6. Gluttony.* Abuse of pleasures attached to eating and drinking of foods required for self-preservation. Do you weaken your moral and intellectual life by excessive use of food and drink? Do you generally eat to excess and thus enslave your soul and character to the pleasures of the body beyond the reasonable needs of the body? Do you kid yourself that you can be a "hog" without affecting your moral life? Did you ever, when drinking or using drugs, become nauseated and vomit only to immediately return and drink or use some more? Did you use so much that your intellect and personality deteriorated; so much that memory, judgment, and concentration were affected; so much that personal pride and social judgment vanished; so much that you developed a spirit of despair?

*7. Laziness.* Illness of the will that causes a neglect of duty. Are you lazy, given to idleness, procrastination, nonchalance, and indifference to material things? Are you lukewarm in prayer? Do you hold self-discipline in contempt? Would you rather read a novel than study something requiring brain work, the Big Book for example? Are you faint-hearted in performance of those things that are morally or spiritually difficult? Are you ever listless, with aversion to effort in any form? Are you easily distracted from things spiritual, quickly turning to things temporal? Are ever indolent to the extent that you perform work carelessly?

## PERSONALITY DEFECTS

1. *Selfishness.* Taking care of one's own needs without regard for others.
    a. Example: The family would like an outing. Dad would like drinking, golf, fishing, or has a hangover. Who wins?
    b. Example: Your child needs a new pair of shoes. You put it off till pay day, but get a fifth that same night.
    c. Afraid to dance because you might appear awkward. Fears any new venture because it might injure that false front you put on.

2. *Alibis.* The highly developed art of justifying our chemical use and behavior through mental gymnastics. Excuses for use such as these:
    a. "A few will straighten me out."
    b. "Starting tomorrow, I'm going to change."
    c. "If I didn't have a wife and family."
    d. "If I could start all over again."
    e. "A drink will help me think."
    f. "Nobody cares anyway."
    g. "I had a hard day."

3. *Dishonest thinking.* Another way of lying. We may even take truths or facts and then though some phony hopscotch, come up with exactly the conclusions we had planned to arrive at. Boy, we are great at that business. No wonder we used chemicals.
    Examples:
    a. My secret love is going to raise the roof if I drop her. It is not fair to burden my wife with that sort of knowledge. Therefore, I will hang on to my girlfriend. This mess isn't her fault. (Good, solid con)
    b. If I tell my family about the five hundred dollar bonus, it will all go for bills, clothes, dentist, and so on. I've got to have some drinking money. Why start a family argument? I'll leave well enough alone.
    c. My spouse dresses well, eats well, the kids are getting a good education. What more do they want from me?

4. *Shame.* The feeling that something irreparable is wrong with you.
    a. No matter how many people tell you it's okay, you continue to berate yourself.
    b. You keep going over and over your mistakes, wallowing in what a terrible person you are.

5. *Resentment.* Displeasure aroused by a real or imagined wrong or injury, accompanied by irritation, exasperation, or hate. Anger and resentment lead to bickering, friction, hatred, unjust revenge. It brings out the worst of our immaturity and produces misery to ourselves and all concerned.
    a. You are fired from work; therefore you hate the boss.
    b. Your sister warns you about excessive drinking. You get fighting mad at her.

   c. A coworker is doing a good job and gets accolades. You have a drug record and fear he may have been promoted over you. You hate his guts.

   d. You may have a resentment toward a person, a group of people, may resent institutions, religions, etc.

6. *Intolerance.* Refusal to put up with beliefs, practices, customs, or habits that differ from our own.

   a. Do you hate other people because they are another race or come from a different country or have a different religion? What would you do if you were that person, kill yourself?

   b. Did you have any choice in being born a particular color or nationality?

   c. Isn't our religion usually "inherited?"

7. *Impatience.* Unwillingness to calmly bear delay, opposition, pain, or annoyance.

   a. A chemically dependent person is someone who jumps on a horse and gallops off madly in all directions at the same time.

   b. Do you blow your stack when someone keeps you waiting over the "allotted time" you gave them?

   c. Did anyone ever have to wait for you?

8. *Phoniness.* A manifestation of our great false pride; a form of lying; rank and brash dishonesty. It's the old false front.

   a. I give my spouse a present as evidence of my love. Just by pure coincidence, it helps to smooth over my last binge.

   b. I buy new clothes because my business position demands it. Meanwhile, the family also could use food and clothes.

   c. The joker who enthralls an AA audience with profound wisdom but hasn't got the time of day for the spouse or children.

9. *Procrastination.* Putting off . . . postponing things that need to be done. The familiar, "I'll do it tomorrow."

   a. Did little jobs, put off, become big and almost impossible later? Did problems piling up contribute to drinking or drug use?

   b. Do you pamper yourself by doing things "my way" or do you attempt to put order and discipline into your life?

   c. Can you handle little jobs you are asked to take care of or do you feel picked on? Or are you just too lazy or proud?

   d. Little things, done for God, make them great. Are you doing the little things for God?

10. *Self-pity.* An insidious personality defect and a danger signal to look for. Stop it in a hurry—it's the build-up to trouble.

   a. These people at the party are having fun with their drinking. Why can't I be like that? This is the "Woe is me" syndrome.

   b. If I had that guy's money, I wouldn't have any problems. P.S. When you feel this way, visit an alcoholic ward, cancer ward, or children's hospital, then count your blessings.

11. *Feelings too easily hurt.*

   a. I walk down the street and say Hello to someone. They don't answer. I'm hurt and mad.

   b. I am expecting my turn at the AA meeting, but the time runs out. I feel like that's a dirty trick.

12. *Fear.* An inner foreboding, real or imagined, of doom ahead. We suspect our use of chemicals, our behavior and negligence, is catching up with us. We fear the worst.

When we learn to accept our powerlessness, ask our Higher Power for help, and face ourselves with honesty, the nightmare will be gone.

13. *Depression.* Feeling sad or down most of the day.

   a. You keep going over all of the things that are going wrong.

   b. You tend to think the worst.

14. *Feelings of inadequacy.*
    a. Feeling like you can't do it.
    b. You hold on to a negative self-image even when you succeed.
15. *Perfectionism.* You have to do everything perfectly all the time.
    a. Even when you have done a good job, you find something wrong with it.
    b. Someone compliments you on something. You feel terrible because it could have been better.

## PHYSICAL LIABILITIES

1. Diseases, disabilities, other physical limitations about how you look or how your body functions
2. Sexual problems or hang-ups
3. Negative feelings about your appearance
4. Negative feelings about your age
5. Negative feelings about your sex

## TIME-OUT

If you have gone through the exercise to this point without coming up for air, it figures. We did our drinking and drugging the same way. Whoa! Easy does it! Take this in reasonable stages. Assimilate each portion of the exercise thoughtfully. The reading of this is important, but the application of it is even more important. Take some time to think and rest, and let this all settle in. Develop some sort of a workable daily plan. Include plenty of rest.

When the chemically dependent person stops using, part of their life is taken away from them. This is a terrible loss to sustain unless it is replaced by something else. We can't just boot the chemicals out the window—it meant too much to us. It was how we faced life, the key to escape, the tool for solving life's problems. In approaching a new way of life, a new set of tools is substituted. These are the Twelve Steps and the AA/NA way of life.

The same principle applies when we eliminate our character defects. We replace them by substituting assets that are better adapted to a healthy lifestyle. As with substance use, you don't fight a defect—you replace it with something that works better. Use what follows for further character analysis and as a guide for character building. These are the new tools. The objective is not perfection, but progress. You will be happy with the type of living that produces self-respect, respect and love for others, and the security from the nightmare of chemical dependency.

## THE WAY TO RECOVERY

*Faith.* The act of leaving that part of our lives we cannot control (i.e., the future) to the care of a Power greater than ourselves, with the assurance that it will work out for our well-being. This will be shaky at first, but in time, there comes a deep conviction.

1. Faith is acquired through application: acceptance, daily prayer, meditation.
2. We depend on faith, we have faith that the lights will come on, the car will start, that our coworkers will handle their end of things. If we had no faith, we would come apart at the seams.
3. Spiritual faith is the acceptance of our gifts, limitations, problems, and trials with equal gratitude, knowing God has a plan for us. With "Thy will be done" as our daily guide, we will lose our fear and find ourselves.

*Hope.* Faith suggests reliance. We come to believe that a Power greater than ourselves will restore us to sanity. We hope to stay clean and sober, regain our self-respect, and love our family. Hope resolves itself into a driving force; it gives purpose to our daily living.

1. Faith gives us direction; hope is the steam to take action.
2. Hope reflects a positive attitude.  Things are going to work out for us if we work the program.

*Love.*  The active involvement in someone's individual growth.

1. Love must occur in action and in truth.
2. "Love is patient, love is kind.  It does not envy, it does not boast, it is not proud.  It is not rude, it is not self-seeking, it is not easily angered, it keeps no record of wrongs. Love does not delight in evil but rejoices with the truth. It always protects, always trusts, always hopes, always perseveres" (1 Corinthians 13:4-7).
3. In its deeper sense, love is the art of living realistically and fully, guided by spiritual awareness of our responsibilities and our debt of gratitude to God and to others.

Analysis:  Have you used the qualities of faith, hope, and love in your past? How will they apply to your new way of life?

## WE STAY ON TRACK THROUGH ACTION

1. Courtesy:  Some of us are actually afraid to be gentle persons. We'd rather be boors, self-pampering types.
2. Cheerfulness:  Circumstances don't determine our frame of mind, we do. Today I will be cheerful. I will look for the beauty in life.
3. Order:  Live today only. Organize one day at a time.
4. Loyalty:  Be faithful to the one you believe in.
5. Use of time:  I will use my time wisely.
6. Punctuality:  Self-discipline, order, consideration for others.
7. Sincerity:  The mark of self-respect and genuineness. Sincerity carries conviction, generates enthusiasm; it is contagious.
8. Caution in speech:  Watch your tongue.  We can be vicious and thoughtless. Too often the damage is irreparable.
9. Kindness:  One of life's great satisfactions. We haven't real happiness until we have given of ourselves. Practice this daily.
10. Patience:  The antidote to resentments, self-pity, and impulsiveness.
11. Tolerance:  Requires common courtesy, courage, and a live-and-let-live attitude.
12. Integrity:  The ultimate qualifications of a person—to be honest, loyal, sincere.
13. Balance:  Don't take yourself too seriously. We get a better perspective when we can laugh at ourselves.
14. Gratitude:  The person without gratitude is filled with false pride. Gratitude is the honest recognition of help received.  Use it often.

Analysis:  In considering the little virtues, where did I fail and how did that contribute to my accumulated problem? What virtues should I pay attention to in this rebuilding program?

## PHYSICAL ASSETS

1. Physical health:  How healthy am I despite any ailments?
2. Talents:  What am I good at?
3. Age:  At my age, what can I offer to others?
4. Sexuality:  How can I use my sexuality to express my love?
5. Knowledge:  How can I use my knowledge and experience to help myself and others?

## MENTAL ASSETS

1. Despite your problems, how healthy are you emotionally?
2. Do you care for others?
3. Are you kind?
4. Can you be patient?
5. Are you basically a good person?
6. Do you want to help others?
7. Do you try to tell the truth?
8. Do you try to be forgiving?
9. Can you be enthusiastic?
10. Are you sensitive to the needs of others?
11. Can you be serene?
12. Sincerity:  Are you going to try to be sincere?
13. Self-discipline:  Are you going to try to bring order and self-control into your life?
14. Are you going to accept the responsibility for your own behavior and stop blaming others for everything?
15. How are you going to use your intelligence?
16. Are you going to seek the will of God?
17. Education:  How might you improve your mind, further your education?
18. Are you going to be grateful for what you have?
19. Integrity:  How can you improve your honesty and reliability?
20. Joy:  In what areas of your life do you find happiness?
21. Are you humble and working on your false pride?
22. Are you seeking the Higher Power of your own understanding?
23. Acceptance:  In what ways can you better accept your own limitations and the limitations of others?
24. Courage:  Are you willing to trust and follow the God of your understanding?

## THE AUTOBIOGRAPHY

Using this exercise, write your autobiography. Cover your life in 5-year intervals. Be brief, but try not to miss anything.  Tell the whole truth. Write down exactly what you did.  Consider all of the things you marked during the exercise.  Read the exercise again if you need to. Make an exhaustive and honest consideration of your past and present. Cover both assets and liabilities carefully. You will rebuild your life on the solid building blocks of your assets. These are the tools of recovery. Omit nothing because of shame, embarrassment, or fear. Determine the thoughts, feelings, and actions that plagued you. You want to meet these problems face to face and see them in writing.  If you wish, you may destroy your inventory after completing the Fifth Step. Many patients hold a ceremony where they burn the Fourth Step inventory. This symbolizes that they are leaving the old life behind.  They are starting a new life free of the past.

# Appendix 22

## Step Five

*Admitted to God, ourselves, and to another human being the exact nature of our wrongs.*

Alcoholics Anonymous (1976)

Before beginning this exercise, read Step Five in *The Twelve Steps and Twelve Traditions* (AA, 1981).

With your first four steps behind you, it is now time to clean house and start over. You must free yourself of all guilt and shame and go forward in faith. The Fifth Step is meant to right the wrongs with God. You will develop a new attitude and a new relationship with your Higher Power. You have admitted your powerlessness and you have identified your liabilities and assets in the personal inventory. Now it's time to get right with God. You will do this by admitting to God, yourself, and another human being, the exact nature of your wrongs. You are going to cover all of your assets and your liabilities in the Fifth Step. You are going to tell someone the whole truth at one time. This person is important because they are a symbol of God and all of humanity. You must watch this person's face. The illness has been telling you that if you tell anyone the whole truth about you they won't like you. That is a lie, and you are going to prove that it is a lie. The truth is this: Unless you tell people the truth, they cannot like you. You must see yourself tell someone the truth and watch their reaction.

It is very difficult to discuss your faults with someone. It's hard enough just thinking about them yourself, but this is a necessary step. It will help to free you from the disease. You must tell this person everything, the whole story, all of the things that you are afraid to share. If you withhold anything, you will not get the relief you need to start over, you will be carrying around excess baggage. You don't need to do this to yourself. God loves you and wants you to be free of guilt, shame, and hurt. God wants you to be happy and to reach your full potential.

> Time after time newcomers have tried to keep to themselves certain facts about their lives. Trying to avoid this humbling experience, they have turned to easier methods. Almost invariably they got drunk. Having persevered with the rest of the program, they wondered why they fell. We think the reason is that they never completed their housecleaning. They took inventory all right, but hung on to some of the worst items in stock. They only *thought* they had lost their egotism and fear; they only *thought* they had humbled themselves. But they had not learned enough of humility, fearlessness and honesty, in the sense we find necessary, until they told someone else *all* their life story. (*Alcoholics Anonymous,* 1976, pp. 72-73)

By finally telling someone the whole truth, you will rid yourself of that terrible sense of isolation and loneliness. You will feel a new sense of belonging, acceptance, and freedom. If you do not immediately feel relief, don't worry—if you have been completely honest, the relief will come. "The dammed-up emotions of years break out of their confinement, and miraculously vanish when they are exposed" (AA, 1981, p. 62). You can be forgiven, no matter what.

The Fifth Step will develop within you a new humbleness of character that is necessary for normal living. You will come to clearly recognize who and what you are. When you are honest with another person, it confirms that you have been honest with yourself and with God.

The person that you will share your Fifth Step with has been chosen carefully for you. You will meet with this person several times before you do the step. You need to decide if you can trust this person. Do you feel that this person is confidential? Do you feel comfortable with them? Do you feel they will be understanding and loving?

Once you have chosen that person, put your false pride aside and go for it. Tell them everything about yourself. Do not leave one dark corner unturned. Tell them about all of the good things you have done, and about all of the bad things. Share the details and don't leave anything out. If it troubles you, even a little, share it. Let it all hang out to be examined by God, yourself, and that other person. Every good and bad part needs to be revealed. When you are finished, say a prayer to your Higher Power. Tell God that you are sorry for what you have done wrong, and commit yourself to a new way of life following the God of your understanding. Many patients like to say the Seventh Step prayer:

> "My Creator, I am now willing that you should have all of me, good and bad. I pray that you now remove from me every single defect of character which stands in the way of my usefulness to you and my fellows. Grant me strength, as I go out from here, to do your bidding." (*Alcoholics Anonymous,* 1976, p. 76)

# *Appendix 23*

## *Adolescent Unit Level System*

Patients participating in the adolescent program will be involved in the Freedom Level System. This system is a simple three-level program designed to be a guide in the development of appropriate treatment attitudes and behaviors. This program is for your benefit and it is the primary means by which you will move forward into a stable program of recovery. You will enjoy more freedom and responsibility as you move up in levels. All we ask is that you try to be honest, open-minded, and willing to participate in your treatment.

### FREEDOM LEVEL 1

All adolescents entering treatment will begin on Freedom Level 1. To be eligible for advancement to Level 2, you must accomplish the following list of goals in a satisfactory manner and identify and implement positive behaviors and attitudes toward treatment.

Treatment Goals

1. Complete the process of orientation to the unit with the assistance of the staff and assigned treatment peer.
2. Participate and cooperate with staff in completing all aspects of the assessment phase of treatment, including clinical and psychological assessments.
3. Review general unit rules with staff or treatment peer and abide by these rules.
4. Cooperate with staff schoolteacher in developing a workable school program. Review and follow all school rules and willingly participate in your continuing education.
5. Become actively involved in all scheduled activities.
6. Complete all written assignments in a timely manner.
7. Verbally participate in groups and begin to take risks.
8. Exhibit a positive attitude both verbally and behaviorally toward staff and treatment peers.
9. Satisfactorily complete all unit assignments and duties such as keeping your room, and the entire unit, clean and organized.

Level 1 Privileges

1. Able to watch "fun" videos.
2. May watch TV during free time.
3. May have recreation room privileges as scheduled.

### FREEDOM LEVEL 2

Adolescents who have satisfactorily completed the goal requirements listed under Level 1 will be promoted to Level 2. Patients on this level may enjoy the Level 1 privileges plus the Level 2 privileges. To maintain Level 2 status, the patient must continue to live up to the Level 1 goals. To advance to Level 2, a patient must demonstrate the following:

Treatment Goals

1. Increased participation in all groups. Take significant risks by being open and honest and providing appropriate feedback.
2. Complete all school assignments and cooperate in all aspects of the school program.

3. Act as a positive role model to your treatment peers by refusing to participate in negative talk or behaviors. Confront your peers on their inappropriate behaviors.

4. Verbalize an understanding of chemical dependency and the components of a recovery program.

## Level 2 Privileges

1. May have radios, tape players, and tapes.
2. Eligible to be a patient sponsor to a new patient.
3. Eligible to be the unit sheriff.
4. May accompany staff away from the facility to help pick out "fun" videos.
5. Snack bar privileges.
6. May leave the unit unescorted with staff approval and you may escort a Level 1 peer to the nurses station or to other functions and appointments in the facility.

## FREEDOM LEVEL 3

### Treatment Goals

Adolescents who have satisfied all goal requirements listed under Level 1 and Level 2 are eligible for Level 3. All Level 3 patients must the complete the following goals:

1. Continue to demonstrate the desire to work a program of recovery.
2. Consistently show by words and actions that you are working on the Twelve Steps.
3. Be a good role model to other patients.

### Level 3 Privileges

1. Participate in scheduled weekend outings with staff and other eligible treatment peers.
2. You are eligible to make one supervised telephone call to a friend each week. Phone calls will have a 10-minute maximum and be made to an individual approved by your primary counselor.
3. You may leave the dining room and return to the unit unescorted.

## PROBLEM BEHAVIORS AND CONSEQUENCES

1. Room restriction
   a. Adolescents are totally restricted to their room for a length of time determined by the staff. They do not attend any activities. No peer visitors are allowed.
   b. No two adolescents are to be restricted to the same room at the same time.
   c. The patient is not allowed breaks.

2. Time-out
   a. The adolescent is restricted to the time-out room for at least one hour. Patient is not allowed peer visitors.
   b. The adolescent loses recreation period and all breaks.

3. Loss of free time: 24 hours or longer determined by staff
   Adolescent has to spend all free time in his or her room.

4. The buddy system

   When a new patient comes into treatment and is on Freedom Level 1 or 2, a Level 3 patient may be assigned to orient the patient to the unit. This would involve introducing the new patient to the other patients and staff and showing them around the center. The buddy should help the new patient to feel more comfortable on the unit.

5. Major consequence
    a. Adolescents who receive a major consequence will automatically be dropped a level.
    b. They will be assigned other consequences as determined by the staff.

6. Minor consequence
    Adolescents who receive three minor consequences will be dropped a level as well as receive consequences determined by the staff.

Adolescents are encouraged to work on respecting themselves, others, and property. They need to be working toward knowing and understanding themselves and developing appropriate and positive social relationships. They need to learn how to identify and deal with their feelings appropriately. All patients are encouraged to develop a sense of responsibility for their actions. The following problem behaviors and consequences deal with these principles.

## MAJOR CONSEQUENCES

1. Adolescents will not use or have in their possession any mood-altering substances during treatment except those prescribed by the physician.

    *Consequence:* Use or possession of mood-altering substances is a serious violation and may result in extended treatment or discharge from the program. If the adolescents are not discharged, they will be placed on room restriction for at least one hour, will be placed on a behavioral contract, and will be returned to Freedom Level 1.

2. Adolescents are not permitted to be verbally aggressive to staff or peers. Behaviors will be individually assessed by the staff member involved to determine if this is a major or a minor consequence.

    *Consequence:* Adolescents involved in a major consequence will drop a freedom level, face possible discharge, and receive room restriction for at least one hour.

3. Adolescents are not permitted to be destructive to or deface any treatment center property.

    *Consequence:* Adolescents involved in this behavior on a major scale (i.e., knocking holes in walls, throwing and damaging items, etc.) will become involved in working for the damage by doing jobs around the center. They will be dropped one freedom level. This may also result in room restriction or time-out.

The patients will present a written report on the incident in contract's group and give a copy of the written report to their primary counselor.

4. Adolescents will not engage in any form of sexual activity while in treatment (i.e., kissing, necking, foreplay, intercourse, etc.). Forming romantic relationships in treatment is not permitted (i.e., holding hands, arms around each other, flirting, inappropriate hugging or touching each other, etc.).

    *Consequence:* Engaging in sexual contact is a serious violation of unit policy and patients who engage in this activity may be discharged from the program. Adolescents not discharged will be placed on room restriction. They will complete a written assignment that they will share with their primary counselor. They may have their time in treatment extended. They will be placed on a behavioral contract. They will lose one freedom level.

5. Adolescents are not permitted to act in a physically aggressive manner toward staff or treatment peers. Anger outbursts (slamming doors, yelling, angrily getting up and leaving a scheduled activity before it is completed, etc.) are prohibited. Physical or verbal aggression toward staff or peers is not permitted (i.e., fighting, throwing items, or making verbal threats of harm).

    *Consequence:* Adolescents involved in physical or verbal aggression may be discharged from the program. Adolescents not discharged from the program will be put on room restriction or time-out. They will make a verbal presentation in contract's group. A written copy of the presentation will be given to the primary counselor. The adolescent will lose at least one freedom level.

6. Adolescents are expected to cope with their problems in a more constructive way than running away from the treatment center.

   *Consequence:* Adolescents who verbally threaten or who are believed to be at risk of running away will be placed on AMA precautions until decided otherwise by their primary counselor with input from the clinical team. Adolescents who leave the center against medical advice and are returned, may be placed on room restriction or time-out. They will be returned to Freedom Level 1. This may result in discharge from treatment or extension of treatment. A urine specimen will be obtained from all patients who inappropriately leave the treatment center.

7. Adolescents are expected to fulfill any consequences they may obtain in a time frame organized by the staff.

   *Consequence:* Adolescents who do not fulfill their consequences will receive loss of free time or be placed on room restriction until the consequence is fulfilled.

## MINOR CONSEQUENCES

1. Adolescents are not allowed to use verbally abusive language to staff or peers (i.e., swearing, hostile language, etc.).

   *Consequence:* Adolescent involved in being verbally abusive will lose free time for up to 24 hours and make a verbal presentation in contract's group. A written copy of the presentation will be given to the primary counselor.

2. Adolescents are not to be involved in horseplay activities (i.e., wrestling, pushing, shadow boxing, etc.). Aggressive horseplay or practical jokes may entail a major consequence. This will be determined by the staff member involved.

   *Consequence:* Involvement in horseplay activities will result in loss of free time up to 24 hours and a verbal presentation to community group. A written copy will be given to the primary counselor.

3. Honesty is a vital part of your treatment and recovery. Being dishonest is not permitted.

   *Consequence:* Involvement in dishonest behavior will result in loss of free time or room restriction. A verbal presentation to contract's group will be required. A copy of this presentation will go to the primary counselor.

4. Adolescents who have possession of unauthorized articles will lose free time for up to 24 hours.

5. Radios and tape players must be kept to an acceptable volume. If you can hear it outside of your room, it's too loud. Radios and tape players played too loudly will be confiscated for 24 hours.

6. Each adolescent late for a scheduled activity will be given a minor consequence. Three such consequences will result in the loss of free time for 24 hours. The patient will be dropped one freedom level.

7. Patients not participating in group will be given a minor consequence. They will present to the next group their reasons for not participating.

# *Appendix 24*

## *Peer Pressure*
### Robert R. Perkinson, Ph.D.

You want your friends to accept you. Sure you do, that's normal. You want to be liked. You want to be loved and accepted by your peers. In treatment, it is important to learn about peer pressure, where it comes from, what is good about it, and what can be dangerous. There are things that you need to watch out for in recovery. If you are not careful, the pressure of your peer group can get you back to drinking or using drugs. Your friends are not trying to hurt you—they just want their old friend back. These friends may have a chemical problem themselves. They may see your recovery as a threat to themselves.

## HOW PEER PRESSURE EVOLVED

The roots of peer pressure evolved in the birds. Birds learned that they were safer if they gathered together in flocks. They could more easily warn others of danger if they stuck together. In a group, they were less likely to be singled out as prey. Birds learned how to stay together for safety. Because this worked so well, birds, over thousands of years, developed a feeling of wanting to be together. They developed social skills used to keep them together. They began to make noises to keep together. Anyone who has heard a flock of geese fly over will testify to the active communication patterns of these birds. Communications became more complicated over the years. They developed a particular sound for relaxation, and a particular sound for danger. The birds developed the feeling of wanting to be together in groups. It felt better to be together. These feelings are what we now call *emotions*.

Higher-order social activity continued to evolve in mammals. Baboons, for example, have very complicated social rituals. These animals groom each other to keep the troop together. The grooming serves to rid them of irritating insects, and it helps them to feel closer together. It is like a back scratch, and it says, If you scratch my back, I'll scratch yours. These social rituals hold a group of animals together. If you go to the zoo, you will see animals rubbing and stroking each other. You will see mothers holding and licking their babies. The species thus becomes bonded together.

Acceptance is a very important feeling because an animal depends on acceptance by the group for survival. If they are rejected by the herd, they have a higher chance of being killed by predators. The animals are all safer if they are in a group.

As we move up the evolutionary scale, we finally get to human beings. Early people, as we know them, were social creatures. They gathered together in groups or tribes for safety. The tribe could function better together. They could specialize and reap the benefits of another person's expertise. It was easier to hunt, fish, and gather food if the tribe worked together. Some would do the hunting, and some would make arrowheads. Each tribe member specialized in a particular function. It was very important for early people to be accepted by their tribe. If they were banished, they would have to fend for themselves. Being alone in the world would put an individual at great risk. So humans developed a desire, a wish, a need to be liked, to be accepted. This was very important for survival.

## THE IMPORTANCE OF PEER PRESSURE

You are beginning to see why peer pressure is so important. If you are rejected by the group, you fear death. Without the acceptance of the group, people feel more vulnerable to the world. Now you can see why we try so hard to get our friends to like us. We need our friends so we can feel safe.

It is very clear that being liked and being accepted by the group is important and good. It is important for all of us to learn the skills necessary to establish and maintain close interpersonal relationships. These are the skills that keep the group together.

Often, symbols or gestures identify the group. Groups may have a flag or a uniform. They may all ride a certain kind of motorcycle or wear a particular hat. All groups have a particular language that is unique to that group. Medical doctors don't use the same words as auto mechanics.

## HOW PEER PRESSURE CAN RISK YOUR SOBRIETY

A few things about peer pressure can get you into trouble. Groups can get you to do things that you wouldn't normally do. They might talk you into doing something that you don't want to do., things like stealing, drinking, or even playing a practical joke on someone. If we always follow the group, we can be led into behavior that we know is wrong.

List five times when you were talked into doing something you didn't really want to do.

1. _____
2. _____
3. _____
4. _____
5. _____

## HOW THE GROUP USES PEER PRESSURE

The group will have a means of pressuring you into cooperating. In formal society, laws govern group behavior. In most groups a member is subject to ridicule and even group expulsion if he or she do not cooperate. "Don't be chicken! What are you scared of?!" There are any number of ways to encourage members to do what the group wants them to do.

List some of the ways your friends try to get you to cooperate with them.

1. _____
2. _____
3. _____
4. _____
5. _____

## HOW TO COPE WITH PEER PRESSURE

It is important to stay in the group, but it is also important for you to make your own decisions. If you don't make all of your decisions, you will be held accountable for the decisions of others.

Here is a new concept for you: The only thing that you owe anyone else is to be different. You must be different from anyone who ever was or anyone who ever will be. You were created for your individuality. The only way you can reach your full potential in life is to make all of your own decisions. If you always follow a group, you cannot be yourself. It is important for you to have the skill to say No. You need to be able to go against the group sometimes. If you are going to be an adult, you have to make all of you own decisions and live with the consequences. That is the only way you can take your own direction. You must think about every choice you make. You cannot let other people make your decisions for you.

When you decide to do something that is different from what the group wants, the group will apply peer pressure. The group will try to get you to conform. They may threaten you or make fun of you. They may get angry at you. But remember: It is your responsibility to yourself, and to everyone else, that sometimes you be different. Once you make a decision, and you believe in it, you must be able to stick to it. If you can't do this, the group will always manipulate your choices. You need to develop the skill of going your own way, even in the face of group opposition.

You do not have to have a good reason for not doing what the group wants. It can just be your choice. You don't have to explain yourself or your opinions to anybody. You do not need an excuse. You can simply say, "Because I want to." This is reason enough.

You must keep the group informed about how you are feeling if they try to pressure you. This holds the group accountable for their behavior. If the group is causing you to feel uncomfortable, you must express this feeling. This will keep their behavior in line. "It makes me feel uncomfortable when you ask me to drink when you know that I'm recovering." Honest statements such as this will usually bring people under control. You must constantly keep people informed about how you are feeling and what you want from them. "I don't want any pot. I would prefer it if you would stop asking me." A simple "No," or "No, thank you," is enough in most circumstances. Say no, and stand your ground. You don't have to explain yourself further. If the group continues to coerce you even after you have said no, you may have to leave the situation. If they do not respect your wishes, you don't want to be with those people anyway. Just excuse yourself and go home. You haven't lost anything—if the group doesn't care for how you feel, they are not the group for you.

People can always get you to feel a certain way if they try. They can get you to feel angry or guilty if they work at it, but even if they have some control over your feelings, they cannot control your actions. That's up to you. If they can get control over your actions by controlling your feelings, they have a slave, they can get you to do anything. Groups will often try to lay guilt on you if you don't cooperate with them, but they can't make you do anything with this guilt. You are in control of your actions.

## MAKE A PLAN TO SAY NO

List 10 ways you are going to say no to alcohol and drugs.

1. _____
2. _____
3. _____
4. _____
5. _____
6. _____
7. _____
8. _____
9. _____
10. _____

Here are some important points to remember: The desire to be accepted by the group is normal and very powerful. The feeling of wanting to be accepted exists deep inside of all of us and this feeling helps us gather together in groups for everyone's mutual gain. Being a part of a group feels good, but our primary responsibility to ourselves and to everyone else is to be different, to be one of a kind. It is therefore crucially important that you take your own direction, make all of your own decisions, and be yourself.

# Appendix 25

## The Behavioral Contract
### Robert R. Perkinson, Ph.D.

Behavioral contracting has been found to be a powerful means of directly influencing behavior (Stuart, 1971). Developing a behavioral contract and living within its limits will create a stable family situation for you and your child. Behavior is defined as any movement. When anyone acts or speaks, it is behavior. We are often asked by frustrated parents, "Why doesn't my child cooperate?" The answer to this question is simple: No behavior exists, nor does it continue to exist, without reward. The child gets good things for the behavior. They might get more freedom by arguing than they do when they behave in a more sociable manner. Many children have been reinforced for antisocial behavior. Parents don't mean to do this—it seems to happen on its own—but psychological laws are at play in all learning.

## REWARD AND PUNISHMENT

A reward is anything that increases the frequency of a behavior. Behavior is reinforced when it gets children something they want or removes something they don't want. A reward might be money, praise, or free time. You can't always tell what is reinforcing to a child—you have to watch the behavior to check it. If the behavior increases, you can assume that what you have done is reinforcing. To most children a hug is reinforcing, but to some it is not—it may even be punitive.

A punishment decreases the frequency of a behavior. You can punish children by giving them something they don't want or taking away something they want. You can verbally reprimand them, send them to their room, or take away their use of the family car. Again, you have to watch the behavior to see what is a punishment. If the behavior decreases, you can assume that you have punished it. The problem with punishment is you can't teach the child anything new, and you get the child's mind off of what they did and onto what you are doing to them. If you want to change a child, reinforcement is much more powerful.

## HABITS

If a child is reinforced for a behavior over a period of time, the behavior will get to be a habit. It will develop a life of its own. This behavior will not go away easily. It will stick like glue. It will take time for new behavior to replace it. In behavioral contracting, you teach your children new behavior by carefully scheduling when they get reinforced. You want to think before you act. Give your children good things when they are acting the way you want them to act. This means your behavior must change as well as theirs.

The family is a powerful force in teaching a child new behavior. All children want to be loved, and you can use this desire to develop the behaviors you want. A behavioral contract is a means by which you control the exchange of positive reinforcement. The contract specifies who is going to do what, for whom, and under what circumstances. The contract makes explicit the expectations of each party. It gives the parent and the child the opportunity to get the things they want. It clarifies the benefits of cooperation by making each person's role in the family clear. The contract makes it more likely that all will live up to their responsibilities. This leads to family harmony and stability.

## LOVE

Love is the active involvement in someone's individual growth. To be loving, you must be actively involved in your children reaching their full potential. Rewards must be earned, they should not be given randomly. If you give your children good things just because they exist, you give them no direction, you don't teach them what works in life. They will think that the world owes them things. This is not fair to the child, and it isn't an accurate view of the world.

All members of a family have rights and duties to each other, and rewards must be exchanged equally. Many times parents feel they are doing all the giving, and the child is doing all the taking. This is a mistake. Happiness comes from giving to others. If you don't teach your child to give, your child will not be happy.

In a healthy family, if you give something, you get something in return. The more you give, the more you get. All the members of a family should want to give all they can. In the behavioral contract, if children act responsibly, they earn specific rewards. Some examples of rewards are free time, time with friends, television time, spending money, and use of the family car. Individual children will have different sets of rewards, and they should actively ask for what they want.

## HOW TO DEVELOP A BEHAVIORAL CONTRACT

The behavioral contract details the behavior necessary for earning each reward. Let's say you are having problems with your children's coming home from school on time. For a variety of reasons they are late and you worry about them. You decide to put this behavior into the behavior contract. If the children get home from school every day on time, they earn a certain amount of television time. If they miss coming home, they don't earn that privilege. Behaviors that you might be interested in are things such as minimum school attendance and performance, curfew hours, and completion of household chores. The responsibilities required must be monitored. You must be able to see if the behavior is occurring. It would be useless for you to forbid your child to see a person at school because you couldn't monitor the behavior. If you want your child to be at school on time and cooperate with school authorities, you can have the teacher keep track for you. You could check with the teacher each week to be sure of compliance. You could send a School Performance Chart with your child to give to the teacher each day. It would look something like this:

The School Performance Chart

Name of Student _____ Date _____

To keep my parents informed about my school progress, I am asking all my teachers to complete this form at the end of each class period. Thank you.

Subject _____

|  | Yes | No |
|---|---|---|
| 1. Student was on time for class | _____ | _____ |
| 2. Student completed homework assignment (Mark only if applicable) | _____ | _____ |
| 3. Student obeyed class rules | _____ | _____ |
| 4. Student was attentive to task | _____ | _____ |
| 5. Student was cooperative with teacher | _____ | _____ |

You must be sure that you are giving your children enough rewards to keep them cooperating with the contract. If they feel like the contract is not good for them, they will resist the whole idea. Each party in the contract must have a full say about what they want, and everyone must be willing to compromise. All parties must agree to the contract and sign it. You must include the consequences that will occur if the children don't comply with the terms of the contract.

Make sure that you verbally reinforce your children as they comply. We are striving for progress not perfection. Statements such as, "Good job! You're doing great! I'm proud of you!" go a long way in getting your children to cooperate cheerfully.

## Detailing What Each Party Wants

The first thing you need to do is determine what all parties want from the family. The children might want to go out on weekend nights and stay out until 11 o'clock. They might want to use the family car. They might want to go out without explaining where they are going. They might want a new bike. They might want to choose their own clothes, or their own style of haircut without your input. Brainstorm with your child about what they want from you. Then decide what you want from your child. You may want them to improve in school. You may want them to come home on time. You may want them to keep you informed about where they are. You may want them to help out with the household chores.

Write all of these things down, and with the counselor, work out what each person is willing to give to get what is wanted from the other. It is important that each person gets the reasonable things that he or she wants from the contract. All parties mutually exchange things that they want from each other. The contract might look something like this:

A Sample Contract

| *Privilege* | *Responsibility* |
| --- | --- |
| In exchange for the privilege of going out one weekend night at 7 p.m. and coming home at 11 p.m. | Robert agrees to maintain a weekly B average in school. |
| In exchange for going out one week night at 7 p.m. and returning by 10 p.m. | Robert agrees to wash the family car once a week. |
| In exchange for the privilege of using the family car once a week. | Robert agrees to wash the dishes at dinner and to take out the garbage. |
| In exchange for the privilege of having Robert cut the grass. | Mr. and Mrs. Jones agree to pay him five dollars each week. |

| *Consequence* | |
| --- | --- |
| If Robert is 1-10 minutes late coming home. | Robert agrees to come home 30 minutes earlier the next time he goes out. |
| If Robert is 10-30 minutes late coming home. | Robert will lose the privilege of going out one weekend night. |

In the above contract, the parents will need to keep a written record of when Robert comes home, and Robert will have to provide the parents a School Performance Chart each day.

The contract can include anything that you want as long as everyone agrees to it. Let your primary counselor help you. If you have any problems with the contract, you can discuss the issues in the aftercare group.

# Appendix 26

## Family Questionnaire
### Robert R. Perkinson, Ph.D.

Your Name _____   Date _____

Patient name: _____   Relationship _____

Address: _____

Home phone: _____

Work phone: _____

The best time for you to be contacted by the family program counselor: _____

Chemical dependency affects everyone it touches. Chemically dependent persons and everyone close to them are adversely affected. No one wants a loved one to be sick, so the family members pretend the disease isn't there. The average chemically dependent person has been ill for years before the family finally realizes that there is a problem. After the problem has been identified, even more years pass before the chemically dependent person receives treatment.

The person you care for is in treatment. That's great! You can relax and know that they are safe. They stand at the turning point, and there is an excellent chance that they will achieve a stable sobriety. They may have further problems, but this is a major step in the right direction. You have done the right thing and you can feel good about it.

The patients may not feel good about coming to treatment right now. They may feel angry or rejected. They may still believe that they don't have a problem. This is denial, it is very common, and it is one of the surest signs that the disease is present. Chemical dependency demands that people lie to themselves. The person is fooled into believing that they are okay even when their life is falling apart.

It is important for you to understand that it is not only the chemically dependent person who is having problems. If you have lived close to a chemically dependent person, you are having problems too. All of these problems have, at their source, subtle distortions of reality. Family members change reality into something that doesn't make them so nervous. Trying to keep the reality of chemical dependency hidden is like hiding an elephant in your living room. The problem is there, and it is big, so it takes large distortions of reality to keep it hidden. The family tries to pretend that there is not a problem. As the problem gets larger, it takes larger distortions of reality to keep it secret.

The distorting begins with minimizing. Family members pretend the problem is not so bad. They believe that other people have more problems than they do. They think that the drinking is not that bad. It could be worse. They minimize to the point that they can't see the real effect of the illness on themselves and the other family members. But the problem is big. They focus on the chemically dependent person and as they do, they become cut off from their own feelings. They have no time for themselves. This sinks the family deeper into an unreal world.

The next lie families tell themselves is there is a good excuse for the problem. This is called rationalization. It's not the drugs, it's the job, or the boss, or maybe even me. The family members, even children, may feel responsible for the chemically dependent person's drinking or drug use. They blame themselves, other people, institutions, money, whatever it takes to take the mind off the real problem. The family actually believes that it is these other things that are the problem, not the chemicals.

The last distortion of reality is called denial. This is where the family members do not experience the full impact of their lives. They have developed such a tolerance for the craziness that they think it is normal. Their lives may be coming apart, but they still think things are in control.

Now is the time to get honest with yourself. Don't make things seem smaller than they were. Don't make excuses. Write down exactly what happened.

---

Why did the patient decide to seek treatment at this time?

_____

_____

_____

What mood-altering chemicals does the patient currently use? (Mark all that apply)

*Chemical*                                          *Amounts Used Per Day*

_____ Alcohol                                       _____

_____ Tranquilizers                                 _____

_____ "Sleeping pills"                              _____

_____ Marijuana (pot)                               _____

_____ Cocaine                                       _____

_____ Amphetamine (Speed)                           _____

_____ Pain medications                              _____

_____ Hallucinogens (LSD)                           _____

_____ Inhalants (gas, paint, glue)                  _____

_____ Over-the-counter medication                   _____

_____ Narcotics                                     _____

Pattern of Use

_____ Continuous (daily)                            _____

_____ Periodic (fairly regular pattern)             _____

_____ Sporadic (off and on with no pattern)         _____

What is the problem as you see it? (Mark all that apply)

_____ Alcohol

_____ Illegal/street drugs

_____ Prescription drugs

_____ Combination of alcohol and drugs

_____ Emotional problems

_____ Family problems

What is the problem as the patient sees it? (Mark all that apply)

_____ Alcohol

_____ Prescription drugs

_____ Illegal/street drugs

_____ Combination of alcohol and drugs

_____ Emotional problems

_____ Family problems

What is the patient's awareness of the problem?

_____ No awareness: "I don't have a problem. It's no worse than anyone else"

_____ Minimal awareness: "Sure, I've had a problem, but I can take it or leave it."

_____ Moderate awareness: "I have a problem, but I can handle it on my own."

_____ Admits to a problem and accepts the responsibility for change.

Duration of the Problem

_____ 0-6 months

_____ 6 months to 1 year

_____ 1-2 years

_____ 2-5 years

_____ more than 5 years (Specify number of years:_____)

Longest Period of Abstinence

_____ Days

_____ Weeks

_____ A month at a time

_____ 6-12 months at a time

When the patient was abstinent, what was the reason he or she stopped using?

_____

_____

_____

Which of the following symptoms of dependency apply to the patient? (Mark all that apply)

_____ Blackouts (cannot remember what they did while drinking)

_____ Hides or protects supply of drugs or alcohol

_____ Cannot stop once they start

_____ Makes excuses for using alcohol or drugs

_____ Has a physical problem associated with use (tremors, nausea, headache)

_____ Personality changes while using

_____ Other, explain

Which of the following behaviors has the patient demonstrated? (Mark all that apply)

_____ Violent, aggressive, or abusive behavior

_____ Unreasonable resentments (holds grudges)

_____ Changing type of friends (changing to friends who use)

_____ Poor school or work performance

_____ Unable to join in family activities

_____ Unable to do things they should do (unable to keep appointments or to get things done at home or at work)

How does the patient obtain money to buy alcohol or other drugs?

_____

_____

_____

How much do you think the patient spends on alcohol or other drugs? Has this created a problem for you, your family, or the patient?

_____

_____

_____

How has the chemical use changed family activities?

_____

_____

_____

What does the patient think about Alcoholics/Narcotics Anonymous?

_____ Critical of AA/NA members

_____ "Good program, but it's not for me."

_____ AA/NA is the answer to the problem

_____ Has no knowledge of AA/NA

Previous treatment. Has the patient participated in any of the following treatments for chemical dependency?

_____ Attended a few AA/NA meetings

_____ Regularly participated for a brief period

_____ General hospital

_____ Psychiatric treatment

_____ Outpatient treatment

_____ Inpatient treatment

Give a brief history of treatment dates.

_____

_____

_____

Are there any other problems in connection with or related to the chemical problem?

_____ Not to my knowledge

_____ School problems

_____ Work problems

_____ Legal problems

_____ Financial problems

_____ Family problems

_____ Psychiatric problems

Explain: _____

_____

_____

_____

Have you or other family members experienced any of the following:

_____ Health problems

_____ School/work problems

_____ Legal problems

_____ Financial problems

_____ Difficulty expressing feelings

Explain: _____

_____

_____

_____

What treatment have you sought for yourself and your family?

_____ AA/NA

_____ Al-Anon/Alateen

_____ Counseling

_____ Psychiatric visits

Explain: _____

_____

_____

_____

Has any of your children been referred to

_____ Social services

_____ Juvenile detention center

_____ Court services

_____ Psychological services

_____ Chemical dependency treatment

Explain: _____

_____

_____

_____

Can you see anything that might interfere with the evaluation or treatment of your family member?

_____

_____

_____

_____

What do you feel are the problem areas that need to be addressed while the patient is in treatment?

_____

_____

_____

_____

In addition to the questions that have already been covered, is there any other information we should know about the patient?

_____

_____

_____

_____

Which types of abuse have occurred in your present family?

_____ Emotional

_____ Verbal

_____ Physical

_____ Sexual

Explain: _____

_____

_____

_____

Did any of the following types of abuse occur in the family in which you grew up?

_____ Emotional

_____ Verbal

_____ Physical

_____ Sexual

Explain _____

_____

_____

_____

Do you believe that chemical dependency is a disease?

Yes _____ No _____

Explain how the chemical problem has affected your relationship with the patient. _____

_____

_____

_____

_____

Write down the names of the members of your family and rate them on how they use mood-altering chemicals: no use = 0; infrequent use = 2; social use = 3; misuse/abuse = 4; dependency = 5.

| Family Member | Chemical Used | Rating |
|---|---|---|
| Yourself | | |
| Present spouse | | |
| Former spouse | | |
| Children | | |
| | | |
| | | |
| | | |
| Your father | | |
| Your mother | | |
| Your brothers and sisters | | |
| | | |
| | | |
| Other family members | | |
| | | |
| | | |

# Appendix 27

## Codependency
### Robert R. Perkinson, Ph.D.

Codependency is what happens to someone who is trying to control someone else. If your loved one is chemically dependent, you have probably tried to help them. You have attempted to fix the problem. But you could not fix it, any more than you could fix them if they had cancer. Chemical dependency is a disease that no one is to blame for. The causes of chemical dependency are so varied and complex that no one has been able to figure it all out—it's too complicated.

In your love for the patient, you may have done some things that were not good for you. It is very common for codependent persons to take better care of the other person than they do of themselves. You may have been so concentrated on the other person's problems that you had no time for your own problems. This is a mistake. This is your turn to stop and concentrate on yourself. What has happened to you in your struggle against this disease? Our experience shows us that family members who look at their own life will immeasurably help the patient achieve a stable recovery. If only the patient is treated, the chance of success is reduced.

There are a variety of codependent traits. These are maladaptive thoughts and behaviors that have been learned in response to the chemically dependent person. It is important that you take a look at each of these traits because they inhibit you from being able to live a normal life. You cannot solve problems accurately when these traits are at work. They distract you. They keep you from seeing the truth.

## DEFENSE MECHANISMS

Defense mechanisms are mental states where we refuse to see reality. We cut ourselves off from reality because the real world is too painful for us. We need to live in a fantasy world of our own creation. The more we use defense mechanisms, the more cut off from reality we are. We feel lonely and helpless because no one can reach us in our self-deceived world.

### Minimization

It begins with minimization. When we minimize, we take reality and make it smaller than it really is. We pretend the problem is not bad when it is bad. We may have become so deluded that we think drinking a six-pack of beer every night is normal. Doesn't everybody drink like this? We may minimize about the financial problems. They don't seem so bad either. Doesn't everyone struggle like this? We minimize about verbal and physical abuse. They were just mad, or out of control, or drunk. That's not really them. They're not really like that. We may minimize by telling ourselves that the addicted person just overdid it at the party; they are really good people, they didn't mean it. When we minimize, we tell ourselves that we have no reason to feel afraid. If the problem was bad, we would have to be frightened and do something about it. But it's not so bad, so we can relax.

List five times when you told yourself things were not bad when they really were.

1. _____
2. _____
3. _____
4. _____
5. _____

## Rationalization

The next defense mechanism we use is rationalization. This is when we make an excuse for the patient. They are drinking or drugging because they have had a hard life, had a fight with their mother, had a bad childhood, got fired, have financial problems, have problems with their brother, or maybe they just aren't understood. Codependents can think up a million reasons why the person is using, but the real reason is that they are chemically dependent. They are sick and need help. We don't want to see this truth because it is frightening. We don't want to believe that our loved one is ill. We want to believe that they are just fine or are only having temporary difficulty.

A rationalization is a lie. It's an excuse for the real problem. Did you ever make an excuse for the chemically dependent person? Did you ever tell the boss that they were sick, or tell the children they weren't feeling well when you knew they were intoxicated or too hung over to function? If you did, you may have believed some of this yourself.

List five times when you made an excuse for the patient's behavior.

1. _____
2. _____
3. _____
4. _____
5. _____

You can see what is happening to the family. By minimizing and rationalizing, they get more and more cut off from reality. They can't see accurately what's going on anymore. They are using the defense mechanisms to cut themselves off from the painful truth.

## Denial

The most characteristic form of defense used in chemical dependency is denial. This is where the mind refuses to experience the full emotional impact of what is happening. Your family is falling apart. Your relationship is shot. You can't talk to your family anymore. You are in severe financial trouble and you still think that you can fix these things. You still think all these problems are something else other than chemical dependency. You may even be so fooled that you think the problems are your fault. If you were a better wife, husband, child, or parent, the chemically dependent person wouldn't be having problems.

In the last few years, list the worst things that happened while the chemically dependent person was using drugs or alcohol.

1. _____
2. _____
3. _____
4. _____
5. _____

In each of these situations, what were you telling yourself that convinced you that things were all right?

1. _____
2. _____
3. _____
4. _____
5. _____

## CARETAKING

Codependent persons focus on the other person. They are obsessed with taking care of the chemically dependent person to the point that they lose contact with reality. They actually think that everything will be all right if they do the right things. They plan everything for everyone. They scold and control. They read self-help books. They feel responsible for everyone's feelings. They go to extraordinary lengths to help. They feel totally drained, as if there is not enough time in the day. They threaten, cry, lie, scream, blame, and shame. They seek counseling, pray, and manipulate. All of these behaviors, and many more, are all designed to bring control to an out-of-control situation. Codependent people think that they can fix things if they just work hard enough. The fact of the matter is we can't control someone else's behavior, no matter how much we try. The more we try, the more frustrating it becomes.

List five ways you tried to control the chemically dependent person.

1. _____
2. _____
3. _____
4. _____
5. _____

## ENABLING

In treatment, you must understand that you can't control anyone but yourself. You are responsible only for your own actions. If you keep chemically dependent people out of trouble, you keep them from suffering the natural consequences of their behavior. If you call the boss and make excuses, they doesn't learn from their mistakes. This is called enabling. By protecting patients from the consequences of their addiction, you help them stay sick. You must no longer protect patients from their maladaptive behavior. You must not pay their bad checks or debts, make excuses, or smooth over ruffled feathers. You must let the patient be responsible.

By caretaking and enabling, codependent persons constantly get chemically dependent persons out of trouble. They protect patients from the consequences of their actions. They may call the boss and say their spouse is sick, when he is too intoxicated or hung over to come to work. They may tell the children that dad or mom needs to rest when he or she has passed out on the couch. They may pay the bail or the bad checks. They call the creditors who are clamoring for payment. They comfort abused family members and try to make everything better.

List five times when you got the chemically dependent person out of trouble.

1. _____
2. _____
3. _____
4. _____
5. _____

You were taking the responsibility for someone else's behavior. By protecting patients from the logical consequences of their own actions, you helped them avoid the pain of their disease. This prevented them from learning that they were sick and needed help. You enabled the illness to stay hidden. You helped the patient to avoid reality. By protecting patients from pain, you prevented them from seeing the severity of their problem. This has got to stop. Each person in a family has to accept responsibility. All must make their own decisions and live with the consequences.

## INABILITY TO KNOW FEELINGS

People who are codependent do not know how they feel. They are so focused on the other person's feelings that they ignore their own. They know how the other person is doing, but they don't know much about themselves. For the most part, codependents think they are fine, but what they are really feeling is frustrated, frightened, and depressed. They are desperately trying to bring order to disorder and confusion.

People who live in a chemically dependent home don't trust how they feel. They feel that something is wrong with them. They try to block out the reality of the nightmare they are living. They may make up what their family is like. John Bradshaw describes this as a fantasy bond (Bradshaw, 1988, 1990). The child or family member creates an idealized family in their mind. They may feel that their father is warm and loving when he is actually abusive. They may feel their mother is a good mother when she is always away at the bar.

In chemically dependent homes, family members learn that feelings are dangerous. If we share how we feel, bad things will happen. We keep our fear, sadness, anger, disgust, and hurt to ourselves. We keep the secrets, sharing them with no one.

List some situations where you kept your real feelings to yourself. Whom were you trying to protect by keeping these feelings secret?

1. _____
2. _____
3. _____
4. _____
5. _____

## INABILITY TO KNOW WHAT YOU WANT

The codependent person is so obsessed with the wants and wishes of the chemically dependent person that they lose what they want for themselves. They become experts at manipulating the family to get the sick person what he or she wants, but they become less and less skilled at getting what they want. They feel that they have no wants. They are trying so desperately to control the situation that they have no time for their own needs.

Stop and think for a minute. What do you want out of life? List five things you want.

1. _____
2. _____
3. _____
4. _____
5. _____

Now write a letter to the chemically dependent person telling him or her how you feel. Ask for what you want. Be thorough. Don't leave any of your feelings or wants out. Be completely honest with yourself and the other person. When you have the letter written, put it aside, we will use it later.

## LACK OF TRUST

Family members from a chemically dependent home have been living in a situation where they could not trust anything. They did not know what was going to happen. Family rules changed when the chemically dependent person was intoxicated or hung over. A father who was loving could turn into a monster. A mother who was quiet could turn loud, aggressive, and pushy. Someone who was usually happy could sob hopelessly. There was nothing the family could trust. Alcohol or drugs could change any rule at any time. The atmosphere is permeated by fear. They live in a constant state of tension. When they come home they don't know what to expect. When the car drives up in the driveway they don't know what is going to happen. Things can get out of control in a hurry and the behaviors can be life-threatening. The chemically dependent person and the people around them constantly lie about what the addicted person is doing. They hide how much they are using. They lie about what they are doing. No one in the home can be trusted. No one knows the truth.

This lack of trust builds an atmosphere heavy with fear. The family members are constantly worried about what's going to happen next. What makes this all the worse is they try to hide the family secret from everyone. This increases their feelings of isolation and helplessness.

List five things that happened in your family that convinced you that you could not trust your family members.

1. _____
2. _____
3. _____
4. _____
5. _____

## PEOPLE PLEASING

Codependent people are people pleasers. They will do virtually anything to keep someone else happy. They feel personally responsible for other people's feelings. People pleasers are never interested in what they themselves want, they are interested in what the other person wants. They want to keep the other person happy. They don't care about how they themselves feel. People pleasers will go to incredible lengths to keep other people feeling comfortable. They tell people that they are feeling fine when they are coming apart at the seams. They have a smile for everybody. They are nice, nice, nice. They rarely, if ever, go against the flow of things. They are incapable of saying no. If they say no, they feel guilty. They will allow people to violate their boundaries. They never rock the boat.

List five times when you did something you didn't want to do just to please some other person.

1. _____
2. _____
3. _____
4. _____
5. _____

## FEELINGS OF WORTHLESSNESS

Codependent persons feel that they are worth less than other people. They don't feel that they deserve the good stuff. They have been treated so badly, and have been taken advantage of so many times, and given of themselves without getting anything back so often, that they have given up. They are tired. They feel burdened. It's like carrying the world around on your shoulders. Somewhere, deep down in a secret part of their minds, they fear that they deserve to be treated poorly. They feel like they are a small person of little worth. They feel like they don't matter. They are not important. These codependent people think they are stupid, unattractive, inadequate, and incompetent. They do not feel capable of dealing with the world. They feel vulnerable, lost, and alone.

When you look at yourself in the mirror, what do you see? (Circle all that apply)

1. I'm stupid.
2. I'm ugly.
3. I'm old.
4. Other people are smarter than I am.
5. I never get the breaks.
6. I hate myself.
7. No one loves me.
8. No one knows me.
9. God made a mistake when God made me.
10. I'm inadequate.

We could go on with the negative self-statements, but you get the idea. Codependents constantly bombard themselves with negative self-talk. The talk is inaccurate and extremely self-damaging. If you use any of the above statements, you must feel terrible about yourself.

Treatment is a time to get accurate. You must learn to live in the real world and see the positive as well as the negative. List 10 positive things about yourself. If you have difficulty, ask someone who knows you to help you.

1. _____
2. _____
3. _____
4. _____
5. _____
6. _____
7. _____
8. _____
9. _____
10. _____

Write these down on a piece of paper and tape it to your mirror. Read them to yourself at least once a day.

## DEPENDENT

Codependent persons are overly dependent. They feel incapable of making good decisions. They don't trust themselves. They get their self-worth from someone else. They may coerce and threaten to leave the addicted spouse, but the thought of leaving fills them with panic. They feel overly vulnerable to the world and everything in it. They don't feel like they can do things on their own. Even if the spouse is incapacitated from the disease, the spouse still feels dependent on that person. "What would I do on my own? What would happen to the children? How would I support myself?" These are all serious questions, and it leaves the codependent person stuck in an intolerable situation. They can't stay and they can't leave. Dependency is fueled by deep-seated feelings of inadequacy and shame. The codependent person doesn't feel capable of doing anything other than holding on.

Do you feel competent to handle life on your own?

_____

_____

_____

## POOR COMMUNICATION SKILLS

Codependents have poor communication skills. They can't ask for what they want or share how they feel. This leaves them incapable of communicating effectively. They are so concerned with how the other person feels, and what the other person wants, that they don't even think about their own needs. Closeness in interpersonal relationships depends on the ability to share the whole truth with someone. You have to be able to tell them how you feel, and ask them for what you want. To be a good communicator you have to be a good listener. You have to probe and question the other person to bring out the whole truth. Codependents don't want to know the truth. The truth is too painful. They are busy keeping the truth from themselves and from everyone else. If they knew the whole truth, they would be terrified.

Codependents feel lonely because they feel like no one knows them. They feel like no one understands them. They try to communicate, but feel the message never really gets across. They feel isolated and trapped.

When is the last time you felt really understood by anybody? Describe the time and person and what it meant to you.

Do you feel the patient understands you?

Yes _____ No _____ Explain your answer.

_____

_____

_____

What are the roadblocks in the way of your communicating openly with others?

_____

_____

_____

## THE TOOLS OF RECOVERY

In treatment you will learn the tools of recovery. The first of these tools is honesty. Without rigorous honesty this program will not work for you. You must tell the truth all the time. You will need to hold family members accountable by constantly sharing your feelings. This takes practice. In treatment you must accept your powerlessness over the disease. If you still think that you can figure it out or work it out, you are still acting codependent.

Alcoholics Anonymous says that probably no human power can remove this disease. The second tool of recovery is a Higher Power. You must choose a Power greater than yourself to turn the problem over to. If you continue to try to handle the problem yourself, you will fail. If you turn the problem over to God, you will succeed. Practice whenever you are faced with a problem. Stop and seek God's will in that matter. Don't try to figure it out for yourself. Ask for God's guidance.

The third tool of recovery is going to meetings. You must attend regular Al-Anon meetings to continue your recovery. If you think that it is only the chemically dependent person who needs to attend meetings, you are off track. You have problems, too. You need treatment to get back on track. Al-Anon groups will give you the support, encouragement, and education that you need for continued recovery.

The fourth tool of recovery is using good interpersonal relationship skills. This means you have to share how you feel and ask for what you want. You have to listen and take the time necessary to develop healthy communication skills. This will not come easily; you have many habits to overcome. You can no longer just do what the other person wants. You can no longer live to please the other person in your life. You must accept the responsibility for your own behavior and allow others to accept the responsibility for their own behavior. You must allow people to suffer the consequences for their actions. You have to stop living for other people and start living for yourself.

Many of you are thinking, "How selfish!" You were taught always to let the other person come first. You were taught it was not right to ask for what you wanted. But you have to love yourself to be happy. If you leave yourself out, you will suffer. God says, love God all you can, love yourself all you can, and love others all you can. That's all we are asking you to do. Bring this exercise and the letter to your family member to the family program.

# Appendix 28

## Personal Recovery Plan

Name: _____    Home Phone: _____

Admission Date: _____    Work Phone: _____

Discharge Date: _____

Name of Concerned Other: _____    Phone: _____

It is important to your recovery to continue to work through your problems on discharge. Your recovery can never stand still. You must be constantly moving forward in your program. Working with your counselor, you must detail exactly what you need to do following inpatient treatment. Each psychological problem or family problem will need a specific plan of action. You must commit yourself to following this recovery plan to the letter. Don't think that your problems are over just because you have completed treatment. Your recovery is just beginning, and you need to work diligently to stay clean and sober.

Make a list of the problems that you need to address in continuing care. Any emotional, family, legal, social, physical, leisure, work, spiritual, or school problem will have to have a plan. How are you going to address that problem in recovery? What is the goal? What do you want to achieve? Develop your personal recovery plan with your counselor's assistance.

A.  Treatment plan for continued sobriety

    1.  Problem 1: _____

        Goal: _____

        Plan: _____

        _____

        _____

        _____

    2.  Problem 2: _____

        Goal: _____

        Plan: _____

        _____

        _____

        _____

    3.  Problem 3: _____

        Goal: _____

        Plan: _____

        _____

        _____

        _____

4. Problem 4: _____

   Goal: _____

   Plan: _____

   _____

   _____

   _____

5. Problem 5: _____

   Goal: _____

   Plan: _____

   _____

   _____

   _____

B. Relapse

In the event of a relapse, list the specific steps you will take to deal with the problem.

_____

_____

_____

_____

C. Support in Recovery

Indicate the AA/NA meetings you will attend each week after discharge. We recommend that you attend at least three meetings per week for the first few months following discharge.

| *Day* | *Time* | *Location* |
|-------|--------|------------|
| _____ | _____ | _____ |
| _____ | _____ | _____ |
| _____ | _____ | _____ |
| _____ | _____ | _____ |
| _____ | _____ | _____ |

D. Indicate when you will attend aftercare group.

| *Day* | *Time* | *Location* |
|-------|--------|------------|
| _____ | _____ | _____ |

E. Who is the AA/NA contact person or persons who can provide you support in early recovery?

Name: _____  Phone: _____

Name: _____  Phone: _____

Name: _____  Phone: _____

F. If you have any problems or concerns in sobriety you can always call the treatment center staff at the following number:

_____

G. If you and your counselor have arranged for further counseling or treatment following discharge, complete the following:

Name of Agency _____

Address _____ Phone _____

First appointment: Day _____ Time _____

H. Make a list of the things you are going to do daily to stay clean and sober.

1. _____
2. _____
3. _____
4. _____
5. _____
6. _____
7. _____
8. _____
9. _____
10. _____

I. You are changing your lifestyle. It will be important to avoid certain people and situations that will put you in a high-risk situation. List the people and places you need to avoid in early recovery.

1. _____
2. _____
3. _____
4. _____
5. _____

## STATEMENT OF COMMITMENT

I understand that the success of my recovery depends on adherence to my recovery plan. The aftercare program has been explained to me and I understand fully what I must do in recovery. I commit myself to following this plan.

_____

Patient's Signature

_____

Staff Member's Signature

Date _____

# *Appendix 29*

## *Sample Discharge Summary*

IDENTIFYING INFORMATION: Mary Louise Roberts is a 45-year-old married white female. She lives in Thomas, Maryland, with her husband Mark and her two daughters. She has lived in Thomas for the last 5 years. She is currently employed as a secretary for Morton Electronics. She was admitted to Keystone Treatment Center on 9-9-91. She was referred by Marcie Frankle, a counselor at the Mandel Mental Health Clinic.

CHIEF COMPLAINT: "Drinking."

ASSESSMENT OF PROBLEM AREAS: The following problems were identified by the clinical staff as needing to be addressed in treatment:

Problem 1. Pathological relationship to alcohol

Problem 2. Depression

Problem 3. Poor interpersonal relationship skills

Problem 4. Unresolved grief

Problem 5. Borderline personality disorder

The following problems were identified and treated by the medical staff.

Problem 2. Depression

Problem 6. Fractured finger

MEDICAL REPORT (This report is completed by the medical staff): Mary's admission lab work and urinalysis were all within normal limits. An admission physical was completed with no significant findings noted. While in treatment, Mary hit a door with her right hand. An X ray was taken on 9-15-91 and it found evidence of a transverse hairline fracture on the radial side of the distal neck of the right fifth metacarpal. No specific treatment was needed. At discharge, Mary voiced no physical complaints. Her hand was observed to be healing. In treatment the patient received a daily multivitamin. We have recommended that the patient continue her multivitamin therapy for at least 6 months following discharge.

Problem 2. Depression

Progress notes: For her major depression, Mary was started on Prozac 20mg q.d. on 9-22-91. No side effects were noted. The medication was reviewed with the patient prior to discharge and a one week supply of Prozac was sent home with her. We have recommended the patient continue to take the medication daily and to see Dr. Frank Smith, of the Mandel Mental Health Clinic, Thomas, Maryland. She has an appointment on 10-5-91 at 3:45 p.m. for a follow-up visit.

TREATMENT PLAN AND PROGRESS NOTES:

Goal 1: Begin a program of recovery congruent with a sober lifestyle.

Progress notes: When Mary first entered treatment, she minimized her drinking behavior and denied the need to be in treatment. She stated that she didn't have a problem with alcohol that was severe enough to require treatment. She completed the Honesty Exercise and she began to see how she was deceiving herself about the extent of her alcohol problem. She was able to trace the family problems that were a direct cause of her drinking behavior. The patient was able to see that the DWI she received last year was directly related to her drinking. During her First Step, Mary was able to share her powerlessness to quit drinking on her own and the unmanageability of her life. Mary began to accept her alcoholism during the second week of treatment. She recognized that she would have to change her attitudes and behaviors if she was going to be able to maintain a sober lifestyle. A major stumbling block to Mary's treatment was her lack of trust. It was difficult for her to trust her interpersonal group for the first

357

few weeks of treatment. As Mary was able to share more in group, she was able to see that the group could be trusted. This was a great relief to the patient and this was a significant move forward in her treatment program. Mary struggled with the same trust issue when she worked through her Second and Third Step. She began to practice prayer and meditation in treatment and this convinced her that there was a Higher Power called God. She completed a Fifth Step with staff clergy and this significantly relieved her. She stated that this was the first time that she had ever told anyone the whole truth. Mary was able to carefully assess high-risk situations for relapse by working through the Relapse Exercise. Her situation of greatest risk appears to be her tendency to become depressed, and this leads her to further drinking. The patient has committed herself to call this treatment center, her sponsor, or her therapist if she begins to feel depressed in continuing care. Mary does state a sincere desire to maintain a sober lifestyle and to live a happy life without alcohol.

Goal 2: To alleviate symptoms of depression

Progress notes: Mary stated on admission that she had been feeling severely depressed for the last 6 months. She had experienced suicidal ideation and had made two suicide attempts before coming into treatment. While in treatment she visited with the staff psychologist and took the Beck Depression Inventory weekly. She read *Coping With Depression* and logged her dysfunctional thoughts. The patient's negative thinking centered around thinking she was ugly, stupid, and inadequate. Once these thoughts were challenged for accuracy, the patient could see that she was pretty, bright, and a capable, wife, mother, and secretary. The patient was placed on medication for her depression. Mary is aware that she has to stay on this medication for at least 6 months. Two weeks after starting the medication and working on correcting her thinking, Mary's Beck Depression Scores began to improve. Her score dropped from severe depression to mild depression over her 4 weeks of treatment. Mary still shows some excessive sadness and she continues to feel overly tired and fatigued. She is sleeping through the night.

Goal 3: Learn and practice healthy interpersonal relationship skills.

Progress notes: Mary has been unable to establish and maintain healthy interpersonal relationships. Her relationship with her husband has been dysfunctional for a number of years. Mary tends to become quickly attracted to men and to think that they are the answer to her problems. When she gets closer to them, she realizes that they have as many problems as she does. She has been involved in several extramarital affairs. In one-to-one counseling, Mary was able to see how alcohol played a significant role in her relationship problems. She usually fought with her husband when drunk and became involved with other men at the bar. The patient was able to see how her parents taught her to keep her feelings to herself. She learned never to ask for anything. The patient completed the Relationship Skills Exercise (Appendix 12) and began to use these skills with her treatment peers. Mary was able to share her feelings with her interpersonal group. Again the trust issue was a hurdle for her. Gradually she was able to ask for what she wanted without feeling guilty. She found out that other people in the program were trustworthy and loyal to her; they could keep information in confidence. Mary was able to work though the Communication Skills Exercise and was able to improve her active listening skills. She began to stop manipulating to get what she wanted and began asking for what she wanted. She worked on developing assertiveness skills and was able to confront people in group about behavior that troubled her. Mary was able to establish many meaningful relationships while in treatment.

Goal 4: Identify her losses and to share her feelings with others. To develop an understanding of the grief process and learn healthy ways of coping with her grief.

Progress notes: Mary lost her mother to cancer 2 years ago and her brother to an automobile accident last March. It became clear to the clinical staff that Mary had not appropriately grieved through these losses in her life. The pain was still very evident in Mary's behavior whenever she would talk about her mother or brother. She would cry for long periods of time whenever these issues were discussed in group. Mary talked about her grief and began to share her feelings in one-to-one counseling and in interpersonal group. Several of her treatment peers had similar losses to report and Mary began to take an active role in getting them to talk about their loss. As she was able to share her pain with the group, Mary's grief began to ease. She wrote a letter of closure to her mother and brother and read these letters to several treatment peers. Mary spoke on several occasions with the staff clergy about the deaths and she began to turn the situation over to the care of God. She began to feel that God was taking good care of her mother and brother and that she would see them again. Mary stated that she felt that her mother and brother would want her to continue with her life and let go of the grief she was feeling. At the end of treatment, Mary was able to talk about the deaths in her family without crying and with new hope about her dependence on God.

Goal 5: Learn coping skills for dealing with symptoms of borderline personality disorder.

Progress notes: Mary has had a persistent affective problem all of her life. She experiences rapid extreme shifts in her feelings from feeling relatively normal to feeling severely angry, depressed, or frightened. The patient had been drinking to relieve herself of these uncomfortable feelings. Her interpersonal relationships have been severely dysfunctional and the patient has felt chronically empty and bored. Mary becomes suicidal and has cut her wrists and arms to relieve herself of her intense psychic pain. During treatment Mary met regularly with the staff psychologist. She learned to identify her feelings and learned what action to take when she was feeling intensely. The patient practiced talking to a staff member or a treatment peer when she was angry or frightened. She learned to get some exercise when she was feeling intense feelings. The patient worked through the Relationship Skills Exercise (Appendix 12) and the Communication Skills Exercise (Appendix 14). She learned how to communicate effectively with others. The patient met with her husband once a week with her primary counselor to work on her marital problems. The patient was referred to Dr. Frank Smith, a psychiatrist who will follow the patient once a week in continuing care.

FAMILY PROGRAM: Mary's husband Mark and her two children Kathy and Tina attended the Family Program. Mary participated in all the family sessions. Mark shared that he has been very frightened by Mary's drinking behavior. He tends to keep his feelings to himself and not to share what he wants from his wife. Mark expressed that he thought that Mary would come around if he could get her to address her alcohol problem. Mark was able to make significant progress in sharing his feelings in the Family Program. He was able to tell Mary of the hurt and the fear he had been feeling when she would go out and stay out all night. He expressed how angry he was at the extramarital affairs, one of which was with his best friend. Mark often openly wept as he shared his feelings. Kathy, the oldest child, age 10, was able to share how she had to take care of her younger sister when Mary was passed out on the couch. She explained how frightening it was to see her mother intoxicated and out of control. Kathy had witnessed one of her mother's suicide attempts and had to call the police to get Mary under control. This child had been more of a mother to Mary than Mary had been to her. It was obvious in the family sessions that this was a very responsible little girl. The youngest child Tina, aged 6, was very quiet during the sessions. She was able to express how frightened she was seeing her father and mother fight. She had also witnessed the suicide attempt. The family had problems severe enough that they were referred to the Mandel Mental Health Clinic for further family counseling. They have an appointment with Marcie Frankle, a marriage and family counselor, on 10-31-91 at 4 p.m.

SUMMARY: While in treatment Mary completed the first five steps of the Alcoholics Anonymous Twelve Step Program. She has been introduced to Steps Six though Twelve. She has worked a daily program of recovery while in treatment and she understands what she needs to do to stay sober. Mary has developed a good understanding of her disease and has made significant changes in her attitudes and behaviors that can be used in a sober lifestyle. She is more honest with herself and with others, and she has learned good problem-solving skills. Mary can now use her feelings to help her to solve problems. Mary has begun to resolve her depression and will continue to work on her psychological problems in continuing care. Her marriage is more stable and she is going to continue marriage counseling. She knows how to cope with her feelings without drinking. She has worked though her grief issues and has established conscious contact with her Higher Power. Mary is willing to take the responsibility for her own life and behavior.

PROGNOSIS: Good. Mary has a positive attitude toward recovery. She made progress in treatment in many areas and she worked hard. She has shown that she is willing to work to maintain her sobriety. She established many supportive relationships in treatment and she plans to build on these friendships in recovery. She has plans to attend AA meetings with a good friend of hers who has 12 solid years of sobriety. Mary will need positive reinforcement in recovery, and she will have to address her depression until it clears. She will need to continue family counseling to stabilize her relationship with her husband and her children. She is aware that she will need to stick close to AA in order to stay in recovery.

AFTERCARE:

1. Complete abstinence from all mood altering chemicals.

2. Attend AA on a regular basis and get an AA sponsor that she can relate to. Mary does have an AA contact person, Cheryl M. 336-2281.

3. Attend aftercare group for a minimum of 6 months on Monday evenings at 7 p.m. at the Thompson Alcohol and Drug Center, 303 Fuller Lane, Thomas, Maryland. Her first appointment has been set with Charlene Schultz on Monday, October 25, 1991, at 1 p.m.

4. Continue to work on a daily spiritual program she began in treatment. Mary will attend church at the Good Faith Lutheran Church. Reverend Bob Luce is the pastor.

5. Continue to check the relapse symptoms daily and work a daily program of relapse prevention.

6. Develop honest and open relationships with others who can aid her in recovery.

7. Avoid old places and people who could trigger relapse symptoms.

8. Continue Prozac therapy and continue to see Dr. Frank Smith for psychotherapy for depression. Her first appointment is at 2:30 p.m. on 10-22-91 at the Mandel Mental Health Clinic, 12 Tigar Street, Thomas, Maryland.

9. Continue family counseling with Marcie Frankle of Mandel Mental Health Clinic, 12 Tigar Street, Thomas, Maryland. The first appointment is 1:30 p.m. on 10-22-91.

10. Continue to trust herself and praise herself in recovery. She will practice self-affirmations daily.

*DSM-III-R* DIAGNOSIS:

| | |
|---|---|
| AXIS I: | 303.90 Alcohol Dependence, severe |
| | 296.25 Major Depression, single episode in partial remission |
| AXIS I: | 301.83 Borderline Personality Disorder |
| AXIS III: | Asthma |
| AXIS IV: | Severity of Psychosocial Stressors: Personal Illness, Death in the family, Severity IV—Severe |
| AXIS V: | Current Global Assessment of Functioning—70 |

# Appendix 30

## Stress Management
Robert R. Perkinson, Ph.D.

Unresolved stress fuels chemical dependency. Addicted individuals deal with stress by using chemicals rather than using other more appropriate coping skills. Everyone has stress and everyone needs to learn how to manage the stress in their life. Stress is the generalized physiological response to a stressor. A stressor is any demand made on the body.

A stressor can be anything that mobilizes the body for change. This can include psychological or physiological loss, absence of stimulation, excessive stimulation, frustration of an anticipated reward, conflict, or the presentation of and anticipation of painful events (Zegans, 1982).

The stress response is good and adaptive. It activates the body for problem solving. Stress is destructive only when it is chronic. The overstressed body breaks down. Initially, the body produces certain chemicals to handle the stressful situation. Initially, these chemical changes are adaptive, but in the long run, they are destructive. Severe or chronic stress has been linked to irreversible disease, including kidney impairment, high blood pressure, arteriosclerosis, ulcer, and a compromised immune system that can result in increased infections and cancer (Selye, 1956).

When animals are put in a situation with an unsolvable problem, they ultimately get sick. They fall victim to a wide variety of physical and mental disorders. Under chronic stress, the organism ultimately dies.

It seems that everyone has a genetic predisposition to break down in a certain organ system when under chronic stress. Some people get depressed, some get ulcers, and some become chemically dependent.

In treatment, you must learn how to deal with stress in ways other than by using chemicals. You must learn to use the stress signals that your body gives you to help you solve problems. If you can't solve the problem yourself, you need to get some help.

Most people who are chemically dependent are dealing with unresolved pain that they have never worked through. They begin drinking or using chemicals to ease the pain and soon they become chemically dependent. Addiction is a primary disease; it takes over the person's life and makes everything worse.

Stress management techniques help addicted individuals to regain the control they have lost in their lives. By establishing and maintaining a daily program of recovery, they learn how to cope with stress. If you are dealing with stress better, you are not as likely to relapse. There are three elements necessary to reduce your overall stress level: a regular exercise program, regular relaxation, and a change in lifestyle.

## RELAXATION

For centuries people have relaxed to quiet the mind and reach a state of peace. When animals have enough to eat and they are safe, they lie down. People don't do that because humankind is the only animal that worries about the future. We fear that if we relax today, we will be in trouble tomorrow.

Herbert Benson (1975) has shown that if people relax twice a day for 10 to 20 minutes, it has a major impact on their overall stress level. People who do this have fewer illnesses, they feel better, and they are healthier. Illnesses such as high blood pressure, ulcers, and headaches can go away completely with a regular relaxation program.

Benson found that the relaxation technique is simple.

1. Sit or lie down in a quiet place.

2. Pay attention to your breathing.

3. Every time you exhale, say the word "one" over quietly to yourself. It's normal for other ideas to come, but when they do, just return to the word "one."

4. Do this for 10 to 20 minutes twice a day.

You don't have to use the word "one," you can use any other word or phrase of your choice, but it has to be the same word or phrase, over and over again. You can get some relaxation tapes or music that you find relaxing. You can pray or meditate. The most important thing is to relax as completely as you can. If you do this, your stress level will be lower, and you will be better able to mobilize yourself to deal with stress when it occurs.

As you practice relaxation, you will learn how it feels to be relaxed. try to keep this feeling all day. When you feel stressed, stop and take two deep breaths. Breathe in through your nose and out through your mouth. As you exhale, feel a warm wave of relaxation flow down your body. Once you have regained your state of relaxation, return to your day, and move a little slower this time. Remember, nothing is ever done too well or too slowly. You don't have to do things quickly to succeed.

When you come to something new that you think you need to do, ask yourself several important questions.

1. Do I have to do this?
2. Do I have to do it now?
3. Is this going to make a difference in my life?

If the new stressor is not that important, perhaps you shouldn't do it at all. Don't decide to overly stress yourself—that doesn't make any sense. Know your limits. Achieve a state of relaxation in the morning, and listen to your body all day long. If anything threatens your serenity, turn it over and let God deal with it.

For the next week, set aside two times a day for relaxation. Go through the meditation exercise we discussed or some other relaxation exercise. Score the level of relaxation you achieved from 1, as little as possible, to 100, as much as possible. Then score your general stress level during the day the same way. Write down any comments about your stress. List the situations when you felt the most tension.

DAY 1
Relaxation Score _____
Daily Stress Score _____
Comments _____
_____
_____

DAY 2
Relaxation Score _____
Daily Stress Score _____
Comments _____
_____
_____

DAY 3
Relaxation Score _____
Daily Stress Score _____
Comments _____
_____
_____

DAY 4

Relaxation Score _____

Daily Stress Score _____

Comments _____

_____

_____

DAY 5

Relaxation Score _____

Daily Stress Score _____

Comments _____

_____

_____

DAY 6

Relaxation Score _____

Daily Stress Score _____

Comments _____

_____

_____

DAY 7

Relaxation Score _____

Daily Stress Score _____

Comments _____

_____

_____

## EXERCISE

The role of exercise in the treatment of chemical dependency has been well established. Significant improvements in physical fitness can occur in as little as 20 days. People who maintain a regular exercise program feel less depressed and less anxious; they improve their self-concept and enhance the quality of their life (Folkin & Sime, 1981).

Most chemically dependent people come into treatment in poor physical and mental shape. They gave up on exercise a long time ago. Even if they were in good physical condition at one time in their lives, the chemicals have taken their toll. They are unable to maintain a consistent level of physical fitness. The mind and body cannot maintain a regular exercise program when a person chronically abuses drugs or alcohol.

An exercise program, while it is difficult to develop, can be fun. You get a natural high from exercise that you don't get any other way. It feels good and it feels good all day.

A good exercise program includes three elements: stretching, strength, and cardiovascular fitness. The exercise therapist will assist you in developing an individualized program specific to you.

Stretching means you increase a muscle's range of motion until you become supple and flexible. Never stretch your muscles to the point of pain. The body will warn you well before you go too far. Let the exercise therapist show you how to stretch each major muscle group. Get into a habit of stretching before all exercise.

In a strength program, you gradually lift more weight until you become stronger. Don't lift more often than every other day. The muscles need a full day of rest to repair themselves. Soon you can increase the load. Three sets of 10 repetitions each is a standard exercise for each muscle group. The exercise therapist will show you how to complete each exercise. Correct technique is very important.

Endurance training means that you exercise at a training heart rate for an extended period of time. This is how the cardiovascular system gets stronger. Your training heart rate is calculated by taking your age, minus the number 220, multiplied by .75.

Cardiovascular fitness is attained when you exercise at a training heart rate for 20 minutes three times a week. Have the exercise therapist help you determine your training heart rate, and develop a program in which you gradually increase your cardiovascular fitness. Usually you will be increasing your exercise by 10% a week.

Many forms of exercise can be beneficial for cardiovascular training. The key point is this: It must be sustained exercise for at least 20 minutes. It can't be a stop-start exercise, such as tennis or golf. It must be something you can sustain. These are exercises such as jogging, walking, swimming, biking, and the like.

After you have worked out your exercise program, keep a daily log of your exercise. Reinforce yourself when you reach one of your goals. You may have a goal of running a mile by the end of the month. If you reach your goal, buy yourself something you want, or treat yourself to a movie to celebrate. Write down your exercise schedule for the next month.

## EXERCISE PROGRAM

Date _____ Training Heart Rate _____

Strength

_____

_____

_____

Stretching

_____

_____

_____

Cardiovascular Fitness

_____

_____

_____

## CHANGING YOUR LIFESTYLE

Along with maintaining a regular relaxation and exercise time, you must change other aspects of your life to improve your stress management skills.

## Problem-Solving Skills

You need to be able to identify and respond to the problems in your life. Unsolved problems increase your stress level. Problems are a normal part of life, and you need specific skills to deal with them effectively. For each problem, work through the following steps:

1. Identify the problem.
2. Clarify your goals. What do you want?
3. Consider every alternative of action.
4. Think through each alternative, eliminating one at a time, until you have the best alternative.
5. Act on the problem.
6. Evaluate the effect of your action.

Work through several problems with your counselor or group while in treatment. See how effective it is to seek the advice and council of others. You need ask for help.

## Developing Pleasurable Activities

One of the things that chemically dependent people fear the most is not being able to have fun clean and sober. Chemicals have been involved in pleasurable activities for so long that they are directly equated with all pleasure. To look forward to a life without being able to have fun is intolerable.

You don't give up fun in sobriety—you just change the way you have fun. You can't use chemicals for pleasure anymore. This is not good for you. But you can enjoy many pleasant activities without drugs or alcohol. If you think about it, this is real fun anyway. The fun you are missing is based on a false chemically created feeling. Once you see how much fun you can have clean and sober, you will be amazed.

Increasing pleasurable activities will elevate your mood and decrease your overall stress level. If you are not feeling well in recovery, it is likely that you are not involved in enough pleasurable activities. If you increase the level of pleasure, you will feel better, and be less vulnerable to relapse.

First, identify the things that you might enjoy doing, and then make a list of the things you are going to do more often. Make a list of the activities you plan to do for yourself each day. Write down your plan. The more pleasurable things you do, the better you will feel.

1. Being in the country
2. Wearing expensive clothes
3. Talking about sports
4. Meeting someone new
5. Going to a concert
6. Playing baseball or softball
7. Planning trips or vacations
8. Buying things for yourself
9. Going to the beach
10. Doing artwork
11. Rock climbing or mountaineering
12. Playing golf
13. Reading
14. Rearranging or redecorating your room or house
15. Playing basketball or volleyball
16. Going to a lecture
17. Breathing the clean air
18. Writing a song
19. Boating
20. Pleasing your parents
22. Watching TV
23. Thinking quietly
24. Camping
25. Working on machines (cars, bikes, motors)
26. Working in politics
27. Thinking about something good in the future
28. Playing cards
29. Laughing
30. Working puzzles, crosswords, etc.
31. Having lunch with a friend or associate
32. Playing tennis

33. Taking a bath
34. Going for a drive
35. Woodworking
36. Writing a letter
37. Being with animals
38. Riding in an airplane
39. Walking in the woods
40. Having a conversation with someone
41. Working at your job
42. Going to a party
43. Going to church functions
44. Visiting relatives
45. Going to a meeting
46. Playing a musical instrument
47. Having a snack
48. Taking a nap
49. Singing
50. Acting
51. Working on crafts
52. Being with your children
53. Playing a game of chess or checkers
54. Putting on makeup, fixing your hair
55. Visiting people who are sick or shut in
56. Bowling
57. Talking with your sponsor
58. Gardening or doing lawn work
59. Dancing
60. Sitting in the sun
61. Sitting and thinking
62. Praying
63. Meditating
64. Listening to the sounds of nature
65. Going on a date
66. Listening to the radio
67. Giving a gift
68. Reaching out to someone who is suffering
69. Getting or giving a message or back rub
70. Talking to your spouse
71. Talking to a friend
72. Watching the clouds
73. Lying in the grass
74. Helping someone
75. Hearing or telling jokes
76. Going to church
77. Eating a good meal

78. Hunting
79. Fishing
80. Looking at the scenery
81. Working on improving your health
82. Going downtown
83. Watching a sporting event
84. Going to a health club
85. Learning something new
86. Horseback riding
87. Going out to eat
88. Talking on the telephone
89. Daydreaming
90. Going to the movies
91. Being alone
92. Feeling the presence of God
93. Smelling a flower
94. Looking at a sunrise
95. Doing a favor for a friend
96. Meeting a stranger
97. Reading the newspaper
98. Swimming
99. Walking barefoot
100. Playing catch or Frisbee
101. Cleaning your house or room
102. Listening to music
103. Knitting or crocheting
104. Having house guests
105. Being with someone you love
106. Having sexual relations
107. Going to the library
108. Watching people
109. Repairing something
110. Bicycling
111. Smiling at people
112. Caring for houseplants
113. Collecting things
114. Sewing
115. Going to garage sales
116. Water skiing
117. Surfing
118. Traveling
119. Teaching someone
120. Washing your car
121. Eating ice cream

Social Skills

What you do socially, can turn people off, or turn them on. If you do any of the following, you might be turning people off.

1. Not smiling
2. Failing to make eye contact
3. Not talking
4. Complaining
5. Telling everyone your troubles
6. Not responding to people
7. Whining
8. Being critical
9. Poor grooming
10. Not showing interest in people
11. Ignoring people
12. Having an angry look
13. Nervous gestures
14. Feeling sorry for yourself
15. Always talking about the negative

You are turning people on if you do the following:

1. Smile.
2. Look into people's eyes.
3. Express your concern.
4. Talk about pleasant things.
5. Be reinforcing.
6. Tell people how nice they look.
7. Be appreciative.
8. Tell people you care.
9. Listen.
10. Touch.
11. Ask people to do something with you.
12. Act interested.
13. Use people's names.
14. Talk about the positive.
15. Groom yourself well.

To have good social skills, you have to be assertive. You can't passive or aggressive. All this means is that you have to tell people how you feel and ask for what you want, even if it makes people feel uncomfortable. You must tell the truth at all times. If you withhold information or distort it, you will never be close to anyone.

Don't tell other people what to do—ask. Don't let other people tell you what to do—negotiate. Don't yell—explain. Don't throw your weight around. When you are wrong, promptly admit it. Happiness is giving to others: The more you give, the more you get.

In the AA/NA program, you never have to be alone. Your Higher Power is always with you. Learn to enjoy the presence of God, and communicate with God as if He were standing right beside you. Call someone in the program every day. Go to a lot of meetings. Reach out to those who are still suffering. Many people in jails or hospitals need your help. Volunteer to be on the AA/NA hotline. Ask people out for coffee after meetings. Don't worry if you are doing all of the asking at first—the reason you are doing this is for yourself. Most people, particularly men, feel very uncomfortable asking others to go out with them, but don't let that stop you. If you don't ask, you won't have the experience of someone saying yes.

Using the pleasant activities list, make a plan for how you are going to increase your social interaction this month. Write it all down and reward yourself when you make progress. Here are a few hints to get you going:

1. Read the activities and entertainment section of your local newspaper. Mark down interesting events that fit into your schedule and go.
2. Offer to become more involved in your AA/NA group.
3. Ask the local Chamber of Commerce for information about groups and activities in the area.
4. Spend your weekends exploring new parts of town.
5. Smile.
6. Join other self-help support groups such as an Adult Children of Alcoholics group or a singles group.
7. Join a church and get involved. Tell the pastor that you want to do something to help.
8. Volunteer your services to a local charity or hospital. Help others, and share your experience, strength, and hope.
9. Join a group that does interesting things in the area, hiking, skydiving, hunting, bird watching, theater group, sports club, senior centers, and so on. Check the local library for a list of such clubs and activities.
10. Ask someone in the program about interesting things to do in the area.
11. Go to an intergroup dance.
12. Go to an AA/NA conference.

The most important thing to remember is that you are in recovery. You are starting a new life. To do this, you must take risks. You must reach out like you have never done before.

# Appendix 31

## The Beck Depression Inventory

*Instructions:* On this questionnaire are groups of statements. Please read each group of statements carefully. Then pick out the one statement in each group that best describes the way you have been feeling the *past week, including today!* Circle the number beside the statement you picked. If several statements in the group seem to apply equally well, circle each one.

Be sure to read all the statements in each group before making your choice.

1. 0   I do not feel sad.
   1   I feel sad.
   2   I am sad all the time and I can't snap out of it.
   3   I am so sad or unhappy that I can't stand it.

2. 0   I am not particularly discouraged about the future.
   1   I feel discouraged about the future.
   2   I feel I have nothing to look forward to.
   3   I feel the future is hopeless and that things cannot change.

3. 0   I do not feel like a failure.
   1   I feel I have failed more than the average person.
   2   As I look back on my life, all I can see is a lot of failure.
   3   I feel I am a complete failure as a person.

4. 0   I get as much satisfaction out of things as I used to.
   1   I don't enjoy things the way I used to.
   2   I don't get real satisfaction out of anything anymore.
   3   I am dissatisfied or bored with everything.

5. 0   I don't feel particularly guilty.
   1   I feel guilty a good part of the time.
   2   I feel quite guilty most of the time.
   3   I feel guilty all of the time.

6. 0   I don't feel I am being punished.
   1   I feel I may be punished.
   2   I expect to be punished.
   3   I feel I am being punished.

Used with permission: A. T. Beck, C. H. Ward, M. Mandelson, et al. (1961), An inventory for measuring depression, *Archives of General Psychiatry, 4,* 561-571. Copyright 1961, American Medical Association.

7.  0   I don't feel disappointed in myself.
    1   I am critical of myself for my weaknesses or mistakes.
    2   I blame myself all the time for my faults.
    3   I blame myself for everything bad that happens.

8.  0   I don't have any thoughts of killing myself.
    1   I have thoughts of killing myself, but I would not carry them out.
    2   I would like to kill myself.
    3   I would kill myself if I had the chance.

9.  0   I don't cry any more than usual.
    1   I cry more now than I used to.
    2   I cry all the time now.
    3   I used to be able to cry, but now I can't cry even though I want to.

10. 0   I am no more irritated now than I ever am.
    1   I get annoyed or irritated more easily than I used to.
    2   I feel irritated all the time now.
    3   I don't get irritated at all by the things that used to irritate me.

11. 0   I have not lost interest in other people.
    1   I am less interested in other people than I used to be.
    2   I have lost most of my interest in other people.
    3   I have lost all interest in other people.

12. 0   I make decisions about as well as I used to.
    1   I put off making decisions more than I used to.
    2   I have greater difficulty in making decisions than before.
    3   I can't make decisions at all anymore.

13. 0   I don't feel I look any worse than I used to.
    1   I am worried that I am looking old or unattractive.
    2   I feel there are permanent changes in my appearance that make me look unattractive.
    3   I believe that I look ugly.

14. 0   I can work about as well as before.
    1   It takes an extra effort to get started at doing something.
    2   I have to push myself very hard to do anything.
    3   I can't do any work at all.

15. 0   I can sleep as well as before.
    1   I don't sleep as well as I used to.
    2   I wake up 1-2 hours earlier than usual and find it hard to get back to sleep.
    3   I wake up several hours earlier than I used to and cannot get back to sleep.

16.  0  I don't get more tired than usual.

 1  I get tired more easily than I used to.

 2  I get tired from doing almost anything.

 3  I am too tired to do anything.

17.  0  My appetite is no worse than usual.

 1  My appetite is not as good as it used to be.

 2  My appetite is much worse now.

 3  I have no appetite at all anymore.

18.  0  I haven't lost much weight, if any, lately. I have been trying to lose weight _____ yes _____ no

 1  I have lost more than 5 pounds.

 2  I have lost more than 10 pounds.

 3  I have lost more than 15 pounds.

19.  0  I am no more worried about my health than usual.

 1  I am worried about physical problems such as aches and pains, or upset stomach, or constipation.

 2  I am very worried about physical problems and it's hard to think of much else.

 3  I am so worried about my physical problems that I cannot think about anything else.

20.  0  I have not noticed any recent change in my interest in sex.

 1  I am less interested in sex than I used to be.

 2  I am much less interested in sex now.

 3  I have lost interest in sex completely.

Score _____

# Appendix 32

## *Biopsychosocial Assessment*
### Robert R. Perkinson, Ph.D.

DATE: ____ ____ 19____

PATIENT NAME: _____

DEMOGRAPHIC DATA:

Age _____ marital status _____ race _____ sex _____ children _____

Residence: _____

Others in residence: _____

Length of residence: _____

Education:

☐ less than sixth grade      ☐ high school graduate

☐ sixth grade      ☐ some college

☐ seventh grade      ☐ college graduate

☐ eighth grade      ☐ postgraduate work

☐ some high school      ☐ postgraduate degree

Occupation: _____

Characteristics of informant:

☐ reliable      ☐ unreliable

CHIEF COMPLAINT:

_____

_____

_____

## BIOPSYCHOSOCIAL ASSESSMENT

HISTORY OF THE PRESENT ILLNESS (age of onset, duration, patterns and consequences of use, current use, last use, previous treatments, tolerance, blackouts, symptoms of abuse or dependence):

PAST HISTORY:

Place of birth: _____ DOB: ____ ____ 19___

☐ Developmental Milestones:      ☐ toilet training

☐ normal      ☐ reading

☐ walking      ☐ spelling

☐ talking      ☐ arithmetic

Specific disabilities _____

Raised with:

☐ mother                              ☐ brothers

☐ father                              ☐ sisters

Birth order: _____

Significant others: _____

Ethnic/cultural heritage: _____

Describes home life as: _____

_____

_____

_____

Grade school: _____

_____

High school: _____

_____

College: _____

_____

Military history:

  Branch: _____

  Highest rank: _____

  Discharge status: _____

  Problems: _____

Occupational history:

  Longest job held: _____

  Length of time at current job: _____

  Employment satisfaction: _____

  Work problems: _____

Financial history:

  ☐ good            ☐ fair            ☐ poor

Current annual income _____

Gambling history:

  ☐ none

  Gambling problems _____

Sexual history:

  Sexual orientation _____

  Physical abuse _____

  Sexual abuse _____

Current sexual history: _____

_____

Relationship history: _____

_____

_____

Recovery environment: _____ family _____ friends

Spiritual history:

☐ believes in God          ☐ agnostic

☐ Higher Power          ☐ atheist

Religious activities: _____

Church:

☐ denomination

☐ attends weekly          ☐ rarely

☐ occasionally          ☐ never

Legal history:

Arrests: _____

Pending litigation: _____

Self-identified strengths: _____

_____

Self-identified weaknesses: _____

_____

Leisure activities: _____

Depression: _____

Mania: _____

Anxiety: _____

Panic attacks: _____

Agoraphobia: _____

Phobias: _____

Eating disorder: _____

## MEDICAL HISTORY

Illnesses:

☐ measles          ☐ pneumonia

☐ mumps          ☐ tonsillitis

☐ chicken pox

☐ whooping cough          ☐ appendicitis

☐ others _____

Hospitalizations:

☐ tonsillectomy and adenoidectomy                    ☐ appendectomy

Chemical dependency

_____

_____

Allergies:  environmental allergens _____

Medications at present: _____

_____

## FAMILY HISTORY

Father:  age: _____

health:

☐ good          ☐ fair          ☐ poor

Described as: _____

_____

Mother:  age: _____

health:

☐ good          ☐ fair          ☐ poor

Described as: _____

_____

Other relatives with significant psychopathology: _____

_____

_____

## BIOPSYCHOSOCIAL ASSESSMENT

MENTAL STATUS EXAMINATION:

Description:

☐ well-developed, well-nourished          ☐ thin

☐ obese                                   ☐ underweight

age _____    race _____    sex _____    hair _____    eyes _____

distinguishing marks or characteristics _____

Appearance:

☐ same as stated age                      ☐ older than stated age

☐ younger than stated age

Dress:

☐ casual                                  ☐ meticulously neat

☐ appropriate                             ☐ seductive

☐ disheveled                              ☐ eccentric

☐ other _____

Personal hygiene:

☐ good          ☐ fair          ☐ poor

Sensorium:

☐ clear

☐ alert                    ☐ lethargic

☐ vigilant                 ☐ drowsy

☐ other _____

Factors affecting sensorium:

☐ alcohol                  ☐ medications

☐ drugs                    ☐ withdrawal symptoms

☐ other _____

Orientation:

person: _____

place: _____

time: _____

situation: _____

Attitude toward the examiner:

☐ cooperative              ☐ distant

☐ friendly                 ☐ aloof

☐ pleasant                 ☐ casual

☐ suspicious               ☐ overly intellectual

☐ hostile                  ☐ neutral

☐ passive                  ☐ apprehensive

☐ dependent                ☐ seductive

☐ withdrawn

Motor behavior:

☐ normal                   ☐ physical agitation

☐ continuous movements, restlessness    ☐ tremor

Unusual and inappropriate movements

☐ slow, retarded           ☐ inappropriate

☐ tics                     ☐ hand wringing

☐ tearful                  ☐ pacing

☐ rigid                    ☐ apprehensive

☐ tense                    ☐ angry

☐ slouched

Eye contact:

- ☐ appropriate
- ☐ poor eye contact with examiner

Gait:

- ☐ normal
- ☐ shuffling
- ☐ other _____
- ☐ wide-based
- ☐ unsteady

Primary facial expression during interview:

- ☐ normal and responsive
- ☐ sad
- ☐ neutral
- ☐ other _____
- ☐ hostile
- ☐ worried

Speech quantity:

- ☐ normal
- ☐ talkative
- ☐ garrulous
- ☐ unspontaneous
- ☐ spontaneous
- ☐ minimally responsive

Speech quality:

- ☐ normal
- ☐ slow
- ☐ rapid
- ☐ pressured
- ☐ hesitant
- ☐ emotional
- ☐ monotonous
- ☐ soft
- ☐ loud
- ☐ slurred
- ☐ mumbled

Speech impairment:

- ☐ none
- ☐ stuttering
- ☐ other _____
- ☐ marked by accent
- ☐ articulation problem

Mood:

- ☐ calm
- ☐ cheerful
- ☐ anxious
- ☐ depressed
- ☐ fearful
- ☐ tearful
- ☐ pessimistic
- ☐ other _____
- ☐ neutral
- ☐ optimistic
- ☐ elated
- ☐ euphoric
- ☐ irritable
- ☐ angry

Client report of depression:

☐ none                    ☐ moderate

☐ mild                    ☐ severe

Episodes of depression:

☐ none                    ☐ frequently in the past 6 months

☐ one or two episodes in the past 6 months    ☐ continuously in the past 6 months

Client report of symptoms of depression:

☐ none                    ☐ sleep disturbance

☐ poor appetite           ☐ fatigue

☐ loss of interests

☐ guilt                   ☐ weight loss

☐ motor retardation       ☐ loss of interest in sex

☐ other _____

Observed signs of anxiety in interview:

☐ none                    ☐ apprehensive manner

☐ physical indications     ☐ problems in attention

☐ other _____

Client report of anxiety:

☐ none                    ☐ moderate

☐ mild                    ☐ severe

Episodes of anxiety:

☐ none                    ☐ frequently in the past 6 months

☐ one or two episodes in past 6 months    ☐ continuously in the past 6 months

Client report of symptoms of anxiety:

☐ none                    ☐ paresthesias

☐ shortness of breath      ☐ muscle aches

☐ palpitations            ☐ cold hands

☐ chest pain              ☐ gastrointestinal symptoms

☐ dizziness

☐ faintness               ☐ muscle twitching

☐ sweating                ☐ dry mouth

☐ other _____

Range of affect:
- ☐ appropriate
- ☐ labile
- ☐ blunted
- ☐ dramatized
- ☐ restricted
- ☐ contradictory
- ☐ flat
- ☐ other _____

Thought processes:
- ☐ logical and coherent
- ☐ neologisms
- ☐ blocking
- ☐ preservation
- ☐ circumstantial
- ☐ evasive
- ☐ tangential
- ☐ distracted
- ☐ flight of ideas
- ☐ loose associations
- ☐ incoherent
- ☐ clang associations
- ☐ other _____

Thought content—preoccupations:
- ☐ none
- ☐ violent acts
- ☐ presenting problem
- ☐ somatic symptoms
- ☐ obsessions
- ☐ guilt
- ☐ compulsions
- ☐ worthlessness
- ☐ phobias
- ☐ religious issues
- ☐ suicide
- ☐ sex
- ☐ other _____

Thought content—delusions:
- ☐ none
- ☐ jealousy
- ☐ persecution
- ☐ grandiosity
- ☐ somatic
- ☐ religious
- ☐ ideas of reference
- ☐ influence by others
- ☐ thought broadcasting
- ☐ control
- ☐ other _____

Description of delusional material _____
_____

Quality of delusional material:
- ☐ systematized
- ☐ poorly organized

Disorders of perception:
- ☐ none
- ☐ auditory hallucinations
- ☐ tactile hallucinations
- ☐ visual hallucinations
- ☐ gustatory hallucinations incorporated into delusions
- ☐ olfactory hallucinations
- ☐ fragmented, not incorporated into delusions

Suicidal ideation:

☐ none  ☐ ideation  ☐ plan

detail of current plans _____

history of suicidal acts _____

_____

Homicidal ideation:

☐ none  ☐ ideation  ☐ plan

detail of current plans _____

history of violent acts _____

_____

Obsessions:

☐ none  ☐ death

☐ illness  ☐ contamination

☐ violence  ☐ doubt

☐ other _____

Compulsions:

☐ none

☐ hand washing  ☐ checking

☐ counting  ☐ touching

☐ other _____

Phobias:

☐ none  ☐ insects

☐ public places  ☐ dogs

☐ closed spaces  ☐ social security

☐ heights  ☐ rodents

☐ snakes  ☐ travel

☐ flying

☐ other _____

Estimated range of intellectual ability:

☐ normal  ☐ below average

☐ above average  ☐ borderline retarded

☐ superior  ☐ retarded

Abstracting ability:

☐ normal  ☐ impaired

Disturbances in consciousness:

☐ no recent disturbances        ☐ recent history of seizures

☐ recent history of loss of consciousness        ☐ recent history of blackouts

Concentration:

☐ normal        ☐ moderately impaired

☐ mildly impaired        ☐ severely impaired

Memory functions:

☐ intact        ☐ recent memory deficit

☐ immediate memory deficit        ☐ remote memory deficit

Confabulations:

☐ none        ☐ suspected        ☐ definite

Amnesia:

☐ none        ☐ less than one month

☐ less than one day        ☐ several months

☐ less than one week        ☐ years

Impulse control:

☐ good        ☐ fair        ☐ poor

Judgment:

☐ good        ☐ fair        ☐ poor

Insight:

☐ minimal, no understanding of problem or acceptance of personal responsibility

☐ insightful, accepts personal responsibility and desires professional assistance

# *Appendix 33*

## *Anger Management*
### Robert R. Perkinson, Ph.D.

Anger is a feeling that helps you to adapt to your environment. It is designed to make stress stop. It helps you establish and maintain boundaries around yourself. It gives you the energy and direction to defend yourself from a physical attack.

Chronic anger is painful. It results in broken relationships. It doesn't help, it hurts. Studies show that people who are chronically angry die years earlier than they have to. They have more colds and flus, more mental and physical illnesses. Chronic anger has many painful consequences.

The reason you are reading this exercise is that your anger sometimes gets out of control. When you are angry you do things that you feel guilty about later. Chronic anger is a shameful cycle of pain. You don't want to hurt others, but you find yourself doing it anyway, over and over again.

A lot of this exercise was taken from *When Anger Hurts* by McKay, Rogers, and McKay (1989). When you have the opportunity, get this book and read it. This exercise will help you manage your anger. It will not be easy, and you will have to work very hard. Learning new behaviors takes a lot of practice. You have had years of training in how to act angry, now you need to learn new skills to deal with problems. Using the techniques described here will enable you to feel angry less often. When you feel angry, you will be able to solve problems rather then make them worse.

### YOUR ANGER JOURNAL

Keep an anger journal every day. Write down every time you feel angry. Write down exactly what happened, in detail, and rate your angry feelings on a scale of from 1 (as little anger as possible) to 100 (as much anger as possible). Rate your aggressiveness from 1 to 100. The more you look at each situation, the more you will learn about yourself and the more you will learn to control your behavior. Your journal might look something like this:

Dec. 4: 8 a.m. Kathy asked me to take out the garbage three times while I was watching TV. I felt like she was trying to drive me crazy. She knew I had had a hard day and needed some time alone. At the same time, the kids were fighting in the other room.
    Intensity of anger felt: 100
    Aggressiveness: 90. I told her to shut up and leave me alone. I threw a pillow against the wall.

Dec. 4: The sales meeting ended before I got a chance to share my concerns with the boss. I needed to talk to him and reassure him about my work. I know my sales have been falling off a bit lately. I felt more hurt than anything.
    Intensity of anger felt: 75
    Aggressiveness: 0. I didn't do anything but boy, was I fuming.

By monitoring your anger, you will be able to observe your progress. You will feel successful as you see yourself handling your anger better.

### THE ANGER MYTH

There is a myth that anger has to be expressed or you will explode into a violent rage. The anger will build up like water behind a dam. If you don't express it, it will come bursting out all at once destroying everything. Research strongly disagrees with this myth. The research shows that anger doesn't work. The more you act angry or think angry thoughts, the more you feel angry. Anger feeds on itself. It never helps to hit walls or pillows, or to yell. It just makes you act more angry.

## WHAT ANGER DOES TO PEOPLE

1. It stuns and frightens them.
2. It makes them feel bad about themselves.
3. The more anger you express, the less effective your anger becomes. People get used to your anger and shrug you off.
4. People distance themselves from you.
5. Anger cuts you off from genuine closeness.
6. The more you act aggressively, the more you want to continue the attack, really rub their noses in it.
7. Anger causes continued aggression from both parties.
8. Anger doesn't stop, it goes on and on, fueling on itself.
9. You resort to anger over and over again. Each episode gets worse.
10. Anger leads to rigidity. Both parties become stuck and inflexible.
11. Anger breeds the desire for revenge.
12. Anger is trying to control the other person, but inevitably you lose control.
13. Anger causes the other person to act defensive and resistive.
14. People shield themselves from you anger by avoiding you.

Angry people feel like victims, caught in a trap. They desire closeness but have a fear of abandonment. Their friends seem selfish and insensitive, employers cheap and uncaring, lovers unappreciative and withholding. Life is no fun.

### Anger Leads to Helplessness in Four Steps

1. You think something is wrong with you.
2. You think the other person should fix you, but they won't.
3. You blow up at them.
4. The other person withdraws even more.

## ANGER IS A CHOICE!

You don't have to act angry. You can solve your problems in other ways. Up till now, anger has been automatic, a decision made without thinking, a choice made out of habit. You spent years thinking anger was saving you, helping you, while all the time it was hurting you. You want to be loved and accepted. Anger will never get you that. Believe it or not, you can feel angry and act in a way that is more productive. Remember, the function of anger is to stop stress. Stress is your problem, not anger.

### Anger Helps You Cope With Stress in Several Ways

1. Anger blocks the awareness of pain.
2. Anger discharges high levels of fear, hurt, guilt, and sadness.
3. Anger discharges the pain that develops when your needs are frustrated.
4. Anger erases guilt.
5. Anger places the blame on someone else.

There are many ways of discharging stress other than acting angry. You can cry, exercise, work, make a joke, write in your journal, go through a relaxation exercise, verbalize your feelings, ask for what you want, problem solve, listen to music, and many other things.

## ANGER IS A TWO-STEP PROCESS

1. You become aware of stress.
2. You blame someone else.

What will not help you is blaming others or thinking about what they should have done differently.
*Blaming:* To blame, you have to believe that the other person purposely did something wrong that hurt you.
*The should:* To "should," you have to believe that the other person should have known better than to do what he or she did.

"The should" and "blaming" are inaccurate thinking. The truth is that if others had known better, they wouldn't have done it. They weren't trying to hurt you—they were trying to meet their own needs.

### To Rid Yourself of Anger, You Must Stop Blaming Others

The only thing that is always true when you are angry is that you are in pain. The trigger thoughts that fuel your anger are usually false. Your anger may have no legitimate basis. If you use inaccurate thinking, you will generate a storm of inaccurate feelings. Armed with the real facts, you might not get angry at all.

It is not anger that builds, it's stress that builds. You need coping skills to deal with stress.

## WHAT IS STRESSING YOU?

Go back to your anger journal and look at each anger-producing situation.

1. Figure out what was stressing you before you got angry. What was the emotional pain, physical pain, frustration or threat that preceded the anger? Prior to feeling angry, were you aware of any internal feeling of hurt, fear, sadness, or guilt? Did you feel uncomfortable physically or psychologically? Write these things down.
2. Try to figure out the trigger thoughts. What you were thinking between the situation and the anger? Did you use the blame or should. Write down exactly what you were thinking.

Bob came home from work to find several Coke cans lying in the middle of the living room floor. He thought, "The kids know better than this. They only think about themselves. Nobody appreciates what I do around here. They don't care if I come home to a dirty house." Bob rated his anger at 100. He yelled at the kids and scored himself aggressively at 85. Later, he felt guilty about yelling at the children and had to apologize.

### How Bob's Inaccurate Thinking Inflamed His Anger

The kids should know better.
They only think about themselves.
They don't care about me.
Nobody appreciates what I do around here.
I live in a dirty house.

Thinking like that, it's no wonder Bob got angry. But he wasn't thinking accurately. His angry feelings came from inaccurate thinking. He ended up feeling angry because of how he interpreted the actions of others.

## BLAMING

The impulse to assign blame lies at the root of all chronic anger. When you decide who is responsible for your pain, you feel justified in acting aggressively. You see yourself threatened and you need to protect yourself. You are the helpless victim of another person's stupidity or selfishness.

There is pleasure in blaming. You can escape the responsibility for your own problems by blaming someone else. You can turn the focus off of your mistakes and concentrate on the other person's mistakes. The problem with blaming is it isn't true. The truth is, people aren't responsible for your life, you are.

1. You are the only one who understands what you need.
2. Other people need to focus on their own needs.
3. People's needs will occasionally come into conflict with yours.
4. Your satisfaction in life depends on how well *you* meet your needs.

## STRATEGIES FOR GETTING YOUR NEEDS MET

You must develop new skills for meeting your needs better. With your counselor's help, develop the following coping skills and practice them often.

1. Learn to give people rewards when they do something you want them to do. Reinforce each person often. The more reinforcing you act toward others, the more reinforcing they will act toward you.
2. Learn to take care of your needs yourself. Don't count on others to meet your needs.
3. Develop new sources for support, nourishment, and appreciation. Join that AA/NA group and go often. Take someone for coffee. Call your sponsor.
4. Learn to say no.
5. Learn how to share how you feel and ask for what you want.
6. Learn to let go and let God.

## TAKING BACK THE RESPONSIBILITY

Go to your journal and examine your anger generating situations.

1. What was stressing you at the time?
2. What were your trigger thoughts?
3. What could you have done differently?
4. How could you have met your own needs?
5. How could you have found other sources of support?
6. What limits did you fail to set? Were you unable to say no?
7. How could you have negotiated better for what you wanted?
8. How could you have let go and let God?

## COMBATING TRIGGER THOUGHTS

Inaccurate thinking leads you to feel inaccurate pain. If you blame, you judge people all day by your own rules. Someone cuts in front of you in traffic, and you fume, "That idiot knows better than that!" But the fact is that many drivers think it is fine to cut in line. The problem with blaming is that people rarely agree with you. They have their own set of rules and judge themselves by their own standards. People rarely do what they think they should do; they do what works for them.

## The Entitlement Fallacy

The entitlement fallacy is the belief that you deserve things because you want them very badly. Your need justifies the demand that someone should give you what you want. The feeling of entitlement engulfs you. How can the other person say no? The truth is, people will give you what they want to give you and nothing more. They are trying to meet their own needs, not yours.

## The Fallacy of Fairness

The idea here is there is an absolute standard of conduct that everyone has to follow. Everyone should know these rules and follow them. If they don't, they are bad and deserve to be punished. The problem with this thinking is that there is no absolute right or wrong standard of conduct. What is fair is totally subjective. The other person could be functioning from an entirely different set of values.

## Blame

Assigning blame lets you escape the responsibility of handing your problems. Blaming triggers anger by making your pain someone else's fault. Blaming labels people as bad when they are doing all they can do with the coping skills they have at their disposal. By blaming, you punish people for doing things they could not help doing.

## Mind Reading

Sometimes you get angry when you try to read people's minds. You think you know why someone did what they did. You think you have them all figured out. You assume the person did something deliberately to harm you. This is almost never true. The other person is trying to meet their own needs.

## Changing Your Trigger Thoughts

Go back to your anger journal and determine what you were thinking between each situation and the anger. Pull out as many of these trigger thoughts as you can and write them down. This is uncovering your automatic thinking.

Once you have a list of the trigger thoughts, go back and develop thoughts that are accurate. What thinking would have been appropriate for that situation?

You will be amazed at how your inaccurate thinking fuels your anger. Keep a record of your thinking for at least 12 weeks. In time, you will be able to catch yourself in the old thinking. Once you are thinking accurately, you will act appropriately. Soon, the old thinking will not sound so convincing or so right. You won't feel like a victim anymore.

## STOPPING ESCALATION

Gerald Patterson of the Oregon Social Learning Center found that anger between people depends on *aversive chains* of behavior where people attempt to influence each other through a rapid exchange of punishing communications. These chains are more likely to occur when the people have relatively equal power, for example, husband and wife, parents and children, and coworkers. Aversive chains usually begin with small events and develop along predictable lines. Early exchanges are often overlooked because they seem unimportant.

## Aversive Chains Are the Building Blocks to Violence

Most aversive chains never pass beyond the first link. Someone in the family teases or insults another, and there is no response.

Since no one reacts to the provocation, the problem stops after a few seconds. Three or four link chains usually last no longer than a half-minute and exist even in healthy homes. When an aversive chain lasts longer than a half-minute, yelling, threatening, or hitting may occur. The longer a chain lasts, the more likely that things are going to get out of control.

Stop an Aversive Chain at the Earliest Possible Moment

The last link in an aversive chain is a trigger behavior. These behaviors usually precede violence. Triggers are verbal or nonverbal behaviors that bring up feelings of *abandonment* or *rejection*. These feelings are too painful to deal with and the person feeling them needs them to stop them right away.

A variety of statements can put the last link in an aversive chain. These are the responses that you need to eliminate, replacing them with your new coping skills.

Verbal Trigger Behaviors

1. Giving sarcastic advice: "Tell them to give you a raise. We need the money."
2. Global labeling: "Women are all like that."
3. Criticism: "You didn't shovel the walk; you made a little path."
4. Blaming: "If you'd just do some work around here."
5. Abrupt limit setting: "That's it, I'm out of here."
6. Threatening: "If you don't like it, get out."
7. Cursing: "Shut the hell up."
8. Complaining: "Ever since I married you, I've been unhappy."
9. Mind reading: "You're trying to drive me crazy."
10. Stonewalling: "There's nothing more to talk about."
11. Sarcastic observations: "Did you dump the trash in your room?"
13. Humiliating statements: "When we got married, you were better-looking."
14. Dismissing statements: "Get out."
15. Put-downs: "Is this what you call clean?"
16. Accusations: "You did it again, didn't you?"
17. Laying on the guilt: "You know I can't stand that."
18. Ultimatums: "If you don't shape up, I'm leaving."

Nonverbal Trigger Sounds

1. Groaning (I've had it with you)
2. Sighing (You are such a burden)

Voice Quality Triggers

1. Whining (irritating tone)
2. Flatness in voice (like you checked out a long time ago)
3. Cold tone (you'll never reach me)
4. Throaty constriction (barely controlled rage)
5. Loud, harsh tone (threatening)
6. Mocking, contemptuous tone (shaming)
7. Mumbling under your breath (the other person has to guess what you said)
8. Snickering (laughing at the other person)
9. Snarling (you better back off)

Trigger Gestures

1. Finger pointing
2. Shaking a fist
3. Flipping the bird

    4. Folded arms

    5. Waving away

## Trigger Facial Expressions

    1. Looking away

    2. Rolling the eyes

    3. Narrowing the eyes

    4. Widening the eyes

    5. Grimacing

    6. Sneering

    7. Frowning

    8. Tightening the lips

    9. Raising an eyebrow

  10. Scowling

## Trigger Body Movements

    1. Shaking the head

    2. Shrugging the shoulders

    3. Tapping a foot or finger

    4. Leaning forward (intimidating)

    5. Turning away

    6. Putting hands on hips

    7. Moving quickly, suddenly

    8. Kicking or throwing an object

    9. Pushing or grabbing

Spend time each evening reviewing your anger journal. Write down your verbal and nonverbal trigger behaviors. In time you will be able to recognize your patterns. Begin eliminating your trigger behaviors and using your new coping skills instead.

## Example of an Aversive Chain

Bob comes home from the office and sees his spouse Patty sitting quietly on the couch. The boss got on his case again and Bob needs some support. Rather than asking her for what he needs, he says the following:

"I can see you had a hard day in front of the television."

"I've been working my tail off." Patty is instantly defensive.

"I know what you do. You lay around all day." Bob crosses his arms sarcastically.

"I work every bit as hard as you do." Patty looks at him angrily.

"Do I have to cook dinner too?" Bob walks to the kitchen.

"What's wrong with you today?" Patty gets up and follows him.

"Don't yell at me!" Bob screams.

"Nothing I do pleases you anymore." Patty begins crying.

"If you don't like it, get the hell out!" Bob is out of control, shaking with fury.

Bob will not get Patty's support now. He needed his wife to help him, but he got the exact opposite of what he wanted. Now his needs are more frustrated. He fumes and primes himself for the next battle.

At every point along this aversive chain, Bob and Patty could have de-escalated the conflict. Remember, anger is a choice.

## BREAKING AVERSIVE CHAINS

### Time-Out

The best thing you can do when you find yourself in a aversive chain is to call a time-out. The first party to recognize an aversive chain makes a time-out sign (a T made with both hands in front of the body). He or she says, "Time-out." The other person only returns the gesture and says, "Okay, time-out." The party who called time-out then leaves the aversive situation for a predetermined amount of time, usually an hour. The person who leaves agrees to return and work on the problem after the time is up, or to make an appointment to work on it later. Time-out should never be used to avoid a problem. Time-out is meant to avoid escalating stress. Time-out says, "It's time to separate. I'll be right back."

Each person should know exactly what is going to happen after a time-out has been called. They need to be certain the other person is going to return. Abandonment and rejection issues are involved here, and they create a lot of fear. A time-out contract needs to be written and signed by both parties. The couple needs to practice the time-out several times in a nonthreatening situation.

After a called a time-out, wait for your feelings to cool down, then try to get accurate in your thinking. Take out these coping statements and read them to yourself.

"Don't blame."
"Don't try to fix the other person."
"What I can do differently?"
"The other person(s) are not trying to hurt me, they are meeting their own needs."
"The other person(s) are doing the only thing they know how to do at the moment."
"If I want the situation to change, I need to change my behavior."

### Rechannel

If you see yourself in an aversive chain, rechannel the conversation to a subject that is nonthreatening. The earlier in the aversive chain this is done, the more effective it will be. Sometimes you can just keep quiet, and that's enough. Don't fuel the anger with your old trigger behaviors, defuse it with your new coping statements.

"There is no absolutely right or wrong answer here."
"We are both partially right."
"It's time to rechannel this discussion."
"Let's go over this later."
"Can we talk about this in an hour?"

### Inquiry

When you see yourself in an aversive chain, seek information from the other person. This makes them feel important and loved. Remember, anger is a response to pain. Ask the other person about how she or he is feeling and thinking.

"What's hurting you?"
"I'm concerned about you."
"Tell me what is hurting you."
"What do you think we need to do to solve this problem?"

## Mind Reading

Mind reading takes a road map from our past and places it unrealistically over the present. We expect people to respond to us the way others did in the past. If our parents were not trustworthy, we assume other people are not trustworthy. If we got hurt by a past relationship, we expect the same thing from the next relationship.

The key to preventing mind reading is to check it out with the other person. Don't assume you know what they are thinking, ask them.

Once you begin asking the other person how she or he feels and what he or she thinks, you will learn a lot about yourself. You will learn about your old maps and how inaccurate they are.

"How do you feel?"
"What do you want me to do?"
"Tell me more about what you are thinking."
"What do you suggest we do to resolve the problem?"

## IMPROVING SELF-TALK

You need to develop many positive things to say to yourself. Make a list of positive self-statements and keep them with you. When you are feeling uncomfortable, take them out and read them over to yourself. Some work better than others. Memorize the ones that work for you.

"I'm a good person."
"I'm smart and capable."
"I am God's creation."
"No matter what happens, I'm going to be all right."
"I can take care of myself."

### Reassure Yourself

You may have to reassure yourself that you are going to be able to get through an aversive chain.

"I can handle this."
"I can call a time out if I need to."
"If I find myself becoming angry, I can deal with it."
"I can find the appropriate coping strategy."
"I believe in myself."

### Stop Trigger Thoughts

Do not allow yourself to fall back into old thinking. You are not a victim. You always have a choice.

"I'm responsible for what happens to me."
"I am never a victim. I have a choice."
"I can take care of my own needs."
"Don't blame."
"People never do what they should do."
"I am free to do anything I want."
"There is no right or wrong answer."
"The amount of support I'm getting is all I can get at the moment."
"Anger will never get me what I want."
"Don't mind read."

### Physiological Coping

Monitor your physiological functioning. If you feel uptight, tell yourself to relax. This reduces your stress and makes you deal with the situation more accurately.

"Take a deep breath."
"Relax."
"Feel your arms and legs become loose and limp."
"Stay calm."
"Visualize one of your favorite places."

Problem Solving

When you have a problem, use these problem-solving skills. Continue to process through the options until everyone agrees to try a solution.

1. Write the problem down.
2. Communicate your feelings.
3. Ask for what you want.
4. Acknowledge the other person's point of view.
5. Develop a list of options.
6. Discuss the pros and cons of each option.
7. Keep working until you reach a consensus.

## YOUR COPING SCRIPT

Prepare for an angry situation with a set of coping statements. Choose the coping statements that seem to work best for you. You may have to change them from time to time and from situation to situation. What are you going to say to yourself the next time you find yourself getting angry?

_____

To reassure yourself.

_____

To stop the trigger thoughts.

_____

To cope physiologically.

_____

To move to problem solving.

Memorize all four sentences and when you find yourself in an aversive chain, say them over to yourself.

## MOTIVATING YOURSELF

Each morning go over the costs of your anger. Explore its toll on you and those you love. Review the consequences of your last anger episode. Make a contract with your significant other to work on practicing the new coping skills, and practice them often. You can do it.

## TIME-OUT CONTRACT

When I realize that my (or my partner's) anger is rising, I will give a "T" time-out sign and leave at once. I will not hit or kick anything, and I will not slam the door.

I will return no more than one hour later. I will take a walk to use up the energy and will not drink or use drugs while I am away. I will try not to focus on resentments.

When I return, I will start the conversation with, "I know that I was partly wrong and partly right." I will then admit to a mistake that I made.

If my partner gives a "T" sign and leaves, I will return the sign and let my partner go without a hassle, no matter what is going on. I will not drink or use drugs while my partner is away. I will try to avoid focusing on resentments. When my partner returns, I will start the conversation with, "I know that I was partly wrong and partly right." I will then admit to a mistake that I made.

Name _____ Date _____

Name _____ Date _____

# Appendix 34

## *Narcissism*
### Robert R. Perkinson, Ph.D.

This might be a difficult exercise for you to read, so you need to be open-minded and willing to learn something new about yourself. You have some narcissistic traits that get you into trouble and lead you to chemical use. For example, you tend to be too sensitive to criticism. Whenever someone criticizes you, even a little, you get hurt and sometimes retaliate. "How dare you criticize me!" Underneath the anger, you feel wounded. You think you have to be the best, or the brightest, or the most beautiful, or the most successful, to be loved. You do not know how to be genuinely close to others, but you have a great need for people to love you. The real problem is, underneath it all, you do not feel good about yourself. You feel ashamed of who you are. You fear other people are better than you are.

Narcissus was a beautiful person in Greek mythology who refused to love others. As punishment for his indifference, the gods made him fall in love with himself. He became so enamored with himself that he could not stop gazing at his reflection in a pool of water. Finally, he fell in the water and drowned. *Narcissism* is a term for people who have an exaggerated need to be admired. Because of this need, they develop an exaggerated sense of their own importance. They exaggerate their talents, accomplishments, and achievements in order to be respected. They stretch the truth to build a fragile self-image. Narcissistic individuals develop an overwhelming need to feel special, and they expect to be treated in special ways. They become excessively concerned with themselves and their needs, losing the capacity to be sensitive to the needs of others. Their relationships start out well, but end up in disaster. At first everything seems fine, the love is wonderful, but when the other person begins to make demands, the anger gets going.

Alcoholics Anonymous says that this self-centeredness is at the root of our addiction.

> Each person is like an actor who wants to run the whole show; is forever trying to arrange the lights, the ballet, the scenery and the rest of the players in his own way. If his arrangements would only stay put, if only people would do as he wished, the show would be great. Everybody, including himself, would be pleased. Life would be wonderful. In trying to make these arrangements, our actor may sometime be quite virtuous. He may be kind, considerate, patient, generous; even modest and self-sacrificing. On the other hand, he may be mean, egotistical, selfish and dishonest. But as with most humans, he is more likely to have varied traits.
>
> What usually happens? The show doesn't come off very well. He begins to think life doesn't treat him right. He decides to exert himself more. He becomes, on the next occasion, still more demanding or gracious, as the case may be. Still the play does not suit him. Admitting he may be somewhat at fault, he is sure that other people are more to blame. He becomes angry, indignant, self-pitying. What is his basic trouble? Is he not really a self-seeker even when trying to be kind? Is he not a victim of the delusion that he can wrest satisfaction and happiness of this world if he only managed well? (*Alcoholics Anonymous,* 1976, p. 61)

As you read this exercise, you might not think you are self-centered. The very idea may make you feel angry. To have any flaw would dent that perfect image you have of yourself. And that's the problem. As long as you need to be perfect, criticism sends you tumbling into shame. If you need to be right all the time, others never seem to respect you. This is what happens: You think you need to be the best at everything, then someone comes along who is as good as, or better than you are, and you feel humiliated. Critical comments by others send you off the edge of sanity—you fume, you rage, you get even. You cannot stand the suggestion that you are not perfect in every way.

To understand the trap of narcissism, you need to understand the narcissistic traits. Let's look at a few and see if any of them fit you.

1. Do you often desire to be the center of attention?
2. Do you want to be the life of the party?
3. Do you feel resentful when your friends achieve something?
4. Do you feel unappreciated?
5. Do you want a beautiful woman or man to hang all over you so other people can see how wonderful you are?
6. Do think you are more intelligent than most?
7. Do you tend to brag about your accomplishments?
8. Do you make a good first impression but have difficulty following through?
9. Do you think people would be better off if they would follow your direction?
10. Do you tend to resent authority figures?
11. Do you try to control people close to you?
12. Do you have difficulty accepting criticism?
13. Do you tend to be unsatisfied in interpersonal relationships?
14. Are you obsessed with money and material things?
15. Are you good at charming others to get what you want?
16. Do you fantasize about big plans and schemes?
17. Do you relish being the big shot?
18. Do you feel you don't get the respect you deserve?
19. Do you believe that the rules and laws are made for other people?
20. Do you want to be God?

These are immature, narcissistic needs, the infantile needs of an individual who wants to be in control. The needs of someone who is desperate for attention. But no amount of love would be enough for you. You would always need more and more and more. Other people have tried to love you, and they have always fallen short, haven't they? Then you blame them without looking at yourself. It's always the other person's fault, never your own. If the other person would just recognize you for the great person you are, and do what you want them to do, things would go fine.

Narcissistic traits are why you are spiritually bankrupt. This is why you have been feeling so empty. This is why you never fit in. Now let's look at the crux of the issue. If you look at these characteristics carefully, you can see that you have been trying to be God. But you are not God, and as long as you try be God, you will fail.

## A FEELING OF WORTHLESSNESS

Underneath your need to be in control is the feeling of worthlessness. You seem to vacillate between being the greatest person and the worst. There is no middle ground. You are either on the top or on the bottom, never in between, never normal. The reason you need constant reassurance from others is you don't feel good about yourself. You feel inadequate. To counteract this feeling, you exaggerate your talents and accomplishments. This is a vain attempt to get people to love you. But people cannot love you until they know you. You cannot lie and feel loved, that is impossible. Intimacy necessitates truth.

Give a few examples of when you lied about your accomplishments or talents to manipulate how someone felt about you.

1. _____
2. _____
3. _____
4. _____
5. _____

Because you feel worthless, you have a difficult time hearing the word *no*. When someone says no, you feel you are bad. Either you are the best or the worst, remember? When someone says no, you get angry and fly into a rage. That makes everything worse.

Give a few examples of when someone told you no and you exploded.

1. _____
2. _____
3. _____
4. _____
5. _____

Because of your feelings of worthlessness, you need to feel that you are special and that other people should recognize your unique abilities. You believe that only special people of high status can really understand you. Because you have a need to be perfect, you tend to routinely overestimate your capabilities. For example, you think you are going to make all A's, and get angry at the teacher when you get lower grades. It's always the teacher's fault, or the boss's fault, or the spouse's fault, never your fault. You need to be admired and respected even when you haven't worked for it. You expect to start at the top, rather than work your way up like other people.

Give an example of when you expected to be respected and you did not deserve to be.

_____
_____
_____
_____

It is important for you to see how these unrealistic ideals set you up to fail. No one is perfect, so when you expect this of yourself, you ultimately fail. When you think your work has to be perfect, you end up feeling humiliated when someone points out that you did something wrong.

Give a few examples of when someone criticized you and you were furious.

1. _____
2. _____
3. _____
4. _____
5. _____

Because of your feelings of worthlessness, you spend a lot of time fantasizing about success, power, brilliance, or ideal love. How wonderful this new job will be, or this new love, or this new ability. This immature need for unlimited success sets you up to fail. You end up feeling more miserable.

Discuss the last romance you had and what happened. How perfect you thought it was going to be, and how it actually turned out.

_____
_____
_____
_____

Love and sex put you at high risk because you put unrealistic expectations on the relationship. You expect the other person to meet your need to feel important, special, loved, powerful, brilliant, and beautiful. But there is no way a person can meet these needs, so the relationship fails and you sink into despair.

Give two examples of how relationship problems lead to chemical use.

1. _____
_____
_____

2. _____
_____
_____

A narcissistic person feels jealous of others and their accomplishments. By constantly comparing yourself to others, you end up feeling bad.

List a number of the people you are envious of, and write down exactly what they have that you want.

1. _____
2. _____
3. _____
4. _____
5. _____

It is important for you to recognize how you constantly compare yourself to others, how you end up feeling either superior or inferior to them. Either way you have separated yourself from love. Intimacy necessitates equality. Both partners need come into a relationship feeling good about themselves.

## TO LOOSEN THE NARCISSISTIC BONDS

These narcissistic traits enslave you. You will never be perfect. You will never be the most brilliant, or the most beautiful, or the most powerful, or the most loved, or the most wonderful, or the most special. Everyone will not worship you. You believe that to be accepted, you have to be the greatest, but you don't. This is a lie.

### You Must Get Honest

Honesty is a wonderful thing. You cannot solve problems without the facts. If you make the facts up, the problems will never be solved, and you will be back in misery. You will never feel loved if you make up who you are. Even if you fool the other person, you know they do not love you. You will never feel known until you tell the truth. The first thing you need to do is not to tell the old lies—you know, as if you were someone special, with special talents. If you never worked for the CIA, don't tell people that you did. If you did not make a lot of money, do not tell people that you did. If you did not save a person from drowning, do not say that you did. You get what I mean. You have a million stories that are not true. You have to stop lying. If you don't, you will be unhappy.

List a few of the lies you told to get people to like you.

1. _____
2. _____
3. _____
4. _____
5. _____

Promise yourself that you will never tell these lies again. Wake up every morning and be grateful that you have not lied that day. Then try to get through the next hour without lying. If you make it, congratulate yourself, that's a victory. Check out how you feel. You will be feeling good about yourself. When you lie, check out how you feel. You will be feeling frightened and bad about yourself. Dishonesty is the main reason you have been isolated. Only by being honest will you begin to feel accepted.

## You Must Go to Meetings

To loosen the bonds of narcissism you must go to meetings and trust someone. This is very difficult because the only person you trust is yourself. But in this illness, if you rely on yourself, you will be sick. You need to turn your will and your life over to someone who can manage your life. Start with anyone you can, maybe your counselor or your group. Put your trust in them, and whatever you do, don't trust yourself. Your best judgment got you into this mess. You don't know the way out. Someone else is going to have to show you the way. Name the person or persons you are going to try to trust.

_____
_____
_____

When you feel like taking the controls back again, don't. When someone makes a suggestion, try it.

## You Must Seek God

You need to seek God. God created you special, and God has a great plan for you. God gave you everything you need to be happy, joyous, and free. There is only one you, and you are special, but you are not better than everyone, you are equal to them. This makes life better, not worse. This alone gives you the opportunity to love rather than rule. Everyone has his or her unique place in God's plan. Whatever you do, God will be there for you, loving you. Take a risk and ask God to come into your life. Say something like this, "God, I don't know if you are out there or not, but if you are, I need you to help me." Then ask God a question. "God, what is the next step in my relationship with you?" Now be quiet, don't be afraid, wait. A word or phrase will come floating through your mind. It will be something like, "Trust me," or "Pray," something like that. That is God speaking to you inside of your thinking.

Write down what happened.

_____
_____
_____

That is the next step. If you take that step, you will feel the peace that AA calls serenity. God will tell you the next step, not the second, or the third. If you follow God's plan, step by step, you are free.

# References

Abelson, H. I., Fishburne, P. M., & Cisin, I. H. (1977). *National survey on drug abuse: 1977. A nationwide study—Youth, young adults, and older adults: Vol. I. Main findings* (National Institute on Drug Abuse, DHHS Publication No. ADM 78-618). Washington, DC: Government Printing Office.

Adams, E. H., Blanken, A. J., Ferguson, L. D., & Kopstein, A. (1990). *Overview of selected drug trends.* Rockville, MD: National Institute on Drug Abuse, Office of Epidemiology and Prevention Research.

Adams, R. D., & Victor, M. (1981). *Principles of neurology.* New York: McGraw-Hill.

Adinoff, B., Bone, G. H. A., & Linnolila, M. (1988). Acute ethanol poisoning and the ethanol withdrawal syndrome. *Toxicology Management Review, 3,* 172-196.

AIDS and Chemical Dependency Committee, American Medical Society on Alcoholism and Other Drug Dependencies. (1988). *Guidelines for facilities treating chemical dependency patients at risk for AIDS and HIV infection* (2nd ed.). New York: Author.

Aigner, T. G., & Balster, R. L. (1978). Choice of behavior in rhesus monkeys: Cocaine versus food. *Science, 201,* 534-535.

Alberti, R. E., & Emmons, M. L. (1986). *Your perfect right: A guide to assertive living.* San Luis Obispo, CA: Impact.

*Alcoholics anonymous.* (1976). New York: Alcoholics Anonymous World Services.

Alcoholics Anonymous. (1981). *Twelve steps and twelve traditions.* New York: Alcoholics Anonymous World Services.

Alexander, E. J. (1951). Withdrawal effects of sodium amytal. *Diseases of the Nervous System, 12,* 77-82.

Alexander, J. F. (1974). Behavior modification and delinquent youth. In J. C. Cull & R. E. Hardy (Eds.), *Behavior modification in rehabilitation settings.* Springfield, IL: Charles C Thomas.

Alexander, J. F., & Parsons, B. V. (1973). Short term behavioral intervention with delinquent families. *Journal of Abnormal Psychology, 81,* 219-255.

American Psychiatric Association. (1987). *Diagnostic and statistical manual of mental disorders* (3rd ed.). Washington, DC: Author.

American Psychiatric Association. (1994). *Diagnostic and statistical manual of mental disorders* (4th ed.). Washington, DC: Author.

American Society of Addiction Medicine. (1991). *Patient placement criteria for the treatment of psychoactive substance use disorders.* Chevy Chase, MD: Author.

American Society of Addiction Medicine. (1994). *Principles of addiction medicine.* Chevy Chase, MD: Author.

American Society of Addiction Medicine. (1996). *Patient placement criteria for the treatment of substance-related disorders* (2nd ed.). Chevy Chase, MD: Author.

Anglin, M. D., & Hser, Y. (1990). Treatment of drug abuse. In M. Tonry & J. Q. Wilson (Eds.), *Drugs and crime* (pp. 339-460). Chicago: University of Chicago Press.

Anthenelli, R. M., & Schuckit, M. A. (1994). Genetic influences in addiction. In *Principles of addiction medicine* (Sec. 1, chap. 6, pp. 1-14). Chevy Chase, MD: American Society of Addiction Medicine.

Appenzeller, O., Standefer, J., Appenzeller, J., & Atkinson, R. (1980). Neurology of endurance training: V endorphins. *Neurology, 30,* 418-419.

Atkinson. R. M., & Kofoed, L. L. (1984). Substance use and abuse in old age. *Substance Abuse, 5,* 30-42.

Balster, R. L., & Chait, L. D. (1978). The behavioral effects of phencyclidine in animals. In R. C. Petersen & R. C. Stillman (Eds.), *PCP phencyclidine abuse: An appraisal* (National Institute on Drug Abuse, DHHS Publication No. ADM 78-728). Washington, DC: Government Printing Office.

Baum, R., & Iber, F. L. (1980). Initial treatment of the alcoholic patient. In S. E. Gitlow & H. S. Peyser (Eds.), *Alcoholism: A practical treatment guide.* New York: Grune & Stratton.

Beattie, M. (1987). *Codependent no more: How to stop controlling others and start caring for yourself.* Center City, MN: Hazelden.

Beck, A. T. (1967). *Depression: Clinical, experimental, and theoretical aspects.* New York: Harper & Row.

Beck, A. T. (1972). *Depression: Causes and treatment.* Philadelphia: University of Pennsylvania Press.

Beck, A. T. (1976). *Cognitive therapy and the emotional disorders.* New York: International Universities Press.

Beck, A. T. (1978). *Depression inventory.* Philadelphia: Center for Cognitive Therapy.

Beck, A. T., & Emery, G. (1979). *Coping with anxiety and panic: SCT method.* Philadelphia: Center for Cognitive Therapy.

Beck, A. T., & Greenberg, R. (1974). *Coping with depression.* Philadelphia: Center for Cognitive Therapy.

Beck, A. T., Rush, J. A., Shaw, B. F., & Emery, G. (1979). *Cognitive therapy of depression.* New York: Guilford.

Beck, A. T., Ward, C. H., Mandelson, M., et al. (1961). An inventory for measuring depression. *Archives of General Psychiatry, 4,* 561-571.

Beitman, B. D., Carlin, A. S., & Chiles, J. C. (1984). Pharmacotherapy-psychotherapy triangle: A physician, a nonmedical psychotherapist, and a patient. *Journal of Clinical Psychiatry, 45,* 458-459.

Benson, H. (1975). *The relaxation response.* New York: William Morrow.

Bettet, P. S., & Maloney, M. J. (1991). The importance of empathy as an interviewing skill in medicine. *Journal of the American Medical Association, 266*(13), 1831-1832.

Block, J. (1971). *Lives through time.* Berkeley, CA: Bancroft.

Bradshaw, J. (1988). *Healing the shame that binds you.* Deerfield Beach, FL: Health Communications.

Bradshaw, J. (1990). *Homecoming: Reclaiming and championing your inner child.* New York: Bantam.

Braunwald, E., Isselbacher, K. T., Petersdorf, R. G., Wilson, J. D., Martin, J. B., & Fauci, A. S. (1987). *Harrison's principles of internal medicine.* New York: McGraw-Hill.

Brostoff, W. S. (1994). Clinical diagnosis. In *Principles of addiction medicine* (Sec. 4, chap. 1, pp. 1-4). Chevy Chase, MD: American Society of Addiction Medicine.

Brown, B. W., Monck, E. M., Carstain, G. M., et al. (1962). Influence of family life on the course of schizophrenic illness. *British Journal of Preventative Social Medicine, 16,* 55-68.

Burant, D. (1990). Management of withdrawal. In A. Geller (Ed.), *Syllabus for the review course in addiction medicine.* Washington, DC: American Society of Addiction Medicine.

Burchard, J. D., & Tyler, V. O. (1965). The modification of delinquent behavior through operant conditioning. *Behavior Research and Therapy, 2,* 245-250.

Burns, D. D. (1980). *Feeling good: The new mood therapy.* New York: Signet.

Burns, D. D. (1990). *The feeling good handbook.* New York: Penguin.

Caracci, L., Megone, P., & Dornbush, R. (1983). Phencyclidine in an East Harlem psychiatric population. *Journal of the National Medical Association, 75,* 869-874.

Carroll, M. E., & Comer, S. D. (1994). Phencyclidine and the halluciogens. In *Principles of addiction medicine* (Sec. 2, chap. 7, pp. 1-9). Chevy Chase, MD: American Society of Addiction Medicine.

Centers for Disease Control. (1988). Smoking-attributable mortality and years of potential life lost—United States. *Morbidity and Mortality Weekly Report (MMWR), 40,* 62-71.

Centers for Disease Control. (1990). *HIV/AIDS surveillance report.* Atlanta, GA: Author.

Centers for Disease Control. (1991a). Alcohol and other drug use among high school students—United States, 1990. *Morbidity and Mortality Weekly Report (MMWR), 40,* 776-784.

Centers for Disease Control. (1991b). Cigarette smoking among adults—United States, 1988. *Morbidity and Mortality Weekly Report (MMWR), 40,* 757-765.

Chatlos, J. C., & Jaffe, S. L. (1994). A developmental biopsychosocial model of adolescent addiction. In *Principles of addiction medicine* (Sec. 17, chap. 1, pp. 1-5). Chevy Chase, MD: American Society of Addiction Medicine.

Chopra, G. S., & Smith, J. W. (1974). Psychotic reactions following cannabis use in East Indians. *Archives of General Psychiatry, 30,* 24-27.

Clinical Institute Withdrawal Assessment Alcohol Scale. (1991). In *ASAM patient placement criteria for the treatment of psychoactive substance use disorders.* Washington, DC: American Society of Addiction Medicine.

Cloptin, P. L., Janowsky, D. S., Clopin, J. M., Judd, L. L., & Huey, L. (1979). Marihuana and the perception of affect. *Psychopharmacology, 61,* 203-206.

Cohen, H. C., Filipczak, J. A., & Bis, J. S. (1965). Case project: Contingencies application for special education. *Progress Report, U.S. Department of Health, Education and Welfare.* Washington, DC: U.S. Department of Health, Education, and Welfare.

Cohen, H. L., & Filipczak J. A. (1971). *A new learning environment.* San Francisco: Jossey-Bass.

Cohen, S. (1979). Inhalants. In R. I. DuPont, A. Goldstein, & J. O'Donnell (Eds.), *Handbook on drug abuse* (pp. 213-220). Washington, DC: National Institute on Drug Abuse.

Committee for the Study and Treatment and Rehabilitation Services for Alcoholism and Alcohol Abuse. (1990). *Broadening the base of treatment for alcohol problems.* Washington, DC: National Academy of Science.

Conte, H. R., Plutchik, R., Wild, K. V., et al. (1986). Combined psychotherapy and pharmacotherapy for depression: A systematic analysis of the evidence. *Archives of General Psychiatry, 43,* 471-479.

Cook, R. F., Hostetter, R. S., & Ramsay, D. A. (1975). Patterns of illicit drug use in the Army. *American Journal of Psychiatry, 132,* 1013-1017.

Creager, C. (1989, July-August). SASSI test breaks through denial. *Professional Counselor,* p. 65.

Csikoszentimihalyi, M., & Larson, R. (1984). *Being adolescent.* New York: Basic Books.

Davidson, W. S., II, & Seidman, E. (1974). Studies of behavior modification and juvenile delinquency: A review, methodological critique, and social perspective. *Psychological Bulletin, 81*(2), 998-1011.

Davis, B. C. (1982). The PCP epidemic: A critical review. *International Journal of Addiction, 17,* 1137-1155.

Dietch, J. (1983). The nature and extent of benzodiazepine abuse: An overview of recent literature. *Hospital and Community Psychiatry, 34,* 1139-1145.

Domino, E. F. (1978). Neurobiology of phencyclidine—An update. In R. C. Peterson & R. C. Stillman (Eds.), *PCP phencyclidine abuse: An appraisal* (National Institute on Drug Abuse, Department of Health, Education and Welfare Publication No. ADM 17-728, pp. 18-43). Washington, DC: Government Printing Office.

*Dorland's illustrated medical dictionary.* (1965). Philadelphia: W. B. Saunders.

Dorus, W., Kennedy, J., Gibbons R. D., & Raci, S. D. (1987). Symptoms and diagnosis of depression in alcoholics. *Alcoholism, 11,* 150-154.

Douvan, E., & Adelson, J. (1966). *The adolescent experience.* New York: John Wiley.

DuPont, R. L. (1994). Laboratory diagnosis. In *Principles of addiction medicine* (Sec. 4, chap. 2, pp. 1-8). Chevy Chase, MD: American Society of Addiction Medicine.

Ellis, A. (1962). *Reason and emotion in psychotherapy.* New York: Lyle-Stuart.

Emrick, C. D. (1987). Alcoholics Anonymous: Affiliation process and effectiveness as treatment. *Alcoholism, 11,* 416-423.

Evans, M. A., Marty, R., Brown, D. J., Rodda, B. E., Kippinger, G. F., Lemberger, L., & Forney, R. B. (1973). Impairment of performance with low doses of marijuana. *Clinical Pharmacological Therapy, 14,* 936-940.

Ewing, J. A. (1984). Detecting alcoholism: The CAGE questionnaire. *Journal of the American Medical Association, 252,* 1905-1907.

Eysenck, H. J., & Eysenck, S. B. J. (1976). *Personality structure and measurement.* London: Routledge & Kegan Paul.

Featherly, J. W., & Hill, E. B. (1989). *Crack cocaine overview 1989.* Washington, DC: U.S. Department of Justice, Drug Enforcement Administration.

Fischman, M. W., Schuster, C. R., Rosnekov, L., Shick, J. F. E., Krasnegor, N. A., Fennell, W., & Freedman, D. X. (1976). Cardio-vascular and subjective effects of intravenous cocaine administration in humans. *Archives of General Psychiatry, 33,* 983-989.

Fisher, D. E., Halikas, J. A., Baker, J. W., et al. (1975). Frequency and patterns of drug abuse in psychiatric patients. *Diseases of the Nervous System, 36,* 550-553.

Folkins, C. H., & Sime, W. E. (1981). Physical fitness training and mental health. *American Psychologist, 36,* 373-389.

Folstein, M. F., Folstein, S. W., & McHugh, P. R. (1975). Mini-mental state: A practical method of grading the cognitive state of patients for the clinician. *Journal of Psychiatric Research, 12,* 189-198.

Frances, R. J., Bucky, S., & Alexopolos, G. S. (1984). Outcome study of familial and nonfamilial alcoholism. *American Journal of Psychiatry, 141,* 11.

Frances, R. J., & Franklin, J. E., Jr. (1988). Alcohol and other psychoactive substance use disorders. In J. A. Talbott, R. E. Hales, & S. C. Yudofsky (Eds.), *The American Psychiatric Press textbook of psychiatry.* Washington, DC: American Psychiatric Press.

Freedman, D. X. (1968). The use and abuse of LSD. *Archives of General Psychiatry, 18,* 300-347.

Freedman, D. X. (1984). Psychiatric epidemiology counts. *Archives of General Psychiatry, 41,* 931-933.

Fultz, J. M., & Senay, E. C. (1975). Guidelines for the management of hospitalized narcotics addicts. *Annuals of Internal Medicine, 82,* 815-818.

Gabel, R. H., Barnard, N., Norko, M., & O'Connell, R. A. (1986). AIDS presenting as mania. *Comparative Psychiatry, 27*(3), 251-254.

Gambert, S. R. (1992). Substance abuse in the elderly. In J. H. Lowinson, P. Ruiz, R. B. Millman, & J. G. Langrod (Eds.), *Substance abuse: A comprehensive textbook* (2nd ed.). Baltimore, MD: Williams & Wilkins.

Gary, V., & Guthrie, D. (1972). The effect of jogging on physical fitness and self-concept in hospitalized alcoholics. *Quarterly Journal of Studies on Alcohol, 33,* 1073-1078.

Gawin, F. H., & Ellinwood, E. H. (1988). Cocaine and other stimulants: Actions, abuse, & treatments. *New England Journal of Medicine, 318,* 1173-1182.

Gawin, F. H., & Kleber, H. S. (1986a). Abstinence symptomatology and psychiatric diagnosis in cocaine abusers. *Archives of General Psychiatry, 43,* 107-113.

Gawin, F. H., & Kleber, H. S. (1986b). Pharmacologic treatments of cocaine abuse. *Psychiatry in Clinical North America, 9,* 573-583.

Geller, A. (1990). Protracted abstinence. In A. Geller (Ed.), *Syllabus of the review course in addiction medicine.* Washington, DC: American Society of Addiction Medicine.

Geller, A. (1994). Management of protracted withdrawal. In *Principles of addiction medicine* (Sec. 11, chap. 2, pp. 1-6). Chevy Chase, MD: American Society of Addiction Medicine.

Gerstein, D. R., & Harwood, H. J. (Eds.). (1990). *Treating drug problems.* Washington, DC: National Academy Press.

Gessner, P. K. (1979). Drug withdrawal therapy of the alcohol withdrawal syndrome. In E. Majchowicz & E. Noble (Eds.), *Biochemistry and pharmacology of ethanol* (Vol. 2). New York: Plenum.

Gilman, A. G., Goodman, L. S., & Gilman, A. (1980). *Goodman and Gilman's The pharmacological basis of therapeutics.* New York: Macmillan.

Glynn, T. J. (1990). Methods of smoking cessation: Finally some answers. *Journal of the American Medical Association, 263*(20), 2795-2796.

Gold, M. S. (1994a). Marijuana. In *Principles of addiction medicine* (Sec. 2, chap. 8, pp. 1-6). Chevy Chase, MD: American Society of Addiction Medicine.

Gold, M. S. (1994b). Opioids. In *Principles of addiction medicine* (Sec. 2, chap. 4, pp. 1-6). Chevy Chase, MD: American Society of Addiction Medicine.

Goldman, A. R. (1989). *Accreditation and certification: For providers of psychiatric, alcoholism and drug abuse services.* Bala Cynwyd, PA: Practical Communications.

Goodwin, D. W. (1985). Alcoholism and genetics. *Archives of General Psychiatry, 42,* 171-174.

Goodwin, D. W., Crane, J. B., & Guze, S. B. (1969). Alcoholic blackouts: A review and clinical study of 100 alcoholics. *American Journal of Psychiatry, 126,* 174-177.

Gorski, T. (1989). *Passages through recovery.* Center City, MN: Hazelden.

Gorski, T., & Miller, M. (1982). *Counseling for relapse prevention.* Independence, MO: Independence Press.

Gorski, T., & Miller, M. (1986). *Staying sober: A guide for relapse prevention.* Independence, MO: Herald House/Independence Press.

Gottochalk, L., McGuire, F., Haser, F., et al. (1979). *Drug abuse deaths in nine cities: A survey report* (Research Monograph No. 29). Rockville, MD: National Institute on Drug Abuse.

Gould, L. C., & Keeber, H. D. (1974). Changing patterns of multiple drug use among applicants to a multimodality drug treatment program. *Archives of General Psychiatry, 31,* 408-413.

Graziano, A. M., & Mooney, K. C. (1984). *Children and behavior therapy.* New York: Aldine.

Greenberg, R. L., & Beck, A. T. (1987). *Panic attacks: How to cope, how to recover.* Philadelphia: Center for Cognitive Therapy.

Greist, J. H., Klein, M. H., Eischins, R. R., Faris, J., Gurman, A. S., & Morgan, W. P. (1979). Running as treatment for depression. *Comprehensive Psychiatry, 20,* 41-54.

Griffith, J. D., Cavanaugh, J., Held, J., & Oates, J. A. (1972). Dextroamphetamine. *Archives of General Psychiatry, 26,* 97-100.

Group for the Advancement of Psychiatry Committee on Alcoholism and the Addictions. (1991). Substance abuse disorders: A psychiatric priority. *American Journal of Psychiatry, 148*(10), 1291-1300.

Gunderson, J. G., & Zanarine, M. C. (1987). Current overview of the borderline diagnosis. *Journal of Clinical Psychiatry, 48*(Suppl. 8), 5-11.

Hamilton, M. (1959). The assessment of anxiety states by rating. *British Journal of Medical Psychology, 32,* 50-55.

Harris, M. J., Jeste, D. V., Gleghorn, A., & Sewell, D. D. (1991). New-onset psychosis in HIV-infected patients. *Journal of Clinical Psychiatry, 52*(9), 369-376.

Havens, L. (1978). Explorations in the use of language in psychotherapy: Simple empathetic statements. *Psychiatry, 41,* 336-345.

Henningfield, J. E. (1984). Pharmacologic basis and treatment of cigarette smoking. *Journal of Clinical Psychiatry, 45,* 24-34.

Herbert, M. (1982). Conduct disorder. In A. E. Kazdin & B. B. Lahey (Eds.), *Advances in clinical and child psychology (Vol. 5).* New York: Plenum.

Hesselbrock, M. N., Meyer, R. E., & Kenner, J. J. (1985). Psychopathology in hospitalized alcoholics. *Archives of General Psychiatry, 46,* 3-5.

Hirschfeld, R. M. A., & Goodwin, F. K. (1988). Mood disorders. In J. A. Talbott, R. E. Hales, & S. C. Yudofsky (Eds.), *The American Psychiatric Press textbook of psychiatry.* Washington, DC: American Psychiatric Press.

Hoffmann, N. G. (1991, June). *Treatment outcomes from abstinence based programs.* Paper presented at the 36th International Institute on the Prevention and Treatment of Alcoholism, Stockholm, Sweden.

Hoffmann, N. G. (1994). Assessing treatment effectiveness. In *Principles of addiction medicine* (Sec, 9, chap. 5, pp. 1-9). Chevy Chase, MD: American Society of Addiction Medicine.

Hoffmann, N. G., & Harrison, P. (1987). A 2-year follow-up of in-patient treatment. St. Paul, MN: Chemical Abuse Treatment Outcome Registry.

Hollister, L. E. (1974). Interactions in man of delta-9-tetrahydrocannabinol I. Alphamethyl-paratyrosine. *Clinical Pharmacological Therapy, 15,* 18-21.

Hollister, L. E. (1986). Health aspects of cannabis. *Pharmacology Review, 38,* 1-20.

Hubbard, R. L. (1992). Evaluation and treatment outcome. In J. H. Lorvinson, P. Ruiz, R. B. Millman, & J. C. Langrod (Eds.), *Substance abuse: A comprehensive textbook.* Baltimore: Williams & Wilkins.

Hubbard, R. L., & Anderson, J. A. (1988). *Follow-up study of individuals receiving alcoholism treatment.* Research Triangle Park, NC: Research Triangle Institute.

Hubbard, R. L., & DesJarlais, D. C. (1991). Alcohol and drug abuse. In E. E. Holland, R. Petels, & G. Knox (Eds.), *Oxford textbook of public health* (2nd ed., Vol. 3). London: Oxford University Press.

Hubbard, R. L., Marsden, M. E., Rachel, J. V., Harwood, H. J., Cavanaugh, E. R., & Ginzburg, H. M. (1989). *Drug abuse treatment—A national study of effectiveness.* Chapel Hill: University of North Carolina Press.

Huges, J. R., & Hatsukami, D. (1986). Signs and symptoms of tobacco withdrawal. *Archives of General Psychiatry, 43,* 289-294.

Hunt, W. A., Barnett, L. W., & Branch, L. G. (1971). Relapse rates in addiction programs. *Journal of Clinical Psychology, 27,* 455-456.

Jacob, J. W., Bernhard, M. R., Delgado, A. et al. (1977). Screening for organic mental syndromes in the mentally ill. *Annuals of Internal Medicine, 86,* 40-46.

Jaffe, J. H. (1980). Drug addiction and drug abuse. In L. S. Goodman & A. G. Gilman (Eds.), *Goodman and Gillman's the pharmacological basis of therapeutics.* New York: Macmillian.

Jellinek, E. M. (1960). *The disease concept of alcoholism.* New Haven, CT: College and University Press.

Joint Commission on Accreditation of Healthcare Organizations. (1988). *Consolidated standards manual.* Chicago: Author.

Joint Commission on Accreditation of Healthcare Organizations. (1992). *Patient records in addiction treatment.* Oakbridge Terrace, IL: Author.

Jones, R. T. (1971). Marijuana-induced "high": Influence of expectation, setting, and previous drug experience. *Pharmacological Review, 23,* 359-369.

Jones, R. T., Bennowitz, N., & Bachman, J. (1976). Clinical studies of cannabis tolerance and dependence. *Annuals of the New York Academy of Science, 282,* 221-239.

Journal of Studies on Alcohol. (1975) A self-administered short Michigan alcoholism screening test. M. Selzer, A,. Winokus, & C. van Rooijen. *Journal of Studies on Alcohol, 36,* 124. New Brunswick, NJ: Rutgers Center of Alcohol Studies.

Juergens, S. M. (1994). Sedative-hypnotics. In *Principles of addiction medicine* (Sec. 2, chap. 3, pp. 1-10). Chevy Chase, MD: American Society of Addiction Medicine.

Kagan, J. (1989). Temperament contribution to social behavior. *American Journal of Psychology, 44,* 668-674.

Kagan, J., Reznick, J. S., & Gibbons, J. (1989). Inhibited and uninhibited types of children. *Child Development, 60,* 838-845.

Kagan, J., Reznick, J. S., & Snidman, N. (1987). The physiology and psychology of behavioral inhibition in children. *Child Development, 58,* 1459-1473.

Kalant, H., Engel, J. A., Goldberg, L., Griffiths, R. R., Jaffe, J. H., Krasnegor, N. A., Mello, N. K., Mendelson, J. H., Thompson, T., & Van Ree, J. M. (1978). Behavioral aspects of addiction: Group report. In J. Fishman (Ed.), *The basis of addiction: Report of the Dahlem Workshop on the basis of addiction* (pp. 463- 495). Berlin: Abakon Verlagsgesellschaft.

Kandel, D. (1978). Antecedents of adolescent initiation into stages of drug use. In D. Kandel (Ed.), *Longitudinal research on drug use.* Washington, DC: Hemisphere.

Karasu, T. B. (1989). *Treatments of psychiatric disorders.* Washington, DC: American Psychiatric Association.

Khantzian, E. J., & Treece, C. (1985). DSM-III psychiatric diagnosis of narcotics addicts: Recent findings. *Archives of General Psychiatry, 42,* 1067-1071.

King, G. S., Smialick, J. E., & Troutman, W. G. (1985). Sudden death in adolescents resulting from the inhalation of typewriter correction fluid. *Journal of the American Medical Association, 253,* 1604-1609.

Kinney, J., & Leaton, G. (1987). *Loosening the grip: A handbook of alcohol information.* St. Louis, MO: Time Mirror/Mosby College.

Klein, D. F., Gittelman, R., Quitkin, F., & Rifkin, A. (1980). *Diagnosis and drug treatment of psychiatric disorders: Adults and children.* Baltimore, MD: Williams & Wilkins.

Klerman, G. L., Weissman, M. M., Rounsaville, B. J., & Chevron, E. S. (1984). *Interpersonal psychotherapy of depression.* New York: Basic Books.

Kosten, T. R., Rounsaville, B. J., & Kleber, H. D. (1985). Comparison of clinical ratings to self reports of withdrawal during clonidine detoxification of opiate addicts. *American Journal of Drug and Alcohol Abuse, 11,* 1-10.

Ledwidge, B. (1980). Run for your mind: Aerobic exercise as a means of alleviating anxiety and depression. *Canadian Journal of Behavioral Science, 12,* 127-140.

Lewinsohn, P. M., Munoz, R. F., Youngren, M. A., et al. (1978). *Control your depression.* Englewood Cliffs, NJ: Prentice Hall.

Lynch, K. R., & Ollendick, T. H. (1977). Juvenile corrections: A model program. *American Journal of Corrections, 39,* 6-7.

Manthey, M. (1991). Commitment to my co-workers. In S. Cox & D. Miller (Eds.), *Leaders empower staff.* Minneapolis, MN: Creative Management. (Available from Creative Management, Inc., 614 East Grant Street, Minneapolis, MN 55404)

Marlatt, A. G., & Gordon, J. R. (1985). *Relapse prevention.* New York: Guilford.

Masterson, J. F., Jr., & Costello, J. (1980). *From borderline adolescent to functioning adult: The test of time.* New York: Brunner/Mazel.

McElrath, D. (1987). *Hazelden: A spiritual odyssey.* Center City, MN: Hazelden.

McKay, M., Rogers, P. D., & McKay, J. (1989). *When anger hurts: Quieting the storm within.* Oakland, CA: New Harbinger.

McLellan, A. T., Luborsky, L., & Woody, G. E. (1980). An improved diagnostic evaluation instrument for substance abuse patients: The Addiction Severity Index. *Journal of Nervous and Mental Disease, 168,* 26-33.

Mee-Lee, D. (1985). The Recovery Attitude and Treatment Evaluator (RAATE): An instrument for patient progress and treatment assignment. *Proceedings of the 34th International Congress on Alcoholism and Drug Dependence* (pp. 424-426).

Mee-Lee, D. (1988). An instrument for treatment progress and matching: The Recovery Attitude and Treatment Evaluator (RAATE). *Journal of Substance Abuse Treatment, 5,* 183-186.

Melges, F. T., Tinklenberg, J. R., Hollister, L. E., & Gillespie, H. K. (1970). Temporal disintegration and depersonalization during marijuana intoxication. *Archives of General Psychiatry, 23,* 204-210.

Miller, G. A. (1985). *The Substance Abuse Subtle Screening Inventory manual.* Bloomington, IN: SASSI Institute.

Miller, J. D. (1983). *National survey on drug abuse: Main findings, 1982.* Rockville, MD: National Institute on Drug Abuse.

Millon, T. (1981). *Disorders of personality: DSM III Axis II.* New York: John Wiley.

Morrison, M. A., & Smith, Q. T. (1990). Psychiatric issues of adolescent chemical dependence. In A. Geller (Ed.), *Syllabus for the review course in addiction medicine.* Washington, DC: American Society of Addiction Medicine.

Morse, R. M. (1994). Elderly patients. In *Principles of addiction medicine,* Sec. 18, Chap. 2, pp. 1-6. Chevy Chase, MD: American Society of Addiction Medicine.

Naditch, M. P., & Fenwick, S. (1977). LSD flashbacks and ego functioning. *Journal of Abnormal Psychiatry, 86,* 352-359.

Nahas, G. G. (1973). *Marihuana: Deceptive weed.* New York: Raven.

*Narcotics Anonymous.* (1988). Van Nuys, CA: World Service Office.

National Institute of Medicine. (1989). *Research effectiveness in the prevention and treatment of alcohol-related diseases.* Washington, DC: National Academy Press.

National Institute on Drug Abuse. (1986). *Drug use among American high school students and other young adults: National trends through 1985.* Washington, DC: U.S. Department of Health and Human Services.

Offer, D. (1986). Adolescent development: A normative perspective. In *American Psychiatric Association annual review* (Vol. 5). Washington, DC: American Psychiatric Press.

Offer, D., & Offer, J. B. (1975). *From teenage to young manhood: A psychological study.* New York: Basic Books.

Offer, D., Ostrov, E., & Howard, K. I. (1981). *The adolescent: A psychological self-portrait.* New York: Basic Books.

Ollendick, T. H., & Cerny, J. A. (1981). *Clinical behavior therapy with children.* New York: Plenum.

O'Malley, S. S., Jaffe, A. J., Chang, G., Schottenfeld, R. S., Meyer, R. E., & Rounsaville, B. (1992). Neltrexone and coping skills therapy for alcohol dependence: A controlled study. *Archives of General Psychiatry, 49,* 881-887.

Patterson, G. R. (1977). *Families: Applications of social learning to family life* (Rev. ed.). Champaign, IL: Research Press.

Patterson, G. R., & Gullion, M. E. (1976). *Living with children: New methods for parents and teachers* (Rev. ed.). Champaign, IL: Research Press.

Perry, S. W., & Jacobsen, P. (1986). Neuropsychiatric manifestations of AIDS-spectrum disorders. *Hospital and Community Psychiatry, 37,* 135-142.

Petersen, R. C., & Stillman, R. C. (Eds.). (1978). Phencyclidine: An overview. In *PCP phencyclidine abuse: An appraisal* (National Institute on Drug Abuse, DHHS Publication No. ADM 78-728, pp. 1-17). Washington, DC: Government Printing Office.

Phillips, E. L. (1968). Achievement place: Token reinforcement procedures in a home-style rehabilitation setting for "pre-delinquent" boys. *Journal of Applied Behavior Analysis, 1,* 213-223.

Pierce, J. P., Fiore, M. C., Novotny, T. E., Hatziandreu, E. J., & Davis, T. (1989). Trends in cigarette smoking in the United States: Projections to the year 2000. *Journal of the American Medical Association, 261,* 61-65.

Plutchic, R. (1980). *Emotion: A psychoevolutionary synthesis.* New York: Harper & Row.

Post, R. M., Kotin, J., & Goodwin, F. K. (1974). The effects of cocaine in depressed patients. *American Journal of Psychiatry, 131,* 511-517.

Reifler, B., Raskind, M., & Kethley, A. (1982). Psychiatric diagnosis among geriatric patients seen in an outreach program. *Journal of the American Geriatrics Society, 30,* 530-533.

Richels, K. Case, W. G., Downing, R.W., et al. (1983). Long-term diazepam therapy and clinical outcome. *Journal of the American Medical Association, 12,* 767-771.

Rosenbaum, J. F., Biederman, J., Hirshfeld, D. R., Bolduc, E. A., & Chaloff, J. (1991). *Journal of Clinical Psychiatry, 52*(Suppl. 11), 5-9.

Sanders, M. R., & Glynn, T. (1981). Training parents in behavioral self-management: An analysis of generalization and maintenance. *Journal of Applied Behavior Analysis, 14,* 223-237.

Schuckit, M. A. (1984). *Drug and alcohol abuse: A clinical guide to diagnosis and treatment.* New York: Plenum.

Schuckit, M. A. (1994). Duel diagnosis: Psychiatric pictures among substance abusers. In *Principles of addiction medicine* (Sec. 6, chap.1, pp. 1-4). Chevy Chase, MD: American Society of Addiction Medicine.

Secretary of Health, Education, and Welfare. (1977). *Marihuana and health: Seventh Annual Report to the U.S. Congress.* Washington, DC: National Institute on Drug Abuse.

Selye, H. (1956). *The stress of life.* New York: McGraw-Hill.

Sharp, C. W., & Brehm, M. L. (Eds.). (1977). *Review of inhalants: Euphoria to dysfunction* (National Institute on Drug Abuse, DHHS Publication No. ADM 77-553). Washington, DC: Government Printing Office.

Sharp, C. W., & Corroll, L. T. (Eds.). (1978). *Voluntary inhalation of industrial solvents* (National Institute on Drug Abuse, DHHS Publication No. ADM 79-779). Washington, DC: Government Printing Office.

Siever, L. J., & Davis, K. L. (1991). A psychobiological perspective on the personality disorders. *American Journal of Psychiatry, 148*(12), 1647-1658.

Siever, L. J., Llar, H., & Coccaro, E. (1985). Psychobiology substrates of personality. In *Biological response styles: Clinical implications.* Washington, DC: American Psychiatric Press.

Sisk, J. E., Hatziandreu, E. J., & Hughes, R. (1990). *The effectiveness of drug abuse treatment: Implication for controlling AIDS/HIV infection.* Washington, DC: Office of Technology Assessment.

Smith, C. M. (1977). The pharmacology of sedatives/hypnotics, alcohol, and anesthetics: Sites and mechanisms of action. In W. R. Martin (Ed.), *Drug addiction I: Morphine, sedative/hypnotics and alcohol dependence. Handbuck der Experimentellen Pharmakologie* (Vol. 45, pt. 1, pp. 413-587). Berlin: Springer-Verlag.

Spalt, L. (1979). Evidence of an X-linked recessive genetic characteristic in alcoholism. *Journal of the American Medical Association, 241,* 2543-2544.

Spelberger, C. D. (1983). *Manual for the State-Trait Anxiety Inventory.* Palo Alto, CA: Consulting Psychologists Press.

Stern, M. J., & Cleary, P. (1981). National Exercise and Heart Disease Project: Psychosocial changes observed during a low-level exercise program. *Archives of Internal Medicine, 141,* 1463-1467.

Stimmel, B., Goldberg, J., Rotkopf, E., et al. (1977). Ability to remain abstinent after methadone detoxification: A six-year study. *Journal of the American Medical Association, 237,* 1216-1220.

Stuart, R. B. (1971). Behavioral contracting within the families of delinquents. *Journal of Behavior Therapy and Experimental Psychology, 2,* 1-11.

Sue, D. W., & Sue, D. (1990). *Counseling the culturally different.* New York: John Wiley.

Suojanen, W. W. (1983). Addiction and the minds of adolescents. In R. C. Bersinger & W. W. Suojanen (Eds.), *Management and the brain: An integrative approach to organization behavior* (pp. 77-92). Atlanta: Georgia State University Press.

Surgeon General. (1979). *Smoking and health* (Office of Smoking and Health, DHEW Publication No. PHS 79-50066). Washington, DC: Government Printing Office.

Talbott, J. A., Hales, R. E., & Yudofsky, S. C. (1988). *American Psychiatric Press textbook of psychiatry.* Washington, DC: American Psychiatric Press.

*Tarasoff v. Regents of the University of California,* 551 P. 2d 334 at 340 (1976).

Tennant, F. S., Jr., & Grossbeck, C. J. (1972). Psychiatric effects of hashish. *Archives of General Psychiatry, 27,* 133-136.

Thacore, V. R., & Shukla, R. S. P. (1976). Cannabis psychosis and paranoid schizophrenia. *Archives of General Psychiatry, 33,* 383-386.

Thompson, T., & Pickens, R. (1970). Stimulant self-administration by animals: Some comparisons with opiate self-administration. *Federal Processes, 29,* 6-12.

Turner, C. E. (1980). Chemistry and metabolism. In R. L. Peterson (Ed.), *Marijuana research findings* (Research Monograph No. 13, DHHS Publication No. ADM AD-1001). Rockville, MD: National Institute on Drug Abuse.

U.S. Department of Health and Human Services. (1984). *Fifth special report to the United States Congress on alcohol and health from the Secretary of Health and Human Services* (Publication No. ADM 84-1291). Washington, DC: Author.

U.S. Department of Justice, DEA. (1983). *Let's all work to fight drug abuse.* Washington, DC: Author.

Vaillant, G. E. (1984). Alcohol abuse and dependence. In L. Grinspoon (Ed.), *American Psychiatric Association annual review* (Vol. 3). Washington, DC: American Psychiatric Press.

Vaillant, G. G. (1977). *Adaptation to life.* Boston: Little, Brown.

Vardy, M. M., & Kay, F. R. (1983). LSD psychosis or LSD induced schizophrenia? *Archives of General Psychiatry, 40,* 877-883.

Volpicelli, J. R., Alterman, A. L., Hayashida, M., & O'Brian, C. P. (1992). *Archives of General Psychiatry, 49,* 876-880.

Wallach, J. (1992). *Interpretation of diagnostic tests: A synopsis of laboratory medicine* (5th ed.). Boston: Little, Brown.

Warheit, G. J., & Buhl, A. J. (1985). Epidemiology of alcohol abuse in adulthood. In R. Michels & J. O. Cavenar, Jr. (Eds.), *Psychiatry.* Philadelphia: J. B. Lippincott.

Washton, A. M., Gold, M. S., & Pottash, A. C. (1984). Adolescent cocaine abusers. *Lancet, 2,* 746.

Weedman, R. (1992). *Dancing the tightrope.* Naples, FL: Healthcare Network.

Weinhold, B. K., & Weinhold, J. B. (1989). *Breaking free of the co-dependency trap.* Walpole, NH: Stillpoint.

Weiss, R. D., Mirin, S. N., Griffin, M. L., & Michaels, J. K. (1988). Psychopathology in cocaine abusers: Changing trends. *Journal of Nervous and Mental Disorders, 176,* 719-725.

Wells, K. C., & Forehand, R. (1981). Childhood behavior problems in the home. In S. M. Turner, K. S. Calhoun, & H. E. Adams (Eds.), *Handbook of clinical behavior therapy.* New York: John Wiley.

Wells, K. C., & Forehand, R. (1984). Conduct and oppositional disorders. In P. H. Bornstein & A. E. Kaydin (Eds.), *Handbook of clinical behavior therapy with children.* New York: Dorsey.

Wesson, D. R., & Smith, D. E. (1977). Cocaine: Its use for central nervous system stimulation, including recreational and medical uses. In R. C. Peterson & R. C. Stillman (Eds.), *Cocaine: 1977* (NIDA Research Monograph No. 13, pp. 137-150). Washington, DC: Government Printing Office.

Westley, W. A., & Epstein, N. B. (1969). *The silent majority.* San Francisco: Jossey-Bass.

Widiger, T., & Frances, A. (1989). Epidemiology, diagnosis, and comorbidity of borderline personality disorders. In *Review of psychiatry* (Vol. 8). Washington, DC: American Psychiatric Press.

Wikler, A. (1976). Aspects of tolerance to and dependence on cannabis. *Annuals of the New York Academy of Science, 282,* 126-147.

Wilcox R. E., Gonzales, R. A., & Erickson, C. K. (1994). In *Principles of addiction medicine* (Sec. 1, chap. 3, p. 4). Chevy Chase, MD: American Society of Addiction Medicine.

Wolf, M. M., Philips, E. L., & Fixsen, D. L. (1975). *Achievement place phase II: Final report.* Lawrence, KS: Department of Human Development.

Woods, J. H., & Carney, J. (1977). Narcotic tolerance and operant behavior. In N. A. Krasnegor (Ed.), *Behavioral tolerance: Research and treatment implications* (National Institute on Drug Abuse, DHHS Publication No. ADM 78-551, pp. 54-66). Washington, DC: Government Printing Office.

Woodward, J. J. (1994). Alcohol. In *Principles of addiction medicine* (Sec. 2, chap. 2, pp. 1-12). Chevy Chase, MD: American Society of Addiction Medicine.

Woody, G. G., Lubrorsky, L., McLellan, T., et al. (1984). Psychotherapy for opiate addicts. Does it help? *Archives of General Psychiatry, 40,* 639-643.

Zegans, L. S. (1982). Stress and the development of somatic disorders. In L. Goldberger & S. Brenznitz (Eds.), *Handbook of stress: Theoretical and clinical aspects.* New York: Free Press.

Zung, W. W. K. (1971). A rating instrument for anxiety disorders. *Psychosomatics, 12,* 371-379.

# Index

Abelson, H. I., 201
Abstinence syndrome, protracted, 17
Adams, E. H., 197, 205
Adams, R. D., 200
Adelson, J., 163
Addiction, physical, 120-122
    cross-tolerance and, 121
    drugs affecting behavior, 121
    drugs affecting cell, 120
    tolerance and, 121
    withdrawal and, 121-122
Addiction clinicians, xvii
Addictionology, 181
Addiction Severity Index (ASI), 5
Addictive relationships, 93-94
    as destructive, 93
    as distraction from pain, 93
    characteristics of, 93
    cycle of, 261
    lies in, 93
    physical abuse in, 93
    verbal abuse in, 93
    *See also* Addictive Relationships Exercise
Addictive Relationships Exercise, 93, 261-262
Adinoff, B., 16
Adolescence:
    as transitional stage, 163
    beginnings of chemical dependency in, 119, 120, 165
    routes through normal, 163-164
    *See also* Adolescents, chemically dependent;
        Adolescents, normal
Adolescent chemical dependency counselors, 166
    good impulse control in, 166
    use of level system by, 166
    use of point system/token economies by, 166-167

use of positive reinforcers by, 167
    *See also* Adolescent treatment
Adolescents, chemically dependent, 165-166
    alcoholic parents and, 165
    death among, 165
    defense mechanisms used by, 165
    depression among, 165
    family conflicts and, 165
    halted emotional development in, 165-166
    incarceration of, 165
    institutionalization of, 165
    loss of self-esteem among, 165
    peer group changes among, 165
    physical deterioration of, 165
    problems with police among, 165
    problems with school officials among, 165
    tumultuous growth group as, 165
    *See also* Adolescent treatment
Adolescents, normal, 163-164
    ages 16 to 19, 164
    ages 13 to 16, 164
    as self-confident, 163
    as well-adjusted, 163
    continuous growth group, 164
    surgent growth group, 164
    tumultuous growth group, 164
Adolescent treatment:
    behavioral contract in, 171
    continuing care after inpatient, 170-171
    continuing education in, 170
    denial court in, 169
    group therapy for, 169-170
    Higher Power in, 169
    learning communication skills in, 167-168
    learning to have sober fun in, 168

413

parents support group and, 171
peer pressure in, 170
phases of, 171-172
physical exercise in, 168
practicing honesty in, 168
primary elements in, 167-172
reinforcers in, 169
rules in, 167
spirituality in, 169
versus adult treatment, 163
Adolescent Unit Level System, 325-328
Affective disorders, causes of, 130
AIDS, 156-157
effects of on CNS, 156
See also AIDS patients
AIDS and Chemical Dependency Committee, 156, 157
AIDS patients, 156-157
AIDS dementia complex in, 156
as high-risk patients, 156-157
confidentiality with, 157
depression in, 156
intravenous drug users as, 156
psychosis in, 156
Aigner, T. G., 203
Al-Anon:
family treatment program and, 179
for family members, 174, 177-178
groups, 352
meetings, 352
Alberti, R. E., 139, 274
Alcohol:
deaths related to, 199
U.S. prevalence of use, 199
use of by children, 199
See also Alcohol hallucinosis; Alcohol idiosyncratic intoxication; Alcohol-induced amnestic disorder; Alcohol-induced intoxication; Alcoholism; Alcohol withdrawal; Alcohol withdrawal delirium; Alcohol withdrawal seizures
Alcohol hallucinosis, 201
Alcoholics Anonymous (AA), 3, 64, 67, 101, 102, 104, 105, 107, 108, 112, 122-124, 138, 139, 140, 170, 178, 243, 287, 297, 299, 303, 306, 307, 308, 312, 313, 315, 323, 324, 395
ABCs of, 149
as nonreligious, 83
beginning of, xix, 123
contact person, 194
definition of sanity in, 104, 299
for adolescents, 172
group, 69, 80, 82, 100, 105, 306, 368
hotline, 80, 368
meetings, 47, 51, 81, 124
national exposure of, 124
slogans, 124
spirituality in, 64
surrender in, 64

U.S. membership of, 101
worldwide membership of, 101, 124
See also specific Steps; Twelve Steps
Alcohol idiosyncratic intoxication, 200
Alcohol-induced amnestic disorder, 200
Alcohol-induced intoxication, 199
Alcoholism:
causes of, 199
genetics and, 199
Alcohol withdrawal, 200
symptoms, 229-232
See also Withdrawal
Alcohol withdrawal delirium, 200-201
Alcohol withdrawal seizures, 200
Alexander, E. J., 198
Alexander, J. F., 171
Alexopolos, G. S., 277
Alterman, A. L., 98
AMA (Against Medical Advice), leaving treatment, 17-19
example of intervention against, 17-18
intervention against, 17
responding to patients for, 19
AMA (Against Medical Advice) team:
description of, 18
using, 18-19
American College of Addiction Treatment Administrators, xx
American Lung Association, Freedom from Smoking clinic of, 208
American Medical Association, recognition of alcoholism as disease by, 112
American Medical Society on Alcoholism and Other Drug Dependencies, 156
American Psychiatric Association (APA), 128, 129, 199, 200, 201, 204, 205, 206, 207, 227
American Society of Addiction Medicine (ASAM), xx, 6, 191
treatment program, xx
Amphetamines:
effects of, 202
patterns of use, 203
toxic psychosis from, 203, 204
Anderson, J. A., 209
Anger:
blame and, 138
fear and, 139
See also Anger Management Exercise
Anger log/diary, 54, 140, 383
Anger Management Exercise, 139, 383-393
Anglin, M. D., 209
Angry patients, 138-141
as fearful, 139
as hurt, 139
assertiveness skills for, 139
counselors remaining calm with, 141
disengagement by, 140

handling, 138-139
handling violent, 138
Higher Power and, 139-140
importance of forgiveness for, 139-140
teaching to recognize own anger, 140-141
time-out by, 141, 390
time-out contract and, 141, 392-393
*See also* Anger; Anger Management Exercise
Anthenelli, R. M., 112
Antisocial patients:
attempts by to split staff, 188
cognitive therapy with, 145
dealing with families of, 145
dealing with rule violations by, 144
empathy disorder in, 143
frustration in working with, 144
impulsive temperament in, 143, 144
in first stage of moral development, 145
keeping honesty log, 144
procrastination by, 144
treating, 143-144
Antisocial personality disorder, 143-145
difficulty in treating, 143
in substance abusers, 143
*See also* Antisocial patients
Anxiety:
benzodiazepine treatment for, 150
definition of, 149
measuring, 150
psychological component of, 150
*See also* Anxious patients
Anxiety disorders, 150
variety of, 150
versus character disorders, 150
*See also* Anxiety; Panic disorder
Anxious patients, 149-153
as avoidant, 149
as responsible, 153
as tense, 149
catastrophizing by, 152
CNS depressant abuse by, 150
cognitive distortions in, 152
cognitive therapy for, 152
coping imagery for, 153
ease in working with, 153
exaggerating by, 152
fear in, 149, 150
giving encouragement to, 150
giving gentle support to, 150
Higher Power and, 151
hypervigilance in, 149
ignoring the positive by, 152
keeping daily relaxation log, 152
multiple somatic complaints in, 150
panic attacks in, 153
physical exercise for, 152
using relaxation techniques with, 151

Appenzeller, J., 99
Appenzeller, O., 99
Atkinson, R. M., 99, 158
Automatic (inaccurate) thoughts:
correcting, 59-63
depression and, 59
*See also* Cognitive therapy

Bachman, J., 206
Baker, J. W., 208
Balster, R. L., 203, 204
Barnard, N., 156
Barnett, L. W., 78, 97, 277, 283
Baum, R., 17
Beattie, M., 174
Beck, A. T., 59, 131, 150, 152, 272, 371
Beck Depression Inventory, 129, 137, 369-371
measuring anxiety with, 150
weekly use of, 130
Behavior:
as movement, 47, 50
consequences of, 52
definition of, 333
*See also* Behavior chain; Behaviors, patient
Behavioral Contract, 171, 333-335
Behavioral contracting, 333
Behavior chain, 52-55, 271-275, 284-285
behavior in, 52
feelings in, 52
thinking in, 52
trigger in, 52
understanding, 96, 98
Behaviors, patient:
changing, 47, 50
*See also* Behavior therapy
Behavior therapy, 50-52
advantages of, 55
for depressed patients, 130-131
for learning to use feelings appropriately, 66
importance of, 55
in group therapy, 73
reasons for using, 50
*See also* Habit; Punishment; Reinforcement
Beitman, B. D., 130
Bennowitz, N., 206
Benson, H., 99, 361
Benzodiazepines, 201
as CNS depressants, 14, 16
as stimulant intoxication treatment, 204
for anxiety, 150
for insomnia, 201
half-life of, 201
low-dose dependence on, 201
PCP and, 204
prevalence of use, 201
protracted withdrawal from, 201

withdrawal from, 122
Bernhard, M. R., 4, 222
Bettet, P. S., 49
Biederman, J., 149
Big Book, The, 77, 107, 111, 123-124, 139-140, 307, 318
Biopsychosocial addictive disease, xvii
Biopsychosocial assessment, 21, 373-382
    biopsychosocial form for, 21
    conducting, 22-27
    diagnosis of problem with, 27
    environment for, 21
    history of present problem in, 22-23
    impressions of acute intoxication in, 27
    impressions of biomedical complications in, 27
    impressions of biomedical conditions in, 27
    impressions of emotional/behavioral complications
        in, 27
    impressions of recovery environment in, 27
    impressions of relapse potential in, 27
    impressions of treatment acceptance in, 27
    impressions of treatment resistance in, 27
    impressions of withdrawal complications in, 27
    patient's concentration in, 27
    patient's family history in, 25
    patient's impulse control in, 27
    patient's insight in, 27
    patient's intelligence in, 26
    patient's judgment in, 27
    patient's medical history in, 24-25
    patient's memory in, 27
    patient's mental status in, 25-26
    patient's motivation for treatment in, 27
    patient's past history in, 23-24
    purpose of, 21
    sample, 28-35, 235-238
    summarizing, 27
    treatment plan and, 28, 35
    using direct quotes in, 22
Bipolar affective disorder, drug treatment for, 128, 129
Bis, J. S., 167
Blackouts. See Alcohol-induced amnestic disorder
Blanken, A. J., 197, 205
Block, J., 163
Bolduc, E. A., 149
Bone, G. H. A., 16
Borderline patients, 146-148
    affective dysregulation of, 146
    attempts to split staff by, 188
    cognitive therapy for, 147
    dealing with countertransference in, 147
    dealing with families of, 147-148
    dealing with transference in, 147
    immaturity of, 146
    intense feelings of, 147
    interpersonal relationships of, 146
    self-destructive behavior of, 146
    setting limits for, 146-147
    temper tantrums and, 146

treating, 146-148
    unstable personality of, 146
Borderline personality disorder, biological component
    of, 146. See also Borderline patients
Bradshaw, J., 85, 348
Branch, L. G., 78, 97, 277, 283
Braunwald, E., 200, 207
Brehm, M. L., 207
Brostoff, W. S., 5
Brown, B. W., 155
Brown, D. J., 206
Bucky, S., 277
Burant, D., 16, 201
Burns, D. D., 62, 67, 272

CAGE Questionnaire, 5, 225
Cannabis, 205-206
    as CNS depressant, 197
    characteristics of intoxication by, 14
    depersonalization from, 205
    effects of, 205-206
    hashish from, 205, 206
    marijuana from, 205, 206
    motor skill impairment from, 205-206
    PCP and, 204
    physical signs of use of, 205
    withdrawal, 122, 206
Caracci, L., 204
Carlin, A. S., 130
Carney, J., 198
Carroll, Lynn, xix, 107, 315
    death of, xx
Carroll, M. E., 204
Carroll, Mitzi, xix, xx
Carstain, G. M., 155
Case, W. G., 201
Case presentation, 185-186
    outline, 185
    purpose of, 186
Cavanaugh, E. R., 209
Cavanaugh, J., 202, 203
Centers for Disease Control, 156, 199, 205, 207
Cerny, J. A., 167
Chait, L. D., 204
Chaloff, J., 149
Chang, G., 98
Chatlos, J. C., 165
Chemical dependency:
    as cause of death, 114
    as chronically relapsing condition, 209
    as family disease, 177-178
    as physiological problem, 113
    as psychological problem, 113, 128
    as social problem, 112-113, 128
    biological component of, 128
    common lies of, 245
    disease process of, 112

genetics and, 112
obsession and, 113
problems from, 114
*See also* Chemical dependency, psychology of; Chemical Use History
Chemical dependency, psychology of:
belief in great lie and, 116-117
never feeling accepted and, 116
promise of the disease and, 117
repression and, 55-56
Chemical dependency counselors, good:
as active listeners, 213-214
as assertive, 215
as constantly reinforcing, 216
as gentle, 212
as loving, 211-212
as patient, 215
as self-loving, 212
as sensitive, 212
avoiding overemotionality, 213
avoiding overinvolvement, 212
feelings about work, 211
interpersonal relationship skills of, 215-216
knowing boundaries with patients, 214
sixth sense of, 213
truthfulness of, 212
*See also* Adolescent chemical dependency counselors; Code of ethics, counseling
Chemically dependent people, thinking by, 55-57
Chemical Use History, 89-90, 239-241
patient diagnosis and, 90
Chevron, E. S., 135
Childhood group, 85-86
exploring early parental relationships in, 85
healing childhood pain in, 86
Higher Power and, 86
writing letters in, 85
Childhood trauma, patients with early, 159-160
cognitive therapy for, 160
dealing with sexual abuse in, 159-160
learning to forgive, 160
need to develop trust, 160
negative self-talk of, 160
posttraumatic stress disorder in, 159
Step Five's importance to, 160
Chiles, J. C., 130
Chopra, G. S., 206
Cisin, I. H., 201
Cleary, P., 99
Clinical Institute Withdrawal Assessment of Alcohol Scale, 16, 229-232
Clinical staff:
activities coordinator, 184
chemical dependency counselor, 183-184
clinical director, 183
clinical supervisor, 183
guidelines for productive interaction, 187
mutual respect in, 181

nurse, 182-183
physician, 181-182
psychologist/psychiatrist, 182
rehabilitation technician/aid, 184
respect for professional boundaries in, 181, 187-188
staff-patient problems and, 188-189
team building by, 186-188
treatment plan input by, 181
*See also* Clinical staffing
Clinical staffing, 184-186
atmosphere of mutual respect in, 185
presenting patients, 185-186
professional atmosphere of, 185
Clopin, J. M., 206
Cloptin, P. L., 206
Cocaine:
as CNS stimulant, 14, 198
crack, 203
effects of, 202-203
freebasing, 203
half-life of, 203
pattern of use of, 203
tolerance and, 203
toxic psychosis, 204
toxic symptoms from use of, 203
treatment for abuse of, 204
*See also* Cocaine abstinent syndrome
Cocaine abstinent syndrome, 203-204
Cocaine Anonymous, 101
Coccaro, E., 143, 146, 154
Code of ethics, counseling, 216-217
Codependency, 174-177. *See also* Codependency Exercise; Codependents
Codependency Exercise, 177, 178, 345-352
Codependents:
caretaking by, 175
chemical dependency's damage to, 174
denial by, 174
enabling by, 175-176
feelings of guilt, 175
feelings of shame, 175
feelings of worthlessness, 176
inability to know feelings, 176
inability to know wants, 176
lack of trust, 176
loss of control, 175
people pleasing by, 176
poor communication skills of, 177
tolerance of for abuse, 174
tolerance of for neglect, 174
*See also* Codependency; Codependency Exercise
Cognitive Capacity Screening Examination, 4, 221-222
Cognitive therapy, 55-63
applying, 57-59
as search for truth, 56
automatic thoughts and, 58-59
comparing inaccurate and accurate thoughts/feelings in, 61

examples of, 62, 63, 132-135
    for depressed patients, 131-135
    getting thoughts accurate in, 60-61
    in group therapy, 73
    scoring accurate feelings in, 61
    scoring inaccurate feelings in, 60
    solidifying accurate thinking in, 63
    uncovering themes in, 61-62
    uncovering thoughts/feelings in, 60
Cognitive triad, depression and, 59
Cohen, H. C., 167
Cohen, H. L., 167
Cohen, S., 207
Comer, S. D., 204
Commitment, 90, 92
    consistency of action and, 64
Committee for the Study and Treatment and
        Rehabilitation Services for Alcoholism and
        Alcohol Abuse, 209
Communication skills, 94
    active listening, 94
    becoming reinforcing, 94
    empathy skills, 94
    positive interactions, 94
    practicing in group, 94
    See also Communication Skills Exercise
Communication Skills Exercise, 94, 263-265
    for borderline patients, 148
    for depressed patients, 136
Community group, 87
Comprehensive Assessment and Treatment Outcome
        Research (CATOR), 209
Compulsions, definition of, 26
Conte, H. R., 130
Contracts:
    as patient homework, 89
    group acceptance of, 89
    group rejection of, 89
    specific objectives in, 89
    See also Behavior contract
Contracts group, 89
    commitment in, 90
    honesty in, 90
    love in, 90
    trust in, 90
Cook, R. F., 208
Corroll, L. T., 207
Costello, J., 165
Counselors. See Adolescent chemical dependency
        counselors; Chemical dependency counselors,
        good
Countertransference:
    borderline patients and, 147
    definition of, 49
    in interpersonal therapy, 66
    narcissistic patients and, 148
    staff-patient problems and, 188
Crane, J. B., 200

Creager, C., 5
Cross-tolerance, 121, 199
Csikoszentimihalyi, M., 163


Davidson, W. S. II, 166, 167
Davis, B. C., 204
Davis, K. L., 143, 146, 149, 153
Davis, T., 208
Defense mechanisms, 56-57, 114-116, 345-346. See also
        Denial; Minimization; Rationalization
Delgado, A., 4, 222
Delirium, organic:
    characteristics of, 14
    length of, 14
Delirium tremens. See Alcohol withdrawal delirium
Delusions:
    definition of, 14
    hallucinogen use and, 14
    length of, 14
Denial, 3, 17, 19, 55, 243, 337, 346
    among chemically dependent adolescents, 165
    as disassociated unreal world, 56
    as most common defense in chemical dependency,
        56, 115-116
    dealing with patients' early, 3
    Honesty Exercise and, 90
Dependence, physical, 16, 198
    characteristics of, 198
    development of, 198
Depressants, central nervous system, 197
    alcohol, 14, 16
    anti-anxiety drugs, 197
    barbiturates, 14, 16
    benzodiazepines, 14, 16
    cannabis, 197
    characteristics of intoxication by, 14
    inhalants, 14, 197
    opiates, 14, 16, 197
    sleeping medications, 197
    withdrawal from, 16, 198
Depressed patients, 128-138
    anhedonia in, 129
    chemically dependent patients as, 128
    See also Depression
Depression:
    acute, 129
    as curable, 137
    assessing, 129
    as treatable, 137
    automatic thoughts and, 59
    chronic, 129
    cognitive triad and, 59
    description of, 128
    genetics and, 130
    inaccurate thoughts and, 59
    in adolescents, 165
    in elderly, 158

interpersonal, 129
life-threatening, 129
logical errors and, 59
measuring severity of, 129
mild, 129
organic, 129
primary symptom of, 129
psychological, 129
psychosis and, 154
rate of in substance abusers, 128
secondary diagnosis of, 127
silent assumptions and, 59
suicide and, 128, 137-138
*See also* Depressed patients; Depression, treatment for
Depression, treatment for:
    antidepressant medications, 128, 129-130
    behavior therapy, 129, 130-131
    cognitive therapy, 129, 130, 131-135
    interpersonal therapy, 129, 135-137
DesJarlais, D. C., 209
Detoxification, 16-17
    description of, 16
    patient reactions to, 16-17
Development, normal, 118-120
    development of insecurity and, 118-119
    fear of abandonment and, 118
    in adolescence, 119
    in adulthood, 119-120
    learning rules and, 118
    peer group and, 119
    primary caregiver and, 118
    struggle for independence and, 118
Diagnosis:
    example of sharing with patient, 13
    primary, 127
    psychiatric, 127
    secondary, 127
    sharing with patient, 12-13
    using DSM for after biopsychosocial assessment, 27
    *See also* Diagnosis, DSM criteria for; DSM-IV
        Psychoactive Substance Use Disorder diagnostic
        criteria
Diagnosis, DSM criteria for:
    of chemical dependency, 8-9
    of drug abuse, 7-8
    of psychoactive substance use disorder, 10, 11, 12
    treatment of and prognosis for recovery, 127
*Diagnostic and Statistical Manual of Mental Disorders*, 128
    types of depression in, 129
    using after biopsychosocial assessment, 27
    *See also* DSM-IV Psychoactive Substance Use
        Disorder diagnostic criteria
Diagnostic summary, 37-38
Dietch, J., 201
Discharge criteria, American Society of Addiction
        Medicine (ASAM):
    inpatient, 193-194
    outpatient, 191-192

Discharge planning, 191
Discharge summary:
    aftercare plan in, 194-195
    description of, 191
    developing, 194-195
    components of, 191
    course of treatment in, 194
    final assessment of patient's condition in, 194
    final primary diagnosis in, 194
    final secondary diagnosis in, 194
    further treatment recommendations in, 194
    initial primary diagnosis in, 194
    initial secondary diagnosis in, 194
    problem list in, 194
    sample, 357-360
    timetable for completing, 194
    writing, 195
Documentation of patient progress, 43-45
    patient record/chart and, 43
    *See also* Progress notes
Domino, E. F., 204
*Dorland's illustrated medical dictionary*, 112
Dornbush, R., 204
Dorus, W., 128, 150
Douvan, E., 163
Downing, R. W., 201
Drug overdose, 14
Drugs Anonymous, 101
Drug use in United States, 197
DSM-IV Psychoactive Substance Use Disorder diagnos-
        tic criteria, 227
DuPont, R. L., 5


Eischins, R. R., 99
Elderly patients, 158-159
    mild cognitive defects in, 158
    reasons for substance abuse in, 159
    recovery of, 159
    *See also* Elderly population
Elderly population:
    depression among, 158
    lack of psychosocial support system among, 158
    prevalence of addiction among, 158
    substance abuse as mental disorder in, 158
    vulnerability of to substance abuse, 158
    *See also* Elderly patients
Ellinwood, E. H., 16
Ellis, A., 131
Emery, G., 59, 131, 152, 272
Emmons, M. L., 139, 274
Emotions, primary, 65
Empathetic statements, examples of, 50
Empathy:
    accuracy of, 49
    definition of, 49
    using in therapeutic alliance, 49
    *See also* Empathetic statements

Emrick, C. D., 101
Engel, J. A., 198
Epstein, N. B., 163
Erickson, C. K., 198
Euphoric recall group, 75-77
    getting real in, 76-77
    uncovering euphoric recall in, 75-76
Evaluating treatment effectiveness, 41
    patient record/chart and, 41
Evans, M. A., 206
Ewing, J. A., 5
Eysenck, H. J., 143
Eysenck, S. B. J., 143

Family members:
    Al-Anon for, 174
    as subject of treatment goals, 39
    handling during initial contact, 2
    of antisocial patients, 145
    of borderline patients, 147-148
    of mildly mentally retarded patients, 158
    of psychotic patients, 155-156
    separating from patient, 2
    See also Codependency; Codependents; Family
        process; Family program
Family process, codependency in, 174-177
Family Questionnaire, 337-343
    for family treatment program, 173
Family treatment program, 177-178
    Al-Anon and, 179
    conjoint sessions in, 178, 180
    first contact in, 173-174
    handling early AMA risk with, 174
    length of, 178
    purpose of, 173
    schedule, 178-179
    working in group, 179
    writing letters in, 178
Faris, J., 99
Fauci, A. S., 200, 207
Featherly, J. W., 203
Feelings, 91-92, 124-126
    as adaptive, 125-126
    core, 253-256
    energy from, 124
    identifying, 125
    motivation from, 124
    movement attached to, 47, 125
    primary, 125
    problem solving and, 47, 65, 79, 80
    purpose of, 253
    using appropriately, 256
    See also Feelings, patient; Feelings Exercise
Feelings, patient:
    changing, 47
    cultural differences in expressing, 65

educating about, 65
sharing, 65, 80
using inappropriately, 66
See also Feelings; Feelings Exercise
Feelings and action group, 79-80
Feelings Exercise, 54, 91, 253-256
Feelings log, 54, 63
Fennell, W., 202
Fenwick, S., 205
Ferguson, L. D., 197, 205
Fifth Step. See Step Five
Filipczak, J. A., 167
Fiore, M. C., 208
Fischman, M. W., 202
Fishburne, P. M., 201
Fisher, D. E., 208
Fixsen, D. L., 167
Flashbacks, 14. See also Hallucinogens
Folkins, C. H., 99, 363
Folstein, M. F., 4
Folstein, S. W., 4
Forehand, R., 171
Forney, R. B., 206
Frances, A., 146
Frances, R. J., 127, 182, 199, 201, 202, 203, 204, 205, 206,
    207, 277
Franklin, J. E., Jr., 127, 182, 199, 201, 202, 203, 204, 205,
    206, 207
Freedman, D. X., 165, 202, 205
Freud, S., 102
Fultz, J. M., 6, 16, 233

Gabel, R. H., 156
Gambert, S. R., 158
Gamblers Anonymous, 101
Gary, V., 99
Gawin, F. H., 16, 204
Geller, A., 17, 122, 201
Gerstein, D. R., 209
Gessner, P. K., 201
Gibbons, J., 149
Gibbons, R. D., 128, 150
Gillespie, H. K., 205
Gilman, A. G., 197, 202
Ginzburg, H. M., 209
Gittelman, R., 153
Gleghorn, A., 156
Glynn, T. J., 171, 208
Goals, treatment:
    and change, 40
    as infinite, 41
    changes in, 43
    definition of, 39
    developing, 39-42
    examples of, 39, 41-42
    examples of developing, 39

objectives and, 40
   patient as subject of, 39
   patient's family as subject of, 39
   selecting, 41
Gold, M. S., 202, 203, 206
Goldberg, J., 202
Goldberg, L., 198
Goldman, A. R., 45
Gonzales, R. A., 198
Goodman, L. S., 197, 202
Goodwin, D. W., 199, 200
Goodwin, F. K., 128, 203
Gordon, J. R., 78, 97, 272, 277, 279
Gorski, T., 81, 97, 277
Gottochalk, L., 201
Gould, L. C., 208
Graziano, A. M., 167
Greenberg, R. L., 131, 152
Greist, J. H., 99
Grief:
   interpersonal therapy for, 135-136
   normal, 136
   pathological, 136
   talking about, 136
   unresolved, 136
   *See also* Grief issues, handling
Grief issues, handling, 67
   delayed grief reaction and, 135-136
   Higher Power concept and, 67
   Step Three work and, 67
   with depressed patients, 135-136
Griffin, M. L., 143
Griffith, J. D., 202, 203
Griffiths, R. R., 198
Grossbeck, C. J., 206
Group for the Advancement of Psychiatry Committee
     on Alcoholism and the Addictions, 16
Groups, treatment center:
   as healthy family, 69
   as microcosm of world, 69
   as powerful motivation for change, 69
   Lord's Prayer to end meetings of, 75
   preparation statement for, 71
   preparing for, 70-73
   running, 72
   serenity prayer to begin meetings of, 75
   *See also specific types of therapy groups*
Group therapy:
   choosing therapy type for, 73
   giving good feedback in, 72
   preparation statement for, 71
   preparing for, 70-73
   receiving feedback in, 72
   *See also* Group therapy, benefits of
Group therapy, benefits of:
   feeling of family, 70
   feel sense of self-worth, 70

feel unconditional acceptance, 70
   free expression of feelings, 70
   gives hope, 69
   helps communication skills, 69
   information exchanged, 70
   learn power of truth, 70
   learn they are not alone, 69-70
   learn workings of interpersonal relationships,
     70
Group therapy agenda, choosing order of, 72
Gullion, M. E., 171
Gunderson, J. G., 146
Gurman, A. S., 99
Guthrie, D., 99
Guze, S. B., 200

Habit:
   as easy pathway to brain, 51, 122
   as learned behavior, 51
   changing, 51
   drinking problem as, 51, 122
   drug use as, 122
Hales, R. E., 137, 182
Halikas, J. A., 208
Hallucinations:
   as transient psychotic state, 14
   during acute intoxication, 14
   during withdrawal, 14
   hallucinogens and, 14
   tactile, 14
   visual, 14
   *See also* Hallucinogens
Hallucinogens, 16, 198, 204-205
   characteristics of intoxication by, 14
   lysergic acid diethylamide (LSD), 198, 204-205
   organic brain syndromes produced by, 205
   psychedelic state from, 205
Hamilton, M., 150
Hamilton Anxiety Rating Scale, measuring anxiety
     with, 150
Harris, M. J., 156
Harrison, P., 209
Harwood, H. J., 209
Haser, F., 201
Hatsukami, D., 207
Hatziandreu, E. J., 208-209
Havens, L., 49
Hayashida, M., 98
Hazelden, 107, 315
   beginning of, xix
Hazelden Foundation, The, xix
   purpose of, xix
Heckman, A. A., xix
Held, J., 202, 203
Henningfield, J. E., 207
Herbert, M., 167

Heroin:
    addicts, 202
    criminal activity and use of, 202
    increased use of, 201
    IV injection of, 202
    methadone programs and, 202
    tolerance to, 202
    treatment of addiction to, 202
    use by affluent people, 201
    use by health care workers, 202
    withdrawal from, 202
Hesselbrock M. N., 128, 150
Higher Power, 64, 302-308, 351
    adolescents and, 169
    angry patients and, 139-140
    anxious patients and, 151
    childhood group and, 86
    grief issues and, 67
    interpersonal therapy and, 137
    narcissistic patients and, 148-149
    panic disorder and, 153
    spirituality group and, 83
    Step Five and, 108
    Step Three and, 105, 106
    Step Two and, 104-105
    stress management and, 99
    trust and, 189
Hill, E. B., 203
Hirschfeld, R. M. A., 128
Hirshfeld, D. R., 149
Hoffmann, N. G., 209
Hollister, L. E., 14, 205, 206
Homicidal ideation, patients experiencing, 141
    reasoning with, 142
Homicidal intent, assessing, 142
Homicidal patients, 141-142
    and counselor's duty to warn intended victim,
        141-142
    transfer of to more secure facility, 141, 142
    See also Homicidal ideation, patients experiencing
Honesty Exercise, 90, 243-245
Honesty group, 73-75
    example of, 73-74
    uncovering lies in, 74-75
Hospitalization, partial:
    as Level II.5 care, 9
Hostetter, R. S., 208
Howard, K. I., 163
Hser, Y., 209
Hubbard, R. L., 209
Huey, L., 206
Huges, J. R., 207
Hughes, R., 209
Hunt, W. A., 78, 97, 277, 283

Iber, F. L., 17
Impulse control, 96-97

assertiveness skills and, 96, 126
    lack of and relapse, 96
    role-playing interpersonal conflict and, 96
    See also Impulse Control Exercise
Impulse Control Exercise, 96, 271-276
    for borderline patients, 148
Inaccurate thinking group, 79
Inhalants, 16, 206-207
    as CNS depressants, 14, 197
    brain damage from, 207
    death from, 207
    frequency of use, 206
    intoxication from, 14
    variety of, 206
Initial assessment, 4-13
    screening for alcoholism, 5
Initial contact:
    choosing words, 1-2
    example of, 3-4
    greeting patients, 1-2
    handling family members during, 2
    touch during, 1
    See also Initial assessment
Inpatient treatment:
    criteria for adolescents, 12
    criteria for adults, 10-11
    See also Inpatient treatment, medically managed in-
        tensive; Inpatient treatment, medically monitored
        intensive
Inpatient treatment, medically managed intensive:
    as Level IV care, 9
Inpatient treatment, medically monitored intensive:
    as Level III.7 care, 9
Interpersonal therapy, 64-67
    changing relationships in, 66-67
    countertransference in, 66
    for building relationship with God, 64
    for building relationships with others, 65-66
    for developing healthy relationships, 64-66
    for developing relationship with self, 64
    for learning relationship skills, 66
    for resolving interpersonal disputes, 136-137
    for treating depression, 135-137
    grief issues in, 67, 135-136
    Higher Power and, 137
    in group therapy, 73
    purpose of, 64
    transference in, 66
Intervention:
    example of AMA, 17-18
    using in-house, 19
    See also Intervention, early
Intervention, early:
    as Level 0.5 care, 9
Intoxicated patient, 14-16
    dealing with, 14, 15-16
    example of conversation with, 15-16
Intoxication, 4

definition of, 14
determining level of, 14
patient's reaction to, 14-15
psychotic symptoms from, 154
*See also* Alcohol-induced intoxication; Alcohol idiosyncratic intoxication
Isselbacher, K. T., 200, 207

Jacob, J. W., 4, 222
Jacobsen, P., 156
Jaffe, A. J., 98
Jaffe, J. H., 198, 201, 202, 203, 204, 206
Jaffe, S. L., 165
Janowsky, D. S., 206
Jellinek, E. M., 112
Jeste, D. V., 156
Joint Commission on Accreditation of Healthcare Organizations, xx, 45, 182, 183
Jones, R. T., 205, 206
Journal of Studies on Alcohol, 5, 223
Judd, L. L., 206
Juergens, S. M., 201

Kagan, J., 149
Kalant, H., 198
Kandel, D., 208
Karasu, T. B., 136
Kay, F. R., 14, 205
Keeber, H. D., 208
Kennedy, J., 128, 150
Kenner, J. J., 128, 150
Kethley, A., 158
Keystone Treatment Center, xix, 75, 107, 315
    counseling staff, xx
Khantzian, E. J., 143
King, G. S., 207
Kinney, J., 199
Kippinger, G. F., 206
Kleber, H. D., 202
Kleber, H. S., 204
Klein, D. F., 153
Klein, M. H., 99
Klerman, G. L., 135
Kofoed, L. L., 158
Kopstein, A., 197, 205
Kosten, T. R., 202
Kotin, J., 203
Krasnegor, N. A., 198, 202

Larson, R., 163
Leaton, G., 199
Lectures:
    flexible schedule of, 111
    length of, 111
    Lord's prayer to end, 111
    on Alcoholic Anonymous, 122-124
    on defense mechanisms, 114-116
    on disease concept, 112-114
    on feelings, 124-126
    on great lie, 116-117
    on normal development, 118-120
    on physical addiction and recovery, 120-122
    serenity prayer to begin, 111
    Twelve Steps in, 111
Ledwidge, B., 99
Lemberger, L., 206
Level of care, 9
    determining necessary, 9-12
Lewinsohn, P. M., 131
Linnolila, M., 16
Llar, H., 143, 146, 154
Logical errors, depression and, 59
Love:
    as action, 64, 92
    as healer in treatment, 3
    in therapeutic alliance, 2, 47
    *See also* Love, Trust, and Commitment Exercise; Love between patients
Love, Trust, and Commitment Exercise, 90-91, 247-251
    for borderline patients, 148
    for patients with early childhood trauma, 160
Love between patients, 161-162
    as crisis, 162
    conjoint counseling and, 162
    countertransference issues and, 162
    dealing with, 161-162
    disciplinary action and, 162
    transference issues and, 162
    treatment center rules discouraging, 161
Luborsky, L., 5
Lubrorsky, L., 127, 182
Lynch, K. R., 167

Maloney, M. J., 49
Mandelson, M., 371
Manthey, M., 187
Maps, internal, 49
    patient's, 49
Marijuana. *See* Cannabis
Marlatt, A. G., 78, 97, 272, 277, 279
Marsden, M. E., 209
Martin, J. B., 200, 207
Marty, R., 206
Masterson, J. F., Jr., 165
McGuire, F., 201
McHugh, P. R., 4
McKay, J., 141, 383
McKay, M., 141, 383
McLellan, A. T., 5
McLellan, T., 127, 182
Mee-Lee, D., 5
Megone, P., 204

Melges, F. T., 205
Mello, N. K., 198
Mendelson, J. H., 198
Men's group, 87
Mentally retarded patients, 157-158
    as good AA/NA members, 158
    Division of Vocational Rehabilitation program for,
        158
    families of, 158
    presenting program orally to, 157
    treating, 157
    using repetition with, 157
Meyer, R. E., 98, 128, 150
Michaels, J. K., 143
Michigan Alcoholism Screening Test (MAST), 5
Miller, G. A., 5
Miller, J. D., 205
Miller, M., 81, 97, 277
Millon, T., 142
Mini-Mental State Exam, 4
Minimization, 3, 17, 114-115, 243, 337, 345
    among chemically dependent adolescents, 165
    as defense mechanism, 56
    reality distortion and, 56, 90, 114
Minnesota Multiphasic Personality Inventory (MMPI),
    185
Mirin, S. N., 143
Monck, E. M., 155
Mooney, K. C., 167
Morgan, W. P., 99
Morrison, M. A., 165
Morse, R. M., 158
Munoz, R. F., 131

Naditch, M. P., 205
Nahas, G. G., 206
Naltrexone, 98
    relapse prevention and, 98
Narcissism, definition of, 395. *See also* Narcissism
        Exercise; Narcissistic patients; Narcissistic
        personality disorder
Narcissism Exercise, 148, 395-399
Narcissistic patients, 148-149
    as interpersonally exploitative, 149
    countertransference and, 148
    description of, 148
    Higher Power and, 148-149
    narcissistic rage and, 148
    need to learn empathy, 149
    sex as relapse trigger for, 149
    *See also* Narcissism Exercise
Narcissistic personality disorder, 106, 148-149. *See also*
        Narcissistic patients
Narcotics Anonymous (NA), 3, 64, 104, 106, 243, 307
    Alcoholics Anonymous and, 101
    as nonreligious, 83

    contact person, 194
    definition of sanity in, 299
    first five steps of, xx
    for adolescents, 172
    group, 69, 80, 82, 100, 105, 306, 368
    hotline, 80, 368
    meetings, 81, 124
    spirituality in, 64
    surrender in, 64
Narcotics withdrawal stages, 233
Narcotic Withdrawal Scale, 16, 233
National Association of Addiction Treatment Providers,
        xx
National Household Survey on Drug Abuse (1988), 197,
        205
National Institute of Medicine, 209
National Institute on Drug Abuse, 203
Nicotine, 14, 207-208
    addiction to as preventable, 207
    deaths from, 207
    diseases and, 207
    effects of, 207
    organized cessation programs for quitting, 208
    self-withdrawal from, 207-208
    tolerance to, 207
    Twelve Step programs for quitting, 208
    withdrawal syndrome, 207
Norko, M., 156
Novotny, T. E., 208

Oates, J. A., 202, 203
Objectives, treatment:
    and change, 40
    as infinite, 41
    as measurable, 40
    changes in, 43
    definition of, 39
    developing, 39-41
    examples of, 41-42
    selecting, 41
O'Brian, C. P., 98
O'Connell, R. A., 156
Offer, D., 163, 164, 165
Offer, J. B., 163, 164
Ollendick, T. H., 167
O'Malley, S. S., 98
Opioids, 201-202
    detoxification, 202
    withdrawal from, 16, 202
    *See also* Heroin
Organic brain dysfunction, checking for, 4. *See also* Cog-
        nitive Capacity Screening Exam; Mini-Mental
        State Exam
Organic brain syndrome:
    characteristics of, 14
    hallucinogen-induced, 205

intoxication as, 14
psychotic symptoms from, 154
withdrawal as, 154
Organic mental disorders, alcohol-induced, 199-201
Ostrov, E., 163
Outpatient treatment:
as Level I care, 9
criteria for adolescents, 11-12
criteria for adults, 10
Outpatient treatment, intensive:
as Level II.1 care, 9
Overeaters Anonymous, 101

Panic disorder:
antidepressant treatment of, 150
Higher Power and, 153
panic attacks and, 153
relaxation techniques for, 153
Parsons, B. V., 171
Patterson, G. R., 171
Peer pressure:
as risk to sobriety, 330
coping with, 330-331
evolution of, 329
how group uses, 330
importance of, 329-330
in adolescent treatment, 170
See also Peer Pressure Exercise
Peer Pressure Exercise, 329-331
Perry, S. W., 156
Personal inventory group, 87
Personality:
character as part of, 142
defining, 142-143
state, 142
temperament as part of, 142
trait, 142
Personality disorders:
age of onset, 143
as chronic, 143
character as major element in, 142
general definition of, 143
maladaptive traits in, 143
temperament as major element in, 142
See also Antisocial personality disorder; Borderline
personality disorder; Narcissistic personality
disorder
Personal Recovery Plan, 195, 353-355
Petersdorf, R. G., 200, 207
Phencyclidine (PCP), 14, 16, 204
effects of, 204
marijuana and, 204
neurological damage from, 204
organic mental disorders from, 204
Phillips, E. L., 166, 167
Pickens, R., 198

Pierce, J. P., 208
Pills Anonymous, 101
Placement criteria, American Society of Addiction
Medicine (ASAM), 6-7
acute intoxication and/or withdrawal complications,
6
biomedical conditions or complications, 6
emotional behavioral complications, 6
recovery/living environment, 7
relapse potential, 7
treatment acceptance or resistance, 6
Plutchic, R., 65, 130, 253
Polysubstances, 208
withdrawal syndromes from, 208
Post, R. M., 203
Pottash, A. C., 203
Praise, practicing skill of giving, 92
Problem list, 35, 37, 38
developing, 38
examples of, 38
Problems:
changes in, 43
definition of, 38
signs and, 38
symptoms and, 28
Problem statements:
as abstract concepts, 28
See also Problem list
Progress notes, 186
date included in, 43
examples of, 44
purpose of, 43
writing, 43-44
Projection, 17, 90
Psychiatric/psychological assessment, 127-128
Psychoactive drugs, reinforcing properties of, 198. See
also specific psychoactive drugs; Cross-tolerance;
Dependence; Tolerance; Withdrawal
Psychosis:
antipsychotic medications for, 155
as chronic, 154
as transient, 154
delusions in, 153
hallucinations in, 153
schizoid personality disorder, 154
schizophrenia, 154
schizotypical personality disorder, 154
Psychotic patients, 153-156
description of, 153
families of, 155-156
lack of motivation in, 155
love and, 156
need for problem-solving training, 155
need for social skills training, 155
treating, 154-155
Psychotic symptoms:
from intoxication, 154

from withdrawal, 154
Psychotropic medication:
    for psychiatric diseases, 128
Punishment:
    and avoiding old behavior, 52
    behavior frequency and, 52
    breaking rules and, 54-55
    definition of, 52
    using, 53-55

Quitkin, F., 153

Rachel, J. V., 209
Raci, S. D., 128, 150
Ramsay, D. A., 208
Raskind, M., 158
Rationalization, 3, 17, 243, 337, 346
    among chemically dependent adolescents, 165
    as blaming, 56, 90, 243
    as defense mechanism, 56, 90, 115
Rational Recovery, xx
Recovery, tools of, 351-352
Recovery Attitude and Treatment Evaluator (RAATE), 5
Reading group, 77
Regier, Carol, xx
Reifler, B., 158
Reinforcement:
    behavior frequency and, 52
    definition of, 52
    existence of behavior and, 52
    importance of, 52
    See also Reinforcing statements
Reinforcers, 52
Reinforcing statements, 53
Relapse, 17
    as process, 82, 97, 277
    high-risk situations for, 279-282
    preventing, 77-78, 82
    rates, 78
    reduced meeting attendance and, 82
    situations triggering, 78, 97-98
    time period between lapse and, 77
    warning signs of impending, 81, 97, 277-276
Relapse prevention, 97-98
    importance of, 97
    See also Relapse Prevention Exercise; Relapse
        prevention groups; Relapse prevention plan
Relapse Prevention Exercise, 97, 98, 277-286
Relapse prevention groups, 77-82
    as weekly, 77
    feelings and action group, 79-80
    inaccurate thinking group, 79
    slips group, 80-82, 283-284
    trigger group, 78-79
Relapse prevention plan, 97

Relationship maps, 66
Relationships, changing, 66-67
Relationship skills, 92-93
    learning, 66
    See also Relationship Skills Exercise
Relationship Skills Exercise, 92, 257-260
    for borderline patients, 148
    for depressed patients, 136
Residential services, clinically managed high-intensity:
    as Level III.5 care, 9
Residential services, clinically managed low-intensity:
    as Level III.1 care, 9
Residential services, clinically managed medium-
        intensity:
    as Level III.3 care, 9
Reznick, J. S., 149
Richels, K., 201
Rifkin, A., 153
Rodda, B. E., 206
Rogers, P. D., 141, 383
Rosenbaum, J. F., 149
Rosnekov, L., 202
Rotkopf, E., 202
Rounsaville, B. J., 98, 135, 202
Rush, J. A., 59, 131, 272

Sanders, M. R., 171
Schizophrenia:
    as chronic psychotic disorder, 154
    difficulty managing, 155
    drug treatment for, 128
Schottenfeld, R. S., 98
Schuckit, M. A., 14, 16, 112, 127, 197, 198, 199, 200, 204,
        208
Schuster, C. R., 202
Secretary of Health, Education, and Welfare, 206
Seidman, E., 166, 167
Self-discipline, 94-95
    problem-solving and, 95
    rules and, 95
    See also Self-Discipline Exercise
Self-Discipline Exercise, 94, 96, 267-270
Self-love, 92
    by chemical dependency counselors, 212
Self-Rating Anxiety Scale, measuring anxiety with, 150
Selye, H., 98, 361
Senay, E. C., 6, 16, 233
Sewell, D. D., 156
Sharp, C. W., 207
Shaw, B. F., 59, 131, 272
Shick, J. F. E., 202
Short Michigan Alcoholism Screening Test (SMAST), 5,
        223
Shukla, R. S. P., 206
Siever, L. J., 143, 146, 149, 153, 154
Silent assumptions, depression and, 59

Sime, W. E., 99, 363
Sisk, J. E., 209
Slips, developing plan for, 98
Slips group, 80-82
    for dealing with slips, 80
    for preventing slips, 80
    role playing in, 80
Smialick, J. E., 207
Smith, Bob, xix, 123
Smith, C. M., 198
Smith, D. E., 202, 203
Smith, J. W., 206
Smith, Q. T., 165
Snidman, N., 149
South Dakota Chemical Dependency Association, xx
Spalt, L., 165
Spelberger, C. D., 150
Spirituality:
    definition of, 64
    in AA program, 64
    in NA program, 64
    surrendering to, 64
    *See also* Higher Power; Spirituality group
Spirituality group, 82-85
    as weekly, 82
    clergy as leader, 82
    developing healthy relationship and, 82-83
    developing healthy relationship with Higher Power
        and, 83
    eleventh-step group and, 83
    Lord's Prayer, 85
    meditation group and, 83-85
    preparation for, 82
    serenity prayer begins meeting of, 85
Staff-patient problems, 188-189
    countertransference and, 188
    patient dislikes counselor, 188-189
    patient dislikes rules, 189
    transference and, 188
Standefer, J., 99
State Trait Anxiety Inventory, measuring anxiety with,
    150
Step Eight, 124
Step Eleven, 124
Step Five, 3, 101, 107, 108-109, 124, 215, 322
    Higher power and, 108
    purpose of, 108
    truth and, 109, 117
    *See also* Step Five Exercise
Step Five Exercise, 323-324
Step Four, 107-108, 109, 124
    forgiveness in, 107
    getting rid of guilt in 107
    identifying character defects in 107
    inventory, 108
    spiritual principles and, 107
    taking responsibility in, 107

*See also* Step Four Exercise
Step Four Exercise, 315-322
Step Nine, 124
Step One, 64, 101, 102-103, 104, 124
    as most important step, 102
    total surrender and, 102
    *See also* Step One Exercise
Step One Exercise, 287-297
Step Six, 124
Step Seven, 124
    prayer, 324
Step Ten, 124
Step Three, 67, 105-106, 124
    helping patients embrace, 106
    Higher Power and, 105, 106
    resistance to, 106
    willingness as key to, 106, 308
    *See also* Step Three Exercise
Step Three Exercise, 307-313
Step Twelve, 124
Step Two, 64, 104-105, 124
    Higher Power and, 104-105
    willingness as necessary for, 104
    *See also* Step Two Exercise
Step Two Exercise, 299-306
Step work:
    as group work, 103
Stern, M. J., 99
Stimmel, B., 202
Stimulants, central nervous system, 197-198
    amphetamines, 14, 198
    characteristics of intoxication by, 14
    cocaine, 14, 198
    withdrawal from, 16
    *See also* Amphetamines; Cocaine
Stress:
    definition of, 98
    disease linked with, 98
Stress management, 98-100
    exercise program and, 99, 361
    Higher Power and, 99
    lifestyle changes and, 361
    meditating as, 99
    practice relaxing as, 99, 361
    *See also* Stress Management Exercise
Stress Management Exercise, 98, 99, 361-368
Stuart, R. B., 333
Substance Abuse Subtle Screening Inventory (SASSI), 5
Sue, D., 23
Sue, D. W., 23
Suicidal ideation, 137
    and transport to psychiatric unit, 137-138
    subsidence of, 138
Suicide:
    by alcoholics, 137
    by drug abusers, 137
    depression and, 128, 137-138

phases leading to, 137
Suojanen, W. W., 165
Surgeon General, 207

Talbott, J. A., 137, 182
*Tarasoff v. Regents of the University of California*, 141
Tennant, F. S., Jr., 206
Thacore, V. R., 206
Therapeutic alliance, 47-49
    being confrontive, 50
    being empathetic, 49-50
    being reinforcing in, 48
    developing positive, 47-48, 49
    encouragement and support in, 47
    importance of trust in, 2-3
    individual treatment and, 47
    love and trust in, 47
    mutual independence in, 50
Therapeutic modality, choosing, 67
Thompson, T., 198
Thoughts, patient, 55
    changing, 47
    *See also* Automatic (inaccurate) thoughts; Cognitive
        therapy
Time-out, 320
    for angry patients, 141, 390
    impulse control problems and, 96
Time-out contract:
    for angry patients, 141, 392-393
Tinklenberg, J. R., 205
Tolerance, drug, 16, 121, 165, 198
Transference:
    borderline patients and, 147
    definition of, 49
    helping patients with, 216
    in interpersonal therapy, 66-67
    staff-patient problems and, 188
Treatment buddy:
    assigning to new patient, 13
Treatment outcome, 208-209
Treatment Outcome Prospective Study (TOPS), 208
    major finding of, 208
Treatment peers, 54
Treatment plan:
    after biopsychosocial assessment, 21, 28, 35
    as measurable, 38
    building, 37
    description of, 37
    diagnostic summary and, 37-38
    problems in, 38
    secondary diagnosis and, 128
    *See also* Problem list; Treatment planning
Treatment planning, 37
    as changing, 37
    as neverending, 37
Treatment plan review, 42-43
    at admission, 43

at discharge, 43
at major change in patient's condition, 43
at point of estimated length of treatment, 43
at transfer, 43
example of, 44-45
formal, 44-45
weekly, 44
Treece, C., 143
Trigger group, 78-79
    drug refusal exercises in, 78-79
    uncovering triggers in, 78
Troutman, W. G., 207
Trust:
    Higher Power and, 189
    importance of in recovery, 189
    in group, 105, 106
    in therapeutic alliance, 47, 189
    resolution of, 189
    truth and, 64
Truth, treatment as search for, 3, 116, 117
Turner, C. E., 205
Twelfth Step work, 13. *See also individual steps*
Twelve and Twelve, The, 77, 111, 287, 299, 307, 315, 323
Twelve Steps, 64, 123, 124, 320
    as core of chemical dependency treatment, 101
    *See also individual steps*

U.S. Department of Health and Human Services, 199
U.S. Department of Justice, 165

Vaillant, G. E., 199
Vaillant, G. G., 163
Van Ree, J. M., 198
Vardy, M. M., 14, 205
Victor, M., 200
Volpicelli, J. R., 98

Wallach, J., 5
Ward, C. H., 371
Warheit, G. J., 199
Washton, A. M., 203
Weedman, R., 45, 163
Weinhold, B. K., 174
Weinhold, J. B., 174
Weiss, R. D., 143
Weissman, M. M., 135
Wells, K. C., 171
Wernicke-Korsakoff syndrome, 200
Wernicke's encephalopathy, 4
Wesson, D. R., 202, 203
Westley, W. A., 163
Widiger, T., 146
Wikler, A., 206
Wilcox, R. E., 198

Wild, K. V., 130
Wilson, Bill, xix, 122-123
Wilson, J. D., 200, 207
Win-win scenario, 93
Withdrawal, 4, 14, 121-122
    acute alcohol, 121, 122, 198
    as organic brain syndrome, 154
    determining, 16
    educating patients about, 15
    from amphetamines, 198
    from benzodiazepines, 122
    from cannabis, 122, 206
    from depressants, 16, 198
    from heroin, 202
    from nicotine, 207-208
    from opioids, 16, 202
    from polysubstances, 208
    from stimulants, 16
    length of acute, 122
    protracted, 122, 201

    psychotic symptoms from, 154
    *See also* Alcohol withdrawal; Withdrawal syndrome, extended
Withdrawal syndrome, extended, 122
Wolf, M. M., 167
Women's group, 87
Woods, J. H., 198
Woodward, J. J., 112, 199
Woody, G. E., 5
Woody, G. G., 127, 182
Work environment, treatment center, 189-190

Youngren, M. A., 131
Yudofsky, S. C., 137, 182

Zanarine, M. C., 146
Zegans, L. S., 98, 361
Zung, W. W. K., 150

# About the Author

**Robert R. Perkinson,** PhD, is the Clinical Director of Keystone Carroll Treatment Center in Canton, South Dakota. He is a Licensed Psychologist, South Dakota Certified Chemical Dependency Counselor, Level III, an Internationally Certified Alcohol and Drug Counselor, Licensed Marriage and Family Therapist, and Nationally Certified Gambling Counselor. He has been practicing in the field of addictions for over 25 years and is listed in *Who's Who in Medicine and Healthcare* and *Who's Who in the World.*